AF607972

WHY CONTROL IMMIGRATION?

CARESS SCHENK

Why Control Immigration?

Strategic Uses of Migration Management in Russia

UNIVERSITY OF TORONTO PRESS
Toronto Buffalo London

Toronto Buffalo London
www.utorontopress.com

ISBN 978-1-4875-0297-3

Library and Archives Canada Cataloguing in Publication

Schenk, Caress, 1977–, author
Why control immigration? : strategic uses of migration management in Russia / Caress Schenk.

Includes bibliographical references and index.
ISBN 978-1-4875-0297-3 (hardcover)

1. Russia (Federation)–Emigration and immigration–Government policy. 2. Immigrants–Government policy–Russia (Federation). I. Title.
JV8190.S34 2018 325.47 C2017-906081-3

Publication of this book was made possible, in part, by a grant from the First Book Subvention Program of the Association for Slavic, East European, and Eurasian Studies.

University of Toronto Press acknowledges the financial assistance to its publishing program of the Canada Council for the Arts and the Ontario Arts Council, an agency of the Government of Ontario.

Funded by the Government of Canada
Financé par le gouvernement du Canada

To Brian, Malcolm, August, and Eloise, my little tribe of misfits and co-adventurers, who keep everything in perspective for me.

Contents

Tables and Figures

Tables

Figures

Acknowledgments

It is both humbling and a great privilege to write a book about immigration that comes at a time when public discourse and political rhetoric about migrants and refugees have reached a fever pitch. Populist and anti-immigration tropes have turned politics in "normal," "civilized," and "modern" countries into terrifying incubators of fear and xenophobia. Responsible citizens throughout the Western world are in a crisis of identity, asking how modern people came to a politics driven by fear and hate. Watching politics and public reaction unfold, I have been both dismayed and heartened by the reaction of friends, family, colleagues, and other experts: dismayed as people on the right and left use their ideology to justify intolerance and reify a polarized political community; heartened by the compassionate responses, again on radically different locations of the ideological spectrum, that drive people to speak and act for justice, life, and humanity. As a political scientist and a person of faith, compelled to think and act according to often contradictory identities, I have long found navigating ideology and politics full of complexity and contingency. The current crisis that pits ideas of what it is to be a modern rational political citizen against the visceral human impulses that drive opinion formation and decision making regardless of level of education or ideological leanings has shown me that my own journey is not unique. As many have become disillusioned with the polarization of politics and limitations of realizing liberal ideals in developed democracies, we are at a crossroads that is full of uncertainty and opportunity.

Many of the discourses of fear we use in the public sphere to talk about security and immigration are similar to how we (in the West) approach Russia. Fear, demonization, and over-simplified caricatures dominate media discourses, drive public opinion, and even seep into scholarly assumptions and framings. Perhaps only by confronting the ugly realities of our own political systems, which seems infinitely more possible in the current context, can we hope to understand Russia for its own sake instead of measuring it against ideals that even Western countries fail to realize. Politics and political societies are not linear and cannot be measured on simple spectrums such as that from authoritarianism to democracy. Many of the analytical tools of social science (especially those based on rational choice) are utterly unable to address current problems because they are both overly reductionist and based on assumptions that do not consider the complex realities of what it means to be human, acting socially and politically. As social scientists, we are driven to simplify complex realities in a way that makes them understandable and translatable to a variety of other contexts. But we must not forget that the main units of our analysis are deeply human and cannot be encapsulated cleanly or perfectly as variables.

I hope I have succeeded in capturing the complex reality that marks immigration control in Russia without being reductionist or dismissing all political developments and outcomes as the inevitable failures of authoritarianism. While I never argue that the differences between politics in the West and in Russia are unimportant, areas such as immigration control reveal tremendous similarities that must be explored and accounted for. I am certainly not unaware of the dangers of the Russian political system, and in no way mean to minimize these as I challenge existing approaches to analysis. In many cases I have obscured the data received from individuals by allowing their comments to inform my approach while not directly quoting them. This is for their protection. Many of my colleagues "live out loud" in Russia, working openly, engaging the government, and being critical when necessary. Some have been jailed for their efforts. Others have been branded foreign agents. Yet they resiliently continue to do their work. They fight for justice, and protect the vulnerable. They are everyday heroes that make Russia an amazing and culturally rich place that deserves to be enjoyed.

Living in post-Soviet Eurasia for over five years has also informed the logic behind this book in substantial ways. Living and working in a place is not the same as field research, when one's energies are focused on pursuing a particular question or topic. Nevertheless, living cross-culturally does offer an extended opportunity for participant observation, exposure to political elites and civil society. It has made me a migrant, and forced me to be the subject of my own research. In this case it has also offered me proximity to my primary research field and the ability to participate in regional initiatives and policy debates. Certainly the experiences in one Eurasian country cannot be directly transferred into conclusions about another, given variation in state structures as well as cultural mores. Nevertheless, there are broad similarities among post-Soviet mentalities roughly analogous to how we conceptualize "Western" mentalities, knowing full well the differences between North American, European, and Oceanian peculiarities. Therefore, being embedded in and continually engaging a post-Soviet state, health care system, work environment, and society (that is in no small part informed and shaped by media from Russia) has forced me to think very carefully about the assumptions that inform my approach to inquiry.

Writing this book has been an analytical exploration as well as an intellectual journey that has taken place with the benefit of a great academic community. I owe a great many mentors and co-travellers thanks for playing their part, providing feedback, guidance, and support. Laura Luehrmann and Venelin Ganev took the raw materials of an inexperienced graduate student and coaxed me to confidently embrace my own ideas. Karen Dawisha, Cynthia Buckley, and Yoshiko Herrara offered the honest advice of strong women who have succeeded in a sometimes difficult profession. Ed Schatz and Ted Gerber were instrumental in helping me break into a career in academia, and have since become candid comrades as I have navigated various stages of idealism and cynicism with the profession. I couldn't ask for a better group of colleagues than those at Nazarbayev University, past and current, and the friends I have collected around the globe who make academic life real, invigorating, and relational.

This project has benefited from the input of many people at various stages, from proposal to final manuscript: Phil Enns, Venelin Ganev, Ted Gerber, Barbara Junisbai, Yoshiharu Kobayashi, Marlene Laruelle, Brenden Pietsch, Ed Schatz, Alexei Trochev, Gerasimos Tsourapas, and especially those who participated in a pivotal book workshop organized by Gulnaz Sharafutdinova at Kings College London, including Bhavna Dave, Paul Goode, and Sherrill Stroschein.

The choice of which press to entrust my manuscript with was not an easy decision. Considerations of prestige, distribution, career politics and pressure, and conflicting advice weighed heavily as I was communicating with a variety of university press editors. Thanks in large part to Richard Ratzlaff at University of Toronto Press, who believed in the project from the first moment and has made the process gratifying, encouraging, and fun, I have never second-guessed my choice.

Last, but certainly not least, are all of the people to whom it doesn't matter one iota whether I've written this book. My forever community of family and friends helps me to understand that the career accomplishments we spend our time striving for are but a drop in the bucket of a meaningful life and the long span of history.

Note on transliteration:

Transliteration of Russian language follows the Library of Congress system, with the exception of spellings that commonly appear in English-language sources.

Abbreviations

CIS	Commonwealth of Independent States
FMS	Federal Migration Service (Federal'naia Migratsionnaia Sluzhba)
FSB	Federal Security Service (Federal'naia Sluzhba Bezopasnosti)
GUVM	General Directorate for Migration (Glavnoe Upravlenie po Voprosam Migratsii)
KMMTs	Krasnodar Intergovernmental Migration Centre (Krasnodarskii Mezhgosudarstvennyi Migratsionnyi Tsentr)
Mintrud	Ministry of Labour (Ministerstvo Truda i Sotsial'noi Zashchity Rossiiskoi Federatsii)
Minzdrav	Ministry of Health (Ministerstvo Zdravookhraneniia)
MMTs:	Multifunctional Migration Centre (Mnogofunktsinoal'nyi Migratsionnyi Tsentr) (Moscow)
MVD	Ministry of Internal Affairs (Ministerstvo Vnutrennikh Del)
MTsTO	Moscow Centre of Labour Exchange (Moskovskii Tsentr Trudovogo Obmena)
OKVED	Unified Classification of Economic Activities (Obsherossiiskii Klassifikator Vidov Ekonomicheskoi Deiatel'nosti)
PVS	Passport Visa Services (Pasportno-Vizovaia Sluzhba)
Rosstat	Federal State Statistical Service (Federal'naia Sluzhba Gosudarstvennoi Statistiki)
Rostrud	Federal Department of Labour and Employment (Federal'naia Sluzhba po Trudu i Zaniatosti)
UFMS	Regional branches of the FMS (Upravlenie Federal'noi Migratsionnoi Sluzhby)

Introduction: Russia as an Immigration Magnet

Headlines proclaiming, "In Russia, the doors are closing. How – and why – Russian citizens are losing their freedom to travel abroad" (Lemondzhava 2016) liken migration control in modern Russia to the tightly monitored regime of the Soviet Union. But while the Soviet Union was famed for closed borders, Russia has some of the most open borders in the world. Receiving millions of migrant workers each year who enter visa-free, Russia has earned its place among migrant-receiving countries in dramatic fashion. Like other major countries of immigration, Russia struggles to balance the economic advantages of migration with public anxieties. In fact, the populist response of Russian elites as they tackle immigration control may be the thing that makes the Russian migration system most "normal."

Russia fell to the third largest country of immigration in 2015, inched out by Germany's decision to accept over a million asylum seekers displaced by war in Syria. However, Russia's immigrant population is chronically underestimated, not capturing many of the millions of Central Asian workers occupied in the informal economy. While migrants from the former Soviet countries of the Commonwealth of Independent States (CIS) can come to Russia visa-free and have simplified access to the labour market, there are a variety of documents and procedures required in order to work.[1] This book chronicles the logic behind these work documents and their actual availability to migrants.

Labour movement to Russia only began demanding the government's attention in the early 2000s, a decade after the fall of the Soviet Union. Though there is some evidence that economic calculations were always important (Radnitz 2006; Tishkov, Zayinchkovskaya, and Vitkovskaya 2005), most migrants in the 1990s were ethnic repatriates seeking citizenship (i.e., ethnic Russians moving from other former Soviet republics to Russia). Recent migrants are not opposed to obtaining citizenship or other permanent and semi-permanent migration statuses, yet these solutions are among a variety of options to legalize their presence and work. The primary goal of many labour migrants is to establish circular patterns where they can move easily between Russia and their home countries. Which documents or migration status a migrant should seek (if any) is often of secondary concern to the exigencies of finding work and meeting economic goals.

Temporary workers from Central Asia (Kyrgyzstan, Tajikistan, and Uzbekistan) and the Caucasus (Armenia and Azerbaijan) are the most politically and socially salient category of migrants. These citizens of CIS countries can come to Russia without a visa for 90 days and obtain permission to work without a prior agreement with an employer.[2] Yet many of these workers are not captured in official statistics. When Russia is advertised as the third largest country of immigration, this is based on its foreign-born population of 11 million. However, these figures do not include temporary labour migrants or any estimate of undocumented migrants.[3] The Russian estimates for foreign-born citizens instead include only naturalized citizen, and non-citizens who either have permanent residence permits, have worked with an official employment contract for over a year, or have studied for at least one year (Rosstat 2010c). Especially because illegal migration is not included, the official numbers underestimate the real number of immigrants in Russia (Zaionchkovskaia, Mkrtchyn, and Tyuryukanova 2009; Zaionchkovskaya 2013). If the government estimates of 3–5 million illegal immigrants[4] plus those on temporary work permits were added to the total foreign-born population in Russia, the number would reach 16–18 million, placing Russia well ahead of Germany's 12 million foreign born.

Increasing numbers of visible (non-Slavic) minorities in many major Russian cities create public anxiety demanding a political solution to labour migration management. The government seeks a set of policies that will not only satisfy anti-migrant sentiments in society but also provide much-needed labour resources to the economy. These two goals often conflict, making any set of policies doomed to lacklustre results that do not meet all parties' interests.

Migration policy and its implementation reflect these tensions and the government's efforts to manage conflicting goals. The development of migration policy further mirrors how public policy has been approached in post-Soviet Russia across various time periods. From the 1990s when there was virtually no attention given to labour migration, reflecting the chaos and fragmentation of the Boris Yeltsin period, to the increasing state coordination and control of the 2000s prioritized by Vladimir Putin, policy reflects broader trends in the government's attitude towards and capacity to accomplish basic tasks of state management. As labour migration has been given greater attention and policies have become more sophisticated, myriad complexities and contradictions have come to the fore, leading the government to seek strategic solutions that balance competing interests among state, economic, and social actors.

Throughout the 1990s, immigration laws were primarily ad hoc (Voronina 2006; Andrienko and Guriev 2005). The legislation was as much liberal (in the sense of low government regulation) as it was piecemeal and incoherent (Ivakhnyuk 2009b; Mukomel 2009). Laws were rarely supported by implementing orders from the government and appropriate ministries, and largely relied on presidential decrees for their management (Mukomel 2005). Rules and laws were at times contradictory (some were even deemed unconstitutional by the Constitutional Court) and left wide latitude for administrative discretion and corruption schemes (Rubins 1998; Katanian 1998).

Legislation in the 1990s primarily focused on regulating the return of ethnic Russians from newly independent states of the former Soviet Union (Voronina 2006). Between 1989 and 2007, 3.6 million ethnic Russians migrated to Russia, comprising two-thirds of migration flows.[5] To a lesser extent, civil wars and unrest in the newly independent Caucasian states and Tajikistan pushed migrants to settle in Russia (Flynn 2004), and these refugees and victims of forced migration were given particular attention by lawmakers (Zaionchkovskaia, Mkrtchyn, and Tyuryukanova 2009). The Federal Migration Service (Federal'naia Migratsionnaia Sluzhba, or FMS) was created in 1992 to oversee the development and implementation of migration policy, and was primarily occupied with protecting the rights of migrants and refugees (Voronina 2006; Gavrilova 2001; Pilkington 1998).

Though by 1996 the FMS had branches in all of Russia's regions that reported directly to Moscow, branches had dual loyalties that typically favoured regional issues (Pilkington 1998). In this sense, the FMS failed to accomplish one of its primary tasks of coordinating migration across the country according to federal priorities. In the 1990s, regional governments dealt with migration issues depending on their own needs;

regions experiencing demographic decline, for example, were more open to immigration than were those already saturated with immigrants (Voronina 2006). In large part this scenario reflects the system of asymmetrical federalism that dominated the entire political landscape during the Yeltsin period, wherein legal space and centre-periphery relations were unevenly developed, and in most cases politics and governance functioned according to local power dynamics rather than federal laws (Burgess 2009; Petrov and Slider 2009; Gill 2007).

As return migration slowed, focus shifted to regulating labour migration, which became the dominant form of migration by 2000 (Korobkov 2008). During Vladimir Putin's first presidency, the FMS shifted focus to combating illegal immigration and regulating labour migration, effectively securitizing the approach to migration (Voronina 2006). The FMS was eventually placed under the Ministry of the Interior in 2002, essentially transforming it into a law enforcement agency (Light 2005; Korobkov and Zaionchkovskaia 2004). This shift coincided with the beginning of the second Chechen war, and a focus on domestic terrorism that received global legitimacy as a result of the September 11, 2001 terrorist attacks in the US (Ivakhnyuk 2013b).

In response to increasing security concerns, major legal changes were introduced beginning in 2002 in an attempt to create a more cohesive (albeit more restrictive) overall strategy for migration (Mukomel 2005). A new law called *On the Legal Status of Foreign Citizens* clarified visa procedures, introduced quotas for temporary residence permits and work permits for foreigners from visa countries, and required registration at a place of temporary stay (for all foreigners without a temporary or permanent residence permit), temporary residence (for those with a temporary residence permit), or permanent residence (for those with a permanent residence permit) within three days of entering Russia.[6] Once registered, CIS citizens could stay in Russia for up to 90 days. Amendments to the law *On Citizenship* limited fast-track naturalization procedures to those born in the Soviet Union who had become stateless, leaving others who had been citizens of the Soviet Union to prove Russian-language proficiency, sufficient income, and surrender of prior citizenships (Shevel 2011).[7]

Despite intentions to create more coherent immigration policy, laws remained "tangled and contradictory" (Ivanov 2013). For example, the regulation of non-visa immigrants was vastly underspecified in the 2002 law.[8] The law explicitly and exhaustively delineated the process for employers to hire a worker from a visa country, including applying for a work visa invitation, permission to hire a foreign worker, and the employee's work permit all at the same time. But no separate process is described for visa-free migrants. In practice, this meant that all foreign workers had to rely on employers to submit the documents required for legal work status, leaving visa-free migrants from CIS countries with little benefit in the labour market.

As a result of the 2002 law, in particular more difficult registration requirements, the rates of illegal immigration and corruption in the immigration sphere spiralled out of control (Mikhailova and Tyuryukanova 2009; Vitkovskaya 2009; Ivakhnyuk 2009b). Expert estimates between 2002 and 2005 asserted that there were 3–5 million illegal migrants in Russia (Ivakhnyuk 2009b, 42; Mukomel 2005, 196), compared to less than 1 million in 1999–2000 (Zayonchkovskaya 2000). In response, Putin signed a presidential decree in 2004 that gave the FMS legal authority to manage migration "until the adoption of relevant federal laws."[9]

After a highly publicized meeting of the Security Council on the theme of migration, where Putin pointed to excessive administrative barriers as the main cause of illegal immigration (Putin 2005), an interdepartmental working group was convened under the leadership of the Ministry of Interior (Ivakhnyuk 2013b). Their efforts produced a major overhaul of *On the Legal Status of Foreign Citizens* in 2006, representing the first changes of any real substance to the law since its initiation. While new procedures allowed CIS workers to apply for work permits on their own and move freely between employers, and allowed foreigners to register either at the place they lived or worked, restrictive elements were also added to the law. In particular, quotas were introduced for all work permits (including those for CIS citizens), and bans prevented migrants from working in some sectors such as retail trade (including in bazaars and markets). Many experts framed the highly publicized bans as a populist election-year strategy in response to complaints that markets were overrun by migrants; they were also framed as a security response to increasing criminality and contraband goods (Vitkovskaya 2009; Mikhailova and Tyuryukanova 2009).

The migrant advocacy community (civil society actors, human rights NGOs and activists, scholars, etc.) was quick to point out the positives of the reforms, hoping they would in fact usher in a new era of regularization for migrants. The immediate result of reforms was a decrease of illegal immigration in 2007 because the initial work permit quota was set at 6 million on the suggestion of experts who argued that it would offer all migrants in Russia the opportunity to legalize their status (Vlasova et al. 2011).[10] Yet the combination of simplified and restrictive procedures marked a departure from the "liberal revolution" that some had hoped for (Grafova 2006). Further, the quota was dramatically decreased year by year, pushing more and more migrants to work illegally, until it stood at 1.6 million in 2014 for its final year.

This book picks up on policy reform once the 2007 reforms took effect. It demonstrates how work permit quotas were strategically reduced to create a publicly acceptable number of legal migrants, while allowing ample numbers of illegal migrants to satisfy labour demand. This scarcity of legal labour, which continued beyond the repeal of work permit quotas, became a valuable resource that could be used to balance a variety of disparate interests across the immigration system. This book traces the repeal of quotas into the first year of the next phase of policy management (2015), when new labour permits called patents became the main policy tool. Across both policy mechanisms, I conceptualize migration management in Russia as a multi-level balancing act powered by patron-client relationships.

As the story of migration management in Russia unfolds in the following pages, the question worth asking at each stage is whether this persistently authoritarian regime is really so different from other major immigrant-receiving countries in its approach to controlling immigration. Given the success of anti-immigrant populism in recent years, reaching a peak in the 2016 Brexit vote in the UK and election of Donald Trump in the US, Russia's characteristically xenophobic attitude towards immigrants finds itself increasingly ordinary in comparative perspective. And while the patron-client relationships that are central to Russia's immigration control reflect a specific approach to strategic management, the underlying tension between various economic, political, and social actors, and the outcomes of increased control leading to increased illegal immigration, make Russia very much at home among major countries of immigration.

Chapter One

Why Control Immigration?

In 2015, conflict in Syria pushed hundreds of thousands of refugees into Europe. Hordes of people crowding onto trains, flooding down motorways, crammed into overflowing boats, and breaking past traffic barriers dominated media coverage. The developments were quickly dubbed a "crisis." Reports of sexual assault, acts of terrorism, and other types of crime by refugees were given top press throughout the world, highlighting a "clash of cultures" between Muslim immigrants and European denizens. Stories of "bogus refugees" seeking to exploit the opportunity to immigrate to Europe resonated with nervous host populations who feared that immigrants would become a drain on their social services. At the same time, tragedies such as the body of a three-year old refugee boy washing up on the shores of Turkey provoked a great humanitarian outpouring. Yet even these benevolent public impulses did not save the European governments from intense criticism on all sides. The need to control immigrants and manage their entry into host countries quickly became palpably felt by governments and societies alike.

Waves of refugees are often unpredictable, stemming from political disruptions such as the wars in Ukraine (2014–) and Syria (2011–), the Arab Spring (2010), economic and political instability in Zimbabwe (2007–), or natural disasters. Governments can do relatively little to plan for these influxes of immigration in the way that they can plan for other types of flows such as labour or family reunification migration. More regular types of flows, be they temporary or permanent, require careful government attention to the various interests represented in society, since they do not occur as the result of tragic events that can mobilize public sympathies and relieve pressure on decision makers, at least in the short term.[1]

Public anxieties about immigrants are standard fare for host states, though they are made increasingly salient through populist rhetoric that plays on fears for electoral or other political benefit. Anti-immigrant populism by many counts was a major reason for the success of the 2016 Brexit vote in the UK and the election of Donald Trump in the US, and is a routine part of right-wing European leaders' discourse. Yet public demands for limits on the number of immigrants in order to protect the security and social stability of their countries pull against economic demand for the cheap labour of immigrants as well as international obligations and humanitarian norms that compel governments not to treat migrants as faceless threats or nuisances but rather to recognize them as people with rights. These "structural contradictions" (Calavita 1992) make it difficult for governments to balance disparate voices, and the task of migration governance becomes an endless attempt to balance fears and realities.

Migration management can all too easily turn into a vicious cycle as competing interests vie for dominance. The vicious cycle of immigration control occurs when the public demands increasingly strict regulations, which inevitably increase illegal immigration because policies do nothing to diminish the structural factors causing migrants to move. Increasing proportions of illegal immigrants create ideal conditions for populists to drum up political support through anti-immigration rhetoric, and if politicians are able to make good on political promises, restrictive policy responses produce ever more illegal immigration.[2] And the cycle goes on and on.

In Russia, the vicious cycle of migration management is all too real, and it leaves the government in a position where they must juggle multiple demands as they create and implement immigration policy. Public anxieties must be addressed because they ultimately affect the legitimacy of ruling elites. Economic demands must be addressed because the current administration has staked its reputation on producing economic growth. The current leadership also prizes stability, and therefore always has a cautious eye open for any potential social, economic, or political disruptions.

This book argues that the Russian government attempts to balance disparate interests by creating a scarcity of legal (documented) labour. Scarcity of legal labour occurs when policies and their implementation do not allow enough migrants to legalize their status to meet labour demand. Low numbers of legal migrants are attractive to the public and become a powerful populist tool that leaders can employ in response to xenophobia, creating the perception that the government is willing to protect society from threats to the labour market and social stability. At the same time, a scarcity of legal labour can be used strategically by actors throughout the political system in various ways, including distributing work documents to those who have connections, offering state officials (law enforcement and bureaucrats) increased opportunities to extract bribes from undocumented migrants and their employers, and allowing the widespread use of illegal labour with relative impunity. Legal labour scarcity forces the majority of migrant workers into the informal sector, where they became a source of cheap labour that can satisfy economic demand.

The scenario I've described, where corruption and illegal immigration run rampant and are countered by populist pronouncements that promise rarely realized results, may seem like an uncoordinated and weak migration state. However, I conceptualize immigration policy management in Russia as a multi-level balancing act that demonstrates the importance of high-level politics, institutional interests and constraints, and the conditions under which government actors at all levels can utilize individual agency and pursue their own interests. The goal is not to produce a controlled immigration environment (i.e., reduced illegal immigration), but rather to exploit opportunities that arise as a result of increased migration. Some few scholars have addressed the question of how and under what conditions immigration policy can be strategically used to create and exploit gaps in policy with the goal of increasing the proportion of illegal immigrant workers, and therefore an in-depth study of the opportunities for instrumental uses of policy in the Russian case is a significant contribution to a little analysed portion of the migration literature.[3]

Can States Control Immigration?

Whether states can control immigration at all in light of various pressures from society, economic need for certain types of labour, and structural factors driving immigration has long been debated in the migration literature. Many have argued that the state's ability to control borders and immigrant flows is not at all absolute, owing to various forces of globalization (Cohen 2001; Sassen 1996; Bhagwati 2003) and the diffusion of international humanitarian norms (Soysal 1994; Jacobson 1996; Sassen 1998). Others point to structural factors such as colonial linkages (Castles and Miller 2009; Messina 2007), persistent inequality resulting from global capitalism (Anderson, Sharma, and Wright 2009; Portes and Walton 1981), and migrant networks and industries of intermediaries that create transnational links and circular migratory patterns (Castles 2004; Tsuda 2003; Basch, Glick-Schiller, and Szanton-Blanc 1994), all of which reinforce migrant flows that are resilient against policy innovations. Another group of scholars focuses on domestic interests that lobby for increased immigration (Money 1999; Freeman 1995) and democratic norms and civil society activists that make rights-based claims for migrants (Bhagwati 2003; Hollifield 2000), even though public opinion as a whole may not prefer increased immigration (Fetzer 2012), and far right party politics push for more restrictive policies (Messina 2007; Schain 2006; Betz and Immerfall 1998).

There is also a contingent of scholars who argue that states have increasing capacity to control immigration and that their efforts are effective by some measure (Brochmann and Hammer 1999; Joppke 1998; Freeman 1994; Bonjour 2011), especially in their ability to impact immigrant flows (Meyers 2004; Cornelius and Rosenblum 2005; Ortega and Peri 2013; Cappelen and Skjerpen 2014; Mayda 2010). These studies do not claim that state control is uniform or absolute, and there is a general consensus in the literature that states cannot balance all demands in a way that satisfies all actors. All things considered, the greatest power states have is to decide which of the immigrants in its territory will be legal and fully documented, and which and how many will be allowed to operate in the shadows with irregular, or undocumented, status (Cornelius and Rosenblum 2005; Dauvergne 2008; Düvell 2011). Though policies rarely have the ability to prevent migrants' attempts at illegal entry and stay (Cornelius et al. 2004), stricter policies have the effect of increasing the proportion of illegal immigrants (Morawska 2001) and making immigrant populations more permanent by restricting temporary and circular migration patterns (Cornelius 2005; Lahav and Guiraudon 2006; Doomernik and Jandl 2008).[4]

The question of whether policies reach their stated aim and how best to assess their effectiveness has received new vigour in the recent migration literature (Czaika and de Haas 2013; Bjerre et al. 2014; Gest et al. 2014). This book reframes the question of policy outcomes to ask what, despite the well-established limitations on state policies, and perhaps even knowing that policies will fail, states and state actors hope to gain through their attempts to control immigration. In other words, "why control immigration?" Though the question of control could be addressed through an ethical framework, such treatment would focus on why states *should* (or *shouldn't*) control immigration.[5] This book rather pursues an instrumental framework that demonstrates why states *do* control immigration, using the case of the Russian Federation. As the third largest country of immigrants, Russia is a crucial case that offers a dynamic and complex picture of potential instrumental uses of immigration control. It is also an essential addition to the migration literature because it contributes to the vastly underdeveloped discussion on immigration control in non-democratic states.[6]

Russia as an Immigrant Destination: Structural Determinants

Migration patterns are influenced far more by structural conditions than by policy efforts to control flows. Current migration into Russia is a direct result of political and border changes following the collapse of the Soviet Union in 1991 and creating a new structural reality. Migration theory tells us that migration flows follow colonial links (Castles and Miller 2009; Cohen 2001; Sassen 1996), are aided by common language and cultural practices (Massey et al. 1993), and are reinforced by the networks created between migrants in the receiving and sending countries (Brettell 2008; Hardwick 2008). These factors are all borne out in the case of Russia following the fall of the Soviet Union (Ryazantsev and Korneev 2013), and further contributed to the political decision to establish a visa-free regime among countries of the Soviet Union's successor organization, the CIS.

Immigration to Russia experienced a fundamental shift in the new millennium, from those seeking permanent status (citizenship) to those migrating temporarily for the purpose of work (Mukomel 2005).[7] Most migrants in the current period are temporary workers from former Soviet Central Asia (particularly Uzbekistan, Kyrgyzstan, and Tajikistan), who comprise the majority of labour migrants to Russia (see table 1.1).[8] Common history, geographic proximity, and the visa-free regime between CIS countries are frequently cited as pull factors driving increasing numbers of labour migrants (Ivakhnyuk 2006). Yet the most important factors driving current migration processes are economic decline in sending countries concurrent with economic growth in Russia, and Russia's declining working-age population. The demand for workers created by these two factors is not satisfied by shifting Russia's current population around (internal migration or urbanization) or programs to attract permanent migrants. Therefore, this book focuses on the much larger contingent of international migrants that come to Russia to work, most often on a temporary basis.[9]

Table 1.1. Documented labour migrants[a]

	2000	2007	2008	2009	2010	2011	2012	2013	2014	2015
All	213,300	1,717,100	2,425,900	2,223,600	1,640,800	1,792,800	2,229,100	2,468,200	3,177,900	1,838,700
China	26,200	228,800	281,700	269,900	186,500	69,500	76,900	71,300	71,700	49,400
North Korea	8,700	32,600	34,900	37,700	36,500	19,300	23,400	27,200	30,700	30,400
Turkey	17,800	131,200	130,500	77,200	45,700	18,900	27,700	27,700	24,100	19,300
USA	1,800	4,800	5,000	5,000	4,300	1,700	800	600	1,100	1,200
Vietnam	13,300	79,800	95,200	97,000	46,000	10,900	12,100	10,300	13,500	14,100
CIS countries	100,900	1,146,000	1,773,800	1,642,700	1,245,700	1,620,400	2,048,400	2,303,500	2,997,800	1,688,900
Armenia	5,500	73,400	101,100	82,000	59,800	98,300	115,400	128,000	179,000	1,700
Azerbaijan	3,300	57,600	76,300	60,700	40,300	64,700	71,600	77,400	110,900	51,300
Kazakhstan	2,900	7,600	10,400	11,200	8,300	9,300	1,700	1,600	1,400	600
Kyrgyzstan	900	109,600	184,600	156,100	117,700	112,400	138,700	173,100	230,300	33,500
Moldova	11,900	93,700	122,000	101,900	72,200	77,400	84,100	94,300	220,700	97,900
Tajikistan	6,200	250,200	391,400	359,200	268,600	327,500	410,000	464,700	589,200	427,500
Ukraine	64,100	209,300	245,300	205,300	167,300	139,800	159,100	167,100	395,800	206,900
Uzbekistan	6,100	344,600	642,700	666,300	511,500	791,000	1,067,800	1,197,300	1,270,500	869,200

Source: Rosstat 2011b; Rosstat 2013b; Rosstat 2015d; Rosstat 2016c.

[a] Documented labour migrants are those who have received a work permit or patent, which are the primary documents required for the majority of foreign workers. These figures do not include migrants who work as highly qualified specialists or individual entrepreneurs; these operate according to different legal rules and are peripheral to the analysis in this book.

Russia as a Land of Opportunity

The decline of the welfare state, economic crises, and rising unemployment have contributed to falling living standards in a number of former Soviet republics, especially in Central Asia and the Caucasus (Korobkov 2008). As a result, labour migration has become an important strategy for reducing poverty, specifically through migrant remittances (Jones, Black, and Skeldon 2007). In this way, the Eurasian migration system experiences migration flows that are typical across the globe as migrants seek higher wages in more economically developed countries (Cornelius et al. 2004; Massey et al. 1993). Tajikistan has become particularly dependent on remittances, the majority of which come from Russia (see table 1.2). Remittances sent through informal channels contribute even more to the receiving economies, and in some cases official data underreports actual remittances by as much as 50% (Karapetyan and Harutyunyan 2013; Quillin et al. 2007; Ivakhnyuk 2009a). Some estimates indicate around 90% of Tajikistan's remittances come from Russia.[10]

Economic migration to Russia is marked by larger and more temporary flows than other types of migration, as well as by large undocumented populations. Officially, there are around 1–2 million temporary labour migrants in Russia each year, yet the government and independent experts estimate an additional 3–5 million undocumented workers at any given time (Zaionchkovskaya 2013).[11] These estimates are not surprising, given the sheer number of people that cross the border into Russia each year, the vast majority of whom are citizens of visa-free CIS states (table 1.3). Greater numbers of illegal migrants accompanied the shift from permanent migration to temporary labour migration in the post-Soviet period. This is natural, considering that permanent migrants require official status to reach their ultimate goal of citizenship. While some labour migrants may eventually aspire to Russian citizenship, most have more immediate goals of finding gainful employment, which is not necessarily dependent on formal legal status.

Migrants are able to find jobs in Russia because of economic growth beginning in 1999, but this growth is not merely an opportunity for migrants as it has also contributed to further economic development. Russia's growth has become fused with the labour of foreign workers, who contribute an estimated 10% of Russia's total GDP (Malashenko 2012; Zaionchkovskaia, Mkrtchyn, and Tyuryukanova 2009). Many

Table 1.2. Remittances (in USD millions)

	2010	2011	2012	2013	2014	2015
Total remittances received % sent from Russia Remittances as a % of country's GDP						
Armenia	1,669	1,799	1,915	2,192	2,079	1,491
	34%	41%	43%	64%	64%	64%
	18%	18%	18%	20%	19%	14%
Azerbaijan	1,410	1,893	1,990	1,733	1,846	1,538
	63%	63%	57%	58%	58%	58%
	3%	3%	3%	3%	3%	2%
Belarus	575	891	1,053	1,214	1,248	1,075
	56%	43%	34%	46%	46%	45%
	1%	2%	2%	2%	2%	1%
Georgia	1,184	1,547	1,770	1,945	1,986	1,625
	43%	45%	37%	59%	59%	59%
	10%	11%	11%	12%	12%	10%
Kazakhstan	226	180	171	207	242	193
	93%	96%	68%	64%	64%	64%
	0.2%	0.1%	0.1%	0.1%	0.1%	0.1%
Kyrgyzstan	1,266	1,709	2,031	2,278	2,243	1,740
	80%	80%	79%	77%	77%	77%
	26%	28%	31%	31%	30%	26%
Tajikistan	2,306	3,060	3,626	4,219	3,854	2,962
	58%	58%	60%	76%	77%	76%
	41%	47%	48%	50%	42%	29%
Ukraine	6,535	7,822	8,449	9,667	7,354	6,212
	48%	48%	43%	52%	52%	51%
	5%	5%	5%	5%	6%	7%
Uzbekistan	2,845	4,262	5,668	6,633	6,206	2,525
					91%	100%
					10%	5%

Source: World Bank 2015; 2010–15 World Bank bilateral remittance data.

migrants find work in the construction industry, which has benefited from the oil boom of the 2000s (Weinthal and Luong 2006), whereas others have found reliable work in Russia's growing service sector. Furthermore, Russia's economy has developed to the point that its labour market is now segmented and there are certain jobs that middle-class Russians do not want (Heleniak 2008; Yudina 2005).[12]

Table 1.3. Entries into Russia

	2008	2009	2010	2011	2012	2013	2014	2015
Total	23,676,140	21,338,650	22,281,217	24,932,061	28,176,502	30,792,091	32,421,490	33,729,187
CIS	15,061,619	12,960,167	13,906,605	15,730,278	17,995,850	19,922,378	21,621,143	22,868,754

Source: Rosstat 2014a; Rosstat 2016a; Rosstat 2012a; Rosstat 2010a

Table 1.4. Remittance outflows from Russia (USD billions)

	2007	2008	2009	2010	2011	2012	2013	2014	2015
Remittance outflow	19.9	29.7	21.2	21.5	26.0	31.7	37.2	32.6	19.7
GDP	1,300	1,661	1,223	1,525	2,034	2,154	2,232	2,053	1,331
	1.5%	1.8%	1.7%	1.4%	1.3%	1.5%	1.7%	1.1%	1.5%

Source: World Bank 2016; World Bank national accounts data.

In the wake of the 2008 global financial crisis, many expected international labour migration flows to decrease, using the logic that the labour market would tighten, causing demand for migrant workers to shrink (Awad 2009; Ivakhnyuk 2009a). The available data shows that while the economic crisis may have had some impact on immigration to Russia, its effects have been less robust than expected. At the beginning of 2009, the World Bank predicted that remittances sent home by migrants would fall by $15 billion due to the financial crisis (World Bank 2009). In the end, remittances declined less than expected and steadily increased after 2009 (see table 1.4).[13] Though some estimate as many as a million Central Asian migrants returned home after the crisis, migrant flows remained robust, causing experts to conclude that migrants did not decide to return to their home countries en masse, but rather stayed and cut living costs in order to keep sending remittances (Ratha, Mohapatra, and Silwal 2009; International Crisis Group 2010). Many migrants chose not to return to their countries of origin in the period of financial crisis, either because of travel expenses or out of fear that they would not be able to return to Russia, given tightening legal space. Migrants remained in Russia and continued to work, often shifting into the shadow labour market (Marat 2009).

It is likely that migration flows following the 2014 ruble crisis will follow these earlier patterns. While migration theory suggests that economic factors are far more powerful than policy reforms in changing migration patterns, we cannot ignore the other structural factors in the Russian case that contribute to resilient migration flows. Though we see declines in remittances and the number of documented labour migrants in 2015, we do not see decreased numbers of foreigners crossing into Russia as we did in 2009. This data, in addition to reports on the ground, suggests that any reductions in migration after 2015 will be short lived.[14] In any case, the trends shown in official data do not capture migrants shifting into the informal sector, and therefore can at best show a partial picture of the migration situation.

Demographic Pressures and Increasing Labour Demand

A major factor contributing to robust labour market demand in Russia is the declining domestic working-age population, which creates employment opportunities at all levels of the economy (Ioffe and Zayonchkovskaya 2010). While the overall demographic picture shows a negative population growth rate, the situation is even more pronounced in the working-age cohort (Vishnevsky and Bobylev 2009). The current population crisis has its roots in declining fertility (Heleniak 2003), high mortality related to alcohol and other health concerns (Shlapentokh 2005), and residual effects of population loss as far back as the Second World War (Ediev 2001), all of which have implications far beyond the current labour market.[15] The government highlighted a number of key policy areas in its *Demographic Policy Concept to 2025*,[16] including pro-natalist incentives, reforms to improve health care and workplace and traffic safety, and an ethnic repatriation (or "compatriot") program to attract certain categories of permanent migrants. These policies have either met with lacklustre results, as in the case of the repatriation program, which has attracted far fewer migrants than expected (Vishnevsky 2013),[17] or have not made an immediate impact on the labour market. Attracting temporary migrants for the sake of filling labour gaps is not mentioned as a solution to the demographic issue. Rather, the government's official position is to focus on ethnic repatriates and highly skilled migrants to fill any labour gaps.

Demographic experts surmise that immigration is the only source of population growth in Russia; they estimate that 500,000 permanent migrants are needed per year to compensate for the demographic decline, and upwards of 1 million are needed annually to bolster the working-age population (Vishnevsky 2013).[18] Yet according to FMS statistics, only 136,000 people became Russian citizens in 2013 and an additional 350,000 were granted temporary or permanent residence permits.[19] This low rate of naturalizations and residence permits compared to the number of labour migrants (including estimates of illegal migrants) indicates that migrant flows are not contributing to permanent population growth. The temporary nature of migration is often reinforced by difficult bureaucratic procedures and the CIS visa-free regime, which allows migrants to establish circular patterns.

Strategic Enforcement Gaps or Unintended Consequences?

Given the structural conditions of demographic decline, a segmented labour market, sending countries' economic dependence on remittances, colonial linkages between Russia and the countries of the former Soviet Union, and robust transnational migrant networks, large migrant flows are inevitable for Russia. These factors alone would be sufficient to produce robust flows of legal and illegal migrants, regardless of policy content (Cornelius and Tsuda 2004). Flows are aided even further by visa-free travel for CIS citizens and an active (yet largely unregulated, and sometimes exploitative) migrant intermediary industry that assists migrants with job placement and documents.

The Russian government is well aware of the acute need for labour as well as the pressures in sending countries that cause immigrants to seek work in Russia.[20] As they have become increasingly sensitized to the structural conditions driving migration, as well as to the need to balance the political demands that come from public fears and economic demand, the government has experimented with a variety of policy mechanisms to manage the labour migration situation.[21] Policies implemented beginning in 2007 have led to dramatic fluctuations in the number of documented labour migrants, but have created an overall policy trajectory that decreases the access of migrants to legal work documents (see table 1.5). The resulting scarcity of legal labour can be framed either as an unintended consequence or as a strategic use of migration management.

In this book, I demonstrate how the scarcity of legal labour is methodically institutionalized by actors in the public administration and by regional executives based on signals from the Kremlin. Scarcity is an essential tool for managing the multi-level balancing act of migration, in an attempt to satisfy interested actors throughout the political system. This strategy is embedded in the institutional structure of authoritarian governance in Russia, in particular the informal networks that exist at all levels of the political system and are essential to its function. An analysis of migration policy can elucidate the inner workings of a sometimes murky Russian system. Furthermore, since Russia is a "world innovator in nondemocratic practices" (Petrov, Lipman, and Hale 2014), this study can illustrate the possibilities of migration management in a non-democratic context.

At the same time, Russia holds much in common with other major immigrant-receiving countries, despite institutional and regime differences. Migration theory is largely based on Western democratic receiving countries (Money 2010; Boucher and Gest 2015). Though there is a growing number of studies on important migrant recipients in the Middle East and Asia, an empirical gap remains beyond OECD countries.[22] The empirical gap has important theoretical consequences, as not all observations taken from the migration literature can be directly applied outside the Western democratic context. In this volume, I probe the limits of migration theory by highlighting aspects of the Russian case that

Table 1.5. Major policy reforms, 2007–15

Law	Date	Reform
On the Legal Status of Foreign Citizens[a]	January 15, 2007	Introduction of work permit quotas for CIS citizens Ban on workers in certain sectors (called "allowable shares") CIS migrants allowed to apply for work permits independently (without an employer)
On Migration Registration[b]	January 15, 2007	Extended period of registration from 3 to 7 days Allowed registration at place of stay/residence or work
On the Legal Status of Foreign Citizens	May 19, 2010	Introduction of patents (allowing CIS citizens to work for individual Russian citizens)
On Compulsory Pension Insurance[c]	January 1, 2012	Obligated certain foreign workers to pay into the pension scheme
On the Legal Status of Foreign Citizens	December 30, 2012	Allowed those on temporary residence permits to work without a work permit or patent
On the Order of Exit and Entry[d]	July 23, 2013	Introduction of 5-year re-entry ban on foreigners who are administratively expelled or who commit two or more administrative violations in a year
Administrative Code[e]	August 9, 2013	Increased penalties for violating migration law, including obligatory administrative expulsion for violating entry, stay, or work procedures in Moscow and St Petersburg (including Moscow and Leningrad oblasts)[f]
On the Order of Exit and Entry	December 21, 2013	Defined fictitious registration as submitting deliberately false information for registration, or registering at a place with no intention to stay there
Criminal Code[g]	December 21, 2013	Defined possible penalties for fictitious registration, including fines of 100,000–500,000 rubles (or 3 years' salary)

(*Continued*)

Table 1.5. Major policy reforms, 2007–15 (Continued)

Law	Date	Reform
On the Legal Status of Foreign Citizens	January 1, 2014	CIS citizens limited to stays of 90 days out of every 180 days (violations can incur re-entry ban of 3 years)
On the Legal Status of Foreign Citizens	April 20, 2014	Simplified access to permanent residence for those able to prove native Russian-language skills
On Citizenship[h]	June 23, 2014	Those able to prove native Russian-language skills given fast-track access to citizenship
Labour Code[i]	December 1, 2014	Employment contracts of foreign workers linked to migration status
On the Legal Status of Foreign Citizens	January 1, 2015	Replaced work permits with patents (and allows work for companies) for CIS citizens
		Required language, culture, and legal norms exam for work permits and patents

[a] Federal Law No. 115 of July 25, 2002.
[b] Federal Law No. 109 of July 18, 2006.
[c] Federal Law No. 167 of December 15, 2001.
[d] Federal Law No. 114 of August 15, 1996.
[e] Federal Law No. 195 of December 30, 2001.
[f] Automatic expulsion for certain violations of entry and stay procedures was later deemed unconstitutional by Constitutional Court Order No. 5-P of February 17, 2016.
[g] Federal Law No. 63 of June 13, 1996.
[h] Federal Law No. 62 of May 31 2002.
[i] Federal Law No. 197 of December 30, 2001.

are parallel to other immigration-receiving states, while exploring the unique mechanisms employed by non-democratic countries.

Reconstructing the Gap Hypothesis

A major commonality between Russia and other immigrant-receiving states is that migration policy is inherently political. While Russia's goal of legal labour scarcity and the informal mechanisms used to manage and enforce it are not common strategies addressed in the migration literature, the fact that this policy course is chosen strategically is simply an attribute of its political nature. Strategic or instrumental uses of policy for political purposes often hinge on enforcement, or more specifically a gap between policies on paper and implemented (or non-implemented) realities. When policies are used strategically, they are often chosen more for their symbolic value than from an expectation that they will change actual migration flows (Cornelius et al. 2004). In the literature, gaps between policy and reality are typically discussed as pathologies. This book reconceptualizes gaps as purposefully, even rationally, chosen strategies that can be used to achieve political aims. The Russian case clearly demonstrates that not only are immigration policies a result of politics, but the *gaps* in policies also serve a political function and can be used strategically by government actors to pursue a variety of interests.

A natural starting point for the discussion of policy gaps begins with Cornelius, Martin, and Hollifield's (1994) "gap hypothesis," which focuses on the differences between policy goals and migration outcomes. The often vast expanse between goals and outcomes can be a result of many different factors, including how different groups' interests coalesce and how they compete for policymaking influence, the process of debating and writing laws, and how policies are interpreted by bureaucrats and institutionalized into everyday practices. Outcomes, which are the response by migrants and other interested actors to policy innovations, can involve changes in migration patterns, the development of alternative strategies to navigate formal paths to legalization (e.g., relying on the services of middlemen to complete legal procedures), informal pursuit of semi-legalization (e.g., use of forged documents to appear legal, or obtaining legal residence but not work documents), or labour activities in the shadow economy.

Given the numerous points at which policy on the ground can diverge from politicians' promises, Czaika and de Haas (2013) consolidated gaps into three locations: between elite discourse and the written content of policies (the discursive gap), between policy and implementation (the implementation gap), and between implementation and outcomes (the efficacy gap). Causes of gaps in these various locations have been attributed to structural factors in the international labour market (Anderson, Sharma, and Wright 2009; Portes and Walton 1981; Cornelius and Tsuda 2004), intermediaries who broker passage across borders and entry into the labour market (Castles 2004; Tsuda 2003; Basch, Glick-Schiller, and Szanton-Blanc 1994), and demands in the domestic economy (Messina 2007; Schenk 2016). Human rights norms and constituencies within democratically governed polities that lobby for increased migration are offered as further explanations of gaps between policy and outcome (Money 1999; Freeman 1995). Other explanations for policy gaps in the migration literature focus on the policy process itself, in particular pointing to ambiguous policy intentions, flawed policy design, inadequate implementation and enforcement, or unintended consequences (Cornelius and Tsuda 2004).

In the Russian case, there is very little discursive gap, as the policies that are adopted in large part follow the populist rhetoric of political elites. Rather the gaps in the Russian case are those of implementation and efficacy. Some of these gaps can be explained by the factors listed above, in particular by specific economic and social conditions that Russia shares with many other immigrant-receiving countries. However, the explanations above do not sufficiently account for the gaps that occur because of political or governance factors, since the mechanisms that Russian elites use to cope with the demands of the multi-level balancing act are not considered in the literature. In particular, the centrality of informal practices in Russian politics (including structurally embedded corruption and reliance on informal networks) presents policymakers with a set of available choices when creating, implementing, and enforcing policies that are different from the choices usually considered in the migration literature (Filippov 2011; Levin and Satarov 2000; Stefes 2007). These informal practices and their pivotal role in the multi-level balancing act are the main focus of this book and are developed in detail starting in chapter 2.

The multi-level balancing act of migration management in Russia, as conceived in this book's account, primarily concerns the decisions and incentives of state actors. Nevertheless, the ability of elites to manage and respond to public opinion is crucial for addressing policy gaps. Russian leaders rely on the type of populist rhetoric common in other receiving states, creating an anti-migrant social contract to quell public dissent. In seeking to navigate between the demands of public opinion and economic need, Russia joins virtually all other immigrant host countries in a pursuit to reconcile a variety of conflicts of interest and the "structural contradictions" (Calavita 1992) between demands from economic and social actors through the creation and implementation of policy (Castles 2004). Moreover, Russia shares a number of important features with the larger pool of major migrant-receiving countries, including demographic and labour market decline, which pull against calls from the public to limit immigration and protect the labour market.

Pursuing an Anti-Migrant Social Contract

The social contract in modern Russia is focused on producing legitimacy for the ruling elite and avoiding any major public backlash. While some have argued that the government's legitimacy, especially in the 2000s, depended on the charisma of Putin (Hill and Gaddy 2013), others have identified the concrete gains of economic prosperity as the cause for the public's support (Feklyunina and White 2011). Building on this latter perspective, the social contract can be defined as a pact where the Russian people give loyalty, political support, and trust in exchange for prosperity and stability (Makarkin and Oppenheimer 2011). However, there are ideational components of the social contract as well, and ideas of patriotism and nationalism have become particularly important during periods of economic uncertainty (Sharafutdinova 2012; Laruelle 2011). In this context, anti-migration populism is a legitimacy-producing strategy that connects the public to state actors in a social contract that aims to keep the population a passive observer of politics.

In order to give elites the latitude to pursue preferred policies while maintaining legitimacy, the social contract is imbued with anti-migrant populism that aims to legitimize immigration policy choices (creating a minimal discursive gap) and ensure that the public will not mobilize against implementation and efficacy gaps that arise from corruption, the use of informal strategies, or bureaucratic rigidity. Populist rhetoric accomplishes these goals because it is based on shared values (between elites and the public) that are compatible with ideas of nationhood or patriotism. Elites view public opinion as something that can be managed through populism without necessitating policy change that is not in their interests, and the public in turn remains passive because their most concrete connection with the migration process is the populist rhetoric of elites rather than direct personal experience with migrants.

Anti-Migrant Sentiment and the National Idea

It is essential to state at the outset that anti-migrant populism and nationalism are not the same thing. The literature on nationalism is vast and varied, encompassing many more and deeper ideas about political identity than are at issue with anti-migrant populism.[23] Nationalism, national identity, and their evolution in Russia since the Soviet period have also been heavily debated, but scholarship has reached little consensus, in part because political elites have treated the topic with great ambivalence.[24] In recent years there has been a more deliberate effort by political elites to reconstitute patriotism as a unifying idea, and some scholars have pointed to a "new Russian nationalism," though the content of these ideas could be interpreted variously (Sharafutdinova 2012; Laruelle 2010; Kolstø and Blakkisrud 2016). As a result, nationalism and patriotism today do not have a cohesive ideational core any more than they did at the fall of the Soviet Union (Tolz 2001; Gerber 2014).

Nevertheless, anti-migrant sentiment is *compatible* in some ways with nationalist discourse. If nationalism is a discourse that defines who belongs (to a nation, ethnicity, or citizenship group) and has a rightful claim on the resources that come with membership, migrants represent a stress on the boundaries of belonging and distribution of resources (e.g., jobs or public goods). Nationalism is also a discourse that seeks to legitimize political elites (Gellner 1983; Goode and Stroup 2015), and in this sense it works towards the same goal as anti-migrant populism.

Anti-migrant rhetoric first appeared among fringe nationalist groups (Laruelle 2010) but was then brought into the mainstream when, after ethnically charged public mobilizations in 2011 and 2012, "the earlier ideological vagueness and ambiguity of official discourse increasingly began to be seen as a potential problem, rather than a strength" (Tolz and Harding 2015). However, anti-migrant rhetoric need not be nationalist. Putin himself only rarely engages in anti-migrant populism, and when he does his statements avoid making links between national identity and immigration. For example, Putin's (2012) editorial *Russia: The National Question*, written during his re-election campaign, criticized "rubber apartments" and promised to introduce language exams for all labour migrants, both of which became major policy issues for international migrants in the following years.[25] Nevertheless, his language about international migrants is extremely careful, separating foreign citizens from issues of identity, and reserving his criticism for internal migrants, conflicts between different groups of Russian citizens, and the migration situation in Europe (Schenk forthcoming). Political elites below the level of the Kremlin much more freely link anti-migrant rhetoric to ideas of nationalism, highlighting the dangers that migrants pose for the identity of Russians by mobilizing certain migration myths.

The utility of anti-migrant populism is that it mobilizes ideas that are compatible with nationalism, without engaging more thorny ideational issues directly. The blurry lines between the two allow discourse to satisfy a larger contingent of people without alienating those of varying commitments or different conceptions of the national idea. Populism is simply the rhetorical packaging that works equally well with a variety of ideologies. For the purpose of the social contract, this flexibility gives elites significant leverage to legitimize preferred immigration policies.

Passivity: Indirect Experience with Migration

For the most part, society remains relatively passive on migration issues in terms of participating in anti-migrant protests or xenophobic violence directed at migrants. Despite an increasing reputation for radical and violent xenophobia in recent years, most Russians experience anti-migrant sentiment indirectly. Surveys that show a majority of Russians favour stricter immigration rules also demonstrate that a large percentage of people do not feel direct ethnic tensions in their city or region (figures since 2005 are consistently above 60%), and that respondents rarely or almost never personally feel tensions between ethnic groups (figures consistently above 80% from 2002 and dipping just below 80% in 2011–12) (Levada Center 2013). This indicates that though there are high levels of perceived xenophobia, it is not a part of people's everyday experience.

A majority of Russians believe migration causes an increase in crime. But official data shows that migrants are responsible for around 50,000 crimes per year, making it impossible that any but a fraction of Russia's 140 million citizens have direct experience with migrant criminality (MVD 2003–9). Rather, the perception of criminality is abstract and delinked in most cases from personal experience, influenced by elite statements and the media's disproportionate focus on migrants involved in criminal activity.

The contradiction between attitudes and experience is particularly acute in Moscow, where 46% of respondents (compared to 17% of respondents nationwide) believe migrants comprise 50% or more of the local population (Neoruss Project 2014). Muscovites' adherence to the idea of "Russia for Russians" is higher (70%) than in nationwide samples (59%), and respondents are more likely to define "Russians" as including only ethnic Russians (43% in Moscow vs 39% nationwide). These findings are corroborated by other surveys that find xenophobic and nationalist attitudes on the whole markedly higher (though not homogeneous in their focus) in Moscow (Gerber 2014). Yet 47% of respondents have no contact of any kind with migrants, and an additional 32% come into contact with migrants only in the course of retail transactions, demonstrating that even higher levels of xenophobia are marked by indirect experience (Neoruss Project 2014).

In a similar way, the Russian public is largely a passive observer of politics (Kudelia 2012). Though the mobilization of the public is important for Putin's approval levels and for electoral turnout, the ruling elite prefers for people to be disengaged (Petrov, Lipman, and Hale 2014). But passivity is not equal to ignorance. The population is often aware of the types of corruption and informal schemes common to the migration sphere, but the social contract requires passivity in exchange for stability and prosperity. In cases where corruption becomes too visible or the public becomes too reactive, the social contract can break down. While corruption scandals can lead to the firing of a governor or ministry-level official, they are often blamed on lower-level officials who can act as scapegoats (and produce a less disruptive episode). This strategy increases the populist capital of the Kremlin by "rescuing" the population from unscrupulous political elites, which is a common strategy of populist leaders.

Public Opinion and Populism: Russia as a "Normal" Country of Immigration

Though early migration research pointed to an "antipopulist norm" in the politics of certain (democratic) receiving states (Freeman 1995), there is ample evidence that immigration politics have generally shifted towards an embrace of populist rhetoric (Messina 2007; Mudde 2012). This shift was first visible in the rhetoric of far-right party leaders, but has become increasingly mainstream in recent years. The term "populism" is widely used in association with anti-immigrant or "nativist" rhetoric.[26] The idea that populism is a direct appeal to the public, often through personalistic means, finds resonance in the Russian case. In fact, populism may be the single distinguishing characteristic that makes Russia a "normal" country of immigration. However, an essential component of Russia's populist approach is that it comes from within the political elite, from state officials at all levels. As a result, populism is a key part of the social contract between the state and society as the state seeks to legitimize political rule and assure the public that their active participation is not necessary to solve immigration problems.

Breunig, Cao, and Luedtke (2012) claim that non-democratic governments are insulated from xenophobic impulses and therefore do not have to factor the public in when formulating immigration policy. But in Russia, there is clear evidence that the government *is* sensitive to public opinion in the process of policymaking (Petrov, Lipman, and Hale 2014), though the mechanism connecting state and society is based on populism rather than electoral accountability. The migration sphere clearly illustrates this sensitivity and demonstrates how Russia manages rhetoric about migration alongside policy in a way that does not create a significant discursive gap.

The discursive gap is particularly small when we consider the statements of Putin and top Kremlin elites. Typically, statements about immigration foreshadow policies that have already been chosen. Putin's language about immigrants is much less inflammatory than that of lower-level elites, meaning any populist moments are important signals for how to approach migration management. For the most part, inflammatory populism is devolved to lower leaders as a part of their responsibility for helping to maintain the social contract (what I call the populist pact). As a consequence, however, there is more discursive gap between the rhetoric of lower officials and the policies that are decided at the federal level. In these cases, it is not necessarily the consistency of policy and rhetoric that is the goal, but rather the management of public mood and creation of the illusion that the government is producing effective migration control.

Anti-immigrant populism finds fertile ground among the Russian population. Populist rhetoric by elites closely tracks with public opinion, both in response to public concerns and in shaping the public discourse through the state-allied media.[27] Public opinion polls record consistently strong and increasing support for anti-immigrant sentiment in Russia. Support for the idea that "Russia for Russians" should be put into policy has been consistently above 50% since 2001, reaching a high of 66% in 2012 and 2013 (Levada Center 2014; Levada Center 2013).[28] Increasing numbers of those polled believe that immigration policies should be restrictive towards immigrants (70% in 2012) and the state should expel illegal immigrants from CIS countries (64% in 2012) (Levada Center 2013).[29] Forty-three per cent of survey respondents in 2013 and 46% in 2014 agreed that all migrants and their children (regardless of legal status) should move back to their home countries (Neoruss Project 2014).

Russians are not alone in their anti-migrant sentiment. Opinion polls in Europe also show significant apprehension towards migration, with 46% of Eurobarometer participants answering that increased labour migration from outside the EU should not be encouraged, though results vary significantly by country from 32% in Romania to 75% in Latvia.[30] Of aggregated European respondents, 42% believe that immigrants do not enrich their countries culturally or economically, again ranging widely from 18% in Sweden to 78% in Latvia. Similar polls in the US show that opinion has varied over time in terms of those favouring more restrictions on immigration, from 65% in 1993 to 35% in 2013, and those favouring deportation of all illegals, from 16% in 2006 to 21% in 2011.[31] While these surveys are not directly comparable for methodological reasons, they establish the fact that immigration is a long-standing target of negative public opinion across receiving countries.

In many ways, the discourses that surround immigration issues in Russia are typical of the myths popular in migrant-receiving countries, focusing on unemployment, security threats, and cultural incompatibility (Mudde 2012). In recent years these myths have been increasingly mobilized through the media in Russia for a variety of populist purposes, and have even become a regular part of election-year rhetoric (Abashin 2017).

The Unemployment Myth

"Immigrants take our jobs!" is a refrain sung throughout the immigrant-receiving world. It is a slogan mobilized by far-right parties in Europe such as the National Front in France, Austria's Freedom Party, and others who fared increasingly well in both national and European election polls.[32] It is a common argument in anti-immigration advocacy circles as well, appearing in the form of analytical-type reports by government and non-government think tanks throughout the US and Europe, and making its way into the speeches of mainstream politicians (Federation for American Immigration Reform 2013; Camarota and Zeigler 2009; Migration Advisory Committee 2012).[33] Russian policymakers are keenly sensitized to fears surrounding unemployment, as chapter 3 will demonstrate.

The credibility of the unemployment myth is in most cases fairly dubious, and at the very least the issue is nowhere near settled in the migration literature.[34] But fact and reason are of minor consequence to populists, who are more interested in mobilizing fear and anxiety for political gain than appealing to scholarly findings.

Rising unemployment in the domestic labour market creates pressure on policymakers in Russia to reduce competition from low-wage immigrant workers (Ivakhnyuk 2009b). The persistent and visible presence of migrants, especially in large urban centres, reinforces the perception that native workers are being pushed out of the labour market by migrant workers. Opinion polls in 2012–13 showed that 67% of respondents believed that migrants were taking Russian jobs (Levada Center 2013). Yet it is interesting that another survey in 2013 revealed that 53% of respondents believed migrants were very much needed in Russia because they did low-wage jobs Russians don't want to do. These results show deep ambivalence on the part of the public when it comes to labour migrants.

Because of perceived labour competition, some scholars point to a rise in xenophobia during periods like the 2008 global financial crisis (Ivakhnyuk 2013a). In Russia, there were widespread calls from mayors, governors, and the chairman of the Federation of Independent Trade Unions for lower migrant quotas surrounding the 2008 financial crisis. Such statements as "We need to preserve jobs for Muscovites" and "We need to close the door to migrant workers and look to the domestic labour market" typify the labour protectionist thrust. Putin, who at the time was prime minister, announced that he would reduce the migrant work permit quota for 2009.[35]

In the wake of the 2014 ruble crisis, we could have expected a similar xenophobic backlash. However, public opinion surveys between 2013 and 2014 show very little evidence for an upsurge in anti-migrant sentiment. In 2015, the media shifted focus to large numbers of migrants leaving Russia because of economic conditions, which could also explain decreasing xenophobic sentiment.[36] The Russian experience illustrates, as other research has found, that there is not a clear causal relationship between crisis and xenophobia (Mudde 2012). Rather, there is latitude for the government to mould crisis rhetoric to different ends.

The Security Myth

The Russian media commonly frames immigration and immigrants as a security threat, portraying migrants as criminals, connected with drugs and organized crime, and posing public health risks (Kozhevnikova 2007). Many Russians do not distinguish between legal and illegal migrants, leading to the widespread perception that *all* migrants are criminals.[37] The increasingly securitized discourse surrounding threats posed by immigrants is not unique to Russia (Alexseev 2006b; Ibrahim 2005; Buonfino 2004), though opinion polls typically show less dramatic results in other countries. Seventy-one per cent of Russians polled in 2012–13 agreed that migrants increase criminality (Levada Center 2013). In the European context, when asked if immigrants are more to blame for crime than other groups, 51% of respondents in Greece, 48% in Germany, 45% in Italy, 36% in France, and 20% in Britain answered in the affirmative (Pew Research Center 2014). Despite the persistence of rhetoric, studies consistently show that migration, criminality, and security threats have few concrete links (Migration Advisory Committee 2012; Bianchi, Buonanno, and Pinotti 2012; Sohoni and Sohoni 2014).

Russian officials often call for restrictive immigration policies on the basis of security threats. Moscow mayor Sergei Sobyanin has several times been quoted as saying that Moscow would be the safest city in the world if it were able to solve its illegal migrant problems (including both foreign and internal migration).[38] Sobyanin's predecessor, Yuri Luzhkov, frequently blamed migrants for increased crime rates, claiming that 36%–50% of crimes in Moscow were perpetrated by migrants, and called for lower work permit quotas as a solution.[39] Statements by officials are rarely debated or analysed in the media, and are instead presented as facts coming from an official source.

Migrants are also linked with threats to public health associated with risky behaviours (i.e., drug addiction and sexually transmitted diseases) (Karachurina 2013), living and working in unsanitary conditions,[40] lack of access to adequate medical care (Kuznetsova, Mukhariamova, and Vafina 2013), and the diseases that are more prevalent in their countries of origin (Ivakhnenko 2013). The former head of Russia's Federal Service for Supervision of Consumer Rights and Human Welfare (Rospotrebnadzor) and lead State Public Health doctor Gennadii Onishchenko made public pronouncements on several occasions linking migrants with the spread of AIDS, tuberculosis, and other diseases, arguing that most migrants are illegal and therefore do not have access to proper health services or sanitary living conditions.[41] He recommended deportation for migrants with serious diseases, passing a directive in 2010 that laid out a procedure for declaring migrants "undesirable" on the basis of health risks.[42]

Cultural Incompatibility Myth

Opinion polls in 2012–13 showed that 46% of respondents believe migrants destroy Russian culture (Levada Center 2013). The idea that migrants are a threat to the social stability of Russia tends to focus on both ethnic and religious aspects. Ethnic concerns focus on non-Slavic identities such as Asians from Central Asia and China and Caucasians from the south of Russia and the countries of Azerbaijan, Armenia, and Georgia. Religious concerns are most often focused on Islam, to which many Central Asians and Caucasians adhere. Both internal (Russian citizens) and international migrants are often collapsed into the same category, which overlaps substantially with religious identifiers and all non-Russian ethnicities (Laruelle 2009; Kozhevnikova 2007; Reeves 2013).[43] Whereas Putin is often very careful to separate internal from international migrants, for the anti-migrant populism mobilized by lower-level officials, nuance (i.e., a migrant's legal status or citizenship) matters very little so long as rhetoric can tap into fears that frame migration in a useful way or legitimize a particular course of action.

The media frequently justifies migration policies in ethnic terms. For example, when new legal measures in 2007 banned migrants from selling goods in markets and bazaars, media outlets connected the reform with ethnic riots in the northwestern city of Kondopoga the previous year. One report explained, "the law is designed to open the way for Russian agricultural producers and vendors to the markets, which have been controlled mostly by migrants from the Caucasus republics, leading to xenophobic sentiments in society."[44]

Even "integration" efforts are often based on highlighting the cultural differences between migrants and Russians. A controversial handbook for migrants published in St Petersburg, criticized for its depiction of migrants as brooms and paintbrushes, recommends that migrants refrain from wearing national clothing or sports clothes (i.e., track suits), especially with dress shoes, sitting in a squatting position on the street, spitting on the street, or preparing food on balconies and in courtyards.[45] All of these are stereotypically Central Asian behaviours or characteristics. The Orthodox Church also issued a guide in the form of a textbook for migrants to assist them in studying for the Russian culture portion of exams introduced in 2015.[46] The textbook focuses on describing Russian customs, but also gives tips to migrants on how to conduct themselves on public transport (e.g., do not spit), and warns that if Russian women aren't treated with respect, their countrymen will come to their defence.

In other cases, cultural threats are cast in religious terms. In 2010 the Moscow city government banned the ritual slaughter of animals within the city limits. The measure came in response to complaints by residents that animals were being slaughtered in outdoor areas around the city by those celebrating the Muslim holiday Kurban Bairam.[47] Reminders have been issued each year from the mayor's office instructing that worshippers must leave the city limits in order to participate in animal sacrifice.[48] Also on the topic of Muslim worship, Mayor Sobyanin has been vocal in his opposition to building additional mosques in Moscow, saying that if mosque attendance were limited to Muscovites or people who had legal residence in the city, nobody would actually be attending services.[49]

Is Russia's Populism "Normal"?

While there are a number of parallels between Russia and other migrant-receiving countries in terms of public opinion and the types of populist rhetoric that resonate with the public, there are also important differences. Despite the recent electoral success of far-right parties in the European Parliament, and the use of anti-immigrant rhetoric by acting executives such as Nicolas Sarkozy and David Cameron, the policymaking process remains deliberative in these Western cases. Populist discourses in this type of political process routinely occur prior to policymaking as a way to mobilize the public around a particular viewpoint that may or may not be eventually adopted into policy.

In Russia, policymaking is not deliberative and most often takes place outside the public eye. Policy is primarily a tool of managing elite interests, and populism is a way of justifying decisions to the public. This is particularly true for the rare populist pronouncements made by Putin, which often indicate a policy course that has already been chosen, producing minimal discursive gap. Sometimes policy is implemented only after public statements, and in these cases, Putin's statements are seen as directives that must be implemented, as will be discussed more fully in the following chapters. The populist discourse of lower-level officials is not strictly connected to policy, as in several of the examples above. In these cases, the rhetorical function of populist statements is to reinforce a social contract between the public and elites that creates legitimacy for the ruling powers.

While public opinion is but one of a number of factors that political elites consider when creating migration policy, it is foundational for the multi-level balancing act in Russia. The creation of migration policy in all states is a matter of trade-offs as states pursue channels of legitimacy that often conflict, including providing security, the conditions for economic prosperity, a sense of justice in economic distribution, and (for some states) institutions that provide for democracy and the rule of law (Boswell 2007). In many states this produces a discursive gap, where the rhetoric of policymakers does not match the policies that are adopted, leaving a number of scholars to conclude that public opinion often has a minimal effect on policy (Freeman 2011; Freeman 1995; Messina 2007). In Russia the highest priority in policymaking is the pursuit of elite interests, and therefore the potential impact of the public must be minimized without threatening legitimacy or the social contract.

Migration policies and rhetoric help to reinforce anti-migrant aspects of the social contract by increasing the populist content of the discourse in certain cases when necessary (e.g., during the 2008 financial crisis, when work permit quotas were decreased) and decreasing it in other cases (e.g., the 2014 ruble crisis, when media coverage focused on migrants leaving Russia rather than on relieving labour market pressure through new policies). Therefore, while public opinion and elite statements may be closely aligned with migration policy adoption, this convergence does not have a demonstrable effect on policy implementation and outcomes, since adjustments to the anti-migrant social contract are made primarily through populist rhetoric rather than by real attempts to change the migration landscape. Attempts to gain legitimacy by policymakers are effective on some level (regardless of the outcome of policies) because populist statements come from within the state and are framed in terms of exercising state capacity.

Scarcity and Informality as Strategies for Migration Management

The major factor setting Russia apart from other major immigrant-receiving countries is the centrality of informal strategies in migration management practices. Using a combination of populism to manage public opinion and a careful mix of formal (law-based) and informal (network-based) mechanisms, government elites can pursue a set of preferred policies that benefit their political and personal interests. Political elites must first fulfil the obligations of the patronage relationships that are central to the political system, and are then free to pursue their personal interests using the resources of their official positions.

This book argues that the state manages conflicting demands from society (based on migration myths), the economy (owing to the demographic crisis), and the political and personal interests of elites by creating restrictive control mechanisms that force many migrants into the informal sector, creating a scarcity of legal labour. Immigration restrictions, primarily those that limit the number of migrants from CIS countries, have broad public appeal.[50] Further, pushing migrants into the informal sector, both through policies and the corruption involved in the implementation process, creates an ample pool of cheap (albeit illegal) labour that employers can draw on.

The scarcity of legal labour acts as a patronage resource that can be deployed in various ways by bureaucratic and regional elites. Decisions about what mechanisms will be used to produce scarcity are made at the federal level. During the 2007–15 period addressed in this book, two major mechanisms have been used to produce scarcity: work permit quotas and labour patents. While the mechanisms are very different in nature, the driving logic behind each is the production of scarcity. Regional leaders and bureaucrats must adapt to federal signals as to the appropriate level of scarcity in order to produce an impression that there is coordination across the administration of the federal system. However, once an illusion of coordination is produced, regional leaders and bureaucrats have significant latitude to decide how scarcity will be deployed.

Because public policy implementation relies on the informal management of patronage pacts, Russia contributes a very different picture of migration management from what is typically considered in the literature; in Russia, devolution is real but is not primarily based on formal principles (e.g., a federal system) and is rather managed by interlocking relationships. While anti-migrant elements in public opinion and populist rhetoric create some parallels between Russia and other migrant-receiving countries, the institutional context and the management of policy gaps are not accounted for in migration theory. The following chapters in this book elucidate how the multi-level balancing act of migration management in Russia creates and utilizes policy implementation and efficacy gaps to satisfy actors throughout the system. As a result, this volume is a major contribution to migration theory because it offers an account of the incentives of policymakers and bureaucrats to strategically pursue a type of enforcement (or non-enforcement) that produces desired outcomes. An in-depth analysis of Russia is appropriate both for the theoretical question of how policy and implementation gaps are used instrumentally and to remedy an empirical gap by analysing a case that is underrepresented in the migration literature.

The following chapters unpack the argument that restrictions on labour migrants coming to Russia are politically motivated by government actors who must translate the federal government's driving desire for stability into reality. Bureaucrats in the federal ministries and in their regional branches must correctly identify and address threats to stability in the creation and implementation of public policy. In the migration sphere, potential threats come from an uncertain balance between society's intolerance of migrants on the one hand and economic demand for a continued supply of inexpensive migrant labour on the other.

The multi-level balancing act, where actors at various levels of the patronage system juggle competing interests, is the institutional structure of migration management. Chapter 2 shows how the patronage ties between state officials create an interdependent system where benefits and obligations are distributed. Regional elites and bureaucrats must fulfil the obligations of patronage pacts in order to retain their positions and benefit from the spoils of migration management. Elites can manage migration with great latitude as long as their efforts appear to follow federally defined prerogatives and do not threaten regional stability by producing visible scandals, public outcry, or social unrest. The multi-level balancing act of migration management acts as a window into how the implementation of public policy and the function of the federal system operate according to the principle of devolution via patronage pact rather than according to written rules and divisions of power.

Chapter 3 analyses work permit quotas as a tool of creating scarcity of legal labour. The quota system that was used for CIS citizens from 2007 to 2014 demonstrates an effort to balance interests in the Kremlin, in regions, and among ministries involved in the migration process. Despite an early liberalizing effect, the quota mechanism was employed in a persistently restrictive manner. Since quotas did little to change labour market demand, signals sent by the federal government as to the appropriate level of quota served to indicate what proportion of illegal immigration would be tolerated. Decreased quotas inevitably led to increased numbers of illegal migrants, informal mechanisms, and corruption schemes used to profit from the migration sphere.

Quotas were based on a complicated system of planning and reporting, mimicking Soviet economic practices. When patents replaced quotas for CIS citizens in 2015, the logic of migration management shifted to a seemingly market-based approach. Chapter 4 illustrates how patents were instituted in order to increase state control over migration management through a state capitalist model. Owing to budget shortfalls caused by falling oil prices and the 2014 ruble crisis, the imperative to create new streams of revenue became a major impetus for migration policy reform. Since patents are fee-based permits requiring monthly tax payments to remain valid, monetizing migrant documents became a reliable way to increase state revenues. Further, the one-stop migration centres, where all of the procedures necessary for obtaining a patent could be completed, attempted to create state-controlled monopolies for migration services in order to displace a diffuse and unregulated system of migration intermediaries.

In order to maintain the scarcity of legal labour that is so crucial for Russian migration management amid a market-based mechanism, a number of new regulations were implemented alongside patents. In particular, the requirement that migrants pass a Russian-language exam and present all the necessary documents to the migration services within 30 days of arrival limited the number of migrants who could legalize their work status. As a result, though the revenue from patents increased in 2015, the number of legal migrants decreased.

Chapters 5–7 go on to explore the ways in which scarcity can be used by regional elites within the context of the patronage rules of the multilevel balancing act. Case studies of Moscow, Sverdlovsk, and Krasnodar demonstrate varying capacities to manage and profit from migration management. In Moscow (chapter 5), the benefits of migration are circulated back into the regional patronage systems, first into the personal networks of Yuri Luzhkov (1992–2010), and then into Kremlin-friendly networks under Sergei Sobyanin (2010–).

The Sverdlovsk case (chapter 6) is marked by a failed patronage pact, both in general and specific to the migration sphere. Under Governor Alexander Misharin (2009–12), the imperative of maintaining a well-coordinated and insulated political system was violated when the regional minister of economics became mired in scandal. The Sverdlovsk case demonstrates the potential of civil society to disrupt regional elites' enjoyment of the spoils of migration management.

Krasnodar (chapter 7) demonstrates an example of anti-migrant populism par excellence by a regional governor who was crucial to stability and legitimacy in the build-up to the 2014 Sochi Winter Olympics. Governor Alexander Tkachev (2001–15) built his reputation on anti-minority rhetoric that was often quite radically beyond the Kremlin's adopted stance. Yet amid several scandals, his tenure demonstrates how federal elites reward those willing to maintain the patronage pact.

These three regions are all important as migrant destinations in Russia. They are some of the largest recipients of migrants, were allocated the largest quotas in the 2007–14 period, and have established themselves as leaders in patent revenue since 2015. Beyond this, the three cases were chosen because they represent varying approaches to migration management and the public reception of migrants. Moscow, as the capital, is the most common migration destination. Because of the intensity of migrants in the local labour market, public attitudes have been relatively hostile. In the Sverdlovsk region, on the other hand, both the government and the public have been comparatively receptive to migrant workers. Krasnodar's location in the south of Russia, which has traditionally struggled with interethnic issues, has earned it a reputation of intolerance towards migrants. And while these were the guiding reasons for conducting field research in each location, I discovered that these general orientations did not always hold true.

The methodological logic of this book is that of political ethnography that uses a wide range of primary and secondary data and methods of analysis. At times, my methodological approach has seemed a far cry from current trends in political science. Often, ethnographic researchers must put on a brave face and use terms like "snowball sampling," "grounded theory," and "process tracing" to give legitimacy to the process of following our noses and using instinct (informed by theory) to sniff out what is important about the things we're discovering in real time. For this reason, reflexivity, or the ability to interject oneself into the research process as agent and interpreter, is an essential part of the ethnographic approach (Pachirat 2009). It is to position oneself both as insider and outsider, and to move between these roles as an iterative unfolding of knowledge. My experience is one of a young, white, English- and Russian-speaking woman travelling on an American passport, with all of the ruggedly individualistic impulses and default rule-of-law assumptions that accompany my passport and cultural citizenship. This identity affects how I encounter my research and how people I meet in the field respond to me. An ethnographic approach drives me to understand the local context deeply and for its own sake, as an insider as much as possible, while using an outside eye to clarify and draw boundaries around practices that are taken for granted or implicit. Reflexivity requires a great deal of reflection and even creativity, which are often underappreciated in social science research, but are necessary in order to think beyond traditional paradigms or fashionable modes of inquiry.

The foundation of this project is fieldwork in four regions of Russia over a period of six years: in Moscow in 2009 and 2012, in Krasnodar and Sverdlovsk in 2012, and in Irkutsk in 2015.[51] Putting down roots in each research location, or creating a temporary non-academic community (often initially formed through existing social networks), has been an essential part of my field research strategy. Through these communities I had the opportunity to play soccer with Tajik kids in Yekaterinburg, spend a week at a family camp in the mountains of Adygea, and join a team of Russian college students providing flood relief for families of Meskhetian Turks in Krymsk. Spending time with people in these various settings created opportunities for conversations, sometimes concretely about migration, at other times more generally about people's thoughts about minorities, politics, local and national leaders, the media, and life in Russia. These interactions did a great deal to inform my understanding about how people interact with the state (especially bureaucratic actors). Field research afforded me the opportunity to engage locals and migrants in everyday settings: while shopping, on public transportation, and in other public spaces. These experiences informed my understanding of the political environment in which migration exists, and produced a wide range of observations not driven directly by my initial research questions.

In addition to informal conversations and participant observations, I conducted 66 formal semi-structured interviews with experts, NGO representatives and human rights activists, human rights lawyers, bureaucrats, government officials, diplomats and consulate workers, and migrants. I found that starting with NGOs and diaspora organizations was an efficient way to gain an initial understanding of the types of problems migrants encounter with the law. As I sat in a café with one migrant advocate, we frequently paused in our conversation so that she could take a phone call and offer words of advice and encouragement to migrants. She told me she gets as many as 70 calls in a day. Organizations and individuals that work with migrants repeatedly interact with state officials and stay abreast of legal changes in order to advise migrants of their legal rights and duties. Some may focus on policy advocacy, while others directly engage bureaucrats, police, the courts, or employers on behalf of migrants. All of them have a ready pool of direct experiences with how migrants and the state interact. I have assembled these snapshots of different levels of generality to create an ordered collage that illustrates the intersection of migrants and the state.

I worked out from a "civil society" core to make contacts with migrants, government officials, and other types of interlocutors. This strategy helped me to identify perspectives and biases across different types of respondents, or to interpret those interpreting the migration situation in the double hermeneutic that ethnographic researchers must engage (Yanow 2009). My interview strategy allowed respondents to identify the most important actors and aspects of the migration landscape, and consequently the direction of this project follows from these conversations. A result of this is that certain aspects of the migration process or experience one might expect to be central (in particular the relationship between migrants and employers, and the impact of business owners on the migration process) do not come to the fore. Rather, what was consistent across interviews was the sense that the most salient issues for migration governance are the law and its implementation through bureaucratic actors.

The book is not an ethnography of the migrant experience, but rather of migration governance. In this sense, my focus is on the ways in which the state interacts (or fails to interact) with migrants. These intersections leave off many aspects of the migrant experience, especially for those migrants living outside the scope of formal law and policy. While some of the strategies migrants use to navigate life outside the formal system are documented in this book, I include them in order to highlight engagement with or avoidance of the state rather than to provide a complete picture of how migrants live and work in Russia.

The core thing I want to understand is how state officials at different levels think about migration. My inferences are based on statements in speeches and the media, the text of laws and other official documents, and elite interviews when possible. As Goode (2010) and Light (2016) note, fieldwork in hybrid or non-democratic regimes like Russia is fraught with difficulties, not least of which is gaining access to government officials. Nevertheless, every interview declined is a data point, and at times keeping a record of government officials who refuse an interview will provide more fruitful observations than the actual interviews.[52] For the handful of interviews I conducted with bureaucrats, the content of their messages was far less important than the impressions they made, including what procedures I had to go through to arrange the meeting (i.e., official letters vs informal contacts), what type of office space they occupied, where it was located, what type of security (or other gatekeepers such as secretaries) I encountered, how long I had to wait outside their office, whether they would let me record the interview, and how they responded to my questions.

Given these limitations, the most important source of data for understanding the logic of officials in this book is the documents produced by different regional and federal-level agencies. Many of these documents were available on various government websites, which is a striking example that public access to data in Russia is much better than some might expect in an authoritarian context.[53] Spreadsheets of official statistical data, searchable text files of laws with hyperlinks to other relevant statutes, spreadsheets with detailed lists of employers permitted to hire migrants, and various migration statistics represent types of data that were previously only available in archives. These electronic documents allow researchers to extend their ethnographic approach beyond the traditional spatial and temporal bounds of field research.[54] These data shouldn't be seen as a poor substitute for elite interviews, but rather as "human artifacts" (Schatz 2009) that reflect micro-level human decision making about how to report bureaucratic activities. As a result, even the multivariate analysis I include in chapter 3 proceeds on a deeply ethnographic logic. The official data used for the analysis was produced by bureaucrats, and is therefore a result of the various logics and goals driving the collection, reporting, and even fabrication of numbers (Kalgin 2016). These logics are not revealed in the statistical analysis because of the limitations inherent in quantification. Nevertheless, the human trace is left on the statistics, and because the bureaucrats themselves use the data they produce to make decisions about migration policy, the analysis reveals a justificatory process that is driven by fear of the political consequences of unemployment. Knowing that public anxieties over unemployment are often tied to immigration, bureaucrats are bound by the dictates of the anti-migrant social contract at the same time as they play an important role in enforcing it.

Chapter Two

The Multi-Level Balancing Act of Migration Management

On a recent trip to Russia, my colleague Robert,[1] an American political scientist, was not able to register in the apartment where he was staying. After several attempts by the landlord to register him, and even a trip with the landlord to the migration office, the local migration officials sent him away with no registration. At this point, his sending organization decided he should register in a hotel. Foreign scholars are often keenly sensitized to the letter of the migration law and well acquainted with the fear of violating regulations, and Robert therefore explained to the organization that registering in a hotel where he was not physically staying was a criminal violation, as opposed to the administrative violation of not having registration documents. But the organization insisted. For a few minutes of his time and the equivalent of $10, he was able to easily secure the registration documents and never encountered any more trouble. As an experiment, he even opted to not hand over his illegally procured registration documents at passport control when he left Russia. It turns out that they did not care about his registration, because the border control agency has nothing to do with this area of migration management. Passport control is a function of the Federal Security Services (Federal'naia Sluzhba Bezopasnosti, or FSB), which are completely separate from the migration services, and the two agencies don't regularly cross-check their records.

This account of much worry for naught is a powerful example of how in Russia it is often better to be illegal with documents than illegal without documents.[2] The power of informal norms such as the need to have documents (complete with official-looking blue stamps) available to show the authorities, and the myriad paths available for obtaining these documents, deserves analytical attention. Different types of formal and informal tools and norms, and the ways in which actors understand and navigate what is truly necessary (i.e., what it takes to be legal *or* how to mitigate risks that come with non-compliance), relying on routine, innovation, or connections, are essential features of the immigration context in Russia.

This chapter shows how the multi-level balancing act of migration management relies on a mix of informal and formal mechanisms. I look at the entire scope of migration actors from the Kremlin to migrants and employers, considering their interests and responses to policy. While various formal mechanisms are used to address the interests of top-level actors (i.e., the Kremlin, ministers, and service heads), informal mechanisms used by low-level actors (i.e., employers, intermediaries, and migrants) add flexibility to the labour market and help people adapt as formal policies change. This process hinges on the middle level, the bureaucracy, which manages the day-to-day interactions between the state and the migrant labour market using a mix of formal and informal strategies.

This chapter shows how labour migration policy in Russia is managed strategically to satisfy actors at multiple levels by using a mix of formal (law-based) and informal (interpretive, network-based, semi-legal, or extra-legal) mechanisms in different arenas. The multi-level balancing act is the institutional structure for migration management in Russia. It utilizes the informal mechanisms that typify Russia's approach to migration and politics more generally, and acts as the playing field on which the spoils of migration can be distributed. In the context of this institutional structure, scarcity-producing mechanisms such as work permit quotas (chapter 3) and labour patents (chapter 4) can be strategically deployed, depending on the political dynamics in various regions of Russia (chapters 5–7).

Mechanisms, Institutions, and Networks

Before I discuss actors and interests, it is essential to lay theoretical groundwork for the tools used to manage and navigate immigration policy and practice. Formal mechanisms are law-based procedures that operate according to written and publicly available documents. In the case of immigration policy, these formal mechanisms are elaborated in federal laws, presidential decrees, government and ministerial orders, and other types of written policy. To the extent that procedures are sometimes clarified on lists and fliers posted physically on the walls of migration service offices, or electronically on the websites of migration services or intermediaries, formal mechanisms can be signalled through less authoritative documents. Nevertheless the public written record is crucial.

Informal mechanisms, on the other hand, are ways that law and practice can be mediated outside formal procedures. From the perspective of immigration policy, important informal mechanisms include the interpretation of formal mechanisms (including bureaucratic discretion and the use of legal loopholes), network-based relations that guide how formal institutions work in practice, semi-legal activities, and extra-legal activities such as corruption schemes, bribe payment, purchase of false documents, and work in the shadow labour market.

According to Tilly (2001), mechanisms are "a delimited class of events that change relations among specified sets of elements in identical or closely similar ways over a variety of situations." Take a corruption scheme as an informal mechanism, which mediates between law and practice by providing government services (e.g., migration documents) through a channel not prescribed by law (e.g., payment to a bureaucrat). A corruption scheme changes the relationship between state and societal actors from one based on written laws and instructions to one that routinely engages alternative or off-the-books methods to accomplish goals. These practices are repeated as long as the corruption scheme continues to function.[3] And while mechanisms produce "uniform immediate effects," in this case the issuing of documents, "their aggregate, cumulative, and longer-term effects vary considerably depending on initial conditions and on combinations with other mechanisms" (Tilly 2001).[4] In other words, because there are many mechanisms working simultaneously (i.e., informal mechanisms such as corruption schemes, intermediaries or document brokers, bureaucratic discretion, and formal mechanisms elaborated by laws), how mechanisms routinize over time varies.

While both formal and informal mechanisms can be reliable and predictable, they are more flexible than institutions, which can be defined as "humanly devised constraints that shape human interaction" (North 1990). Because the migration sphere is constantly changing (e.g., the primary migration law was changed 85 times from its inception in 2002 to the end of 2015), the use of mechanisms to conceptualize adaptations in behaviour is useful. Whereas much of the literature discusses informal practices as indistinguishable from informal institutions (Grzymala-Busse 2010; Gel'man 2004; Koehler 2008),[5] interjecting mechanisms into the discussion adds an important layer of nuance, since institutions (formal and informal) represent rules (North 1990; Helmke and Levitsky 2004), but mechanisms present opportunities or means used to navigate and potentially change institutions.

Formal and informal mechanisms are embedded in institutions, which give important cues for how mechanisms can operate. Key institutions in Russia include laws and other legal instruments (e.g., presidential decrees, government orders);[6] legal divisions of power (often constitutionally defined) such as elected or appointed positions throughout the government, administration, and federal system;[7] and informal networks, particularly of the patron-client variety, but also of a more horizontal sort, which refer to the ways in actors rely on ties with family or kin, friends, and acquaintances in order to solve a variety of problems.

The dominance of network ties is well established in analyses of Russian politics and society (Ledeneva 2013; Ledeneva 2006; Hale 2014; Sharafutdinova 2010a; Gel'man 2016; DeBardeleben and Zherebtsov 2010).[8] Though labels range from neopatrimonialism to clientelism to patronalism,[9] the constant theme of these works is that politics relies on personal relationships to accomplish tasks, and that the interests of network insiders do not always align with their professional obligations, especially if they are state officials. When network ties are fused with state structures as they are in Russia, patron-client patterns emerge.[10] The repeated practice of informal mechanisms in this context allows clients the possibility of carving out spheres of autonomy and control and reinforcing their utility to the patron in a system that would otherwise be exclusively top-down. Informal mechanisms also offer a more predictable and reliable set of options for interacting with government officials and economic actors than is often considered in the literature, which focuses on informality as a departure from Weberian bureaucratic norms.

Inherent in patron-client relationships is a pact whereby patrons agree to give benefits (in particular job tenure, and access to the formal and informal benefits, or "spoils," of that position) to clients in exchange for loyalty and producing beneficial outcomes (e.g., favourable election results or meeting administrative targets). As long as clients are able to manage the obligations of the pact, they can keep their position and continue to access the spoils it provides, which could include prestige, potential for promotion, fringe benefits, access to the proceeds of corruption, etc.

The patronage pact could be divided into numerous sub-pacts, all of which must be balanced by actors at various locations throughout the political system. What I refer to as the populist pact is one such sub-pact, where political elites at various levels are responsible for upholding the anti-migrant social contract described in chapter 1. Other sub-pacts are related to public policy areas such as welfare, security, or, as this book illustrates, migration. Often sub-pacts are overlapping and intertwined. As I will argue throughout this book, the populist pact has important links to the migration pact, which will be elucidated below.

Generally, pacts are informal and implicit, and the mix of sub-pacts a political actor is responsible for varies according to formal position (i.e., job title) and regional or geographic dynamics. The mechanisms and priorities that actors use to balance their pact responsibilities also vary. These dynamics highlight the complexity of the patronage system as a multi-level balancing act, since actors at each location in the political system have multiple responsibilities and must decide, often with little explicit information, how to prioritize their activities. Often it is only when a patronage pact breaks down (either by dissolving altogether or resulting in sometimes very public censure from patrons) that it becomes clear what imbalances patrons are willing to tolerate. Though, in most cases, patronage breaks down when personal interests (i.e., clients using the spoils of their positions) overshadow the professional obligations of juggling sub-pacts, patrons are generally conservative and unwilling to punish imbalances (i.e., corruption) as long as clients can continue to contribute to the priority goals of stability, economic growth, and legitimacy.[11]

Equilibrium (an indicator of stability) occurs when clients can juggle a variety of pact demands and keep the relevant social, economic, and state actors relatively satisfied, and is most visible through an absence of pact breakdown. When the social contract and patronage pacts are functioning, anti-migrant social mobilization will be minimal, and elites will maintain their positions and will make an attempt to keep corrupt activities minimally visible. The biggest threat to equilibrium is not necessarily the lack of transparency inherent in the system, but rather the short-term horizons that typically define elite interests and patronage relationships.

This chapter demonstrates for the Russian migration context what numerous scholars have noted more generally: a political system dominated by network relationships utilizes both formal and informal mechanisms for accomplishing its goals. A conventional scholarly perspective holds that the reliance on informal strategies is a way to compensate for

Table 2.1. The multi-level balancing act of migration management

ACTOR	INTERESTS	MECHANISMS
State actors		
Kremlin	Stability, economic growth, and legitimacy	Rhetorical guidance (speeches, articles, etc.) Devolution via patronage pact (federalism disciplined by patronage rules) Political appointments (cabinet, governor, etc.) and direction of the party
Ministry and Service Heads	Control over policy areas	Draft laws Press statements Implementing orders
Regional executives (governors; mayors of federal cities)	Tenure, promotion, and spoils	Quiet management of social and inter-elite conflict Production of votes for United Russia Regional cabinet appointments Populist connection with public (Appearance of) a coordinated/disciplined administration Reproduction of federal policy prerogatives
Bureaucrats (career)		
– high-level bureaucrats	Tenure, promotion, and spoils	Development of regional directives and reports Implementation of federal orders Production of on-paper discipline Organization of high-level corruption schemes
– mid-level bureaucrats	Tenure, promotion, and spoils	Production of on-paper discipline Management of personnel Organization of low-level corruption schemes
– street-level bureaucrats	Tenure, promotion, and spoils	Meeting administrative goals Enforcement of the rules Petty corruption (i.e., taking bribes)

Table 2.1. The multi-level balancing act of migration management (Continued)

ACTOR	INTERESTS	MECHANISMS
Marketplace actors		
Employers	Profit and cost savings Avoiding trouble with law	Following rules to hire legal migrants Using connections/bribes to hire legal migrants Hiring illegal migrants (not providing contract, not reporting to tax services)
Migrants	Income Reducing risk and insecurity Avoiding trouble with law	With or without paying bribes and with or without using an intermediary: Obtaining all registration and work documents Obtaining some documents (i.e., registration, but not work permit/ patent) Obtaining false documents Seeking other migration status (temporary or permanent residence; citizenship)
Migrant intermediaries	Profit Avoiding trouble with law	Organizing the sale of documents Forging relationships with state officials to facilitate activities

the deficiencies of a weak state (Gel'man 2004; Ledeneva 2013). I argue that network and patron-client ties are used to signal the acceptable use of formal and informal mechanisms so that actors can balance the responsibilities and benefits of the patronage pact. These signals often originate from the upper echelons of the political system and are transmitted downward through networks that function within the federal system and state administration.

In the migration context, the interests of actors and the tools they have available to meet the obligations of the patronage pact are slightly different at the various levels of state administration and in the marketplace, depending on actors' interests and what they can provide to patrons (see table 2.1). Key to all of these relationships is the Kremlin's driving priorities of stability, economic growth, and legitimacy.

I will discuss each of these actors listed in table 2.1, from those with most to least formal power in the state, and then marketplace actors. Though this treatment in many ways reinforces the discourse of politics in Russia as a vertical hierarchy, it should not be concluded that horizontal ties (both formal and informal) are unimportant. While patron-client network ties are necessarily and by nature vertical, they can be disrupted or reinforced by horizontal processes, as in the case of civil society actors in Sverdlovsk, who were able to disrupt a corruption scheme and upset the patron-client relationship between the governor and regional minister of economics.[12] While the nature of the patronage pact between marketplace actors and the state is quite different from that among state actors, the role of employers and migrants in producing stability, growth, and legitimacy cannot be dismissed. Because of their essential role in the economy, marketplace actors, even at the low level, exercise significant agency because of the flexibility provided by corruption, which is often overlooked in the literature.

High-Level Politics: The Kremlin and the Ministries

At the heart of the social contract and patronage pacts with elites are the concepts of stability, prosperity, and legitimacy, as these are the key interests of the Kremlin (Kononenko 2011). The primary goal of the Putin administration,[13] from his initial term in the presidency until the current period, has been the pursuit of a strong state, which is typically analysed through the policy efforts to centralize power (Isakova 2001; Gorenburg 2010; Sakwa 2014) and the pursuit of a mercantilist or state capitalist model of economic development (Klimina 2014; Lane 2008). Legitimacy comes from convincing the public that these projects have succeeded.

Stability has been another driving goal of the Putin administration (Ledeneva 2013; Smyth, Lowry, and Wilkening 2007), which is intertwined with the concept of a strong, legitimate, and prosperous state. Owing to the chaotic transition from the Soviet era that persisted through the 1990s, the goal of pursuing a more coordinated system with a strong central state has been a key component of the social contract between Putin and the public. The general social contract is similar in form and function to the anti-migrant social contract discussed in the previous chapter. It is the ruling elite's responsibility to produce stability and security, and the public in exchange gives loyalty and trust of a sort, measured through high approval ratings and electoral outcomes, but also the tacit understanding that the administration should be allowed to operate according to its own rules.[14]

The stability and security that the public wants involve reliable access to jobs, control over crime, access to public goods, and generally the benefits of a prosperous society. It is the task of political leaders throughout the country at various levels of the patronage pact to produce stability, which can be measured as political support for the Kremlin and a lack of public backlash, either through protest, open conflicts, or visible scandals. At their disposal are the populism of anti-migrant rhetoric, as discussed in the previous chapter, and other rhetorical tools that assure the public that the state is strong and in control. Breakdowns in stability signal a violation of the social contract and various patronage sub-pacts, which can provoke a direct response from top political elites (Schenk 2013).[15]

Prosperity includes economic growth, increases in overall quality of life, and/or economic freedom (Wegren 2003; Greene 2012). Since the recovery from the 1998 financial crisis and the rise in world oil prices, prosperity has primarily been investigated in terms of natural resource wealth (Åslund 2005; Treisman 2010; Rutland 2008). However, it could be argued that a sense of prosperity also comes from having a developed economy, and that migrant labour is crucial to the development Russia has achieved. Advanced industrial economies are marked by certain features, including a segmented labour market. The majority of labour migrants in Russia work in the lower sector of this segmented market, providing essential functions in the economy and the added value of serving as a potential scapegoat in times of economic crisis.

Stability and prosperity ultimately contribute to the current leadership's legitimacy, which is key to maintaining the social contract between the public and the ruling elite. Legitimacy is the public's belief that the political elites are fulfilling their duties. In the immigration arena, legitimacy comes from presenting a policy agenda to the public that is consistent with other key discourses, such as those on national identity, and the strong state that promotes law and order.

In the pursuit of stability, prosperity, and legitimacy, the Kremlin uses a combination of formal and informal mechanisms that show political elites' preference for a network-based state rather than a law-based state, despite political rhetoric embracing the latter. A network-based state presents decidedly different opportunities and incentives for actors throughout the political system because the most crucial aspect of producing equilibrium is staying connected to important patrons and proving one's loyalty. The mechanisms producing connection and loyalty are not always clearly elucidated and can thus be difficult to anticipate (even for insiders); nevertheless, they operate reliably and predictably more often than not and produce recognizable institutional patterns.

Direction from the Top? Alternative Views on the Origins of Public Policy

When Putin was elected president in 2000, immigration flows were shifting from ethnic repatriation to labour migration. As discussed in the Introduction, migration was seen with new interest, and an active period of policymaking followed. Several key labour migration reforms since 2007 have directly followed speeches given by Putin. There are two ways of interpreting Putin's impact on formal policy outcomes. One follows the logic that Putin speaks from the high reaches of the Kremlin, and policymakers scramble to implement his wishes (Gontmakher 2015). The other is that policies in the interests of certain ministries are formulated and passed up for Putin's endorsement through policy speeches. This section looks at examples that support each interpretation.

Migration control became a key theme of Putin's 2012 re-election campaign. He made a number of specific recommendations to increase integration and to get tough on false registrations or "rubber apartments," the common practice of registering citizens from other regions of Russia and migrants in an apartment where they did not actually stay.[16] Upon his inauguration in May, Putin immediately passed a series of presidential decrees, one of which stipulated that by November 2012 language exams should be instituted for labour migrants.[17] By December 2013, new clauses were added to the criminal code making fictitious registration a criminal offence.

According to the top-down interpretation, Putin sets the course for policy innovations through his statements and decrees. This view argues that ministers and bureaucrats often don't know about possible policy reforms until Putin makes pronouncements, and then are left to implement policies based on vague ideas of what he intended (Gontmakher 2015). While policies can be written by experts or bureaucrats, in reality the "top political leadership is the sole mastermind" (Gel'man 2016).[18] There are certainly times that Putin intervenes to "manually control" policy (Schenk 2013; Petrov, Lipman, and Hale 2014), but the running of day-to-day politics in this way is not feasible. A more moderate view is that policymaking starts with Putin (in the form of often quite generally stated presidential decrees), but then must be developed and implemented into policy by the cabinet and ministries, who have their own interests that influence the overall effectiveness of the policy course (Remington 2014).

Top-down perspectives do not allow for the nuance and contingency that are demonstrated by the actions and interests of ministers and bureaucrats in the arena of immigration policymaking. Even if top elites give macro-level direction, it is within the ministries and administrative bodies that the details of the policies take shape and can be used to promote a particular set of interests. Because the Kremlin has limited information about policy implementation (Petrov, Lipman, and Hale 2014; Gontmakher 2015), its support of specific policy agendas is based on which ministers have access to the Kremlin and can craft their preferred messages from below. Kremlin officials can then accept suggested policy directions as part of their overall plan to pursue prosperity and stability, to be sealed by a public endorsement from Putin.

Often it is the initiative of a single ministry that results in new policy directions. For example, a major innovation to the migration law in 2010, allowing migrants from CIS countries to purchase monthly labour permits (called patents) and simplifying procedures for highly qualified migrants, came at the initiative of the FMS. The draft bill was originally formulated by Anatoly Kuznetsov, deputy head of the FMS, and prior to its initiation was vigorously debated in the Tripartite Commission on Social and Labour Relations, which brings together representatives of the government, trade unions, and employers.[19] All three parties represented in the Tripartite Commission were categorically opposed to the initiative; nevertheless, the draft was pushed through primarily because of the support of Commission Head and Deputy Prime Minister Alexander Zhukov.[20]

The new patent system benefited the FMS more than any other agency. First, it created much-needed revenue. Migrants paid 1,000 rubles per month under the original system, and revenue for the first two years of patents totalled 8.3 billion rubles ($277 million at the time) or $11.5 million per month.[21] Furthermore, patents circumnavigated the Labour Services (within the Ministry of Health), who were in charge of managing migrant quotas, giving the FMS sole control over the migration process (Lukanin 2010). Therefore, when a 2013 speech by Putin contained the same technocratic language as a later draft bill from the

FMS, it suggests that the policy originated in the FMS and made its way up to Putin for endorsement. Because the Ministry of Labour (Mintrud) was simultaneously preparing legislation that would increase its control over the migration sphere, Putin's endorsement of the FMS bill marks a major victory for the migration services.

The scholarship on Russian politics has paid a great deal of attention to the *siloviki*, or politicians who lead "power ministries," such as the Ministry of Interior (Ministerstvo Vnutrennikh Del, or MVD) and Ministry of Defence (Sakwa 2010; Kryshtanovskaya and White 2003; Rivera and Rivera 2006; Dawisha 2015), and to the factions within them (Taylor 2011). An examination of elite competition between less studied ministries such as the FMS and Mintrud offers important insights into the Russian political system. We can expect that the same logic of personal relationships, and the importance of proximity to Putin for policymaking influence, will govern all competition at the cabinet and ministerial level (Bremmer and Charap 2007; Gel'man 2016; Renz 2006). As several scholars have noted, Putin plays the key role as arbiter between any conflicting groups in his cabinet (Hale 2014; Taylor 2011).[22] But different ministries have their own goals that are not defined by the Kremlin, and pursuing their interests involves ensuring that certain policy areas are under their control. The logic is simple: if a ministry has control over a key policy area, it can then deploy an array of formal (e.g., ministerial orders) and informal mechanisms (e.g., gathering the spoils corruption schemes) to its advantage.

The competition for control over immigration policy has been particularly acute between Mintrud and the FMS. Since 2005, the FMS has been directed by Konstantin Romodanovskii, a former FSB lieutenant general (Sakwa 2010). In 2012, the FMS was taken out of MVD and placed directly under the authority of the government, and in 2013 Romodanovskii was given the rank of minister.[23]

What is now the Ministry of Labour and Social Protection (Mintrud) has gone through several reorganizations since the first Putin administration. As the result of a cabinet shuffle in 2004, the Ministry of Labour and Social Development was renamed the Ministry of Health and Social Development (Minzdrav) and placed under the leadership of Mikhail Zurabov (2004–7), who was a member of the liberal St Petersburg faction of Putin's inner elite (Kryshtanovskaya and White 2005). Responsibility for labour migration was located within the Federal Service for Labour and Employment (Federal'naia Sluzhba po Trudu i Zaniatosti, or Rostrud) as a part of Minzdrav from

2004 to 2012 and then transferred to the current Mintrud. For much of the time since 2004, labour migration was a responsibility of Maksim Topilin, first as the head of Rostrud from 2004 to 2008, as vice-minister of Minzdrav from 2008 to 2012, and as minister of labour from 2012 to the present.

Migration experts consider the FMS a conservative organization that favours a more securitized migration policy, whereas "civilian" ministries such as the Ministry of Economic Development (Mineconomiki), Minzdrav, and Rostrud represent a more "liberal" thrust (Ivakhnyuk 2013b).[24] This is consistent with Kryshtanovskaya and White's (2005) division of liberal cabinet members (including former Minister of Health Zubarov), who prefer market competition, and *siloviki* (including former Minister of Interior Nurgaliev and FMS head Romodanovskii), who prioritize a strong state that controls the economy and projects a narrow definition of national identity that privileges cultural homogeneity.

With this context in mind, it is curious on first glance that it was the FMS that led the charge to overhaul the patent system (a more market-based system) and eliminate work permit quotas for visa-free workers (a system focused on planning and government control). The most plausible explanation is that the more widespread use of patents shifted bureaucratic authority over migration from Mintrud (which coordinated the quota process) to the FMS itself, giving the agency and its regional branches direct control over all aspects of the labour migration process.

The combination of Zurabov's departure from Minzdrav, Romodanovskii's elevation to the cabinet, and the success of FMS-initiated policies shows that the power of the FMS vis-à-vis Mintrud increased during the years addressed in this analysis. I will discuss this competition in more detail in chapters 3 and 4. For now it is important to emphasize that these struggles are driven by a desire to control formal mechanisms. Control of policy allows an agency to deploy a whole host of informal mechanisms that bring direct personal benefit to its personnel at many levels. Once formal policy control is achieved, it is diffused across the territory through the institutions of the federal system, and down through the regional branches of the administration. Each of these locations plays a role in the patronage pact, and signals are given directly from the Kremlin and more routinely through networks about when it is appropriate to pursue personal interests.

Regional Elites: Presidential Envoys, Governors, and Regional Cabinets

Because of Russia's vast territory, federalism is a logical choice for governance. How (and whether) the federal system functions, however, is highly debated. Following the "federal in form, unitary in function" Soviet Union, federalism after Yeltsin's offer to the regions that they "take as much sovereignty as they can swallow" developed unevenly.[25] Therefore, when Putin was first elected in 2000, one of his driving goals was to increase coordination across the regions (creating a dictatorship of law) and accountability to Moscow (a vertical of power). Towards this end, a number of policies were introduced with the goal of adding administrative oversight and decreasing the autonomy of regional elites (Chebankova 2010; Goode 2007; Sharafutdinova 2010b; Ross 2003; Sakwa 2014).[26]

Russia currently has 83 regions (85 counting areas of Ukraine annexed in 2014) led by governors (or mayors in the case of federal cities Moscow, St Petersburg, and Sevastopol), which are divided into 8 federal districts each led by a presidential envoy (*polnomochnyi predstavitel' prezidenta*, often shortened to *polpred*). The presidential envoys have been surprisingly absent from discussions on migration policy and practice. By many counts, though their installation was considered critical for the creation of the vertical of power campaign, they were marginalized when gubernatorial elections were rescinded in 2004, bringing governors directly under the authority of the Kremlin (Ross 2011).

Governors, on the other hand, are pivotal elites who are instrumental in maintaining the patronage pact between the regions and federal leaders.[27] Governors are responsible for ensuring that the goal of stability and legitimacy is produced at the regional level. In the big picture this requires producing stable regions, which requires careful management of any social unrest, political scandal, or elite competition (Sharafutdinova 2010b; Slider 2014; Turovskii 2010). Governors must also meet basic benchmarks of loyalty, typically measured by producing votes for United Russia candidates (Reuter and Robertson 2012). Under the conditions of a fulfilled pact, governors retain their posts or are promoted to a federal position (Semenova 2011).[28]

Because migration management is a potentially contentious public policy area, governors must pay careful attention to its dynamics at the regional level. In practical terms this means that there are certain priorities governors must demonstrate to uphold the government's priorities in the migration arena. Specifically, they must make a populist connection with their constituents, present a unified administrative front, and contribute to the overall goal of producing a scarcity of legal labour. I will refer to governor's duties in this regard as the migration pact, which can be conceptualized as a sub-pact of the overall patronage relationship.[29]

As discussed in chapter 1, the strategy of managing social discourse on migration is heavily dependent on the populist messages of elites. The populist pact, as a sub-pact of patronage relations that overlaps with the migration pact, requires that regional elites increase or decrease the anti-migrant content of their rhetoric in order to manage public opinion. In this way, regional elites are responsible for upholding the social contract and ensuring that the public remains passive in their anti-migrant attitudes. As a result, governors are an important conduit for promoting the federal government's interests *and* ideas.

Governors are also responsible for putting forward the picture of a coordinated regional administration that includes control (or insulation, more specifically) of any major corruption that could be connected to state actors, and a disciplined bureaucracy in pursuit of the policy goals set out by the federal executive. The management of corruption is important, not for the sake of eliminating or reducing it, but rather for making sure it does not erupt into public scandals that could upset stability or legitimacy. A coordinated regional administration involves managing elites in the region so that any corruption that occurs as a result of enjoying the spoils of the patronage pact remains elusive to the public.

Governors must also produce the activity of a bureaucracy that is disciplined by federal goals. This involves interpreting the policy prerogatives of the Kremlin and putting them into practice at the regional level. During the quota period, projecting discipline meant creating a regional planning mechanism that conveyed a sense of rationality and coordination across agencies. In the patent era, those regions that embraced the role of a disciplined bureaucracy created new migration centres that could be used to streamline the issuing of documents (and more importantly, the collection of revenues from patents).

In both of these eras, this bureaucratic effort helped to realize the primary goal of producing a scarcity of legal labour, which is necessary to balance interests across society and the economy. During the patent era, loyal bureaucracies under the oversight of governors worked towards the additional goal of creating state capitalism and increasing budget revenues. Scarcity in turn produced patronage resources that could be used by a variety of regional actors, as will be more fully explored below. So long as the governor fulfils his patronage duties, he and his regional clients are free to use migration resources to their own benefit. If he fails to keep himself insulated from public backlash, or if regional inter-elite struggles or other factors that could threaten equilibrium are not contained, the patronage pact could be potentially interrupted.

The patronage pact does not require uniformity across the regions, and therefore does little to promote the formal goals of centralization through the vertical of power and dictatorship of law. Devolution via patronage pact illustrates how the Kremlin relies on network loyalty to strategically manage the country. What is important is not the legal uniformity or even degree of direct control over regional affairs by the Putin administration, but rather producing equilibrium where social, economic, and state actors are relatively satisfied by their ability to access a mix of formal and informal mechanisms as they pursue their goals. In other words, it is the job of the governors to reproduce at the regional level what federal executives produce in the centre. In this sense the institution of the federal system is not a method of dividing power, but rather defines the positions and roles that will be dominant actors in the patronage pact. This argument counters the dominant discourse that claims Russia has become increasingly centralized during Putin's tenure, joining a contingent of scholars who see regional politics as varied and resilient to centralization (Baranov et al. 2015; Reisinger 2013; Chebankova 2010).

Federal patronage relations were largely unaffected by the reintroduction of gubernatorial elections in 2012 because of the de facto control over patronage networks retained by the Kremlin (Slider 2014; Blakkisrud 2015; Moses 2015). The consolidation of this control has been primarily attributed to the successful creation of a dominant party system through United Russia (Reuter 2013; Reuter and Remington 2009; Gel'man 2010). And while the party system is the most visible manifestation of the patronage pact, the logic of this book pushes the argument further to demonstrate that formal institutions, whether the federal system, elections, or parties, are indeed disciplined by the patronage pact and are therefore more subject to informal rules than to their formal status. The signals and duties of the patronage pact go far beyond the party system to include public policy arenas such as migration management.

The Bureaucracy

State administration has a critical role to play in producing state stability (Stoner-Weiss 2006). Bureaucrats in the regional FMS offices who issue migration and work permit documents, bureaucrats in the employment and tax services who register the employment of migrants and the tax liability of employers, and inspectors of various offices and police who enforce laws and investigate violations all have a vital role in determining whether legislation is put into practice as written. All of the actors in this category could be thought of as "career bureaucrats," those whose position comes from within the state administration. In some countries career bureaucrats are strictly non-political appointees, but in the Russian system this cannot be ruled out, since the informal networks that penetrate the bureaucracy fuse politics and administration (Huskey 2011).

It is important to recognize different interests and functions of the various players in the bureaucracy, what types of formal and informal tools they use, and how the system contributes to migration management. The patronage pact of each bureaucrat is with their direct supervisor, creating a top-down network structure within the state administration. In many cases these relationships create "many disparate narrow verticals poorly related to each other" (Petrov 2011) that not only are uncoordinated in their policy tasks but also often compete directly for control over potential revenue streams (Pryadilnikov 2009). In general, bureaucrats seek tenure (Gontmakher 2015), promotion, and spoils (Gel'man 2016). In exchange, they provide "on paper" stability and discipline (fulfilling administrative targets, usually set by upper-level bureaucrats or ministers) (Gel'man 2016).

One of the key informal mechanisms used by the bureaucracy is various types of corruption. Public officials and civil servants are considered the largest arena in Russia affected by corruption, and it is generally considered easy to obtain permits or avoid fines through payment of bribes to officials. The largest corruption markets are higher education and traffic police, and while the frequency of bribe paying on the everyday level has decreased in recent years, the size of the average bribe has increased substantially (Levin and Satarov 2013). These sectors have a direct impact on migrants.

A 2008 survey showed that 40% of migrants paid bribes as a result of random document checks by police (Tyuryukanova 2009a). Of migrants who were not legally registered, 50.9% reported paying bribes to the police, yet only 20.5% had been arrested (Zaionchkovskaia 2009, 106). This is compelling evidence that police are more interested in collecting bribes than they are in directing illegal migrants through legal channels to either regularize their status or be deported. Over 40% of migrants and employers reported that they can solve any problems that arise in the migration process by paying bribes (Zaionchkovskaia 2009, 108).

Informal mechanisms are not the only tool of bureaucrats, of course. Fees are a good example of a formal mechanism that can be used at the discretion of regional authorities, directly benefiting regional budgets. Some fees are explicitly devolved to regional governments (e.g., regional governments can decide on the monthly charge for patents), while others are more implicit in the sense that there is no federal statute allowing or forbidding them. Fees for language exams and courses fall in this implicit category, which could also be considered a legal loophole, allowing regional governments to increase budget inputs. Fines are another discretionary category that is used with great regularity. Payers often talk about fines and bribes as indistinguishable. The difference is important, however, for the discussion of formal versus informal mechanisms. Fines are paid to banks and involve paperwork (the issuing of a bill, which must be taken to the bank for payment, and a receipt that acts as proof of payment back at the bureaucrat's desk). Bribes are paid in cash or gift directly to a state official.

Although there are a number of bureaucratic agents that are involved in various aspects of the labour migration process, including labour inspectors, police, and border agents, I will focus primarily on those within the migration services and those involved with labour planning. Looking at an arena that is not typically considered on the forefront of corrupt practices will add new insight into the scope of corruption in Russia. Since corruption is often taken as a given in Russia's bureaucracy, even by top-level political elites, it is not surprising to encounter corruption in everyday practice.[30] What is surprising is when corruption is not present. In the case of migration, variation in corruption depends on the level of the bureaucracy.

Upper Management: Regional Heads of UFMS and Labour Planning Committees

Those at the top of the bureaucratic hierarchy are the heads of regional offices. Some of these positions are the regional representatives of federal ministries (e.g., Ministry of Economics) and therefore serve the function of a governor's cabinet or government at the regional level. Others are the heads of agencies like the FMS (whose local branches are called UFMS, Upravlenie Federal'noi Migratsionnoi Sluzhby), or the Department of Labour and Employment, which may or may not be a strict duplication of federal-level agencies. Though these positions are usually occupied by career bureaucrats, they are often gubernatorial appointments and therefore have an essential political role.

It is the task of upper management to ensure that the efforts of the people in their organization produce the appearance of a disciplined agency, which is a component in producing the stability needed by the Kremlin at the regional level. One key task for upper management has been reporting on and planning for labour migration. This is often accomplished by reports from individual agencies and work done through interdepartmental commissions on migration.

One example, planning for migration quotas, which will be discussed in greater depth in chapter 3, involves a bureaucratically intensive process that centres on regional interdepartmental commissions appointed by governors. These groups of upper-level regional bureaucrats are responsible for compiling applications to hire foreign workers from employers, weighing them against reports on the migration situation from regional agencies, and recommending a quota number to federal authorities in Moscow. Often at this level, those producing administrative outputs operate on the logic of avoiding the production of data that might raise red flags (Kalgin 2016).

Based on my interviews with members of interdepartmental commissions in the regions, these groups have a technocratic mind frame. They gave the impression that the labour market is a relatively simple arena that can be managed through government planning. But findings in chapter 3 indicate that bureaucrats make decisions based on simplified calculations, in the case of work permit quotas focusing solely on fluctuations in regional unemployment.

In some cases bureaucrats have used their positions on these commissions to create corruption schemes, as in the case of Sverdlovsk regional Minister of Economics Evgenii Sofrygin in 2012. Sofrygin was both the head of the interdepartmental commission defining regional quotas and responsible for the region's migration centre. Because of pressures to relieve budgetary shortfalls, Sofrygin and the director of the migration centre began to sell quota allocations. This was a common practice throughout Russia whereby migrants and employers were told the quota was exhausted unless they paid.[31] Some suspect that the Sverdlovsk Regional Migration Centre was renamed the United (or "Single") Migration Centre so that all migrant business would be diverted there.[32] Sofrygin then used his position as the head of the interdepartmental commission to reduce the 2012 quota. In doing, Sofrygin created scarcity of quota that could be used to further the corruption racket through the United Migration Centre.

Mid-Level Bureaucrats

There are numerous UFMS offices in each region, and often multiple offices in the capital city of each region. The head of each of these offices serves the important function of coordinating the activities of the office. In Krasnodar, I made an appointment with an UFMS official through informal channels. When I asked to record the conversation, he scolded me, saying that if I'd wanted an official interview, I should have written a letter to the head of the office and received official permission. The clear message in this conversation was that the informal should remain informal.

Mid-level bureaucrats are the office heads and the heads of departments within those offices. In other words, it is those bureaucrats who have desks and offices with doors. They are interested in job tenure and enjoying the spoils of their positions (Gel'man 2016). While promotion might be a motivating factor in some cases, such promotions would usually entail either relocation to a different city or agency (cross-agency rotation is quite common in the Russian administration) or transition into the private sector.[33] Job tenure, on the other hand, comes with the continued benefits of salary plus access to whatever spoils of corruption the bureaucrat can produce within the confines of the patronage pact, which at this level is between the mid-level and upper-level bureaucrats.

Tenure at this level is based on correctly interpreting the cues from higher-level officials about how policies should be implemented and avoiding the appearance of corruption that could lead to scandal. In the end, being removed from office is often political, based on broken pacts, or when a scapegoat is needed. While there are constant efforts to check the work of bureaucrats, the information that is gathered during audits can be used to provide justifications for sacking certain officials at key moments of pact breakdown.[34] The purpose of audits at this level is not necessarily to identify those who use their position opportunistically through various forms of corruption, but rather to gather information for future use: to save face when a patronage pact has been violated, or against political opponents.

Mid-level bureaucrats have a position within the agency that allows them to organize corruption schemes with relative impunity, such as those providing official documents either for a price or through informal networks. For example, in Krasnodar there is a company called the Intergovernmental Migration Centre, which arranges documents for foreigners as an intermediary. While intermediaries like this are widespread, this office is directly next door to the main UFMS location and is run by the spouses of UFMS officials.[35] In some cases it is a high- or mid-level bureaucrat who is plied with material benefits by the leader of a group of migrants, perhaps through a fancy lunch meeting where additional gifts are given,[36] to make the path clearer for the migrants in that network.[37] There is commonly the expectation from above that bribe proceeds will then be passed up to higher-level officials within the administration (Cheloukhine and King 2007), or up a "semi-feudal chain of command" (Shlapentokh 2003).

Street-Level Bureaucrats[38]

It is the lower-level bureaucrats who have the most regular interactions with migrants. These bureaucrats sit at the windows and reception desks of UFMS branches, receive migrants' documents (passport, migration card, verifications of completing medical checks and language exams, receipts of payments of taxes, etc.), and process permits such as temporary residence permits, work permits, and patents.[39] What is striking about these actors is that they are rarely involved with corruption directly. In all of the interviews I conducted with migrants and NGOs, I did not hear even one story about a bribe being given directly to the person who was processing migrant documents.[40] Every account of corruption I heard involved upper- or mid-level bureaucrats. While we can't rule out point-of-sale corruption entirely, it seems there is reduced opportunity for spoils among lower-level migration bureaucrats in UFMS offices.

The guiding interest at this level is job tenure and promotion, which depends on bureaucrats doing their job as their superiors want. They are often guided by the fear that they will be reprimanded for not following instructions, so they follow the letter of the law/procedure. They avoid making decisions that could be seen as suspicious or discretionary, and are careful to meet whatever goals are set (usually informally) by their bosses, for example the minimum number of fines that should be levied in a given period.[41] This type of attitude has been explored both in historical and current iterations by Rowney and Huskey (2009), who explain that lower-level bureaucrats are conditioned not to make independent decisions but rather to always appeal to a higher level of authority. By deferring to higher officials, they can avoid making decisions that could get them in trouble. As a result, these bureaucrats follow the letter of the "law," whether that is the law itself, formal implementing instructions, or informal directions.

I encountered this scenario when preparing for a Fulbright research trip in 2012. My host university encountered difficulty obtaining a visa invitation from the local UFMS branch in Yekaterinburg because I (as an American citizen) wanted to process my visa through the Russian embassy in Kazakhstan. Despite having obtained a short-term visa at this same embassy a few months prior on the basis of an invitation from a university in Moscow, the Yekaterinburg UFMS refused to issue the invitation unless I travelled to the United States and applied for the visa there, which in the end I did. When I finally arrived at the research site, weeks after originally planned, via the US, my host explained that their local UFMS had become much more restrictive in recent years because bureaucrats were afraid of being reprimanded by the federal FMS in Moscow. She explained that the Moscow UFMS was much more powerful and consequently much freer to interpret the law and various government and ministerial orders as they saw fit.

The perception that laws should be implemented more strictly than federal law requires can in this case be attributed to what I call the "fear of the audit" or the idea that bureaucratic actors do not want to act in a way that could be criticized by their superiors or central authorities, and so their behaviour becomes decidedly conservative. Though I characterize the conservative behaviour of street-level bureaucrats as driven by a "fear of the audit," this should not be taken to mean these actors are powerless. Since street-level bureaucrats are on the forefront of providing (or refusing) services to migrants, even if it looks as though their hands are tied they have a real and continual impact on how laws and policies work in practice.

In 2015 in Irkutsk, I encountered this "fear of the audit" mentality both through a personal interaction with an UFMS bureaucrat and via the experiences of a number of migrants and diaspora leaders I encountered. My own experience concerned registration in the apartment where I was staying. Though the apartment owner was happy to register me, in the end the woman at the UFMS would not register me because my visa was arranged through an organization in Moscow. She explained that in order to be registered by a private apartment owner, I would need to produce some sort of document from my host in Moscow that explained why my work required me to be in Irkutsk. If the bureaucrat registered me without this document, she could receive an official reprimand (*protokol*). However, she assured me that since I was leaving Russia a few days later (though well after the 7-day period within which registration was required), I would be fine without registration.

On that same trip, I encountered a number of people who shared their own experiences with the UFMS in Irkutsk, in particular its general unwillingness to stray from the letter of the law. A Tajik migrant I spoke with had lived for over 10 years in Moscow and moved to Siberia because it was quieter and a more relaxed place to live. The only negative part of his experience was the orientation of the UFMS, who were much more restrictive than in Moscow. He and others were not willing to accept my framing of the bureaucrats as afraid of receiving punishment, but were rather convinced that the UFMS looked for every opportunity to fine migrants.

Migrants I interviewed in Irkutsk described how UFMS agents would confiscate documents while levying fines until the time that the migrants could produce proof of payment (a receipt from a bank that shows the fine had been paid). Sometimes the banks would complain that there was no specific violation indicated on the payment request, making it difficult to process the payment properly. Even with proof of payment, the UFMS officials would sometimes require additional paperwork (e.g., registration documents of other relatives living in the same apartment) before releasing the migrant's documents. The drive to increase revenues from fines is related to the fear of the audit mentality, as often agencies have goals for tasks such as collecting fines, and it is the responsibility of street-level bureaucrats to make sure targets are reached.

The demand for additional documents not specifically stated by law is a common occurrence, which makes it necessary for applicants to resubmit paperwork several times before it is successfully accepted. A number of employers (25%–30%) surveyed in 2008 reported that, when registering on behalf of migrant workers either at the post office or FMS, officials required the presence of the migrant, despite the laws that stipulate that migrants can have a third party register for them

(Zaionchkovskaia 2009, 107). Another practice immediately following a 2007 liberalization of the migration laws was the recording of a specific employer on the work permits of CIS migrants despite their legal right to get a work permit prior to finding employment. This practice left the migrants essentially tied to an employer, which was the very situation the law had been amended to prevent.[42]

Even if street-level bureaucrats in the migration services are the least involved with direct corruption, the theoretical relationship between government red tape and the increase in corruption has been established by those well acquainted with the Russian context (Guriev 2004). Experts agree that there are direct implications of this relationship in the migration sphere, and that these bureaucratic problems have created the incentive and opportunity for migrants and employers to seek documents through informal means (Vitkovskaya 2009). It is logical that the difficulties of the procedures create incentive, yet, in order for the opportunity to arise, either bureaucrats must be complicit or there should be a third party willing to intercede with either false papers or a connection through which they can produce official documents. All of these scenarios have a place not only in the migration sphere but in everyday bureaucratic interactions in Russia more generally.

On the Ground and in the Market: Employers, Migrants, and the Intermediary Industry

The literature on corruption and the informal economy supports the hypothesis that, as legislation becomes increasingly restrictive and is managed arbitrarily by corrupt officials, more migration is managed through informal channels.[43] Irregular migrants generally cost less than legal workers because they can be employed for lower wages, do not require social benefits such as health care, and allow evasion of employment and income taxes (Jahn and Straubhaar 1999, 17).[44] As long as these economic benefits remain, the demand for illegal migrants will persist, and increased immigration restrictions will not lead to decreased illegal immigration (Dmitriev and Piadukhov 2009, 277). For the worker, the situation is also beneficial: although wages are below what would be paid to a native worker or legal immigrant, they are often significantly above the earning potential in the country of origin.[45] Society benefits from cheaper prices for goods and services that result from the use of illegal labour (contributing to the social contract).[46] Russia's large informal sector (comprising 48% of the GDP by some estimates) provides ample economic opportunity to illegal immigrants (Schneider 2004).

Economic actors are the most affected by changes in migration policy, but they are resilient and flexible. In all immigration systems, illegal immigration is an informal market response to the narrowing of legal channels (Samers 2004, 28). In Russia, there is the added "benefit" of corruption and the uneven regulation that provide employers and migrants additional options to solve problems and a different assessment of risk and consequence than in rule-of-law contexts. These factors offer marketplace actors agency that is often overlooked in the literature.

State officials give marketplace actors certain latitude because of the crucial role economic growth and prosperity play in the social contract. As I will demonstrate in further chapters, violations of migration rules are very, very unlikely to be uncovered. Immigration enforcement is at best intermittent and is often random. Employers and migrants who have informal connections to state officials are best poised to navigate the system, yet even those without connections can often find ways to manage problems through a variety of informal mechanisms.

Employers

The driving interest of business owners is the bottom line. Hiring migrants instead of locals can be a cost-saving measure on some level. However, hiring migrants in a fully legal way (i.e., through registration with tax services) can put a significant tax burden on employers. A 2006 survey showed that 77% of migrants had no work contract and were paid under the table, and for those migrants who had no migration registration or work permit, 90% were paid under the table and only 3% had a work contract (Tyuryukanova 2008). This situation was largely a result of the 30% income tax rate for foreigners at the time, compared to the local tax rate of 13% (Ivakhnyuk 2009b). When social benefits were included, the tax burden of a foreign worker could be as much as 56%.[47]

The primary calculation of employers in regard to migrant workers is whether to hire migrants legally and follow all state procedures, or to hire migrants without completing all required elements (i.e., signing a contract, reporting to the tax services, etc.). Employers must make calculated decisions in order to strike a balance between saving costs and avoiding penalties associated with hiring illegal migrants. A number of employers have reported that they have not formalized their working relationship with migrants because they wish to avoid dealing with corrupt administrative officials. One employer reported that as a result of going through official channels, inspections from Interior Ministry officials seeking bribes became a regular part of life (Tyuryukanova 2009b, 23).

Despite employer fears, evidence from court cases shows that punitive measures are typically enacted on migrants rather than employers. Two groups of court cases from Krasnodar analysed in chapter 7 show that employers are prosecuted far less than migrants, and punishments are less severe, involving temporary suspension of certain activities, rather than the large fines allowed by law.

Migrants

While this book focuses on the institutional constraints (both formal and informal) created by the state, it is essential to recognize that migrants have agency. Working within the constraints posed by the law and informal institutions such as corruption, which limit access to formal legal status, migrants have developed a set of skills that help them navigate life and work in Russia.

For labour immigrants, the primary interest is making enough money to live on and send back to relatives in the home country. Like employers, migrants are motivated by the desire to avoid the detection of any labour violations and any resulting penalties. Many migrants make an effort to complete the necessary legal procedures, either themselves or through the help of their networks or a paid intermediary. Yet there are many times when a migrant is unable to get proper documents and works either with no documents or with false documents (Tyuryukanova 2009b; Kroschenko and Zibarev 2009).

Even migrants who hold work documents (work permits or patents) do not always work legally, because they do not have a written contract or because they are not registered with the tax services. In 2007, the FMS reported that a majority (53%) of migrants with legal work permits worked in shadow jobs (without a formal contract). A 2008 survey shows an even larger percentage of illegal immigrants (85%) working in shadow jobs (Tyuryukanova 2009a).

Despite widespread informality in the migration sphere in Russia, there is the very acute sense that it is better to be illegal with documents than illegal without documents, as in the opening story of my colleague. Whether the documents are appropriate to the situation is not always particularly important. For example, when the patent system was introduced in 2010, it was advertised as an easy way to come to Russia and work legally. However, migrants would frequently purchase a patent because it gave them valid registration status for a year, but they wouldn't work. Other migrants holding patents worked for legal entities (companies), despite the stipulations at the time that limited patent holders to working for individual Russian citizens in a personal or domestic capacity. Sometimes this occurred simply because migrants didn't understand the law. Related to this, it was not uncommon for migrants to arrange their documents through a service agency or middleman, who promised a work permit but delivered a patent instead. Other times, migrants were simply willing to take a calculated risk that they would not be caught working for the wrong type of employer, and chose the simplest possible work document to obtain.

Some migrants opt to pursue a different status to reduce risk. For example, until 2012, gaining temporary residence allowed migrants to register as individual entrepreneurs instead of as foreign workers. After 2012, those with a permanent *or* temporary residence permit could work without a work permit or patent. In order to obtain a permanent residence permit, a foreigner must first get a temporary residence permit, which is regulated by a quota. Because of limited access to these permits, there are many accounts of obtaining false or illegally procured documents from intermediaries (Tyuryukanova 2009b, 14).

Intermediaries

Because the bureaucratic tasks required of migrants are significant, a thriving system of intermediary agencies has stepped in to facilitate.[48] The intermediary sector of migration management is large, diverse, and essentially unregulated. Though there have been a number of attempts by the government to either regulate or eliminate certain aspects of the intermediary market,[49] it has been nearly impossible because of its sheer size as well as its integration on some level with bureaucrats who benefit from colluding with intermediaries.[50] Though many employers (42.3%) and migrants (43.2%) alike are willing to pay bribes directly to officials in order to solve problems that arise in the migration process, an equal number (51.9% of employers and 43.2% of migrants) use intermediaries to solve problems (Zaionchkovskaia 2009, 108). The migrant services industry generates an estimated 30 billion rubles annually (United Russia 2009).

Since 2009, the Passport-Visa Services (Pasportno-Vizovaia Sluzhba, or PVS), formally an agency of the FMS, has operated as an intermediary. It is authorized to assist migrants in all legal aspects of the migration process, and works on a paid basis. Yet the various branches throughout the country work in markedly different ways. Some are closely connected to the UFMS branch that they serve, as in the case of the Irkutsk PVS, which simply printed up a registration application for me to carry across the hall to the UFMS official (for a fee of 1000 rubles). Others are quite independent and use their position to work for the benefit of migrants by providing services and advocating for their rights.

A number of agencies operate on a purely commercial basis and range in their reliability from a well-respected Kyrgyz diaspora leader registered as an individual entrepreneur in order to fill a need in the community, to the Intergovernmental Migration Centre in Krasnodar closely (and corruptly) associated with the UFMS. That organizations take payment for their services does not mean they are corrupt. In fact, recent interviews with a number of NGOs in Russia revealed that in the context of serious funding problems, owing to an undeveloped tradition of private donations combined with the 2012 foreign agent law restricting organizations' access to foreign funding, commercial activities may be the best option for agencies hoping to assist migrants.[51]

Many intermediary agencies post advertisements in public transport with only a phone number. Other agencies have established offices and recruit business via the internet. One such example is called Slavic Right, whose website warns of unscrupulous middlemen who offer fake documents at cheap prices.[52] The company offered a variety of services as of 2017, including work permits (for a fee of 750–1,500 euros),[53] temporary and permanent residence permits, citizenship, and other related services, including helping those who have encountered trouble with the police (for 1,500 euros) or with tax inspectors (500 euros), or need representation in court (1,500 euros). The company also specializes in helping companies avoid fines levied by the FMS, for a fee of "60,000–500,000 rubles depending on the number of migrants that were arrested."[54] A quick internet search will return many similar services, even those that provide transport to the nearest border in order to obtain a new migration card (a strategy many migrants use in order to reset the period of stay).[55] However, most migrants in Moscow (61.5%) find an agency through personal acquaintances (Dmitriev and Piadukhov 2009, 282). At the beginning of 2015, intermediary services were charging as much as 30,000–40,000 rubles for patents (including language exam, medical checks, etc.).[56]

There are also those intermediaries who act as employment brokers, offering job placement for a fee. While private employment agencies operate throughout the world, the International Labour Organization has identified two peculiarities with private employment agencies in Russia currently. The first is that they charge migrants rather than employers for their services. Employers are often unwilling to pay the associated costs or to risk receiving workers they are not satisfied with only to find that the employment agency has vanished with the placement fee. Second, the agencies contract migrant labour to large companies who take on no legal relationship with the workers.[57] In these cases, the migrant's relationship is with the intermediary or a sub-contracting company, and the workers do not exist to the parent company and therefore receive no social benefits or labour rights.[58] It is not uncommon for shadow intermediaries to confiscate migrants' passports and force workers to repay the cost of transportation from their home countries through unpaid labour, often under threat of physical abuse or being reported to the police.[59]

Informal mechanisms develop at the marketplace level to cope with an increasingly narrow and uncoordinated legal space. Actors adapt to the circumstances with a short-term focus of reducing a variety of risks, and therefore strategies are not uniform across Russia's expanse. What is persistent across Russia's migration sphere is the strategy of using informal mechanisms either in pursuit of legal status or in pursuit of circumventing legal requirements. Foreign workers who utilize well-developed migrant networks can find it easier to navigate life, work, and interactions with the state in Russia. Since millions of Central Asian migrants go to Russia each year, many migrants rely on friends and family to help them. Migration is not without risks, and stories of exploitation are readily available, especially given the attention of human rights organizations to the migration situation in Russia. Nevertheless, risk or vulnerability does not eliminate agency, which is strengthened through a variety of informal mechanisms including networks and even corruption.

Conclusion: Ensuring Informality through Scarcity

This chapter has detailed the various actors in the multi-level balancing act of migration management and described the informal and formal mechanisms available to each. The scope of migration actors reaches from the upper echelons of the Kremlin to the streets of Russia where migrants work. At each level, actors have a role to play in the patronage system and social contract, which helps to define their interests and how they will respond to policy. At each level, actors use a mix of formal and informal mechanisms to balance their interests and obligations. The driving goal of the multi-level balancing act is to create a scarcity of legal labour that increases the informal benefits that can be used and distributed across the system at all levels.

The exposition of informality in this chapter challenges the literature in some important ways. Many scholars frame informal solutions as pathologies, acts of desperation, or survival strategies (Kim 2013; McMann 2014). Sometimes actors are excluded from participating in the formal sector because of heavy regulations or high costs (Perry et al. 2007). In these cases, corruption (i.e., payment of bribes) acts as a survival strategy, for example a payment to an inspector or law enforcement agent so that they will overlook irregularities in an immigrant worker's status, a company's tax violations, etc. But these perspectives obscure the agency that is available to actors even at the lowest level. Perhaps an actor prefers not to pay a bribe because it is expensive or is extracted in a manner that imbues a sense of powerlessness. But we cannot ignore the fact that corruption also increases the agency of actors when paying a bribe is a reliable alternative to engaging bureaucratically cumbersome official procedures.

At times, therefore, informal strategies provide the most flexible and best options for navigating the system. Furthermore, in a system where corruption is common and a reliable solution to problems, actors may prefer to take a calculated risk and avoid official procedures (e.g., hiring a migrant through the formal legal channels), knowing they can pay a bribe to solve any problems they may encounter. Yet informal strategies should not be reduced to corruption-related practices. This chapter has elaborated a wide array of informal strategies used in combination with formal mechanisms throughout the migration governance structure. Informal strategies can include network ties (between migrants, between state officials, or cutting across state and economic actors), bureaucratic or institutional culture (e.g., setting internal targets for administrative tasks such as collecting fines), or any other mechanism that is not a part of the formal (written) legal structure.

A natural question in light of the preceding discussion is whether the increased informality in the migration labour market is an intended or unintended consequence of policy decisions. While decision makers at the federal level are often disconnected from the specifics of migration processes on the ground and insulated from the impact of their decisions in the regions, they are not unaware of the informal strategies that arise to meet policy contexts.[60] If we focus on legal consistency as the goal of policymaking, the Russian migration management system looks uncoordinated and full of gaps between policy goals and outcomes. However, this chapter has reframed Russia to show a complex network of interlocking actors and interests that use a variety of formal and informal tools to balance their responsibilities and interests. This focused activity serves a function in the federal system, producing devolution that is disciplined by multiple overlapping patronage pacts and sub-pacts.

For policymakers it is important to retain control of the migration process in a formal institutional capacity, as demonstrated by the manoeuvring between Mintrud and the FMS. At the upper levels, the primary emphasis is on control (or the illusion of control) rather than on producing legality. Elites in the ministries respond to higher political pressures and work to produce the impression that the policies are functioning, which they do primarily by passing down the task of day-to-day management to regional actors. Regional bureaucratic actors take their task of producing "on paper" compliance with executive goals seriously, but are narrowly focused on a particular set of goals and tasks that may not be connected with the realities of the labour market. All of these actors operate on signals given from higher-up officials, sometimes even directly from the Kremlin, about the appropriate level of scarcity. Given the clear signals documented in this chapter and elaborated in the next two chapters, it is equally clear that scarcity is an intended outcome of policy decisions. Policymakers not only expect but rely on the informal mechanisms that are part and parcel of the institutional structure of governance in Russia to balance any conflicting interests that arise and smooth over the appearance of policy gaps.

The strategies at play in Russia have links to Soviet practices. The iterative process between federal and regional actors, each focused narrowly on their own interests, mimics the Soviet practice of economic and labour planning, which will be discussed more fully in the following chapter. During the Soviet period rigid policies were strategically used to increase the direct benefits to those with positions of power (Shleifer and Vishny 1992). The strategies outlined in this chapter show

how these patterns persist and permeate the system in an attempt to balance disparate interests. The historical patterns of informal networks and economic exchange across the Soviet and post-Soviet periods make informal strategies a reliable option. This context makes migrants from former Soviet countries particularly adept at navigating the uncertainty that arises from a scarcity of legal labour permissions.

The scarcity of legal labour is an essential mechanism for signalling the appropriate mix of formal and informal mechanisms in the management of migrant labour. The following two chapters look at two successive policy packages that were used to institute a scarcity of legal migrant labour. Both work permit quotas (2007–14) and patents (2015–present) are policies that specifically target migrants from CIS countries, the largest suppliers of low-skilled labour to Russia. Though the policies are fundamentally different, quotas being based on the principles of central planning and patents reflecting market ideas, both have been used to institute scarcity and ensure the continued use of informal mechanisms. The appropriate level of scarcity relies on cues from Putin. Both while Putin was president (2000–8, 2012–present) and prime minister (2008–12), he gave important signals indicating the acceptable number of legal migrants (in the case of quotas) and the degree of regional autonomy that could be exercised over migration management (in the case of patents). These signals have an impact on the types of informal mechanisms that develop among actors at all levels.

Chapter Three

Scarcity Mechanism #1: Quotas as a Legacy of State Planning

What started as a bar fight in the small northern town of Kondopoga in September 2006 became an iconic warning of the potential dangers of migration in Russia. When two ethnic Russians turned up dead as a result of the fight with Chechens, there was violent backlash by locals that left several Caucasian-owned businesses destroyed. Protests demanded the deportation of migrants from the Caucasus, notwithstanding the fact that those hailing from north Caucasian regions are often natural-born Russian citizens. Nationalist organizations like the Movement against Illegal Immigration (Dvizhenie protiv nelegal'noi immigratsii – DPNI) made Kondopoga their rallying cry, and the media maximized the nationalist message, in one report rearranging the text of a Putin speech to locate comments on Kondopoga next to statements about protecting Russians (Schenk 2010). Though major new reforms to migration policy had already been adopted in July 2006, they were later framed as a response to Kondopoga and larger patterns of xenophobia and labour market competition owing to migrants from the Caucasus.[1] In response to Kondopoga, Putin recognized the need to "increase order" in the spheres of migration and labour relations, though he also warned against provocateurs who might blow the issue out of proportion (Putin 2006). Other than these fairly vague comments, Putin had very little to say about the new migration policies. It is particularly important to emphasize that, when the policies were introduced, Putin was completely silent on the issue of quotas that are central to this chapter's analysis. Only when the 2008 global financial crisis hit did he speak out about how quotas should be managed.

Changes to the migration law that came into force on January 15, 2007 introduced work permit quotas for migrants coming from CIS countries. Quotas for 2007 were set at 6 million with the goal of allowing enough work permits for migrants already in Russia as well as newcomers (Vlasova et al. 2011). When quotas are set in line with labour market realities, as in 2007, scarcity of legal labour should not occur. Therefore, the puzzle of migration quotas in the Russian context is why some of the largest quotas in the world became a key mechanism for producing scarcity.[2] Tracing this quota over its lifespan from 2007 to 2014 demonstrates how instituting scarcity can be used to indicate a permissible level of informality for use by state and marketplace actors. In the Russian case, quotas not only set a numerical limit for the number of migrants allowed to work each year, but also reproduced Soviet central planning practices. These practices, operating on signals from Putin, produced scarcity and created and reinforced informal practices.

The focus of this chapter is the quota for work permits (*razreshenie na rabotu*) specifically for migrants from CIS countries that was in place from 2007 to 2014. To be clear, it is not the only quota that is used in the migration sphere, though it has been the most politically contentious. Quotas for visa invitations (*priglashenii na v"ezd*) were introduced for foreign workers coming from visa countries in 2002 and remain to the present day. During the 2007–14 window, the visa invitation quotas became a sub-quota of the work permit quota.[3] Another important quota is that regulating temporary residence permits (*razreshenie na vremennoe prozhivanie*, typically shortened to RVP), which allow a foreigner to work without a work permit (as of 2012). Determining each of these yearly quota uses similar procedures that I will elaborate below. However, the work permit quotas were the most visible and controversial because of their relative size (see table 3.1). They are particularly interesting because, though they were the largest quota (in Russia and in comparative perspective), they became a key tool in producing a scarcity of legal migrant status.

There were two ways for a CIS migrant to get access to work permits during the 2007–14 period. One path was through an employer who had applied for a quota allocation in the previous year (typically at least six months in advance). The other was for migrants to apply by themselves or through an intermediary (see figure 3.1). This latter possibility was an innovation of the package of amendments that went into effect on January 15, 2007. Lawmakers, migration officials, and migration advocates in the non-governmental sector alike framed these aspects of the law as a liberalization because migrant workers could obtain work permits on their own and move freely between employers.

Table 3.1. Quotas compared

	Temporary residence permits	Visa invitations	Work permits
2007	52,723	308,842	6,000,000
2008	140,790	1,140,633	3,384,129
2009	200,345	1,250,769	3,976,747
2010	159,515	611,080	1,944,356
2011	105,000	499,650	1,745,584
2012	105,807	460,510	1,745,584
2013	95,800	410,126	1,745,584
2014	160,687	357,894	1,631,586

Source: Government Orders defining yearly quota.

Figure 3.1. How to get a work permit

For non-CIS citizens (to be completed by employers)

Apply for permission to hire a foreign worker[a]

Apply for quota[b]

Apply for visa invitation

For all migrant workers (CIS workers could apply themselves)

Submit to UFMS:

- Application form
- Migration card
- Registration (verifying work or residence location)
- Passport (translated and notarized)
- Colour photo (passport style)
- Payment receipt[c]
- Medical certificate[d]
- Employment contract[e]

[a] Some regions (e.g., Moscow) required employers to get permission even for CIS citizens.

[b] Though CIS migrants didn't need to apply for quota ahead of time, their work permit was counted against the overall quota in the region. In some regions, employers were required to apply for quota (a separate process from applying for permission to hire a foreign worker) ahead of time even to hire a CIS worker.

[c] Payments are made to a bank, and receipts presented to the UFMS.

[d] Verifying that the migrant has no infectious diseases (tuberculosis, AIDS, etc.) or drug dependence.

[e] For CIS migrants, a contract was only required to extend a work permit beyond 3 months.

This innovation had the potential to interject flexibility into the system and protect migrants from labour exploitation and slavery.

Any employer could theoretically hire a migrant who had obtained a work permit on their own, and this introduced elements of contradiction into the system. If employers could hire a CIS worker without previously applying for a quota allocation, why should they apply in advance? However, since quotas for each region were determined in large part based on employer applications, if employers did not participate in the yearly quota application drive, the region would not have a realistic estimate of labour market needs.

This and other contradictions in the quota system reflect divergent interests and a lack of cooperation between the FMS and Minzdrav/Mintrud, which, combined with signals from the Kremlin as to the maximum allowable level of quota, produced a resilient scarcity of legal labour. Populist intervention by Putin in 2008, declaring an acceptable maximum level of quota, served the purpose of maintaining legitimacy in a time of public anxiety. Putin's quota was well below labour market need, however, causing an inevitable increase in illegal migrants. The scarcity-level quotas also required very careful management by bureaucratic actors in the federal ministries and regional governments to ensure an "on paper" discipline that lined up with the political prerogatives of the Kremlin.

Soviet Labour Planning and Responses to Scarcity

The 2007–14 work permit quotas not only drew legitimacy from international practice but also found familiar territory, given Soviet economic and labour planning practices. While Russian politics cannot (and should not) be reduced to Soviet legacies, the practices that were established during that time have some important continuities with current procedures. Soviet practice included institutionalized procedures for involving local and enterprise-level leaders when deciding on yearly production quotas that parallel the procedure for work permit quota formulation.[4] Nevertheless, the ability of the central planning apparatus to truly control economic affairs on the ground was limited, resulting in scarcity and shortages, which had to be strategically managed at the local level.

A persistent view of Soviet economic planning is that all decisions were given directly from Moscow in a hyper-centralized, top-down process (Harrison and Kim 2006). While scholars have identified how decision making was driven largely by political considerations (Robinson 2013; Gregory 2001), it is important to acknowledge that input from local enterprises was an important part of planning (Nikitin 1969; Harrison and Kim 2006). These processes were not contradictory, but rather represented an iterative process where both local and central needs were considered (Vlachoutsicos and Lawrence 1990). Economic plans began with draft plans created at the enterprise level, which were then weighed against preliminary targets issued from the central authorities. A number of intermediary agencies such as ministries and their regional branches then worked to reconcile the needs of the two ends (Richman 1969; Gregory 2004). Central planning also involved a number of corrective opportunities, which incorporated thousands of requests for amendments from the local and regional level into the plans (Richman 1969; Gregory 2001).

A key part of central planning dealt with manpower planning, which involved numerical limits on workers and wages for every enterprise or agency in the Soviet Union (Brown 1957; Hough 1979). Meeting planned labour targets necessarily involved not only mobility within and between enterprises but also migration across the country (Malle 1987). From the perspective of state planners, migration served the sole purpose of balancing labour supply and demand, and fulfilling central plans for worker distribution (Brodersen 1966; Lewis and Rowland 1979).[5] Yet the state only rarely compelled workers directly to move across the country to fill labour gaps.[6] More frequently, the state used market-style mechanisms to entice workers with higher wages, education opportunities, housing, pension and disability payments, or appeals to ideology, patriotism, and worker discipline (Grossman 1979; Brown 1957; Manevich 1968; Brodersen 1966; Hough 1979). However, more often than not, job recruitment started and finished at the local level by employers posting jobs on public bulletin boards and hiring "at the gates" of their enterprises (Malle 1987; Brown 1957). This type of hiring frequently relied on informal network connections (Lane 1987).

Though manpower planning involved targets or limits for each workplace, labour shortages were chronic during the Soviet period.[7] Shortages in turn had implications for both the development of migration patterns and the informal strategies used to cope with the consequences of scarcity. In the context of increased labour demand, workers could seek better conditions if they were not satisfied in their current jobs. Much of the resulting migration was to urban areas, where there were better employment opportunities and greater access to consumer goods.

Despite administrative controls meant to prevent over-population in large cities, people continued to move to urban areas, either finding creative ways to circumvent barriers, such as marriage to a city dweller, obtaining false residence permits, or living illegally without proper documents (Buckley 1995; Rutland 1985; Light 2016).[8]

To prevent workers from leaving their positions amid conditions of shortage, managers often used informal mechanisms to entice workers to stay. Though wages were determined by central plans, there were numerous ways for managers to exercise discretion over wage distribution or raise additional funds to use for worker incentives.[9] Workers were also plied with lax working conditions (Rutland 1985).

Because both rural-urban migration and informal inducements for workers were often managed outside planning mechanisms, they found themselves by default in the realm of the informal or second economy, which operated on market and network principles. Examples of economic activity occurring outside the plan are ample (Gregory 2004), and a robust second economy of informal economic exchange existed alongside the planned economy (Grossman 1977). Many scholars argue that the plans issued by the centre were of secondary importance and that "impulsive 'resource management,' largely outside the realm of formal planning, was the principal instrument of resource allocation" (Lazarev and Gregory 2002). Though most accounts of the Soviet second economy focus on industrial and consumer goods, informal labour was also important.

Like the Soviet experience, the work permit quota system used in 2007–14 included both market-based (economic opportunity) and policy-based (visa-free regime) incentives to migrate, at the same time as there were significant points of control (registration and work permit requirements). We also see a parallel situation that tightening the legal space did little to influence actual flows of migrants, as migrants persistently find ways to bypass migration controls through the use of informal mechanisms. Nevertheless, the activity of planning is crucial. The process of submitting regionally defined targets to the central apparatus is similar across both periods, as are the political signals sent from the top.

Just as central planning and shortages produced informality during the Soviet period (Kim 2013), work permit quotas demonstrate a repeat of historical dynamics. In both eras, the state produces a planning-oriented system that does not adequately provide needed resources, creating shortages, which are then solved through informal procedures.

Both the institutionalization of scarcity, imposed at the top levels of government for political purposes, and the use of that scarcity to distribute informal resources have precedent from the Soviet experience.

Signalling Scarcity: The View from the Top

The Soviet system was criticized for its inability to connect realities on the ground with political goals, and in the end deferring to the needs of central planners in Moscow. A similar argument has been made about the 2007–14 work permit quotas because they were not in line with labour market need. Rather, political factors drove a complicated and non-transparent procedure (Ioffe and Zayonchkovskaya 2010; Vlasova et al. 2011; Mikhailova and Tyuryukanova 2009). This chapter pursues these critiques by assessing the political context of quotas, the process used to produce "on paper" discipline by regional administrations, and how actual practice diverged from the formal picture.

It is clear that quotas were political because of Putin's personal involvement in determining an acceptable quota level. The signals from the Kremlin serve the important function of indicating an appropriate mix of formal and informal mechanisms, and they further show that at key points the system needed direction from the highest levels in order to set it on a preferred course. When Putin announced a quota that was below labour market demand, he instituted a scarcity of legal labour. This scarcity ensured robust activity in the shadow labour market and the use of informal mechanisms by state and marketplace actors. For state actors, the use of informal mechanisms is a patronage resource because it increases spoils available for personal use as long as all other patronage pact responsibilities are attended to.

The 2007 work permit quota was set at 6 million based on expert recommendations of the number of work permits needed to accommodate migrants already in Russia as well as those expected to arrive within the year, providing a telling estimate of real labour market need in Russia.[10] Following that year, employer applications were the starting point for determining quota, but because employer participation was initially quite low, the 2008 quota was only 1.8 million (Kroschenko and Zibarev 2009).[11] In a number of regions (including Moscow), the 2008 quota was exhausted by May, indicating that it did not meet labour market demand. The FMS announced in August 2008 that additional quota would be added, and it was eventually increased to 3.4 million.[12]

When the 2009 quota of 4 million was announced, based on increased participation by employers, there was an immediate backlash in the media, and from regional governors and representatives of trade unions who questioned the increase in quota in the wake of the global financial crisis. The issue garnered national attention during the annual publicly televised question and answer session "A Conversation with Vladimir Putin" in December 2008, when a woman asked why migrant quotas were so high, given unemployment rates amid the financial crisis. Putin sympathized with her query, saying, "I recommend that the quota be reasonably reduced by no less than 50%." Following Putin's statements, numerous stories appeared in the media with headlines such as "quota for migrants decreased twofold,"[13] to around 2 million.[14]

Putin's statements stand as a key moment in the development of work permit quotas. In prime populist fashion, they represent a sympathetic leader protecting the needs of citizens against an unresponsive bureaucracy and market-driven employers who would seek to hire the cheapest possible labour at the expense of domestic workers. An announcement such as this by Putin serves the function of increasing legitimacy at the same time as it signals to the administration how labour market priorities should be set. Because Putin rarely indulges directly in the anti-migrant populism typical of lower elites, his statements show the importance of the issue. In a moment of populism par excellence that only a state insider could pull off, Putin not only promised to rescue the people from the threat of migrants but seemingly swept aside bureaucratic procedures and labour market signals from employers. This episode had a lasting effect on how quotas would be set for the remainder of the 2007–14 period.

However, the public rhetoric did not match the policy reality, producing one of the few discursive gaps we see in the Russian migration system. Analysing the quota numbers as set in government documents presents a different picture from the one crafted in the media. Beginning in 2003 (with quotas for visa invitations), quotas included a yearly "reserve," or a pool of quota set aside and not allocated to a specific region.[15] This allowed for mid-year adjustments of quotas, if a particular region needed additional foreign workers, without changing the overall nationwide numbers. In 2008, both the overall and the reserve quotas were quickly used up, causing the government to add additional quotas as discussed above (see table 3.2 and figure 3.2).[16]

Table 3.2. Work permit quota

	2007	2008	2009	2010	2011	2012	2013	2014
Total quota	6,000,000	1,828,245	3,976,747	1,944,356	1,745,584	1,745,584	1,745,584	1,631,586
(year end)		(3,384,129)						
Reserve	1,064,321	492,588	1,988,373	583,307	523,751	477,606	521,399	489,476
(year end)		(847,995)	(2,174,023)	(526,807)	(377,441)	(256,194)	(296,869)	(263,287)
To regions	4,935,679	1,335,657	1,988,374	1,369,030	1,221,833	1,267,978	1,224,185	1,142,110
(year end)		(2,536,134)	(1,802,724)	(1,417,549)	(1,368,143)	(1,489,390)	(1,448,715)	(1,368,299)

Source: Government orders defining yearly quota; Minzdrav/Mintrud orders defining yearly regional allocation and mid-year adjustments.

Figure 3.2. Quota and reserve

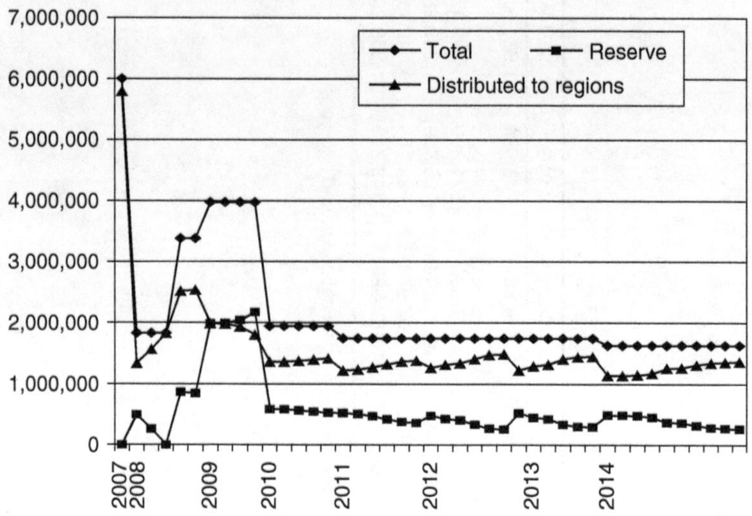

In 2009, the overall quota was never actually reduced in the official documents as Putin recommended. Rather, the 2 million (or 50%) figure that Putin suggested and that was widely publicized was the allocation of quotas to the regions at the beginning of the year. The overall quota remained 4 million, with a reserve of 2 million. During 2009, the overall quota remained stable, though there were three mid-year reallocations of the regional numbers (see appendix table A3.a). These served to further reduce regional-level quota to the point that the overall reserve was larger than the actual regional allocation (see table 3.2).[17] Contrast this to the situation in 2008, when over the course of five mid-year adjustments not a single region reduced its quota. By the end of 2009, fewer work permits had been issued than in 2008, despite an initially higher quota based on requests from employers (see table 3.3).

After 2009, the quota became relatively more stable, with the overall quota more closely matching the levels suggested by Putin in 2008. The quota for 2010 was set at 2 million, though a reduction to 1.3 million was announced in the final days of 2009 after a meeting between Putin and the head of the Federation of Independent Trade Unions, Mikhail Schmakov.[18] Headlines of "Putin has reduced the quota for labour migrants" again evoked the feeling that protecting the local labour market was receiving the personal attention of Putin.[19] Though the media widely reported the 1.3 million figure, this "reduction" was again simply a choice to focus on the regional allocations (excluding the reserve) and not the overall quota number, which remained at 2 million.[20] Thus the regional allocation decreased less than 500,000 between the end of 2009 and the beginning of 2010, despite the rhetoric of an overall decrease from 4 million to 1.3 million. It is also interesting to note that while most regions had smaller quotas for 2010, 17 regions increased their quotas from 2009.[21]

From 2011 to 2013, the federal-level quota stayed at 1.7 million each year, and in 2014 it was reduced to 1.6 million. In these years, any variation occurred within and between regions. Each year there were between four (in 2011) and nine (in 2014) mid-year adjustments of regional quota numbers, with the overall effect that the reserve decreased and more quota was dispersed to the regions with each adjustment (see appendix table A3.a). However, regions did not uniformly participate in the mid-year adjustments, nor did they always increase their quota; in certain cases, regions used the opportunity to decrease their quota.

Putin's direct intervention in the quota system in 2008 and 2009 sent important signals about the mix of formal and informal mechanisms that would be allowed going forward, by defining how much of the migrant labour market should operate in the formal (documented) sphere. Putin's signals were also given with a keen eye towards producing legitimacy. When a quota of 2 million didn't produce any great public backlash (both in 2009 and 2010), there was no need for further personal intervention. The government (presided over at the time by Putin as prime minister) settled on a quota just under this equilibrium point in the ensuing years, in effect institutionalizing Putin's intervention into a policy that decreased the maximum number of legal labour migrants.[22]

Given relatively stable migrant populations, measured both in terms of remittances being sent out of Russia and entries into the country (table 3.4),[23] decreased quotas inevitably caused increased illegality. Therefore institutionalizing a quota below labour market demand also institutionalized the scarcity of legal labour. And while the reasons for this strategy were political and even populist in nature, it relied on careful and particular bureaucratic management. Because any major adjustments to the quotas were shifted from the widely publicized federal-level quotas to the regions after 2009, it is necessary to look in

Table 3.3. Quota and work permits

	2007	2008	2009	2010	2011	2012	2013	2014
Total quota (year end)	6,000,000	1,828,245 (3,384,129)	3,976,747	1,944,356	1,745,584	1,745,584	1,745,584	1,631,586
To regions (year end)	4,935,679	1,335,657 (2,536,134)	1,988,374 (1,802,724)	1,369,030 (1,417,549)	1,221,833 (1,368,143)	1,267,978 (1,489,390)	1,224,185 (1,448,715)	1,142,110 (1,368,299)
Work permits issued	1,717,137	2,425,921	2,223,596	1,640,801	1,027,929	1,148,725	1,111,494	1,043,834

Source: Rosstat 2011b; Rosstat 2013b; Rosstat 2015d; Government orders defining yearly quota; Minzdrav/Mintrud orders defining yearly regional allocation and mid-year adjustments.

Table 3.4. Estimating migrant population

	2007	2008	2009	2010	2011	2012	2013	2014	2015
Remittance outflow[a]	19.9	29.7	21.2	21.5	26.0	31.7	37.2	32.6	19.7
Entries	22,908,625	23,676,140	21,338,650	22,281,217	24,932,061	28,176,502	30,792,091	32,421,490	33,729,187
–from CIS	16,082,555	15,061,619	12,960,167	13,906,605	15,730,278	17,995,850	19,922,378	21,621,143	22,868,754

Source: Rosstat 2014a; Rosstat 2016a; Rosstat 2012a; Rosstat 2010a; World Bank 2016.

[a] USD billions.

greater detail at the regional quota picture. A deeper analysis of the quota mechanism demonstrates the role of the bureaucracy in migrant management as well as the interaction between bureaucratic procedure and political elites.

Setting Work Permit Quotas: The Bureaucratic Machine at Work

Once the Kremlin signalled the appropriate level of quota, it was the responsibility of the ministries to produce a palatable picture of the quota for public consumption. Regional governments also played a role in assuring that the quota mechanism proceeded in a disciplined manner that fulfilled federal prerogatives. Though this bureaucratic coordination was primarily an "on paper" type of discipline, it contributed to the projection of stability by producing a cohesive picture of regional quota distribution.

This section elaborates and evaluates the quota procedure used to produce the "on paper" discipline required by the patronage pact. According to migration experts in Russia, quotas were "determined through a complicated and multi-layered mechanism not backed by any serious methodology" (Ioffe and Zayonchkovskaya 2010). Others suggested that the procedure was complicated and non-transparent, allowing ample room for political and administrative discretion (Mikhailova and Tyuryukanova 2009). As a consequence, the quotas did not reflect real demand for foreign workers, and were based on political factors rather than economic prerequisites (Vlasova et al. 2011).

Whatever criticisms could be made of the quota methodology, the seriousness with which bureaucrats approached the task could not be doubted. The task of formulating quotas was indeed bureaucratically intensive, and from my observations and discussions with those involved, a process that was taken quite seriously. Through a number of interviews with bureaucrats involved in the quota formulation process in various regions, it became clear to me that the attitude towards the process was technocratically oriented. Nevertheless, this is not sufficient evidence to establish that the methodology itself is feasible or that it will produce a rational estimation of the migrant labour market. The following section evaluates the government procedure and methodology in light of common criticisms in order to assess whether quota allocations across regions follow macroeconomic, labour market, and other indicators. While interviews with bureaucrats created some initial impressions of how they approached their tasks, their descriptions of the quota-planning process often lacked the detail necessary to understand the full picture. Therefore, I rely on a number of documents issued by government agencies at various levels. I approach these extremely technical documents as "human artifacts" (Schatz 2009) that reflect micro-level human decision making about how to implement bureaucratic tasks.

Procedure

After the expert-recommended limit of 6 million was set for 2007, work permit quotas were decided on the basis of a procedure driven by regional bureaucrats. The government defined a detailed schedule that began each May to determine the following year's quota (see appendix table A3.b).[24] The process started with applications from employers, which were analysed by regional interdepartmental commissions established by, and under the authority of, regional governors. Representatives of a variety of regional ministries and departments also assessed employer applications and gave recommendations to the interdepartmental commission, who then submitted a regional quota for federal approval and assigned quota to individual employers.

The first several years of quota planning met with a number of coordination and implementation delays. For example, both in 2007 and 2008, regions weren't notified of how much quota they would receive until several months into the year (the last column of appendix table A3.a shows when the regional distributions were issued each year). For the 2008 quotas, forms for employers to use in their applications were issued only four months after the May deadline for submission.[25]

The forms for interdepartmental commissions to use for submitting regional quota requests to Minzdrav in Moscow, on the other hand, were issued well before the deadline to set 2008 quotas. This shows a priority for creating internal bureaucratic procedures over and above defining procedures involving interaction with the public. In other words, it demonstrates that administration in Russia first and foremost serves the state rather than embracing the idea of public service. In order to complete the forms by the July (2007) deadline, regional commissions were guided by general criteria set out in the migration legislation.[26] However, the methodology that would be used in following years to estimate the impact of migrant workers on the regional labour market was not ready until September, and therefore was not considered when creating 2008 quotas.[27]

Another disruption occurred when the federal ministries were reorganized and responsibility for quota formulation was transferred from the Ministry of Health (Minzdrav) to the Ministry of Labour (Mintrud) in 2012.[28] Procedures for employer applications and instructions for interdepartmental commissions were particularly affected by these developments. When responsibility for quota formulation was transferred to Mintrud, the agency issued new rules that reduced the role of employer applications and centralized the quota process under the authority of Mintrud elites in Moscow.[29]

Eventually, all application forms were automated and made accessible through an online portal. Regional governments made significant efforts both to publicize the application drive and to assist employers in filling out online applications.[30] These efforts increased the participation of employers, but in many regions this meant that the interdepartmental commissions received many more applications than they could approve once Putin signalled the appropriate level of federal quota.

Once all of the instructions for interdepartmental commissions were established, the resulting methodology included consideration of numerous factors related to the labour market, macroeconomic indicators, social and security considerations, and the infrastructure capacity of the region (see appendix table A3.c). While the exhaustive list of indicators aimed to create a comprehensive picture of the immigrant labour market and the overall impact of immigrants on society, the methodology was problematic for reasons of data reliability and availability, contradictory indicators, and a lack of specificity, especially in terms of measurement.

One of the frequent justifications for not including Russia in cross-regional immigration studies is a lack of reliable data (Ruhs 2013). However, in a 2013 OECD report, the Federal State Statistical Service (Federal'naia Sluzhba Gosudarstvennoi Statistiki, or Rosstat) was deemed to have made significant improvements, and in some areas it is now on par with OECD minimum standards, especially in terms of independence and public accessibility of data. Nevertheless, remaining weaknesses are the coordination and sharing of data across ministries and the coordination of data from subordinate statistics agencies (OECD 2013). These critiques are palpably observed in the case of migration data since many categories of migration data are missing in the Rosstat databases.

While regional branches of the FMS collected detailed statistics, which were sent to the federal level, the statistics section of the FMS website only presented a limited snapshot (often less than a year) of migration statistics at any given time. Because the FMS statistics were updated frequently, removing previous reports from the website, compiling comprehensive data is challenging.

Data availability poses certain obstacles to replicating the quota-planning methodology. In some cases, the data required to create an estimate of the need for foreign workers is not available to the public, and it is unclear whether the data exists at all. Were the procedure as rational, even scientific, as bureaucrats indicated to me in interviews, there should have been no barriers for independent analysts wishing to replicate the results. However, given the lack of specificity of the methodology, as well as the unavailability of many categories of the data, replication can at best be partial.[31]

Even if data were fully available, the methodology directed interdepartmental commissions to consider multiple factors that at times could be contradictory. For example, if a region had insufficient housing and social infrastructure to absorb foreign workers, yet its only alternative prospect for filling labour demand was internal migrants from other Russian regions, the impact on infrastructure would not be diminished. Some of the criteria included in the methodology had a minimal impact on the labour market, and were more related to considerations of national identity or security. For example, given the smaller than expected numbers of ethnic return migrants through the government-sponsored "compatriot" program, the overall labour market effect of the program has been minimal, though there is symbolic value in favouring these foreign workers over non-"compatriots."[32] Another factor, namely the need to consider a foreign worker's country of origin, is not related to the labour market and can only be explained as a political consideration of bilateral relations with particular sending countries. And while the migration law specifies that national security issues (e.g., public health threats involved in accepting migrants from particular countries) should be considered in quota formulation, the combination of indicators driven by competing logics left bureaucrats without a clear set of instructions.

Because there was no clarification on how data points should be weighted, regional bureaucrats were left to interpret measurements on their own. For example, there were no specific instructions on whether migrant crime or cost to the health care system should be weighted more or less heavily than migrant contribution to economic growth.[33] Further, the methodology did not indicate whether the given variables should be considered as increasing or decreasing demand for migrant workers. For example, are lower relative wages of migrant workers a justification for increasing the quota (to contribute to further economic development in certain sectors) or decreasing the quota (to protect the native labour force)? Left with unclear directions, bureaucrats had to interpret and prioritize on their own. Yet, as the following analysis will show, the latitude the methodology might have afforded was not realized in quota planning because bureaucrats across Russia systematically used simplified considerations of the labour market to make their decisions.

Trends: Testing the Methodology

Despite data limitations, I will demonstrate that quota trends followed a sort of rational, if simplified, calculation that considered selected indicators from the government methodology. Using a panel data set for 83 regions of Russia across the years 2006–14, I regress quotas at the beginning (*quota1*) and end of each year (*quota10*), as well as the number of work permits (*wkpt*) on major labour market and socio-economic indicators that approximate the government quota methodology (see appendix table A3.c for full discussion of variables and methods).[34] Assessing different dependent variables on factors that the government methodology indicates *should* impact quota allocation allows me to compare the impact of macroeconomic, social, and labour market indicators on the quota at the beginning and end of year (reflecting initial quota and adjustments throughout the year) and on the number of work permits issued in a given year. This serves to demonstrate whether Minzdrav/Mintrud and the interdepartmental commissions follow a consistent logic within each region when setting and adjusting quota, and whether regional UFMS branches follow a similar logic when issuing work permits.

Results

Model 1 shows that for initial quota allocations (*quota1*), the most important factor that bureaucrats considered was unemployment

Table 3.5. Determinants of quota and work permits

	quota1		*quota10*		*wkpt*	
Migrant contribution to gross regional product	0.000***	(0.000)	0.000**	(0.000)	0.000	(0.000)
Unemployment rate	–8.33***	(3.16)	–11.5***	(3.68)	–1.97**	(1.00)
Average wages	0.28	(0.21)	–0.47***	(0.15)	–1.28***	(0.14)
Informal workers	0.66	(1.74)	–0.71	(1.16)	–1.05	(0.86)
Job vacancy rate	5.81	(3.95)	11.9***	(1.16)	5.80*	(3.57)
Graduates entering the labour market	0.24	(0.43)	0.39	(0.40)	–0.57**	(0.26)
Migrant contribution to GDP	1.18	(5.25)	–0.05	(3.64)	0.62	(1.22)
Migrant work permits	0.27	(0.24)	0.06	(0.15)	0.40***	(0.04)
Housing density	0.003	(0.003)	–0.001	(0.003)	0.004**	(0.002)
Schools	0.000	(0.000)	0.000	(0.000)	0.000	(0.000)
Hospital beds	–0.001	(0.004)	0.003	(0.004)	0.004*	(0.002)
Constant	1.52	(6.04)	9.73**	(4.86)	22.8***	(3.55)
Observations	664		664		581	
R2 within	0.52		0.56		0.57	
R2 between	0.86		0.65		0.34	
R2 overall	0.76		0.63		0.35	

Note: fixed effect coefficients are presented with robust standard errors in parentheses; all independent variables are lagged by one year; logged values shown for quota, work permits, wages, and graduates; * = p < .10, ** = p < .05, *** = p < .01

rates (see table 3.5). The negative coefficient indicates that as unemployment within a region increased, the overall quota decreased. Migrant contribution to gross regional product is the only other significant variable. Despite having an intricate (albeit not well defined) methodology for constructing quota, at the end of the day the biggest factor influencing bureaucratic decision making was unemployment rates. This finding corroborates previous research on migration patterns among Russian regions (Andrienko and Guriev 2004; Gerber 2006) and gives further credence to the importance of the unemployment myth in upholding the populist pact. For bureaucrats, it was important to produce a disciplined view of quota planning on paper (best accomplished through a simplistic calculation of the labour market) that also aligned with populist demands from the public. A technocratic approach to migration management, therefore, need not be nuanced (or well grounded in migration theory) in order to reach the goals of state actors.

As bureaucrats adjusted quota within each year, demonstrated by using the year-end quota as dependent variable, wages became important. As average monthly wages increased within a region, quotas decreased. Workplace vacancies were also important. When vacancies increased, quota was adjusted upward. In model 2 we see again that bureaucrats made decisions about increasing or decreasing quota based on a simplistic understanding of the labour market that only considered migrant workers' place in it to a very small degree. Nevertheless, these results indicate that quota amendments were adapting to real labour market changes and that regional bureaucrats adjusted quota in a logical, if not entirely comprehensive, manner.

When comparing the logic of formulating and adjusting quotas (by the interdepartmental commissions and Minzdrav/Mintrud) with the logic of issuing work permits (by the FMS), model 3 demonstrates that bureaucrats in the UFMS branches also relied on labour market factors (unemployment rate, average wages, vacancy rate, and number of graduates entering the labour market). In addition, the number of work permits issued in the previous year had a significant impact on the number of work permits that would be issued in a given year. It is natural on some level that UFMS branches would use their own internal data as a guideline for procedures.

When looking at the predictive value of the models included in this chapter, which is a partial replication of the government methodology, there is strong evidence that the relationship between quota and basic labour market indicators was robust and meaningful. Given the criticism of the quota formulation process by migration experts, it is surprising to find that the quota followed a fairly rational calculation, albeit one that was overly reductionist and focused on just a few key indicators, especially unemployment.

What is important to remember in the bigger picture is that, despite a fairly disciplined allocation of quota across regions, the overall federal-level quota numbers were not at all in keeping with labour market demand as defined by experts in 2007. Therefore, in all regions, in all years from 2008 to 2014, regional interdepartmental commissions were managing scarcity. While this chapter demonstrates that they allocated scarcity in a rational and disciplined way, reflecting the attitude of bureaucrats that the job they have been given to do is meaningful and should be taken seriously, in a very real sense this was an exercise in façade building.

Bureaucrats did the important job of producing quotas that looked rational and could be justified in terms of macroeconomic and labour market indicators, fulfilling their part of the patronage and migration pacts. And while the on-paper version of quota allocation served a very important function, it consistently underestimated the need for migrant workers in order to follow the political directives of the Kremlin. By creating scarcity of legal labour and fulfilling the patronage pact, bureaucrats assured that there would be the political latitude for regional actors to use "off the books" migrants as they wished.

Use of Quota: A Disconnected Reality

Once quota allocations were assigned to employers, the job of the labour planners in the regions and at the federal level was done.[35] The work of issuing work permits to migrants occurred in the offices of the UFMS. These two processes, planning and issuing, were largely divorced from one another, especially for work permits issued to CIS migrants. This situation was a result of the 2007 changes allowing CIS migrants to obtain a work permit on their own, without first having a relationship with an employer. Though these work permits counted against the quota, migrants were not legally obligated to work for an employer who received quota allocation.

In theory, this gave migrants the upper hand in terms of receiving work permits and choosing a place of employment. In reality, migrants who attempted to get quota on their own were often given the runaround by officials who demanded various documents not required by law, such as a labour contract or other proof of an employer who had received quota.[36] A migrant rights activist in Moscow told me that it was virtually impossible in practice for migrants to get a work permit on their own during this time.[37] Migrants consistently found it easier to use the services of an intermediary rather than deal with the migration services themselves. Intermediaries for their part either had their own quota allotment, subcontracted with companies who received quota, had good relations with bureaucrats in order to process paperwork without undue requirements, or provided migrants with false documents.

Federal officials were fully aware of this situation and on occasion made attempts to eliminate or regulate intermediary activity.[38] In 2009, the FMS clarified the procedures for issuing a work permit, specifying that work permits could not be issued to migrants for more than 90 days unless they signed an employment contract, in which case they could extend their stay for up to a year.[39] According to this procedure, the work permit issued with the employment contract would be issued outside the quota.[40] While this stipulation is logical in that a single migrant shouldn't count against the quota twice, it further separated the actual use of migrants from the process of quota allocation granted to specific employers because nowhere in the federal law or implementing orders was it specified that a contract must be signed with an employer who had received a quota allocation.[41]

Employers were required submit a notification when they hired a visa-free foreign worker, but nowhere in the forms or instructions for the notification was the quota mentioned.[42] Thus, as a result of processes that didn't entirely match up, those employers who applied for quota allocation and those employers who actually hired migrants were not necessarily one and the same, a fact admitted by Maxim Topilin (head of Rostrud) in 2010.[43] According to Topilin, this was because in the UFMS offices the bureaucrats did nothing to ascertain whether the employer with whom a migrant had signed a contract was on the list of approved employers (issued by Rostrud based on employers who had completed the quota application and were approved by the regional and federal government).

Increased Scarcity, Increased Informality

In a scarcity situation, where quotas were set below labour market demand, employers could choose to engage in the process of applying for quota or bypass the procedures by hiring migrants who could get work permits on their own or by hiring illegal migrants. From the perspective of employers, having at least some quota was useful to provide legitimacy and cover. Expert interview respondents repeatedly emphasized that companies often employed more migrants than they had permission for, yet employing a portion of their migrant workforce legally produced at least a guise of compliance.[44] Furthermore, quota gave employers a tremendous amount of power because they were in possession of a scarce resource, which they could then use for themselves, give to an associate, or sell to the highest bidder.

There were also a number of intermediaries who acted as speculators, buying and selling work permit quota. Speculators often created companies, requested large numbers of quota, and then sold it (Di Bartolomeo, Makaryan, and Weinar 2014).[45] In many cases, if a migrant had an employer's name associated with their work permit it was not the company they actually worked for.[46]

Even if quotas had been established in accordance with labour market needs as they were in 2007, migrants continually had problems accessing the work permits that were available. For example, even in 2007, when the quota was 6 million, only 1.7 million migrants (1.2 from CIS countries) actually obtained work permits. This means that, of the estimated 6 million migrants in Russia at the time, less than one-third were eligible to work legally. However, migrants with work permits did not always work legally, because they did not have a written contract, because they were not registered with the tax services, etc. In 2007, the FMS reported that a majority (53%) of migrants with legal work permits worked in shadow jobs (without a formal contract). A 2008 survey shows an even larger percentage of undocumented migrants (85%) working in shadow jobs (Tyuryukanova 2009a). Once quota was institutionalized at scarcity level, the reduced number of work permits guaranteed that large portions of the migrant population would work outside the legal sphere in the informal economy. At the same time, bribes paid to police and labour inspectors for them to turn a blind eye to violations have become a reliable strategy for both employers and migrants alike.[47]

In the bigger picture, it is essential to establish that decreased legal space does in fact lead to increased informality. Several data points are important for making this case. First of all, the number of estimated migrants in Russia at any given time has not changed during the period in question. Experts estimate that there are around 6 million immigrants in Russia. This is a conservative estimate based on 1–2 million legal labour migrants plus 4–5 million illegal migrants (Zaionchkovskaia, Mkrtchyn, and Tyuryukanova 2009; Zaionchkovskaya 2013), but is in line with the logic that the 2007 quota was set with the goal of offering legal documents to all migrants in Russia. Given the resilient flows of remittances and border crossings shown in table 3.4 despite times of financial downturn, it is plausible that the estimate of 6 million remains robust.

Given a fairly static number of migrants in Russia, decreasing access to legal work documents naturally increases illegality (table 3.6). Once scarcity was instituted as a result of signals from Putin, the proportion of immigrants who did not have legal work status increased, especially from 2008–10 before patents were introduced. If patents were not included in the numbers of legal workers, the percentages of illegal migrants would have increased across the quota period (82.9% in 2011, 80.9% in 2012, 81.5% in 2013, and 82.6% in 2014).

Though the number of patents increased in each year, the idea that this trend actually increased the proportion of legal migrants is dubious. Up until 2014 patents were only permitted for migrants who worked for private individuals, yet it is simply unrealistic to believe that in 2014 the number of migrants working for private individuals was more than double the number working for companies. Rather it was common during this period for migrants to obtain patents, yet work for companies. This situation did nothing increase the legality of migrants' work, though it often improved their registration status. If anything, the increase of patents confirms the estimates that migrant stocks remained robust despite increasing scarcity of work permits.

Conclusion

State and marketplace actors both used formal and informal mechanisms to establish and navigate conditions of scarcity during the quota years 2007–14. State actors used informal mechanisms, including signals from Putin about the acceptable level of scarcity and the rules of the patronage, migration, and populist pacts, to ensure that they would be able to enjoy the spoils that arose from being in control of a scarce resource (in this case work permits). Bureaucrats also used the formal mechanisms of quota planning (directed by informal signals and patronage rules) to create a rational picture of quota on paper. Marketplace actors used informal mechanisms to hire migrants legally (using network connections or corrupt practices such as bribes to more easily procure documents) or to avoid detection or punishment when hiring illegal workers.

Scarcity and informality play an essential role in the multi-level balancing act of migration management. Low quotas have an important populist function, assuring the public that the government is concerned enough about their labour market prospects to intervene in the policymaking process. This is signalled unquestionably by Putin's direct intervention, playing the populist role par excellence by promising to rescue the people from the migrant threat. Though his language is indirect and dispassionate, his statements send a clear message to the public and to bureaucrats about how quotas should be set.

Table 3.6. Quota and labour migration

	2007	2008	2009	2010	2011	2012	2013	2014
Quota	6,000,000	1,828,245	3,976,747	1,944,356	1,745,584	1,745,584	1,745,584	1,631,586
(year end)		(3,384,129)						
Allocated to regions	4,935,679	1,335,657	1,988,374	1,369,030	1,221,833	1,267,978	1,224,185	1,142,110
(year end)		(2,536,134)	(1,802,724)	(1,417,549)	(1,368,143)	(1,489,390)	(1,448,715)	(1,368,299)
Work permits	1,717,137	2,425,921	2,223,596	1,640,801	1,027,929	1,148,725	1,111,494	1,043,834
(% of allocated quota)	(34.8%)	(95.7%)	(123%)	(116%)	(75.1%)	(77.1%)	(76.7%)	(76.3%)
Patents	—	—	—	—	764,900	1,080,430	1,356,675	2,134,079
Total legal migrants	1,717,137	2,425,921	2,223,596	1,640,801	1,792,829	2,229,155	2,468,169	3,177,913
Estimated illegals[a]	4,282,863	3,574,079	3,776,404	4,359,199	4,207,171	3,770,845	3,531,831	2,822,087
(% of migrant population)	(71.4%)	(59.6%)	(62.9%)	(72.7%)	(70.1%)	(62.9%)	(58.9%)	(47%)

Source: Rosstat 2011b; Rosstat 2013b; Rosstat 2015d Government orders defining yearly quota; Minzdrav/Mintrud orders defining yearly regional allocation and mid-year adjustments.

[a] These estimates are calculated based on a static number of 6 million labour migrants on the Russian Federation territory at any given time.

Yet if scarcity was so carefully established by Putin, as this chapter has shown, why would the government introduce a mechanism (patents) in 2010 that worked in the opposite direction? The answer to this question, as will be demonstrated in the following chapter, is a continued quest for balance among ministerial, regional, and big picture political interests. In this case the FMS found in patents a way to increase revenues to compensate for budget shortfalls. During the first several years of patent use, the mechanism functioned more informally than formally, since migrants did not limit themselves to working for individuals as required. Once patents replaced quota for CIS migrants in 2015, it was necessary also to introduce mechanisms that would ensure scarcity so that (especially state) actors could continue to pursue their interests through a mix of formal and informal practices.

Chapter Four

Scarcity Mechanism #2: Patents as State Capitalism

In the spring of 2015, a few months after new patent laws had gone into place, I sat down to tea with an Uzbek diaspora leader in Irkutsk. I dropped by the bustling office without an appointment or any prior contact, hoping I would be lucky enough to spend a few minutes hearing how migrants were adapting to the new rules. Everyone in the office graciously paused in their work to put on the kettle and sit down for a chat to explain some of the complications of the reforms. Without a doubt, the single greatest challenge migrants faced was the "30-day rule," the head of the diaspora emphasized, or the fact that a bevy of documents should be procured and submitted within 30 days of arrival to Russia. If the procedures were not completed in time, migrants faced fines up to 15,000 rubles, or the expense of leaving and re-entering Russia to reset their 30-day window. The diaspora leaders were quick to point out that most procedures were fairly easy, with the exception of newly instituted language exams. In many cases, passing the exam and obtaining a certificate of completion were simply impossible within 30 days.

Patents were introduced in 2010 as a fee-based monthly permit for CIS citizens, allowing them to legalize their registration status and giving them the right to work for individual Russians in a domestic capacity. In 2015 the patent system was expanded to allow work for companies, and replaced work permits (and therefore quotas) for CIS citizens altogether. The shift from a planning-based mechanism (quota) to a market-based mechanism (patents) would seemingly liberalize the migrant labour market and make it easier for migrants to achieve legal status. However, this chapter will show that the shift to patents did not reflect a market mentality that would legalize enough migrants to meet labour demand. Rather, in the context of economic crisis and budget shortfalls, the fee-based system was driven by elite interests in response to signals by Putin as a way to increase revenues and meet economic targets. As such, the shift to patents shows how the multi-level balancing act experiences periods of change and adapts to internal (elite interests) and exogenous (economic crisis) factors. At the same time, scarcity remained a valuable resource, and therefore new federal and regional mechanisms were put in place to ensure a continued scarcity of legal labour.

The 2015 reforms to the patent system mark a shift to a model of migration management through state capitalism. Evidence shows that the state benefited tremendously from the direct cash influxes through the sale of patents. Tax revenue from patents grew from 18 billion rubles in 2014 to 34 billion rubles in 2015. Furthermore, through the creation of state-affiliated migration centres, profits that resulted from processing migrant documents represented a new stream of revenue for the government.

The introduction of state capitalism, or "Kremlin capitalism," marked a turning point in the early 2000s as the Putin administration worked to bring the chaotic market economy of the 1990s under state discipline and control. In the same way that the Kremlin reined in the oligarchs of the 1990s in industries such as banking, media, and natural resources, the move towards patents shows the state asserting itself in an area that had become dominated by ultra-entrepreneurial migrant intermediaries. Because the state was well aware of the various profiteering schemes surrounding migration management, patent reform represents an attempt by the state to bring all of the proceeds of the intermediary market more firmly under the control of state agencies. And while the mechanisms of migration control shifted from quota to patent, the logic and the institutional structure of the multi-level balancing act remained largely the same: scarcity managed through patronage-disciplined devolution. The goal of patent reform was not increased control of migration, since the careful balance between legal and illegal labour remained. Rather, the goal was revenue and reducing manoeuvring space for entrepreneurs who could compete with the state for profits.

Patent Era #1: A Move towards Marketization (2010–14)

When patents were introduced in May 2010, they were advertised as a simple way for CIS citizens to legalize their status. Migrants could obtain patents directly from local branches of the UFMS with only a migration card and passport. There was no limit to the number of patents that could be issued either regionally or nationally. The only restriction at the time was that patents limited migrants to working for an individual Russian citizen (*fizicheskoe litso*) in a personal, domestic, or non-business-related capacity. For 1,000 rubles per month (referred to as a tax or fee), a migrant could work in the region where the patent was issued. Patents were issued for 1–3 months, and could be renewed for additional periods of 1–3 months up to 12 months, so long as the monthly fees were paid in advance. When patents were introduced in 2010, work permit quota had reached a stabilization point at lower-than-market-demand level. Patents immediately began to act as a pressure valve for the scarcity of labour permission produced by quotas.

Prior to 2010, individual Russian citizens could apply through the regular process to receive quota and could hire a migrant with a work permit for the type of domestic work eventually covered by patents. From 2008 to 2014, Rostrud issued lists of employers approved to hire foreign workers (i.e., recipients of quota), which can help to establish a picture of the demand for the type of domestic workers who could be legalized through patents. The number of migrants approved to work in household services provides an estimation of the pre-2010 demand for (documented) patent-eligible labour.[1] The quotas issued at the beginning of 2010 give the most direct measure of demand, since they are most temporally proximate to the institution of patents. Yet of the 1.9 million quota allocated at the beginning of 2010, only 290 are designated for household services (51 in Moscow, 123 in Tula, 95 in Perm, 8 in Udmert, 2 in Krasnoyarsk, 1 in Sverdlovsk, and 10 in Tyumen).

Given this data, a plausible conclusion is that the migrants who went on to obtain patents represent a category of workers who had never before been legalized. Whether patent numbers reflect an increased demand for legal workers in *domestic* service, however, is an altogether different question. If demand for patents truly reflects demand for domestic workers, it rose from 203 workers in 2010 to 764,900 workers in 2011 (an increase of 377,000%) and to 2,134,079 in 2014 (a 1,000,000% increase) (see table 4.1).[2] But it seems highly unlikely that this many employers were simply waiting to legalize their domestic service workers once the regulations became easier. It is also unlikely that the demand for domestic workers in 2014 was double that of migrants in the traditional labour market (i.e., construction, agriculture, retail, etc.), reflected by the quota numbers for that year.

A more plausible explanation for the patent trends from 2010 to 2014 is that they reflect a demand *by migrants* for legal status. Because patents were relatively easy to obtain, many migrants began to purchase patents even if they weren't employed. Without a work permit or patent,

Table 4.1. Quotas vs patents

	2010	2011	2012	2013	2014	2015
Quota	1,944,356	1,745,584	1,745,584	1,745,584	1,631,586	275,856
Work permits	1,640,801	1,027,929	1,148,725	1,111,494	1,043,834	182,370
Patents	—	764,900	1,080,430	1,356,675	2,134,079	1,656,288
Total legal migrants	1,640,801	1,792,829	2,229,155	2,468,169	3,177,913	1,838,700

Source: Rosstat 2011b; Rosstat 2013b; Rosstat 2015d; Rosstat 2016b; Government orders defining yearly quota.

CIS migrants were limited to 90 days' stay in Russia before they had to leave the country and re-enter with a new migration card.[3] After 2013, migrants were limited to staying 90 days within each 180-day period unless they had work documents. Purchasing a patent became an easy alternative to managing these limited periods of stay, even if the migrant did not work. Since there was no concrete connection between a patent holder and an employer, there was no way to verify that the reported work was being carried out.

It was also common for patent-holding migrants to work for companies or legal entities (*iuridicheskoe litso*) even though a work permit (regulated by quota) was required for this type of employment. Sometimes this occurred simply because migrants didn't understand the law. It was not uncommon for migrants to arrange their documents through a service agency or middleman, who promised a work permit but delivered a patent instead. Other times, migrants were simply willing to take a calculated risk that they would not be caught working for the wrong type of employer. This is another example of how in Russia there is the perception that it is better to have some sort of documents, regardless of whether they are the proper ones or not.

Revising Patents: Big Politics and Ministerial Interests

Patents were originally introduced as an amendment to the main migration law *On the Legal Status of Foreign Citizens*. The draft bill was formulated by Anatoly Kuznetsov, deputy head of the FMS, though there are some indications that the initiative came from Medvedev's Presidential Administration.[4] Even before it went to the Duma, the draft was heavily debated in the Tripartite Commission on Social and Labour Relations, which brings together representatives of the government, trade unions, and employers. All three parties represented in the Tripartite Commission were categorically opposed to the initiative; nevertheless, it was pushed through primarily with the support of Commission Head and Deputy Prime Minister Alexander Zhukov.[5] In January 2010, the government submitted the amendment for consideration by the Duma Committee on Constitutional Legislation and Development and the Committee on Budget and Taxes.[6] It was then passed by the Duma and Federation Council, and signed by the president in May 2010.

Not long after the institution of patents, Maksim Topilin (at the time vice-minister of health and social development) reaffirmed the necessity of the quota system, saying that it was "the right of the government" and that any problems with the system simply needed to be addressed through interministerial coordination.[7] He expressed faith in the ability of quotas to regulate the migration situation if planned properly, and spoke out against any efforts to cancel them.

However, the utility of the patent system, and in particular its benefit to the FMS, could not be ignored. The patent system was in the interests of the FMS for several reasons. First, it created much-needed revenue. With migrants paying 1,000 rubles per month, revenue for the first two years of patent proceeds totalled 8.3 billion rubles ($277 million at the time) or $11.5 million per month.[8] Furthermore, patents allowed the labour migration process to circumnavigate the labour agencies in charge of quotas (Minzdrav/Mintrud, Rostrud) and come under the sole authority of the FMS (Lukanin 2010).

In January 2012, as a part of his re-election campaign, Putin published several articles in major newspapers outlining future policy in key areas. *Russia: The National Question* appeared in *Nezavisimaia Gazeta* on January 23, 2012, addressing a number of migration-related issues.[9] In particular, Putin recommended policies for reining in illegal immigration (increasing penalties for violating migration registration) and increasing integration (introducing exams on Russian language, history, literature, and legal norms). Upon his inauguration in May, Putin immediately passed 12 presidential decrees to implement his campaign promises.[10] One decree stipulated that by November 2012 Russian language, history, and legal norms exams should be instituted for labour migrants (with the exception of highly qualified migrants).[11]

Other targets included in what came to be known as the "May decrees," while not directly related to migration regulations, set the context for an expanded patent system. Together they called for increases in social and military spending in parallel with reduced dependence on oil revenues. Just as with Putin's proclamation of acceptable migrant quotas discussed in the previous chapters, the May decrees were an important indicator of the direction that ministers and bureaucrats should take. As Remington (2014) notes, the decrees set out an unrealistic course of action that created pressure on state officials at various levels. In the first post-decree round of budget planning, it became quickly apparent that meeting the targets, given current state revenues, was not feasible. Putin's response, however, was to officially reprimand several ministers, including Topilin (who by this time had been promoted to the post of minister of labour).[12] Though the reprimands were reversed a year later, the pressure on ministers to meet decreed targets continued unabated.[13] The budget crunch created a context that was amenable to adopting measures, such as patents, that would bring additional sources of revenue into state coffers and help the Kremlin to save face amid unrealistic targets.

Putin's election promises also put pressure on the government commission on migration policy, which had been working on a new migration concept since 2009 (Ivakhnyuk 2013b; Romodanovsky 2013). Though initial work on the concept had involved significant input from civil society actors and migrant advocates, the end result was a rush to finish the *Concept of State Migration Policy to 2025*, approved by Putin in mid-2012, which reflected a securitized approach advocated by the Ministry of Interior (and its corollary agencies the Federal Security Service and Anti-Drug Service) (Ivakhnyuk 2013b).[14]

The *Concept of State Migration Policy to 2025*, approved by both the FMS and Mintrud, identified the need to improve the quota system, but did not specify a particular course of action. Though there are some indications that earlier drafts penned by the FMS envisaged doing away with quotas, the final text made no such indication.[15] Given the successful institution of patents in 2010, administered under the sole control of the FMS, it is not surprising that the migration services would favour increasing the scope of patents. By the same logic it is natural that Mintrud, which administered the quota process, would prefer to keep migration management in their sphere of influence. In July 2013, Topilin came out strongly against the idea of removing quotas, saying, "We are categorically opposed to the abolition of quotas. We consider this recommendation to be incorrect and economically unreasonable. It will lead to the collapse of the labour market."[16] But Topilin's promises and warnings in the end could not compete with the money-making potential of patents.

Another important signal about the future direction of patents came in December 2013 during Putin's annual address to the Federal Assembly. Putin's speech, essentially a state of the union address, specifically addressed patents, yet also highlighted the need to improve local government. In the speech, Putin pointed to a lack of order in the labour market that could potentially lead to national conflict and criminal activity.[17] To solve the problem, he suggested streamlining access to the labour market for visa-free migrants and gave very specific suggestions to

> change the current patent system. Currently, foreign workers must obtain a patent for work with [an individual]. I recommend that legal entities and individual entrepreneurs should also have the opportunity to hire a foreign worker on the basis of a patent. The price of a patent will be determined by subjects of the Federation themselves, depending on the situation in the regional labour market and the average income of the population in the area. The system of patents should be differentiated and should stimulate the flow of professional, educated specialists, who know the Russian language and who are close to our culture. Let me stress that patents should only be valid in the regions they are purchased. I expect that if we competently organize this work it will be an economic instrument to regulate the flow of migrants. Do you understand? An economic instrument – meaning the cost of a patent in various regions of Russia. And finally, we need to increase control over the stated reasons for entry of foreign citizens. All civilized countries do this. The state should know why and for what period foreigners are coming to Russia. Therefore it is necessary to solve the problem of visa-free foreigners who have come and stayed for a long period of time without a particular purpose. They likely have a purpose in mind, but the state knows nothing about it. The period of their stay in the country should be limited, and those that violate the rules of stay should be banned from entry, depending on the severity of the violation, for a period of 3 to 10 years. These measures will create additional barriers for foreigners who, frankly speaking, work in the shadows, and even in criminal activities, or who work illegally, often in inhumane conditions, and themselves, unfortunately, become victims of criminals. (Putin 2013)

Notwithstanding the contradictory message at the end, collapsing all migrants (victim and criminal alike) into a category that should be met with increased barriers, the tone of the speech is clear that the regulation of migration should be made more strict. This is all the more contradictory given Putin's (2012) statements in *Russia: The National Question* that "simply tightening the screws on migrants won't solve the problem. In many countries, such crackdowns only spur the flow of illegal migration." The recommendations about regions having control over the price of patents is in alignment with an earlier portion of the same 2013 speech, in which Putin highlights the need to build "strong, independent, and financially wealthy local authorities." This sentiment is also in line with other statements by Putin that the realization of the May decrees is heavily dependent on regional decision makers and supports the need to have real (albeit disciplined by patronage) devolution.[18]

The specificity with which Putin addresses patent regulations is illustrative of behind-the-scenes activity working to reform migration policy. Because the tone and verbiage of this section of Putin's speech are quite technocratic, addressing specific policy nuances, it suggests that the speech and its signals were carefully prepared by speech writers in the Presidential Administration. Using the forum of the Federal Assembly to speak specifically to this policy issue is a clear signal to migration policymakers, but also represents the ability of some of those policymakers to get their preferred policies on the president's agenda. It is not clear whether the initiative originated in the Presidential Administration or in the FMS, but the proposal was clear in its intent to create revenues for the state and was likely successful because it linked up nicely with goals already promoted by Putin. For this reason, patent reform easily gained traction.

The work of drafting the resulting amendments to *On the Legal Status of Foreign Citizens* fell to the FMS, which began speaking publicly about their work even before the amendment was introduced in the Duma.[19] The FMS recommendations were announced at a roundtable in March 2014, attended by government representatives, experts from the academic community, and the International Organization for Migration. The press release from this event, posted on the FMS website, was a reproduction of portions of Putin's speech nearly verbatim.

Despite his earlier statements, Topilin made an immediate shift after Putin's 2013 speech to the Federal Assembly. The very same day, Topilin made statements in the press arguing that when patents were extended to cover a wider variety of employers, it would be essential to put some restrictions in place with the goal of increasing control over foreign workers. He suggested differentiating patent prices by region and increasing the price overall, in part to cover deductions that would be taken to cover medical insurance (a strange justification, since the law required migrants to have insurance through their employer or an individual contract with an insurance company, neither of which would require payments by the state).[20] This is consistent with Topilin's previous urgings that migrants pay more into social funds, including the pension system.[21] Yet when the FMS began discussing the draft bill that included the total abolition of quotas and work permits for CIS migrants in early 2014, Mintrud renewed their protest that the move would lead to a lack of coordination and control in the labour market.[22]

Once quotas for CIS citizens were cancelled, Topilin began to discuss proposals for Mintrud to retain a stake the migration process. In February 2015, he announced that regions that did not demonstrate they were making an effort to replace migrant workers with local workers would have federal funds for unemployment payments suspended.[23] In April 2015, Topilin stated that because the rules now required migrants to get health insurance and pay into the pension system, "we have the instruments to verify whether immigrants are working legally from the perspective of labour legislation, not just migration status."[24] He went on to indicate that migrants found in violation of the pension contribution scheme (managed by Mintrud) could be expelled from Russia. These statements demonstrate efforts of Mintrud to regain some control over migrant workers and the migration process.

At the same time, the FMS continued its efforts to consolidate further control over the migration situation throughout the period of this book's analysis. In particular, they drafted an entirely new piece of legislation with the tentative title *On Migration Control in the Russian Federation*, which would transfer the authority for ensuring that employers follow migration legislation to the FMS (instead of the labour inspectorate under Mintrud). Nevertheless, the FMS is not immune to other interministerial rivalries and power manoeuvres. After the analysis for this book was complete, the FMS was transferred to the MVD and renamed the General Directorate for Migration (Glavnoe Upravlenie po Voprosam Migratsii). It is unclear how much of their previous mandate the FMS will retain under this arrangement, but in the meantime Mintrud has continued lobbying to transfer the regulation components of labour migration to its authority.

Patent Era #2: Towards State Capitalism (2015–Present)

Amendments to the legislation on patents fundamentally changed the way the migration system worked. On the one hand, they added clarity to migration procedures by shifting CIS labour migrants to a totally separate mechanism from migrants from other destinations who continued using work permits regulated by quotas.[25] On the other hand, what was a fairly simple and straightforward mechanism before 2015 became infinitely more bureaucratic.

Since 2015, patents are issued for between one and 12 months, and can be renewed for one addition period of 12 months, pending pre-payment of income taxes. In order to receive a patent, a migrant must collect and present a number of documents (see figure 4.1). First is a migration card, received at the border, that specifies the purpose of entry as "work." Migrants must then present proof of registration, a certificate showing they have passed a Russian language, history, and legal norms test, a medical certificate clearing them of drug addiction and infectious diseases (including HIV), proof of medical insurance either through their employer or in the form of a private policy from a provider approved by the regional government, a receipt showing payment of taxes and fees, a translated and notarized copy of their passport, and, for patents lasting more than two months, an employment contract. These bureaucratic requirements and their management are crucial for the government to achieve the goal of increasing revenues while maintaining scarcity of legal labour.

Figure 4.1. How to get a patent (2015)

Submit to UFMS within 30 days of arrival:

- Migration card (purpose of visit must specify "work")
- Registration (verifying work or residence location)
- Passport (translated and notarized)
- Colour photo (passport style)
- Payment receipt for patent fees and first month of taxes[a]
- Medical certificate[b]
- Certificate verifying a passing grade on Russian language, culture, and legal norms exam
- Medical insurance policy

Submit to UFMS within 2 months of receiving patent:

- Employment contract[c]

[a] Payments are made to a bank, and receipts presented to the UFMS.
[b] Verifying that the migrant has no infectious diseases (tuberculosis, AIDS, etc.) or drug dependence.
[c] Without submission of the contract, a patent can be annulled.

Mechanisms for Maintaining Scarcity

Increased bureaucratic requirements make patents much less accessible to migrants than they were in the previous period. When I spoke with diaspora leaders from Kyrgyzstan, Tajikistan, and Uzbekistan in Irkutsk in spring 2015, they all agreed that the 30-day rule had become the single greatest barrier to migrants' legalization. The most commonly cited problems with the patent procedure were the cost involved and completing the language, culture, and legal norms exam (and especially receiving verification of passing within the given time frame).

In certain regions there was simply no infrastructure to conduct the exams, nor a budget to pay local examiners, and so special testing teams would come from Moscow or St Petersburg.[26] In Irkutsk, once the tests had been completed, the testers would give the migrants a receipt declaring they had passed the exam, but the official certificates could only be distributed after the team had return to their main offices to process all of the test scores. However, the UFMS refused to accept the receipt because the law specifies that a "certificate" must be presented as proof of passing the exam. Many of these certificates did not arrive until after the migrants' 30-day period had already lapsed, leaving migrants unable to obtain a patent.

It is important to acknowledge that temporary coordination issues such as developing testing centres that could accommodate migrants are short-term mechanisms of scarcity. Other short-term issues made it difficult for migrants to get patents in 2015, but should not produce ongoing barriers to legalization. Examples include the requirement for migration cards to specify "work" as the purpose of entry into Russia, and new rules requiring international passports for all categories of migrants. However, there are also long-term mechanisms of maintaining scarcity, including bans on workers in certain sectors, migrant "blacklists," employment contracts, and monthly patent fees.

Short-Term Barriers

One example of a short-term barrier is new migration card requirements. In order to receive a patent, a migration card that specifies "work" as the purpose of visit is required. Prior to 2015, migration cards technically should have listed "work," but in practice many migrants working in Russia had entered on a migration card listing "private" as the reason for their trip. Increased enforcement of this procedure meant that all migrants who were in Russia with a stated purpose other than work had to leave the country and re-enter with a new migration card in order to get a patent.

A related issue had to do with new regulations on documents, requiring an international passport rather than the internal identity documents that had previously been accepted for some CIS citizens.[27] In practice, these new rules meant not only that new or returning migrants needed international passports to enter Russia, but also that migrants who were in Russia when the rules took effect in January 2015 could not leave the country without an international passport, even if they had entered Russia on an internal passport.[28] Though in theory there was sufficient time between the enactment of these new procedures and their entry into force in January 2015 so that those who were already in Russia could either leave the country or apply to their embassy for an international passport, this assumes migrants are able to learn of legal changes in a timely manner.

Unless migrants are legally employed with an employer who carefully watches migration legislation, or unless they receive updates from their embassies, they are in the situation where they must hear about changes through word of mouth (i.e., friends and co-nationals, etc.). Though the FMS had a section on their website with updates to laws, this was only helpful for migrants who had reliable internet access. Without these updates, migrants risk approaching a border point or migration office without full information (and potentially being found in violation of the laws). Presumably, this is one of the justifications for having migrants take a legal norms test in order to get a patent as of January 2015. However, with the volatility that is part and parcel of migration legislation, these exams can at best give migrants a snapshot of legal norms at one moment in time.[29]

While not ongoing mechanisms of scarcity, issues related to migration cards and passports are important to mention because they have an impact on the 2015 statistics. Barriers that migrants faced when seeking patents in 2015 contributed to a decrease in the number of patents issued from 2014 to 2015. Though the government explains this trend as a result of decreased demand for migrant labour because of the ruble crisis, it is important to acknowledge that the numbers of legal migrants were also depressed by administrative barriers.

Long-Term Barriers

The presence of long-term barriers, such as bans on workers in certain sectors, migrant "blacklists," employment contracts, and monthly patent fees, is likely to ensure the continued scarcity of legal labour. Through the use of these mechanisms, the government can ensure the continued availability of resources that can be deployed strategically for the benefit of actors at various levels in the patron-client chain.

Each year, the government sets limits on how many migrants can work in certain professions. These "allowable shares" regulate jobs related to sports, the sale of alcohol and pharmaceuticals, and other retail tasks. Many of these categories have zero quotas, effectively banning foreign workers in these sectors (see table 4.2). Other professions, such as private security guards, are regulated by separate laws.[30]

The addition of agricultural workers and drivers to allowable shares allocations in 2015 targets two key areas of migrant employment. Nevertheless, we cannot expect that it will actually reduce the number of migrants working in these sectors. After allowable shares were instituted in 2007, migrant workers coped by working illegally, registering as individual entrepreneurs, or shifting their work to fit within the letter of the law. For example, when I was buying a coat at a bazaar, the bulk of the transaction was conducted by an Asian man with a Chinese accent. He helped me try on the coat, offered alternative selections, and haggled with me over the price. Yet when it came time to pay, he wouldn't touch the money, waving his hands in front of him in refusal, and indicating that I needed to pay his Russian colleague. This type of arrangement, and others in which migrants work hauling and stocking merchandise behind the scenes, are examples of how migrants have adapted to the legal requirements without exiting the labour market.

At the end of 2012, and subsequently in July 2013, changes to *On the Order of Exit and Entry* increased the length of time migrants who had committed administrative violations, had been administratively expelled or deported, or were on a list of "undesirables" could be barred from entry or re-entry. These categories have become colloquially referred to as "blacklists,"[31] and the number of migrants who have not been permitted to enter Russia has risen markedly since their institution (see table 4.3). A related change was made to *On the Legal Status of Foreign Citizens* in July 2013, which added provisions for revoking or denying work permits, temporary residence permits, and permanent residence permits. Any of these permits could be revoked or denied if

Table 4.2. Allowable shares

	Sales						Sports	Transport[a]
	Alcohol[b]	Pharmacy	Markets	Stores	Vegetables[c]	Tobacco		
2007	0%	0%	40%[d]	40%[e]	—	—	—	—
2008	0%	0%	0%	0%	—	—	25%	—
2009	0%	0%	0%	0%	—	—	25%	—
2010	0%	0%	0%	0%	—	—	25%	—
2011	0%	0%	0%	0%	—	—	25%	—
2012	0%	0%	0%	0%	—	—	25%	—
2013	25%	0%	0%	0%	—	—	25%	—
2014	15%	0%	0%	0%	—	—	25%	—
2015	15%	0%	0%	0%	50%	15%	25%	50%[f]
2016	15%	0%	0%	0%	50%	15%	25%	35%–40%[g]

Sources: Government orders defining yearly allowable shares.

[a] Passenger and cargo.

[b] Excluding beer.

[c] Including production.

[d] 0% after April 1.

[e] 0% after April 1.

[f] A 2013 amendment to the law *On Road Safety* (Federal Law No. 196 of December 10, 1995) made it illegal to drive on a foreign or international licence for entrepreneurial purposes (i.e., formal or informal taxis, public transportation, etc.), though the entry into force of this amendment has been repeatedly delayed. All categories of foreigners are eligible to take the exams necessary for a Russian driver's licence.

[g] passenger: 40%, cargo: 35%

the migrant had, any time in the prior 5 years or twice within 10 years, been administratively expelled or deported. Further reasons for revocation or denial of temporary and permanent residence permits include criminal drug activity, administrative violations related to drugs, or violations of public safety and security, employment regulations, or terms of a residence permit.[32] The FMS does not publish data on the number of work permits or residence permits that have been revoked, yet it is clear that the authorities use the expulsion/deportation mechanism less frequently than the new blacklists.

According to *On the Order of Exit and Entry*, migrants can be also denied entry for reporting false information about their identity or purpose of visit. Increased border scrutiny, along with a growing list of Central Asian migrants barred from re-entry, creates disincentive for migrants to return home for visits if doing so could jeopardize future trips when they could simply remain in Russia and work in the

Table 4.3. Blacklists and deportations

	2011	2012	2013	2014	2015
Blacklisted migrants[a]	64,933	88,748	459,337	644,918	490,893
Migrants barred entry	n/a	73,816	456,434	682,893	481,404
Migrants expelled or deported	28,585	35,115	82,413	139,034	117,493

Source: FMS statistics.
[a] Decisions made about barring the entry of foreign citizens (adding migrants to the blacklist).

shadows. This is an almost certain law of immigration, which has been observed repeatedly in other migrant-receiving countries: when laws become more restrictive, circular migration decreases, migration stocks become more permanent, and, unless there is an amnesty mechanism, the number of illegal immigrants increases (Martin 2014; Massey and Pren 2012; Hollifield 2014).

Re-entry bans and increased administrative expulsions have attracted a great deal of scholarly attention because of their securitized focus (Kubal 2016a; Troitskii 2016). Indeed, the increase in expulsions, deportations, and denials of entry is significant. However, from the literature we know that even securitized policies rarely have the effect of bringing immigration under control. The FMS data in table 4.3 shows that 598,897 migrants were administratively expelled, deported, or barred from entering Russia in 2015. Yet this is only 3.5% of the total number of foreigners entering Russia that year.[33] While the symbolic value of increased expulsions and entry bans is crucial, both for the populist pact and for how migrants' calculate risk, the real impact on migration control is limited.

In order to extend a patent beyond two months, a migrant must produce an employment contract. In December 2014 an entirely new chapter was added to the Russian Labour Code regulating the work and contracts of foreign citizens. Because the Labour Code is primarily the domain of Mintrud, this further demonstrates the struggle between ministries for control over the migration process. Under the new rules, labour contracts are tied to the migration status of foreign workers and can be annulled if there are irregularities in the migration status. In cases where the medical insurance policy required by the Labour Code lapses, the contract can also be annulled. If a contract is annulled, a person's migration status is in further jeopardy. Not only do these changes fuse migration status with employment status, they also signal the increasing importance of contracts for migrants' legal status.

For low-skilled migrants, signing contracts has not been a traditional part of the working arrangement in Russia, and therefore the primacy of contracts is an important development. Because many employers have traditionally been reluctant to sign contracts and thus formalize the working relationship in a way that will obligate them to pay taxes and social insurance, tying migration status to a formal labour contract could be an ongoing barrier to migrant legality.

One of the most important long-term barriers to legalization, ensuring ongoing scarcity of legal labour, is the fees that migrants must pay for patents. Prices rose significantly from a standard monthly price of 1,000 rubles in 2010–14 to prices that vary widely by region (see table 4.4). These monthly fees are on top of initial costs of the language exam, medical checks, health insurance, and other associated costs, which can reach up to 10,000 to 20,000 rubles depending on region and whether intermediary services were used to process documents. Though some of these represent one-time fixed costs (the language exam), the sum of yearly taxes can in some cases exceed migrant wages. Yearly tax payments for 2016 are anywhere from 21,801.60 (in regions that have adopted the federal minimum tax rate) to 98,085.60 rubles in Yakutia, which charges the highest patent prices.[34]

A Picture of Scarcity

Given all of the short- and long-term barriers migrants face when seeking patents, it is not surprising that we observe a decrease in the number of patents issued from 2014 to 2015. The media was quick to report declining migration rates, based on the number of patents issued. The framing of events was important for the populist pact because it reflected the government's desire to manage any anti-migration moods that could have arisen from a perceived liberalization of the labour market through patents. Most often, the reason cited for decreasing migration was economic crisis rather than a change in migration law, reflecting a potentially risky strategy of focusing on the economic situation that citizens themselves could not escape. Nevertheless, the economic crisis has not had as negative of an impact on the government as some expected, primarily because of careful populist management, which has primarily focused on blaming the impact of the crisis on the West.

Table 4.4. Cost of patents by region, 2015–16

Federal District	2015	2016		2015	2016		2015	2016
Central			**Southern**			**Ural**		
Belgorod	3,192.00	3,938.80	Adygea	1,568.00	1,530.20	Kurgan	1,568.00	3,416.00
Briansk	2,500.00	3,088.56	Kalmykia	1,568.00	2,316.80	Sverdlovsk	2,400.00	2,860.00
Vladimir	3,000.00	3,000.00	Krasnodar	2,800.00	3,244.80	Tyumen	3,999.00	4,139.00
Voronezh	3,000.00	3,088.56	Astrakhan	1,568.00	2,316.80	Khanty Mansi	1,568.00	3,475.00
Ivanovo	1,568.00	3,106.00	Volgograd	2,666.00	2,600.00	Yamalo Nenets	6,629.00	7,412.50
Kaluga	3,842.00	3,900.00	Rostov	1,568.00	1,816.80	Cheliabinsk	3,500.00	3,500.00
Kastroma	1,568.00	2,485.40	**North Caucasus**			**Siberian**		
Kursk	3,294.00	3,815.30	Dagestan	1,568.00	—	Altai republic	1,568.00	1,816.80
Lipetsk	3,137.00	3,633.60	Ingushetia	3,999.00	1,816.80	Buriat	1,568.00	4,269.50
Moscow (oblast)	4,000.00	4,000.00	Kabardino-Balkaria	1,568.00	1,816.80	Tuva	1,568.00	3,475.50
Orlov	2,039.00	3,172.10	Karachay-Cherkessia	1,568.00	1,816.80	Khakassia	3,137.00	3,633.60
Riazan	2,807.00	3,325.60	North Ossetia	1,568.00	1,816.80	Altai krai	1,568.00	2,761.53
Smolensk	2,750.00	3,186.00	Chechnya	1,568.00	1,816.80	Zabaikalski	1,568.00	4,269.50
Tambor	2,500.00	3,000.00	Stavropol	1,568.00	3,088.60	Krasnoyarsk	1,568.00	3,034.00
Tver	3,000.00	3,475.20	**Volga**			Irkutsk	1,568.00	3,470.00
Tula	3,000.00	3,500.00	Bashkortostan	1,568.00	2,906.90	Kemerovo	3,000.00	3,475.50
Yaroslavl	3,000.00	3,270.00	Mari El	1,568.00	1,816.80	Novosibirsk	1,568.00	3,034.60
Moscow (city)	4,000.00	4,200.00	Mordovia	3,046.00	3,528.20	Omsk	2,500.00	2,896.00
			Tatarstan	2,839.00	3,288.40	Tomsk	4,000.00[a]	2,500.00

Northwest			**Volga (con't).**			**Far East**		
Karelia	1,568.00	3,651.80	Udmurt	1,568.00	3,000.00	Sakha/Yakutia	7,056.00	8,173.80
Komi	1,568.00	2,216.50	Chuvash	3,137.00	3,633.60	Kamchatka	1,568.00	4,996.20
Arkhangelsk	2,666.00	3,088.60	Perm	1,568.00	3,243.00	Primorski	3,137.00	3,706.30
Nenets	1,568.00	7,000.00	Kirov	1,568.00	3,010.40	Khabarovsk	2,756.00	3,179.40
Vologda	3,640.00	4,215.00	Nizhnii Novgorod	2,274.00	1,816.18	Amur	4,270.00	4,946.30
Kaliningrad	2,666.00	3,543.00	Orenburg	2,580.00	3,197.60	Magadan	3,921.00	4,542.00
Leningrad	3,000.00	3,000.00	Penza	1,568.00	2,725.20	Sakhalin	1,568.00	3,179.40
Murmansk	1,568.00	—	Samara	2,500.00	2,999.50	Jewish	2,756.00	3,851.60
Novgorod	3,294.00	3,815.00	Saratov	3,136.00	3,088.60	Chukotka	8,000.00	4,542.00
Pskov	1,568.00	—	Ulianovsk	1,568.00	2,616.20			
St Petersburg	3,000.00	3,000.00						

Source: Regional laws.

[a] Reduced to 2,500.00 mid-year.

Data from the FMS supports the argument that the 2014 ruble crisis resulting from Western sanctions has had an impact on migration rates.[35] Even with an influx of Ukrainian refugees, migration rates were already decreasing in 2014, as indicated by fewer foreign citizens entering Russia, according to some FMS estimates (see table 4.5).

Yet even if the number of entries decreased in 2014, legal labour migration was at an all-time high, as were migrant registrations. In 2015, even with decreased entries and registrations, both figures are higher than in 2011, the only year with similar figures of legal labour migrants. This indicates that the number of legal labour migrants in 2015 is not a result of fewer migrants crossing the border, but rather of a smaller number of migrants being legalized than in any other year since patents were instituted. If we look at legal labour migrants as a percentage of entries, migration registrations, and foreign population, all of which are at their lowest point in 2015, it further demonstrates that there were not fewer foreigners in Russia, though a smaller number of them legalized their status as labour migrants. This data shows a convincing picture of continued scarcity of legal labour.

Increasing State Budget Contributions

Though fewer patents were issued in 2015, the revenues earned from the sale of patents nearly doubled (see table 4.6). This is simply a factor of the new fee structure discussed above. Higher fees continued a trend where the patent revenue as a percentage of what the FMS contributes to the state budget increased every year, quickly outstripping the proceeds coming from administrative fines. Not only that, the overall level of patent revenue increased over 850% from 2011 to 2015, leading to a more than twofold increase in the overall size of the budget contributions during this period, from 26,171,266,500 rubles in 2011 to 57,415,810,000 in 2015. While this is a relatively small portion of overall GDP (around 0.04% in 2015), in some regions (such as Moscow) the tax revenue from patents surpassed that collected from oil companies.[36]

Patent fees are an important part of increasing state revenues. However, for the state to truly capitalize on the profits involved in migration management, it also had to decrease the market share of migrant intermediaries. Though there have been legislative efforts to reduce the ability of intermediaries to operate, these have been only

Table 4.5. A picture of scarcity (FMS data)

	2011	2012	2013	2014	2015
Foreigners entering Russia	13,831,860	15,870,340	17,785,910	17,281,971	17,083,849
(alternative figures)				(18,201,509)[a]	
—% growth		14.74%	12.09%	−2.83%	−1.15%
(alternative figures)				(2.34%)	(−6.14%)
Registrations	6,068,473	6,627,847	7,370,628	8,680,930	7,868,441
Foreign citizens in Russia[b]	n/a	10,085,049	10,847,352	10,969,093	9,948,099
Work permits	1,195,169	1,340,056	1,273,984	1,303,258	216,969
Patents	865,728	1,289,204	1,537,323	2,386,641	1,788,201
Total legal labour migrants	2,060,897	2,629,260	2,811,307	3,689,899	2,005,170
—as a % of entries	14.90%	16.57%	15.81%	21.35%	11.74%
(alternative figures)				(20.27%)	
—as a % of migration cards	33.96%	39.67%	38.14%	42.51%	25.48%
—as a % of foreigners in Russia	—	26.07%	25.92%	33.64%	20.16%
GDP (current prices,. billions of rubles)	59,698.12	66,926.86	71,055.39	77,893.10	80,412.55
Remittance outflow (USD billions)	26	31.7	37.2	32.6	19.7

Source: FMS statistics; World Bank 2016.

[a] The FMS data provides statistics for the current year and the previous year. For example, the 2015 data also includes figures from 2014 for comparison. In some cases, a particular year's figures are reported differently in the following year, though in most cases, the numbers aren't substantially different. In those cases, the latest available figures are used. However, in the 2015 data, the number of foreign citizens entering Russia in 2014 was reported as 18 million, whereas the earlier publication of 2014 data reports 17 million. In this case the difference is likely a result of adjusting the figures to reflect the numbers of Ukrainians entering as a result of unrest there.

[b] These figures are very similar to foreign-born population, which is typically a reference to more permanent categories of immigrants, as discussed in this book's Introduction. Yet FMS labels them as "foreign citizens," not foreign-born citizens.

Table 4.6. Patent revenue, thousands of rubles

	2011	2012	2013	2014	2015
Patents	764,900	1,080,430	1,356,675	2,134,079	1,788,201
Proceeds of patents	3,558,532	6,674,917	8,395,776	18,311,660	34,060,896
(% contribution to budget)	(13.60%)	(20.34%)	(22.66%)	(40.82%)	(59.32%)
Proceeds of fines	5,921,831	6,142,339	6,449,666	9,168,527	8,753,081

Source: FMS statistics

marginally successful. More successful have been the state's efforts to direct migrants through state-affiliated intermediaries.

In 2009 the government established the commercial enterprise Passport Visa Service (PVS) within the structure of the FMS for the express purpose of managing passport and migration documents.[37] Since then, offices have opened in 49 regions and in Kyrgyzstan. Though there are no data on the revenues created by the PVS, its primary purpose is to provide fee-based services such as filling in the forms necessary to submit to UFMS branches for registration, work permits, patents, etc.

In some cases, a regional PVS or UFMS office will have a "migration centre," which is essentially a location separate from the main office serving Russian citizens, for matters concening foreign citizens. However, a number of other types of migration centres were opened in 2014–15, many of them government-affiliated in some way. Together with the PVS-affiliated centres, these new offices represent a clear new trend towards expanding state services in the migration sphere.

At times the lines between these centres and the PVS offices are blurry. For example, in Moscow Oblast the United Migration Centre and PVS branch have separate websites, but the location (and even the map image) is the same.[38] This particular centre, opened in 2014, houses a branch of the UFMS and a number of different organizations offering the services that migrants need to complete the patent process (see table 4.7), demonstrating how central the issuing of patents has become to the function of the migration services. The United Migration Centre has the legal designation of a federal state unitary enterprise (*federal'noe gosudarstvennoe unitarnoe predpriiatie*), as do all PVS affiliates. This is a commercial designation where the organization's property is owned by the state and a portion of any profits earned are paid to the state, though the purpose of the organization should not be to profit itself but rather to serve the needs of the public.[39] The majority of the other

Table 4.7. Services provided at the Moscow Oblast United Migration Centre/PVS

Individual services	Company providing services
Medical exam	OOO United Medical Centre (Edinyi Meditsinskii Tsentr)
Document translation	OOO Migrant Alliance (Migrant Al'ians)
Photos and copying	OOO Centre of Labour Migration (Tsentr Trudovoi Migratsii)
Medical insurance	OOO Rosgosstrakh
	SAO[a] BSK
	SPAO RESO-Garantiia
	OOO Renaissance Insurance Group (Gruppa Renessans Strakhovanie)
Language exam	State Institute of Russian Language Named after A.S. Pushkin (Gosudarstvennym Institutom Russkogo Iazyka Imeni A.S. Pushkina)

[a] Strakhovoe (Publichnoe) Aktsionernoe Obshchestvo (Public Joint Stock Insurance Company).

organizations on site are designated as Limited Liability Companies (*obshchestvo s ogranichennoi otvetstvennost'iu* or OOO), which are privately owned, for-profit businesses.

Centres like the United Migration Centre, where many services are housed under one roof, are part of a larger movement in Russian public administration pursuing the principle of "one window" services through Multifunctional Centres. By law, Multifunctional Centres are for the express purpose of providing state or municipal services, though they can have various legal organizational designations, including commercial, non-profit, or state or municipal institutions.[40] Since 2010, a network of Multifunctional Centres called My Documents (*moi dokumenty*) has been established across Russia, which focuses on services to Russian citizens, including payment of taxes, registration of births, and managing social benefits.[41] In total there are over 3,000 Multifunctional Centres throughout Russia.[42]

A few Multifunctional Centres added special packages of services for migrants in 2015. In South Sakhalin, a migration centre was opened in October 2015 as a department of the Multifunctional Centre, specifically for the purpose of helping migrants with patent documents.[43] While there is not an UFMS branch on site, as with the PVS-affiliated centres, the migration centre is located separately from the main Multifunctional Centre and is within a few blocks of an UFMS office. Similar arrangements exist in the Multifunctional Centres in Moscow, Tula, and

St Petersburg, offering a range of services for patent-seeking migrants.[44] As of February 2016, all Multifunctional Centres can process migrants' registration documents.[45]

A number of other migration centres were opened throughout Russia in 2014–15, in Moscow, Voronezh, Novosibirsk, Kaluga, Kirov, Tomsk, Altai, Tver, Yamalo Nenets, Volgograd, Magadan, Krasnoyarsk, Karelia, Vladivostok, and Tambov. Most of these are legally separate from the FMS and PVS or Multifunctional Centres mentioned above, but either are officially endorsed by the regional government or migration services, or have a legal designation marking them as a state institution. Several of the centres, such as the one in Kirov, are constituted as a part of an existing language school or centre, highlighting the centrality of the language exams in the documentation process. Many of the centres offer additional services such as fingerprinting and application for a tax identification number. Some, such as the centre in Barnaul, even offer hotel services where migrants can stay while they are waiting for their documents, and issue the registration document required for a patent.

Many of these centres were promoted as a way to provide migrants with services while eliminating middlemen and corruption.[46] As we will see in the following chapters, however, migration centres are not without their own problems, including violations of anti-monopoly legislation and the development of new corruption schemes. Nevertheless, the centres are an important tool in the regional management of migration and the distribution of spoils. Since the centres are under the control of regional governments, they give regional elites continued access to the proceeds of migration documentation.

Increased Regional Autonomy?

Not only are migration centres a distinctly regional initiative (to date there are no federally operated migration centres), with profits benefiting regional budgets, but the monthly tax rate for patents is also defined by regional authorities. In addition to financial prerogatives, regional leaders are given the authority to suspend the issue of patents at any time for a variety of purposes. The devolution of authority to regional decision makers to set the price for patents and suspend the issue of patents at their discretion is perhaps the most surprising and controversial aspect of the new patent regulations because it seems to break any formal links between the federal powers and the regional migration situations, leaving the migrant labour market completely in the hands of regional leaders.

In the context of the patronage pact that is integral to the function of politics in Russia, this is a curious moment. As elaborated in chapter 2, the job of governors in the patronage pact is to produce stability and loyalty in their region. Yet many scholars have argued that this stability is part and parcel of the vertical of power and Putin's desire to increase central authority across Russia. In this light, a total devolution of formal power to regional leaders is nothing short of shocking.

The incentives for regional leaders in this new status quo cannot be underestimated. Both because scarcity of legal permission is tangibly advantageous to regional leaders, and because federal leaders have given visible signals as to acceptable levels of immigration, it is in the interests of regional leaders to keep the numbers of legal immigrant workers low. The combination of patent fees with administrative barriers allows elites to keep legal migration within scarcity range while still increasing budget revenues. Since regional leaders are in more direct control of migration resources, they also have direct access to any spoils that can be generated from the new migration institutions.

As the next chapters will show, the shift away from formal federal levers over migration is actually a sign of the strength of the patronage pact rather than of its weakness. There are indications that the patronage pact is strong enough to withstand a weakening of formal ties and still produce the desired results of stable regions that produce loyalty to the Kremlin elite, in this case continuing the federally signalled levels of acceptable legal migrant labour. Evidence from gubernatorial elections after 2012 shows a similar stability in that the restoration of elections did not lead to a reduction in Kremlin-loyal governors (Slider 2014; Blakkisrud 2015; Moses 2015).

Turning to three cases studies, I explore the limits of regional independence in the context of the federal-regional patronage networks. In the next three chapters, this book will explore how and under what conditions regional leaders have access to the spoils of the migration system. The cases of Moscow, Sverdlovsk, and Krasnodar show how migration management develops differently depending on the insulation of regional elites from civil society, relationships between state officials and business elites who profit from the use of migrant labour, the ability of elites to mobilize populist anti-migrant sentiments, and the centrality of migrants in the regional labour market as well as use of migrant workers for state-funded jobs. Moscow, Sverdlovsk, and

Krasnodar are major migrant destinations within Russia, receiving large numbers of migrants, high quota allocations during the 2007–14 policy window, and among the largest patent revenues since 2015.

I originally selected the three cases for field research because of the intensity of migration as well as the varying public attitudes towards foreigners and ethnic minorities. As the largest recipient of immigrants and the primary destination of labour migrants from CIS countries, Moscow represents an intensified picture of immigration relations in Russia. Not only are there more migrants in Moscow than in any other location in Russia, but Muscovites have more intensely anti-migrant attitudes than residents of other regions (Gerber 2014).[47] In contrast, the Sverdlovsk region has been remarkably receptive to migrants in terms of both regional government policy and public attitudes. While the region is not without its problems, it is also marked by an embrace of tolerance and multiethnic cooperation. Krasnodar has a reputation for intolerance and interethnic conflict, both at the level of regional policy and in social attitudes (Tishkov, Zayinchkovskaya, and Vitkovskaya 2005). I expected that these attitudes would be especially intense during preparations for the 2014 Sochi Olympics, which saw an increase in migrants working in construction and related industries.

The case studies of migration politics on the ground in Moscow, Sverdlovsk, and Krasnodar further demonstrate the benefits and obligations of the migration pact, where leaders must produce a populist connection with the public, a coordinated political system, and the disciplined implementation of the government's preference for scarcity. When these pact obligations are upheld, a variety of strategies are available to regional elites to use the spoils of migration for their personal benefit.

The Moscow case illustrates a system with a strong municipal patronage network and a coordinated administration that is insulated from public accountability. Mayors Luzhkov and Sobyanin have both produced highly coordinated administrations. For the most part, each leader has been able to insulate his administration and related elites from scandal or undue scrutiny, with the exception of the end of the Luzhkov period. The spoils of migration management also shifted, yet through both periods we see the persistence of both petty corruption schemes and a dominance of state actors in migrant management (i.e., policy creation and implementation) as well as the use of migrant labour for state enterprises.

Sverdlovsk is a case of failed migration and patronage pacts during Governor Misharin's administration. Misharin was unable to produce a well-coordinated and insulated political system, and as a result a series of corruption scandals led to pact breakdown. Patronage broke down in part because of strong civil society in the region, which was able to expose corruption and the benefits it provided to regional leaders. A sense of strong civil society is palpable in Sverdlovsk, and it had a marked impact on my field research. First, it was easier to find a university that would host my visit, which reflects a greater openness and willingness to engage with foreign scholars. Second, interviewing using a snowball strategy was far more fruitful than in other regions because the community of activists and scholars is larger and more tightly knit.

In Krasnodar, I found a firmly controlled regional government marked by intense anti-migrant populism, and a weak and diffuse civil society. The practically impenetrable regional fiefdom of Alexander Tkachev (2001–15) was a comparatively difficult place to conduct research and complete basic tasks such as registration. Krasnodar is marked by well-concealed corruption schemes that utilize the spoils of migration management, yet rarely erupt into scandals because of the strictly administered regional government. Even when the occasional scandal occurred, the governor was able to demonstrate his utility to the Kremlin by producing regional stability, especially important amid preparations for the 2014 Sochi Olympics.

Because of the obligation of the patronage pact that corruption should not create public scandals, concrete evidence of schemes that elites use to create spoils is most available in cases where the migration pact has broken down. The three cases demonstrate various types of patronage breakdown. In each case, though migration management is not the driving reason for pact breakdown, various failures in the migration sphere offer a window into the larger relationship between centre and region. In Moscow, Luzkhov's personal business interests were one of the key reasons for pact breakdown, leading to his dismissal. In Sverdlovsk, mismanagement of the government and inability to control other regional elites led to Misharin's ouster. The migration scandal centred on the minister of economics indicates that it is not the presence of corruption that is the primary problem leading to pact breakdown, but rather the inability of executives like Misharin to insulate elites from having their corrupt activities exposed by civil society actors. Misharin's resignation and exit from public life altogether demonstrate his lack of stamina for the demands of politics. Krasnodar is a slightly ambiguous case because Tkachev is transferred to Moscow as minister of agriculture, but only after the Sochi Olympics are complete. Whether

Tkachev's transfer is a promotion, and thus a reward for fulfilling his regional pact, or a way of reining in a too-independent regional leader is not entirely clear.

One of the most important lessons from assessing regional management of migration is that the Kremlin relies on network loyalty to manage the federal system. Devolution via patronage pact, rather than the traditional idea of devolution as a power-sharing mechanism, means that producing legal uniformity is secondary to reproducing the regime's goals of stability, legitimacy, and prosperity at the regional level. The most important aspect of the federal system, then, is that it defines which actors will be responsible for fulfilling the patronage pact by producing equilibrium and distributing the spoils of migration and other policy areas.

Chapter Five

Local Politics of Immigration in Moscow

Headlines in early 2016 quoted Moscow mayor Sergei Sobyanin as saying, "the sale of patents to migrants brings more income into the budget than oil companies."[1] In the same speech, Sobyanin claimed that the city had reduced illegal immigration and decreased the risk of infectious diseases through migrant health screenings. These statements demonstrate an inherent tension underlying Sobyanin's words. On the one hand, he is using the language of migration myths to assure the public that the government has produced concrete improvements. On the other hand, he is highlighting the fact that migration is big business, a fact that requires significant numbers of migrants to be true. Sobyanin quite poignantly demonstrates the delicate equilbrium of the multi-level balancing act as he pitches his comments both to the public and to federal leaders who expect increased budget revenues.

If proximity were the key to managing federal relations, Moscow could be held up as a prototype of centralization and vertical power. The Kremlin's location, a five-minute walk from the mayor's office, gives the federal level ample opportunity for oversight and monitoring. Nevertheless, governance in Russia's capital is a complex mix of Kremlin and municipal power and can therefore serve as a window into the dynamics of Russian federalism as the institutional framework used for distributing patronage resources. Both because the stability of Moscow is of paramount importance to politics in Russia and because migration is particularly intense in Moscow, migration management is particularly salient for the patronage pact. Beyond the duties of the general patronage pact, which requires the mayor to produce stability, growth, and loyalty, fulfilling the federal mandate in the migration arena demands that Kremlin policy prerogatives are implemented, public opinion is managed, and the city administration appears coordinated. When the pact is maintained, the spoils of migration can be used to benefit those in the mayor's networks. If migration issues become destabilizing, the patronage pact suffers stress.

The populist pact is crucial for managing migration in Moscow, and is clearly demonstrated in the rhetoric of its mayors. In addition, it is the responsibility of regional executives to fulfil other requirements of the migration pact, namely producing scarcity of legal labour following the cues of Kremlin elites, and producing the appearance of a coordinated migration administration. The Moscow case demonstrates how the patronage pact between the Kremlin and regional executives affects the implementation and distribution of legal labour scarcity. A main beneficiary of this scarcity in the Moscow case has been the state itself, including state actors, as well as elites close to the municipal authorities. This chapter outlines the populist path taken by two different mayors, assesses their patronage networks, and demonstrates links between these networks and the administrative process of setting and distributing quotas and managing patents. These informal mechanisms have been instrumental in securing the spoils of migration for state and state-connected actors.

Both Yuri Luzhkov (1992–2010) and Sergei Sobyanin (2010–present) faced similar pressures to balance robust labour needs in an increasingly cosmopolitan city with a thriving service sector and booming construction industry, alongside demands from the population to limit immigration. Consequently, both have been strident about the need to control both the number of migrants and some associated cultural practices (e.g., the construction of new mosques, and some holiday traditions). Luzhkov's public rhetoric reaffirmed the need for low quotas and increased measures to combat illegal immigration. Sobyanin, after an initially soft approach towards migration, adapted to the demands of the populist pact and increased his anti-migrant rhetoric, showing a populist learning curve.

The administrations of Luzhkov and Sobyanin offer the opportunity to compare how patronage and the spoils of migration management vary across patronage networks. Luzhkov had traditionally not only been loyal to the Kremlin but also provided a great deal of growth and stability that benefited the federal government. Yet he had significant stores of personal power and a cadre of clients, which had both direct and indirect consequences for the migration sphere. Towards the end of his tenure, these consequences began to outweigh Luzhkov's utility to the federal government. Luzhkov's dismissal and replacement with Kremlin loyalist Sobyanin was a warning to political and business elites not to act independently and to keep patronage networks in line with Kremlin-approved boundaries. The Sobyanin administration consolidated a shift from personal networks to networks that are more firmly Kremlin-allied.

The Moscow administration has reliably implemented the Kremlin policy prerogative of scarcity through quota and then patents across both mayors. Experts estimate, and this chapter will confirm, that the number of migrants (legal and illegal) has remained well over one million in Moscow. The quota for Moscow continually decreased from 750,000 in 2007 to just under 200,000 in 2014, pushing increasingly more migrants to work illegally. Once patents became the only method of legalizing a migrant's labour status in 2015, the number of documented labour migrants decreased by over 50% to just 551,320 (see table 5.1). Sobyanin's administration fully embraced the state-capitalist model for patent distribution and was able to create a near-monopoly on the patent industry by directing all migrants through a new Multifunctional Migration centre in the suburb of Sakharovo.

The Luzhkov Period

Throughout Luzhkov's tenure, he took an activist stance against labour migration. As early as 1994, he passed an order requiring that all applications to hire foreign workers be approved directly by top leaders in the city administration.[2] Luzhkov was a vociferous critic of the 2007 migration legislation that allowed migrants to apply for work permits themselves and move freely between employers, claiming it was too liberal. He instead proposed the creation of a new police force dedicated to immigration control.[3] For the duration of his tenure he continued to speak out against federal legislation, consistently demanding lower and lower quotas for Moscow.[4] In 2010, he proposed shortening the period that visa-free CIS citizens could stay in Russia from 90 days to 15 days.[5]

Further, Luzhkov was actively critical of the FMS, which led to very public disagreements played out in the media. FMS representatives argued that Luzhkov's rhetoric justified opaque dealings with migrants, reinforcing the idea that managing migrants through informal mechanisms is a deliberate strategy on the part of government actors.[6] When Luzhkov passed an initiative in 2009 requiring all migrants to sign a rental contract with their landlord as a stipulation for registration with the Moscow UFMS, the FMS cancelled the procedure, saying that regional UFMS offices did not have the right to add additional requirements to the federal laws.[7] This sort of visible disagreement between different actors in

Table 5.1. Labour migration, Moscow

	2007	2008	2009	2010	2011	2012	2013	2014	2015
Quota	750,000	244,309	392,157	250,000	128,803	136,384	101,546	95,020	12,505
(year end)		594,886	392,157	250,000	181,336	209,513	215,479	188,225	21,621
Work permits	482,900	623,200	522,429	345,142	182,958	211,084	242,891[a]	340,843	66,549
(% of quota)	(64%)	(105%)	(133%)	(138%)	(101%)	(101%)	(113%)	(181%)	(308%)
Patents	—	—	—	19,185	115,133	172,597	292,490	811,072	484,771
Total labour migrants	482,900	623,200	522,429	364,327	298,091	383,681	535,381	1,151,915	551,320

Sources: Moscow UFMS statistics; Minzdrav/Mintrud orders defining yearly regional allocation and mid-year adjustments.

[a] Data on the UFMS website records the number of work permits issued at 339,978, while the lower number is recorded in the Rosstat statistics.

the multi-level balancing act of migration management discredits the uniform legal and political space that the Putin administration purports to advance. Nevertheless, federal elites allowed Luzhkov's activism without public reprimand or possible loss of tenure as long as it served their political ends of producing stability and loyalty.

Luzhkov consistently couched his arguments in the language of protecting the labour market for native workers and cutting down on crime. This type of rhetoric resonated with xenophobic segments of society and thus served an important function in gaining popular support and legitimacy. At the same time, the scarcity resulting from low quotas was a benefit to industries that relied on migrant labour. Luzhkov's patronage network included a number of oligarchs with controlling interests in the construction and retail industries, which at the time were the largest employers of migrants. Furthermore, the city directly employed a large number of migrants, many of whom had at least some degree of irregularity in their status. With this in mind, it is natural that Luzhkov continually spoke out for lower quotas in order to obtain ample informal labour for the city and regional oligarchs.

Luzhkov's long tenure allowed him to construct a powerful municipal patronage network and act as a pivotal figure between federal political elites and local oligarchs. Luzhkov had both mass and elite appeal that contributed to his popular legitimacy and ability to provide patronage resources for economic elites. He accomplished these tasks by using his loyalty to the federal government to negotiate benefits for those in his sphere of interest.

Luzhkov proved to be both a popular mayor and a reliable ally of the Kremlin for most of his tenure, retaining his post from 1992 to 2010 across periods of election and appointment. He received a high percentage of votes in elections (89.6% in 1996 and 71.5% in 1999) before his position, along with all regional executives, became subject to appointment after 2004 (Medvedev 2004). Luzhkov's success owes to his ability to act as a powerful stabilizing force, ushering in enormous growth and development despite the instability of the 1990s. It is this stability, as well as Luzhkov's ability to deliver votes for the Kremlin's candidates in national elections,[8] that helped produce legitimacy for the Kremlin and secured the patronage relationship between the federal and city governments. As long as Luzhkov provided the federal government with continued legitimacy, his position was secure and he received patronage resources such as the use of informal migrants for state enterprises and the businesses of economic allies.

Luzhkov's Patronage Network: Economic Elites

Luzhkov's relationships with economic elites were persistently controversial, and many believe the scale of corruption he allowed was a driving cause of his eventual dismissal. While Luzhkov's networks were vast, a few key examples will serve to illustrate the types of relationships and privileges that patronage brings, and demonstrate how these processes have a potential impact on the migration sphere.

One of the most controversial and public relationships was between Luzhkov and his wife, construction baron Elena Baturina, who consistently topped Forbes lists of the richest people in Russia. The two were often criticized for not complying with anti-corruption legislation that requires public officials to disclose their income and property holdings (Nemtsov 2009). During Luzhkov's tenure as mayor, Baturina owned and was acting president of the construction and development company Inteco. While some of Inteco's projects are relatively modest and public-oriented in nature (e.g., projects for Moscow State University), the bulk of its work has focused on high-impact luxury facilities. Inteco received a number of government contracts while Luzhkov was in office, either directly or through its subsidiaries. It grew to control building projects covering one million square metres in and around Moscow, and around 20% of the city's housing market. According to a January 2010 Levada Center poll, a majority of Muscovites (65%) believed that Baturina's success was only realized with the help of Luzhkov (Levada Center 2010). These allegations became the subject of intense focus and may have contributed to Luzhkov's firing in September 2010. Baturina moved to London not long after Luzhkov's dismissal. At the time, she was implicated in a corruption scandal that involved transfers from the city budget into an Inteco account (via a loan from the Bank of Moscow to a property company called "Premier Estate").[9] In February 2011, Inteco's offices were raided by police in the course of the investigation, and in in September 2011, Baturina sold all of her shares in the company.[10]

The implications of the Luzhkov-Baturina empire are important for the issue of migration. The construction industry in Russia has traditionally been the largest sector of employment for migrant workers, employing 40% of all labour migrants, according to 2008 figures (Tyuryukanova 2008). Of the 5 million total construction workers in 2008, 13% (and as many as 19% in Moscow) were migrant workers (International Labour Organization 2009; Tyuryukanova 2008).[11] Experts estimate that if illegal immigrants were included in these calculations, migrants would comprise at least 50% of all construction workers. If migrants truly comprised half of all construction workers (or 2.5 million) and this number were 40% of the total migrant population, a quota of less than 6.25 million would inevitably lead to illegality. During the Luzhkov period, quotas provided ample illegal labour to contribute to Baturina's fortunes, decreasing construction costs and maximizing profits.

Aside from ties to Baturina and the construction industry, Luzhkov had ties to business elites that were powerful in other sectors that traditionally employ migrants. The 2009 scandal over the closing of Cherkizovskii market brought one of these relationships to light. Cherkizovskii market, the largest open-air market in Eastern Europe at the time, was owned by Telman Ismailov, Russia's 61st richest man with a net worth of $600 million.[12] When it was closed by the federal government on account of unsanitary conditions and in connection with contraband goods, many interpreted this as a sign that Luzhkov had let his allies take too much latitude.

Since 2006, the city government had repeatedly threatened to close Cherkizovskii because of its association with underground trading practices.[13] Luzhkov delayed the market's closure several times, announcing as late as April 2009, amid a federal investigation, that it would not be closed until 2010.[14] The delays allowed the market to remain open and profitable for Ismailov. Federal agencies became directly involved starting in 2008, when the FSB took up a case that investigated police involvement in smuggling of counterfeit goods to markets throughout Russia, including Cherkizovskii.[15] In June 2009, days after Ismailov threw a lavish grand opening at his new $1 billion hotel in Turkey (a party whose guest list included a number of Hollywood stars as well as Luzhkov and Baturina), Putin (2009) spoke sharply against illegal imports as a threat to the federal budget and vowed a crackdown. This type of direct intervention by Putin is sometimes referred to as "manual control" (Petrov, Lipman, and Hale 2014; Schenk 2013), which can be used to discipline unruly members in the patronage network, and in this case it stood as a warning to Luzhkov and Ismailov. Federal agencies closed the market later that month, bypassing any city jurisdiction. Many suspect that the federal government was angered by the fact that Ismailov was spending the fortune he earned in Russia abroad;[16] Russian TV coverage at the time included montages combining coverage of the market closing with the grand opening of Ismailov's Turkish hotel.

In 2007, the introduction of "allowable shares" (discussed in chapter 4; see table 4.2) effectively banned foreign workers in retail markets. Yet the legislation was largely ineffective.[17] At the time of its closing, Cherkizovskii was manned primarily by migrants from the CIS, China, and Vietnam. In the weeks following the market closing, 900 migrants were found to be without documents,[18] to say nothing of those with counterfeit documents or documents procured by paying bribes to corrupt bureaucrats. Several of my interview respondents explained that the market had been run by mafia bosses who employed the migrants and paid off police inspectors to turn a blind eye to illegal activities. This account also helps to explain the estimated $2 billion worth of contraband goods recovered from the premises of Cherkizovskii after its closing.[19]

At the time, many believed that the closing of Cherkizovskii was a signal to Luzhkov from the Kremlin that his influence and ability to protect the interests of those around him were waning. The episode stands as an example of how federal-regional patronage networks break down when regional leaders do not keep their side of the bargain, maintaining stability and a coordinated, well-behaved elite. In addition to the problematic relations with business elites, Luzhkov and then-president Dmitry Medvedev had engaged in a heated public exchange in the months preceding Luzhkov's September 2010 dismissal, showing further stress on the patronage pact.[20] Luzhkov refused to resign and was thus fired by Medvedev, who said, "It's not just a suspension, it's a removal from office. That means I have fired him … I, as the president of the Russian Federation, have lost trust in Yuri Mikhailovich Luzhkov as mayor of Moscow."[21]

Transition of Power

After a brief interim administration led by Luzhkov's deputy mayor Vladimir Resin, Medvedev appointed Sergei Sobyanin, who was approved by the Moscow City Duma on October 21, 2010.[22] However brief, the administration of Resin warrants a few words. First, Resin very quickly became a member of the ruling party United Russia, likely because a show of loyalty to the Kremlin was necessary to be considered for the permanent appointment of mayor, to which Resin aspired.[23] During his three weeks in office, from September 28 to October 21, Resin actively continued the work of the office, signing numerous mayoral orders (*ukazy*) and regional government orders (*postanovlenii*). Among these were changes to personnel and changes to the composition of the interdepartmental commission in charge of migrant quotas.[24] Some consider Resin's activism, his shows of loyalty and his housecleaning, as a sort of campaign for the permanent mayoral position. Nevertheless, in the end, Resin was passed over in favour of Sergei Sobyanin. Once Sobyanin was appointed mayor, Resin returned to his position as deputy major until December 2011, when he took up an elected position in the State Duma, as a member of the United Russia party list.

The Sobyanin Period

The appointment of Putin's chief of staff Sergei Sobyanin to the mayoral post indicates the importance of Putin's patronage networks. Sobyanin's appointment represented an opportunity for federal leaders to disrupt regional patronage networks. However, with the exception of visible figures like Luzhkov, Ismailov, and Baturina, there was significant continuity in both personnel and public administration in the sphere of migration management. There are two reasons for this. First, entirely dismantling the municipal patronage network would be too destabilizing for the political and economic system. It was more efficient and expedient to keep the majority of the network intact but to remove a few key figures in order to test the loyalty of elites and remind them of the power of the Kremlin. This is a lesson that Resin, for example, learned quickly and thoroughly as he threw his lot in with federal leaders.

Second, there was continuity in the migration sphere not least because the establishment of quota at scarcity level had already been institutionalized by federal elites, as demonstrated in chapter 3. The quota for Moscow never rose above 250,000 during the Sobyanin period, and was reduced to the lowest-ever level of 95,000 in 2014. This is important evidence that the removal of Luzhkov was not an anti-corruption move, but rather aimed to eliminate a too-independent political elite. Therefore, the scarcity of legal migrant labour as a patronage resource continued to flow from the federal government to municipal elites as a reward for their ongoing loyalty, maintained through low quotas (2007–14) and bureaucratic barriers to obtaining patents (2015–).

Migration continued to be an issue requiring political attention during the Sobyanin period, though Sobyanin faced a steep populist learning curve. Immediately after his appointment in 2010, Sobyanin caused some controversy when he declared that there were 2 million migrants working illegally in Moscow, as opposed to the 200,000 cited by the FMS. His statements were a direct criticism of decreased quotas, though at the same time he promised further scrutiny of employer applications in future quota formulations.[25] Just over a year later, however, Sobyanin declared the illegal immigration situation in Moscow had stabilized despite reports from the procuracy that there had been no reduction in illegal immigrant numbers.[26] Sobyanin further stated that "Moscow cannot manage without migrants," because of the 2 million work vacancies at the time, yet he emphasized the importance that migrants "be registered, pay taxes, and not commit crimes."[27] Later in 2012, he promised that migrant quotas would be kept within 3.2% of the working population of Moscow, and that rumours of increasing the quota were completely unfounded.[28] In the early months of 2013, amid record snowfalls, Sobyanin personally conducted inspections of snow removal processes after widespread complaints of slow service. Some pointed to an insufficient number of street cleaners (*dvorniki*) as the reason for backlogs in snow removal. In Moscow, there is a visible presence of migrant street cleaners, yet Sobyanin's inspections included photo ops with road crews made up of Slavic workers and assurances from the head of the company Avtomobil'nye Dorogi that his workforce included "practically no people from CIS countries."[29] Even months later, Sobyanin stated that Moscow was managing perfectly well without migrants as street cleaners.[30]

The migration issue became particularly visible during the 2013 mayoral race as Sobyanin and opposition figure Alexei Navalny focused their campaigns on typical populist themes such as social services for immigrants, protecting the domestic labour market, illegal immigration, migrant crime, etc.[31] During the three-month campaign season, hundreds of newspaper articles were published detailing each candidate's views on the migration situation.[32] The immigrant issue was especially charged at least in part because of a conflict between police and internal "immigrants" from Dagestan that set off a wider campaign of raids, the establishment of migrant camps, and a rash of deportations.[33] One observer called it an "imitation fight against illegal immigration," which was more of a publicity stunt on the part of Sobyanin than a real effort to improve the migration situation.[34] Nevertheless, other key points of the mayoral campaign reflected ongoing efforts by Sobyanin to address migration problems such as "rubber apartments."

Even after Sobyanin won the elections, migration remained a salient issue in the public sphere. In October 2013, riots broke out in the Moscow suburb of Biriulyovo after the murder of an ethnically Russian teenager by an Azerbaijani immigrant. The events provoked anti-immigrant protests in Moscow and several other regions, demanding immigration reform. The government took a dual-pronged approach in order to respond to migration concerns without indulging nationalist voices deemed too radical. The government acted decisively to end riots and unsanctioned protests by nationalist elements, and then arrested over 1,000 immigrants in an ensuing anti-immigrant campaign.[35] Sobyanin also fired several prefect-level city administrators for allowing their regions to spin out of control.[36] In particular, he criticized the illegal sale of alcohol and counterfeit goods in markets, again allowing markets to become a focal point for tensions involving migrants and crime.

Throughout these events, Sobyanin consistently played into a variety of migration myths, including the idea that migrants take jobs, present health and security risks, and are culturally incompatible with the local population. The fight against "rubber apartments" was often framed as a sanitary issue, and fears of social unrest and cultural incompatibility were evoked by the Biriulyovo events as well as by the debate over the construction of mosques and the ritual slaughter of animals discussed in chapter 1. In this way, there is significant continuity between the Luzhkov and Sobyanin periods in the use of populist rhetoric. Though Sobyanin was initially less resolute in his use of populism, over his tenure he has increased the anti-migrant nature of his rhetoric in order to fulfil the populist pact and uphold the social contract.

Though populism remained central, there was a profound shift from personal patronage networks under Luzhkov to Kremlin-allied networks under Sobyanin. Though Luzhkov's networks at the administrative level (i.e., vice-mayors and heads of prefects) remained largely the same, the networks were disciplined by a few visible replacements, not the least of which was Luzhkov himself. In many ways the process of bringing regional elites into alignment with the Kremlin was a continuation of Putin's efforts to bring the federal system into vertical alignment, or devolution disciplined by patronage. Luzhkov was one of the regional leaders who held onto his power longest, and one of the last to be brought into line. The year 2010 marks the time when some of the last most powerful regional leaders, including long-standing governors in Tatarstan, Bashkortostan, and Sverdlovsk, were removed to make way for a more Kremlin-aligned set of governors.

In the migration sector, Sobyanin's first five years as mayor mark a holding of the policy line, preserving the status quo of labour scarcity through quotas and ensuring that the city government was the primary beneficiary of migrant labour. He then led the charge towards a disciplined implementation of federal prerogatives in grand fashion with the shift to patents and the construction of a new multifunctional migration centre, all of which put substantial new flows of money directly into the city budget.

A Closer Look at Quota Allocation in Moscow

Composition of Interdepartmental Commissions

Both Luzhkov and Sobyanin kept the interdepartmental commission responsible for defining quotas at arm's length. While the mayor appointed commission members, there are few other concrete links between his office and the commission or its members. Nevertheless, the commission was stocked with city officials and included no civil society representatives. Moscow has had an interdepartmental commission on questions of migration since 1999, which originally consisted of 5 members led by the vice-mayor of Moscow and included 3 representatives from the city migration services. The original commission was expanded substantially in 2003 (when quotas for visa migrants were established) and 2007 (when quotas were extended to CIS migrants).[37] Yet since 2003, there has been surprisingly little representation from the UFMS, which reflects ongoing struggles between the mayor's office and the migration services.

For the most part, the members of the commission have represented key agencies, including the city administration, prefectures, and organizations such as Moscow Centre of Labour Exchange, the Interregional Information-Business Centre, and the Moscow House of Compatriots.[38] In a few cases, individuals have remained on the commission regardless of what institution they represent.[39]

From 2012, the city Department of Labour convened a working group that liaised with the interdepartmental commission.[40] The working group was primarily composed of staff members of the Moscow Centre of Labour Exchange (Moskovskii Tsentr Trudovogo Obmena, or MTsTO), which has had a representative on the interdepartmental commission from 2007 onward.[41] The Moscow Centre of Labour Exchange is a subsidiary organization of the Moscow Department of Labour. It has been integrally involved in both migration planning and the quota system as well as in implementation of migration policy.

In 2008, MTsTO received permission to hire 29,100 workers across a number of professions.[42] In 2010, the centre was allotted 80,000 work permits, by far the largest allocation of quota to any single entity in that year.[43] Being a direct recipient of quota put MTsTO in the position of being a migrant intermediary and allowed it to redistribute its quota allocation to interested employers and workers. While there is no direct evidence that MTsTO engaged in corruption related to redistributing the quota, a number of my interview respondents characterized the quota industry as one where there was a great deal of buying, selling, and trading. It is in fact quite unlikely that a major clearinghouse for quota could keep itself free of corruption, and at the very least there was a conflict of interest between MTsTO's role in the interdepartmental commission and as a quota recipient. Even if MTsTO was not directly involved in corrupt practices (i.e., selling of quota to the highest bidder or to those with connections), the organization still benefited in these years from increased business, and from having a position of central importance to the migration process. In 2009 and 2011–14, the centre received no quota. However, since 2010 MTsTO has had the sole responsibility for accepting and processing all employer applications for the quota drive, cementing its centrality in migration planning.[44]

Quota Allocations: Bureaucratic Processes

The story of MTsTO provokes the larger question of who gets quota and who doesn't. As this book has argued, quota allocation after 2007 was at scarcity level, meaning that many employers who wanted to hire migrant workers were not given quota. For 2008, despite employer requests for over 600,000 migrant workers, the Moscow quota was set at 244,309. For 2009 the Moscow quota was 250,000, despite requests by employers for over 1 million foreign workers. For 2010, employers requested over 600,000 workers, yet the quota was further reduced to 200,000.[45] For 2012, 13,500 employers requested 834,000 workers, and quota was set at 136,384.[46]

In a scarcity situation, employers can choose to engage in the process of applying for quota or bypass the procedures and either hire migrants who can get work permits on their own (CIS citizens) or hire illegal migrants. From the perspective of employers, having at least some quota is useful to provide legitimacy and cover. Expert interview respondents repeatedly emphasized that companies often employed more migrants than they had permission for, yet the legally hired employees produced a guise of compliance. Furthermore, quota gave employers (or intermediaries, as in the case of MTsTO) a tremendous amount of power because they were in possession of a scarce resource, which they could then use for themselves, give to an associate, or sell to the highest bidder.

Each year from 2008 to 2014, the Department of Labour (Rostrud) posted spreadsheets on their website detailing which companies were granted quota in each region. These documents provide a rich source of data as well as important insight into the bureaucratic process and mentality surrounding quota allocation.[47] Approaching the documents as "human artifacts" (Schatz 2009) that reflect how bureaucrats make and record decisions reveals how data entry varies from person to person and region to region, demonstrating various propensities to require different types of information and at different levels of detail from employers applying for quota (see appendix to chapter 5 for a fuller analysis of these issues). The meticulous hand-analysis of the spreadsheets further shows how different regional commissions and bureaucrats reallocate quota within a given year.

The analysis shows that the key industries given quota in Moscow are trade (15%–68% of quota), construction (10%–39%),[48] real estate (7%–23%), and manufacturing (4%–26%) (see table 5.2). This allocation is consistent with other expert estimates that migrants often find work in trade and construction. The real estate sector, however, warrants a few words of explanation. In Moscow, this sector comprises a much greater share than in the other cases analysed (an average of 1.4% of quota in Krasnodar, and 10.2% in Sverdlovsk). According to the Russian Classification of Economic Activities (Obsherossiiskii Klassifikator Vidov Ekonomicheskoi Deiatel'nosti, or OKVED), these jobs include real estate transactions as well as a number of service-related jobs ranging from machine and equipment rental, computer and IT-related activities, scientific research and development, accounting, legal services, architecture, and public relations. In practice, the real estate sector becomes a catch-all category for a diverse group of workers, from engineers to street cleaners, and from general directors to geologists. Employers in this category range from construction and auditing companies to Goldman Sachs, BP, and Conoco Phillips. The decision of how to classify a particular migrant worker can be determined by the employer, the bureaucrats who accept the employer applications, the interdepartmental commission who reviews applications, or even by the individuals who compile the spreadsheets.

Quota Allocation to Specific Companies and Organizations

In addition to the sectoral breakdown, it is also important to take a closer look at key companies that receive quota. First, given Yuri Luzhkov's business connections as well as the centrality of the construction industry to migrant employment, Yelena Baturina's company Inteco is of particular interest. Inteco itself never received any quota; however, its general contracting company "Strategy" (a part of Inteco since 2002)[49] was allotted quota ranging from 91 to 690 workers each year, with the exception of 2010 when they had no quota. Not surprisingly, greater quota numbers were allotted in 2008 (690) and 2009 (542), when overall quota numbers were much higher. What is notable, however, is that in 2008 and 2009 Strategy received quota to hire 2–3 times the average number of workers allotted to construction companies, while towards the end of the quota period (after Luzhkov's dismissal) its quota is within average range (see appendix table A5.b).

One of Inteco's major projects was a new building called City Palace, commissioned by the city government to house the mayor's office and city Duma (Medvedev 2004). The building is located in the business district called Moscow City, a pet project of Luzhkov's that involved a host of public works developments, including roads and utilities as well as a new subway line. In 2005, Inteco purchased shares in the developing companies City Palace and ST Group and held them until 2010, when they were sold to construction magnate Viktor Rashnikov, who completed the renamed Evolution Tower in 2014 using a Turkish construction company called Renaissance Construction.[50] Renaissance Construction received quota in 2008 (3,000), 2011 (100), 2012 (2,066), and 2014 (997). These allotments were also far above the average granted to construction companies, as high as 13–14 times in some years (see appendix table A5.b). Renaissance Construction was also exempted from a ban on hiring Turkish workers enacted in 2016 as a result of sanctions against Turkey, showing that it has remained well connected enough to survive any politicizations of migration policy (Schenk 2016), and it has been resilient to changes in patronage at the municipal level.

Given the document record alone, quota allocations to individual companies are merely suggestive of patronage ties that provide business advantage. This is particularly true in the construction industry, where there are many layers between developing companies like Inteco and migrant workers, including construction companies and myriad subcontractors. What is perhaps more interesting, and far more suggestive, is

Table 5.2. Quota allocation by sector, Moscow

	2008	2009	2010	2011	2012	2013	2014
Starting quota	300,000	392,157	250,000	128,803	136,384	101,546	161,252[a]
Year-end quota	594,886	392,157	250,000	199,778	209,513	215,479	—
MANUFACTURING							
Approved quota[b]	—	26,581 (7%)	11,531 (5%)	33,392 (26%)	8,765 (6%)	3,736 (4%)	13,458 (8%)
Year-end	25,925 (4%)	—	19,066 (7%)	13,355 (7%)	11,375 (5%)	12,023 (6%)	—
CONSTRUCTION							
Approved quota	—	153,133 (39%)	62,258 (25%)	27,584 (21%)	29,856 (22%)	27,281 (27%)	41,321 (26%)
Year-end	192,068 (32%)	—	79,065 (32%)	19,846 (10%)	59,461 (28%)	58,241 (27%)	—
TRADE							
Approved quota	—	116,602 (30%)	36,258 (15%)	18,974 (15%)	34,780 (26%)	32,035 (32%)	54,088 (34%)
Year-end	138,355 (23%)	—	61,032 (24%)	132,474 (66%)	50,094 (24%)	71,153 (33%)	—
HOSPITALITY							
Approved quota	—	19,198 (5%)	7,928 (3%)	3,356 (3%)	6,492 (5%)	3,904 (4%)	5,680 (4%)
Year-end	13,514 (2%)	—	10,605 (4%)	2,863 (1%)	10,564 (5%)	8,927 (4%)	—
TRANSPORTATION							
Approved quota	—	18,187 (5%)	10,354 (4%)	7,668 (6%)	10,087 (7%)	11,437 (11%)	12,223 (8%)
Year-end	30,336 (5%)	—	12,917 (5%)	6,154 (3%)	12,759 (6%)	13,413 (6%)	—
REAL ESTATE							
Approved quota	—	39,143 (10%)	27,832 (11%)	23,643 (18%)	30,790 (23%)	20,538 (20%)	25,404 (16%)
Year-end	116,637 (20%)	—	40,002 (16%)	15,754 (8%)	44,793 (21%)	35,307 (16%)	—
GOVERNMENT							
Approved quota	—	0	80,033 (32%)	0	0	0	0
Year-end	29,257 (5%)	—	8,383 (3%)	0	155 (0.07%)	0	—
SERVICES							
Approved quota	—	9,850 (3%)	6,197 (3%)	2,795 (2%)	9,452 (7%)	4,742 (5%)	4,582 (3%)
Year-end	20,884 (4%)	—	8,627 (4%)	3,773 (2%)	12,403 (6%)	7,672 (4%)	—

Source: Rostrud spreadsheets; Moscow UFMS statistics.

[a] Does not reflect beginning of the year figures, but is the first spreadsheet issued for the year.

[b] % total quota in parentheses

the use of quota and migrant workers by government and state institutions. In 2009, FMS spokesman Konstantin Poltaranin asserted that, as with construction and trade, Moscow's municipal service sector would not function without migrant labour.[51] Kremlin critic and mayoral hopeful Alexei Navalny claimed in 2013 that the city of Moscow was the biggest employer of migrants, either directly or through intermediaries.[52]

The city of Moscow employs a number of migrants across many sectors, including municipal services such as street cleaning. The situation is curious in that *On the Legal Status of Foreign Citizens* stipulates that migrants have no right to work in municipal services. Yet there has been a visible presence of Central Asians as street cleaners (*dvorniki*) during both the Luzhkov and Sobyanin periods. According to one Muscovite I spoke with, these jobs were filled by Tatars during the Soviet period, who at that time were seen as outsiders in much the same way as Central Asians are now.

In some cases, municipal departments received quota directly, though this was rare. In 2008, the Department of Trade and Services was allowed 400 workers in 10 professions across manufacturing, trade, and construction, the largest single share being 50 vegetable growers. More often, the city employs migrant workers through subsidiary municipal institutions.[53] Each municipal department has a number of subordinate organizations that implement a variety of tasks. For example, the Moscow Department of Housing and Communal Services uses 22 different subcontractors in the areas of engineering infrastructure, gardening, road maintenance and repair, waste management, housing, and coordination and development of industry.[54] The Moscow Department of Labour and Employment uses 16 subcontractors, one of which is MTsTO, discussed above. The city Department of Transportation's subsidiaries include the Moscow Metropolitan (metro system) and the above-ground public transportation system, Mosgortrans. Of these public institutions, Mosgortrans and the MTsTO have consistently been the largest recipients of quota for foreign workers, receiving far greater quota allocations than any company in any economic sector. Mosgortrans received between 33% and 81% of the entire transportation allotment across all quota years.

While there has been some minor attention in the media to migrant drivers for Mosgortrans, the attention did not come close to the level of scrutiny given to Avtomobil'nye Dorogi during the snow cleanup débâcle of 2012–13 discussed above.[55] This is despite a comparatively small quota allocated to Avtomobil'nye Dorogi (see table 5.3).

Table 5.3. Quota for government institutions, Moscow

	2008	2009	2010	2011	2012	2013	2014
Mosgortrans	9,976	9,159	7,000	5,000	5,825	4,562[a]	4,900
MTsTO	29,100	—	80,033[b]	—	—	—	—
Avtomobil'nye Dorogi	—	—	—	—	222[c] (307)	363[d] (530)	30
All municipal and federal institutions	42,047	11,110	89,353	6,172	7,793	6,097	—

Source: Rostrud spreadsheets.

Note: The numbers in parentheses represent "hidden" quota, which may well be a clerical error, but nonetheless reflects a greater number of migrants recorded in the categories that disaggregate migrants by housing, skills, etc. than in the spreadsheet column reflecting the total number of migrants.

[a] Year-end allocation. In the first iteration of quota distribution in 2013, Mosgortrans received no quota.

[b] Beginning of the year allocation. There were 3 spreadsheets issued for Moscow in 2010, despite the overall quota remaining at 250,000, in February, September, and October. In each issue, the number of quota for MTsTO decreases (to 14,346 and then 8,350), which suggests that they were reallocating their quota throughout the year rather than using it to hire migrants directly.

[c] Year-end allocation. At the beginning of 2012, no quota was allotted.

[d] Year-end allocation. At the beginning of 2013, a quota of 200 was assigned.

Furthermore, the large quota allocation to MTsTO in 2010 received no press at all. The fact that an allocation of 80,000 quota, or one-third the total regional quota for the year, received no public attention, yet the organization remains a part of the system, says something very important about the ability of well-connected institutions to easily capitalize on migrant labour, and the inability of civil society and media in Moscow to root out any related corruption.

On some level, it is logical that the city would receive large allocations of quota, because government actors need to demonstrate that they are playing by their own rules when hiring foreign workers. Construction companies like Strategy and Renaissance meanwhile are tacitly expected to hire illegal migrants, according to customary practice in the industry. However, a disproportionate allocation of quota to a government institution, as in 2010 to MTsTO, gives a small group of actors a significant amount of control over an already scarce resource.

The allocation of quota serves the important function of conferring legitimacy on companies who hire migrants and justifying the continued use of a specific bureaucratic mechanism. The analysis in the appendix to chapter 5 shows the depth of this bureaucratic process. The fact that both bureaucrats and companies actively participated shows that engagement with the state was seen as necessary on some level. Companies receiving quota could either diversify their risk (by hiring a portion of their migrant labour force legally) or profit from their quota allocation by selling it. Yet while the discussion of quota allocation is important, it is only part of the story. Who actually received work permits is the other important part of the equation.

Quota vs Work Permits

The *use* of quota in reality, through obtaining a work permit from the FMS, is quite different from the *allocation* of quota by the bureaucratic actors of the interdepartmental commission.

Data on which companies received work permits for their migrant workers is non-existent, and therefore cannot help tease out the variety of formal and informal procedures used to obtain documents. There are also no data on how many work permits were registered with the tax services. However, the available data shows that in Moscow, the number of work permits issued exceeded quota in every year except 2007, when quotas were determined by experts rather than by interdepartmental commissions. This is true both overall and in key economic sectors such as manufacturing and trade (see table 5.4).

These data demonstrate not only that federal-level ministries are disconnected from one another, but also that they are disconnected from regional realities. While federal-level agencies such as Mintrud and FMS are primarily motivated by increasing their control over policy areas, they seem less interested in the concrete realities of implementation. The situation suggests a de facto devolution of decision making to regional authorities, leaving entities like the UFMS to exercise discretion and autonomy by issuing work permits far in excess of quotas allocated to the region. On the one hand, this situation produces an uncoordinated policy space that can be used strategically by actors both inside (e.g., MTsTO) and outside (e.g., companies and intermediary firms) the state. On the other hand, this space for strategic uses of migration management is critical for the health of the multi-level balancing act, giving regional actors sufficient space to enjoy the spoils of their positions so long as stability and the anti-migrant populist pact are not violated. Therefore simply looking at an uncoordinated policy space as a pathology of state function misses the crucial utility

Table 5.4. Quota use by sector, Moscow

	2006	2007	2008	2009	2010	2011	2012	2013	2014
Year-end quota (Moscow)			594,886	392,157	250,000	181,336	209,513	215,479	188,225
Work permits issued		482,900	623,200	522,429	345,142	182,958	211,084	242,891[a]	340,843
(% of quota)		(64%)	(105%)	(133%)	(138%)	(101%)	(101%)	(113%)	(181%)
AGRICULTURE									
Approved quota	—	—	375	217	838	305	826	1,693	2,299
Work permits issued	645	—	10,223	—	14,732	—	—	—	—
(% of quota)	—	—	(2,726%)	—	(1,758%)	—	—	—	—
MINING									
Approved quota	—	—	2,569	1,899	1,864	108	328	380	183
Work permits issued	295	—	4,972	—	2,773	—	—	—	—
(% of quota)	—	—	(194%)	—	(149%)	—	—	—	—
MANUFACTURING									
Approved quota	—	—	25,925	26,581	19,066	13,355	11,375	12,023	13,458
Work permits issued	13,609	—	37,117	—	24,071	—	—	—	—
(% of quota)	—	—	(143%)	—	(126%)	—	—	—	—
CONSTRUCTION									
Approved quota	—	—	192,068	153,133	79,065	19,846	59,461	58,241	41,321
Work permits issued	110,769	—	174,087	—	70,528	—	—	—	—
(% of quota)	—	—	(91%)	—	(89%)	—	—	—	—
TRADE									
Approved quota	—	—	138,355	116,602	61,032	132,474	50,094	71,153	54,088
Work permits issued	133,297	—	196,408	—	98,830	—	—	—	—
(% of quota)	—	—	(142%)	—	(162%)	—	—	—	—
TRANSPORTATION									
Approved quota	—	—	30,336	18,187	12,917	6,154	12,759	13,413	12,223
Work permits issued	24,321	—	29,013	—	18,994	—	—	—	—
(% of quota)	—	—	(96%)	—	(147%)	—	—	—	—

Source: Rosstat 2011a; Rosstat 2009b; Minzdrav/Mintrud orders defining yearly regional allocation and mid-year adjustments; Rostrud spreadsheets.

[a] Data on the UFMS website records the number of work permits issued at 339,978, while the lower number is recorded in the Rosstat statistics.

and flexibility that is provided by favouring informal mechanisms in migration management.

Patents

Because of Moscow's orientation towards municipal use of migration resources, the move to state capitalism as the Kremlin's preferred policy strategy was a natural one, not least because the state was already the primary beneficiary of migration management. This is evident in that the Multifunctional Migration Centre (Mnogofunktsinoal'nyi Migratsionnyi Tsentr, or MMTs), which opened in November 2014 expressly to manage the issue of patents, issued 455,000 of the city's 484,771 patents in 2015, quickly creating a near-monopoly of migration services.[56] In addition to the 11 billion rubles collected in taxes, the centre collected 1.6 billion rubles from the 3,500-ruble service fee every migrant pays to the centre.

When it opened, the MMTs in Moscow could serve up to 2,000 migrants per day, working 24 hours a day. In early 2016, it expanded its capacity to 7,500 migrants during business hours (8:00 a.m. to 8:00 p.m.).[57] The centre is advertised as a one-stop centre that allows migrants to complete all necessary procedures, including medical checks, language exams, the purchase of a medical insurance policy, payment of taxes, notarization of documents, etc. The website claims that "all you need is two documents to receive a patent," and that if migrants come with their passport and migration card, all other services can be performed on site, including registration.[58]

The centre is located in "New Moscow," a new prefecture of the city, annexed from Moscow oblast in 2012. Because of its distance from the centre (60 kilometres outside the MKAD, or ring road, surrounding Moscow), there is a direct bus that runs from metro station Annino for a cost of 300 rubles ($5) for a round-trip ticket. In 2015, payment for all services started at 14,500 rubles ($240), most of which was paid directly into the city budget.[59] A monthly fee of 4,000 rubles ($67) was paid to the Federal Tax Service, and since patents can be issued for up to 12 months, contingent on the prepayment of taxes, migrants could pay the full 48,000 rubles ($800) for a one-year patent.[60]

Despite a website full of information, there are parts of the patent process that remain fuzzy. One concerns registration. Though migrants can register at the centre, the details for this process are not entirely clear, especially since the centre advertises that all documents can be processed with only a passport and migration card. Typically, registration requires a rental agreement or other proof of permission to live at a particular address. While migrants can also be registered at their place of work, this does not clarify how they can register themselves with only a passport and migration card when employment contracts are only required after the first two months of a patent's duration.[61]

The payment of taxes is also not clear. Monthly taxes should be prepaid to the tax services, either online or at any bank that processes tax payments. Patents are issued with a maximum one-year validity, but remain valid only as long as taxes are paid on time (there is no expiration date printed on a patent, only a date of issue).[62] The FMS does not publish figures on terminated patents at the federal level,[63] and this fact highlights the massive coordination effort that would be required between the FMS and tax services to track patents that were no longer valid on account of non-payment. The enforcement mechanism for tax payment is simply that migrants must produce proof of payment anytime an official (e.g., labour inspector, police officer, migration official) asks to see their documents; thus legal experts advise that migrants "save all receipts, and make copies, since the ink on the receipts is likely to fade over time."[64] This situation creates opportunities for migrants either to take a calculated risk that their documents will not be checked or to purchase false receipts as a cost-saving mechanism. The practice of purchasing false receipts quickly became common practice, causing the migration centre to post on its website, "do not purchase vouchers outside of banks, it is a scam."[65]

Aside from issues related to taxes and registration that are likely relevant far beyond the Moscow case, a more concrete problem with the MMTs is charges of monopolistic practices lodged by the Federal Antimonopoly Service. In December 2015, the migration centre was charged with violations of anti-monopoly legislation over insurance companies issuing health policies at the centre. The centre held an ongoing competition for contracts with insurance companies to sell policies at the centre.[66] However, the Federal Antimonopoly Service found the centre at fault for imposing additional requirements on the insurance companies, beyond what was specified by law.[67] The centre denied the allegations, saying that the additional requirements (in particular that there could be no ongoing litigation between shareholders of the company) were posted in error and were removed quickly.[68]

What is particularly interesting about these anti-monopoly charges is that they focus on the potential lost opportunities for companies rather than on the possibility of offering migrants more competitive

Table 5.5. Migrants served from 2015 to the beginning of 2016, Multifunctional Migration Centre, Moscow

Medical insurance policies issued	230,000
Medical checks completed	130,000
Language exams conducted	440,000
Patents issued	More than 455,000

Source: "Sobyanin: Prodazha patentov migrantam prinosit v biudzhet bol'she dokhodov, chem neftianye kompanii [Sobyanin: The sale of patents brought more income to the budget than oil companies]."

products. This becomes clear when we note that, while 230,000 medical insurance policies were issued at the centre through the contracted companies, nearly twice as many language exams were conducted (see table 5.5). Yet there is no discussion of monopolistic practices regarding language exams because by law the exams must be managed by a state-approved organization, whereas medical policies can be purchased from any insurance company. There were also no claims of monopolistic practices when in February 2016 the Moscow city government passed an order requiring that the medical checks needed for patents be conducted only at the migration centre.[69] According to the migration law, regional executives are required to issue a list of approved medical organizations that can conduct medical checks. By reducing the approved organizations to one, the Moscow city government ensures that all patent-seeking migrants will be channelled through the migration centre, consolidating the profits of the migrant intermediary sector that have connections to the city government.

Moscow stands as *the* example of how to turn the migration industry to state capitalism. Though there are still migrant intermediaries, they advertise that they now help migrants prepare their documents for the migration centre.[70] Many of the intermediaries are located near the MMTs and have connections to people in the centre, according to local activists, who also report that a number of these intermediaries provide false documents to patent seekers.[71] Given the nearly 25,000 administrative violations related to labour migration registered by the Moscow UFMS in 2015 and the over 2,000 recorded violations related to patents, the migrants who choose unreliable intermediaries or choose to risk working without valid documents remain numerous.

Not only has Moscow shown its competent loyalty through state capitalism, but in order to fulfil the parallel goals of the state it also

Table 5.6. Labour migrants among foreigners, Moscow

	2013	2014	2015
Migrants registered	2,299,346	2,948,310	3,415,265
–visa-free	1,650,892	2,407,472	2,951,106
Work permits	242,891[a]	340,843	66,549
Patents	292,490	811,072	484,771
Total documented labour migrants	535,381	1,151,915	551,320
Purpose of entry			
–study	72,000	91,500	115,400
–tourism	397,300	332,100	324,200
–private	673,900	654,700	479,400
–work	923,100	1,676,000	2,352,900
–other	182,200	169,300	114,600

Source: Moscow UFMS 2016.

[a] Data on the UFMS website records the number of work permits issued at 339,978, while the lower number is recorded in the Rosstat statistics.

continues to produce the crucial scarcity of legal labour. This scarcity is necessary to balance the interests of those who benefit from illegal labour with the interests of those who gain from migration management. The picture of scarcity becomes stark when the decrease in patents issued in 2015 is observed alongside an increase in the number of foreigners registered in the city (table 5.6). What is particularly striking about these figures is that despite the ruble crisis and the decrease in documented labour migrants, both of which corroborate the official position disseminated in the media that migrants were leaving Russia, the number of foreigners registered increased substantially.[72]

The labour market potential of registered foreigners becomes clearer when we consider the purpose of entry. These figures reflect new rules stating that, in order for the migrant to receive work documents, the purpose of entry must be written as work on their migration card. In this sense, any migrant who has even the smallest intention to work should declare their purpose of entry as employment. It is simply unlikely that more migrants are coming with the intent to work but fewer are working. Rather it is more likely that the demand for migrant labour remains strong despite economic crisis, yet those migrant workers are increasingly unable to obtain the necessary documents to work legally.

Conclusion

The move towards marketizing patents came at the same time that Russia was hit hard by economic crisis. Falling oil prices combined with Western sanctions over Crimea led to declines in GDP growth and value of the ruble. In this context, the argument that economic factors are more powerful than policy factors (i.e., patent reform) in shaping immigration flows, combined with decreasing numbers of legal labour migrants, could lead to overly simplistic explanations of trends in Russia. While the media and government quickly latched onto the idea that migrants were leaving Russia in droves as a result of the downturn in the economy, this argument has more to do with populist wishful thinking than with the realities of the migration situation.

Migration research supports the idea that economic crisis can decrease flows of new migrants *but* that migrants already in the host country are not induced to return home in response to decreasing economic opportunities (Cornelius et al. 2010). Combined with findings demonstrating that restrictive policies tend to create more permanent (and less temporary or circular) migration (Hollifield, Martin, and Orrenius 2014; Martin 2014; Massey and Pren 2012), there is strong support for the proposition that the migrant population in Russia has not left, but has simply gone underground. According to a migrant advocate in Moscow, while there was indeed a wave of migrants that returned home in response to the crisis, it was temporary, lasting no more than six months.[73]

Nevertheless, the government and press were able to get considerable mileage out of the argument that migrants were leaving, and it seemed to truly calm people's anxiety on some level. This only highlights the central importance of the populist pact in Russia, which relies far less on fact and nuance than it does on quelling the public's fears. In the multi-level balancing act of migration management, it is the responsibility of the Moscow mayor to secure this populist connection. Both Luzhkov and Sobyanin (after a period of adaptation) have actively embraced anti-migrant rhetoric when necessary to manage public opinion.

To fulfil the migration pact, the Moscow mayor must not only make a populist connection with the public but also put forward a coordinated administration and produce a scarcity of legal labour according to the signals given by the federal government. These requirements must be fulfilled in order to keep the multi-level balancing act of migration management at an equilibrium, where the public, regional elites, and federal decision makers are relatively satisfied with the status quo. Because of the intensity of migration in Moscow, the migration pact is a crucial part of the overall patronage pact. While pact breakdown in the case of Luzhkov cannot be explained solely by his violations of the migration pact (in particular his failure to present a coordinated political system that kept major migration-related corruption out of the public eye), migration-related activities and interests contributed to his inability to fulfil the promises of the overall patronage pact.

While Sobyanin's appointment was advertised as an anti-corruption move, his tenure demonstrates the more important goal of bringing corruption into more disciplined compliance with the rules of the patronage pact, in particular making migration profitable for the city while avoiding any major public scandals. Actors inside the city's administrative structures or closely allied to city officials are able to use the spoils of migration management such as the management of scarce resources (e.g., MTsTO and MMTs) or providing preferential contracts (e.g., medical insurance providers). Most importantly, the Moscow municipal authorities have shown an eager willingness to implement the ruling elite's project of balancing scarcity with increased revenues by embracing the state capitalist model of patent distribution.

Moscow provides an important picture of labour migration in Russia. Migrant labour is an important resource available to businesses as well as for the municipality, so long as it does not provoke public scandal like that surrounding Cherkizovskii market. But despite Moscow's central importance to migration management, what occurs in Moscow cannot be assumed for the rest of Russia. While the requirements of the patronage, migration, and populist pacts are the same throughout Russia, their application is not uniform. The cases of Sverdlovsk and Krasnodar provide important contrasts to Moscow. Both are important migrant-receiving regions, but they have markedly different orientations towards migrants and minorities. They also display different levels of adherence to the migration pact, which produces concrete consequences for regional executives.

Chapter Six

Regional Politics of Immigration in Sverdlovsk

On a summer day in 2012, a few friends and I sat in an empty field near Taganskii market in Sverdlovsk's capital of Yekaterinburg with a group of Tajik kids and their moms. As the kids played, we asked the women about their life in Russia. Many spent their time divided between Russia and Tajikistan, and while in Russia kept their children at home because they didn't have the right documents to send them to school. While we were talking, a Russian man grabbed one of the kids and hauled him off towards the market. The migrant women and remaining kids scattered in the opposite direction. While I was quite alarmed, not having any idea what had just happened, the situation quickly became clear. The man, a plain-clothes police officer, came back to explain to my friends and me that the police regularly received complaints from the public about kids begging on the street corners near the market. They had to address the complaints, and were further concerned about the safety of the kids, since the traffic in the region was quite intense. The police officer assured us that they would hold the kid for a couple of hours and then release him, and this was a pattern they followed with some regularity. He further urged us to tell the migrant women that they should make sure they had all of their documents in order. His words did not come across as a threat, but rather a plea for the migrants to protect themselves and their children. It was clear that the officer was sympathetic, yet obligated to enforce the law "just enough" to demonstrate that something was being done.

"Just enough" compliance characterizes how regional elites in the Sverdlovsk region relate to the migration pact. On the three elements of the migration pact, Sverdlovsk demonstrates some elements of populist management of the public, and a general adherence to the federal elites' goals of creating a scarcity of legal labour and increasing revenues through the sale of patents. However, an episode under Governor Alexander Misharin in 2012 demonstrates a weakly coordinated administration and an elite whose corruption was not well insulated. This opened the door for the patronage resources stemming from migration management to be disrupted by the whistle-blowing efforts of migration activists in civil society. In general, Sverdlovsk ranks higher than other Russian regions on measures of interethnic tolerance as well as democracy and civil society (McMann and Petrov 2000; Uhlin 2006; Alekseeva and Fitzpatrick 1990; Fish 1995; Fadeicheva 2009). Consequently, regional leaders must balance an activist public and civil society with the priorities of the federal government.

During my field research in Yekaterinburg (the capital of Sverdlovsk and the main migration destination in the region), I often asked people about the region's reputation for tolerance. Nearly everyone pointed to long-standing relationships between ethnic minority groups. Nevertheless, Sverdlovsk has also been at the forefront of policies and measures to attract and assist both internal and international migrants. For example, in 2004 Governor Eduard Rossel established a regional migration centre in Yekaterinburg to help migrants with entry and adaptation. The centre even included an on-site dormitory to house migrants until they found longer-term options. In 2010 a resettlement program was initiated to attract internal migrants from Ingushetia to Sverdlovsk. The non-governmental sector has also been actively involved in migrant advocacy work since 1997, supported by a variety of funding sources including the International Organization for Migration.

This chapter first explores the orientation of the regional executives towards migration, assessing their attitudes and policies. It discusses three governors, Eduard Rossel (1991–2009), Alexander Misharin (2009–12), and Evgenii Kuivashev (2012–), and also considers Yekaterinburg Mayor Evgenii Roizman (2013–), who more actively engages in anti-migrant populism than any of the governors. The chapter then proceeds to an analysis of the quota and patent eras in turn. During the quota period, Misharin's weak administration was not able to keep the migration administration working in a disciplined fashion, nor was he able to keep corruption out of the public eye. A corruption scheme led by the regional minister of economics came to light as a result of the whistle-blowing efforts of civil society actors, triggering a breakdown of the migration pact and exposing the weakness of the overall patronage pact between Misharin and the Kremlin. During the patent era, the projection of a disciplined bureaucracy was recovered, and the region was able to proceed along the path towards state capitalism, though to a lesser extent than in Moscow.

Regional Government Actors

While this book focuses on the top regional executives (governors of regions and mayors of federal cities) as the main pivot point in the multi-level balancing act of migration management, the Sverdlovsk case offers insight into how additional levels can also become important. In this case, while the governors refrain from taking a resolutely populist stance on migration, the mayor of Yekaterinburg has stepped up to fill the void. By devolving the populist pact even further down the hierarchy of power, governors are able to balance between liberal elements in society while still allowing a pressure valve for any migration-related anxieties among the public.

The Governor's Office

The position of governor in Sverdlovsk has seen a number of changes since 2009, when long-standing governor Eduard Rossel was removed. Alexander Misharin's administration was continually under criticism for his ineffective leadership and inability to manage corruption, and he was eventually replaced by Evgenii Kuivashev in 2012. Both Rossel and Misharin were removed amid larger campaigns by the Kremlin, in 2009 amid a purging of Yeltsin-era heavyweights, and in 2012 ahead of the reintroduction of direct gubernatorial elections.[1]

Governor Rossel had an open orientation towards migration and in particular had a constructive working relationship with the Tajik government.[2] Rossel's stance changed somewhat in the wake of the 2008 financial crisis, when he made a rare foray into populism. In keeping with the rhetoric throughout the country, Rossel declared that the work permit quota for foreigners was far too high and should be reduced to protect the local population from rising unemployment, saying "the Ministry of Economics of the Russian Federation gave us a quota of 170,000 gastarbeiters for this year, but we refused, asking for no more than 50,000 people."[3] Rossel went so far as to write a letter to the federal government requesting that they cancel quotas altogether.[4] Around the same time, he spoke of the need to combat the drug-related crime that is often associated with migrants.[5] Rossel's statements about quota are notable, since, at the time, Sverdlovsk was well on its way to issuing over 100,000 work permits to foreign workers by the end of 2008,[6] and for 2009 was assigned a quota of 133,402.

Many people in the region were disappointed when Misharin replaced Rossel. Not only had Rossel been quite popular, but Misharin was very quickly seen as an ineffective leader who could not unite the regional government.[7] His administration was mired in scandal, including accusations of nepotism and a number of resignations and removals due to corruption.[8] During the three years he was in power, Misharin changed his administration three times and reshuffled the structure of ministries several times. These changes would have a dramatic impact on the quota formulation process, as will be discussed in further detail below. It was precisely because of Misharin's inability to coordinate and insulate the regional government, combined with the activism of civil society leaders, that a major migration-related corruption scandal occurred. It is not the corruption itself, but rather Misharin's inability to keep it contained, that led to a breakdown of the migration pact. While the spoils of corruption can act as a reward for upholding the migration pact, the Misharin administration demonstrates that the inability to coordinate and insulate those in the government and the instability that occurs as a result of corruption scandals are violations of pact obligations and disrupt any potential benefits for political insiders.

When Misharin applied for early retirement, he was replaced by Evgenii Kuivashev, a Kremlin insider who had experience in the vicinity as governor of Tyumen (2007–11). In 2009 Kuivashev was added to the president's cadre reserve list,[9] and in 2011 he was appointed as the Ural Federal District presidential envoy (2011–12). And while Kuivashev's administration was able to coordinate efforts in the migration arena, his support for the United Russia mayoral candidate in Yekaterinburg's 2013 election was not able to overcome the support for an opposition candidate. Kuivashev has not been immune to corruption scandals, leading to his being named the least effective governor in Russia in 2015.[10] Neither has he stood for election since his appointment, despite the reintroduction of gubernatorial elections in 2012, indicating that there is concern about his ability to consolidate public support.

On the issue of migration, Kuivashev has not embraced a populist stance. Rather his public statements focus on encouraging the integration of migrants into society, and expressing support for the activities of minority groups.[11] Importantly, in 2015 Kuivashev advocated to extend the 30-day period for migrants to complete patent requirements.[12] Despite the isolated examples of Rossel's statements about quota, the Sverdlovsk governors have taken a stance on migration that is decidedly less populist than in Moscow or Krasnodar. A stark contrast is found in the figure of Yekaterinburg mayor Evgenii Roizman, demonstrating how in some cases the populist pact is accomplished by devolving its responsibilities.

Mayor of Yekaterinburg

Evgenii Roizman, elected mayor of Yekaterinburg in 2013, has actively used populist rhetoric to appeal to his constituency. Though the mayor's office has no official role in setting migration policy and does not have any concrete connection to regional offices implementing and managing migration, the 2013 election campaign took on an anti-migrant tenor that highlights important contours of public opinion.

That a political outsider was elected to the position of mayor had many people proclaiming a victory for democracy (Leighton 2013). However, while Evgenii Roizman is an outsider in the sense that he is not a member of United Russia, he is well known among the political elite, having served in the federal Duma from 2003 to 2007.[13] Though Roizman framed his candidacy as an anti-Kuivashev challenge, it is important to note that a "win for democracy" is unlikely to be a win for migrants and their related issues. This is because Roizman has long been associated with anti-migrant attitudes and activities.

A long-standing project of Roizman's is the organization City without Drugs (Gorod Bez Narkotikov), which has operated in Yekaterinburg since the 1990s as a rehabilitation program for drug addicts. Roizman claims that he had support from the Rossel administration, though his relationship with the following two governors was marked by various conflicts.[14] Notably, during my field research in Yekaterinburg in 2012 (soon after Kuivashev was appointed), Roizman was under investigation by the authorities for the deaths of two women participating in his drug rehabilitation programs. According to one Yekaterinburg resident, Roizman was in a difficult position during this time because the government didn't approve of his activities, though he remained extremely popular, with every tenth car sporting a Gorod Bez Narkotikov sticker.[15]

The Gorod Bez Narkotikov website for many years included a section that compiled publications related to the "Tajik problem." Here one could find a compendium of newspaper articles from 2003 to 2007 that connected citizens of Tajikistan with drug-related crimes.[16] Roizman earned a reputation as a nationalist because of public statements along these lines, which resonate with members of the public who are prone to anti-migrant sentiment.[17] Media monitoring in Sverdlovsk found that when migrants are considered negatively, nearly 70% of the time they are labelled as Tajiks (the more general terms "migrant," "foreigner," or "guest worker" tend not to garner as negative connotations) (Fadeicheva 2009).

During Roizman's time as a federal Duma deputy from 2003 to 2007, he spearheaded an initiative to institute a visa regime with Tajikistan, with the stated aim of reducing drug trafficking.[18] While he maintained that his efforts did not discriminate against Tajiks,[19] his language engages many of the migration myths outlined in chapter 1. In a 2012 interview, Roizman maintained the necessity of a visa regime with Tajikistan, claiming that all heroin entering Russia was transported by "citizens of Tajikistan or ethnic Tajiks" and that "almost all Tajik cultural societies [diaspora groups] that I have encountered during my work in Cheliabinsk and Sverdlovsk were created to coordinate drug trafficking," engaging the myth that migrants are a health and security risk.[20] On the possibility of Tajiks integrating into Russian society, Roizman said, "Tajiks have their own country, it is called Tajikistan," engaging the cultural incompatibility myth.[21] Roizman went further to comment that Russians face extinction due to the overwhelming immigration of foreigners. In later statements, he argued that migrants from Central Asia take Russian women and Russian jobs, leaving locals unable to compete on either account.[22] Evoking fear-based justifications, he maintained that "migration is only okay when it does not cause fear or anxiety among the local population," and that that the only way to more easily deport migrants would be in the context of a visa regime.[23]

In August 2013, Roizman voiced vocal disapproval over a decision by the federal Health Ministry to stop mandatory drug testing for migrant work permits.[24] On his blog, he argued that plenty of Central Asian migrants were drug addicts and therefore migrant workers should all be drug tested.[25] Anti-drug rhetoric resonates with the Sverdlovsk public, and contributed to Roizman's victory in the mayoral election. Survey results show a third of migrants encounter discrimination from police, local residents, and the media, based on assumptions that they are involved with narco-trafficking (Vandyshev et al. 2009). In an analysis of regional media and its orientation towards migrants and migrant issues in Sverdlovsk from October 2008 to February 2009, 28% of coverage focused on the theme of narcotics (Fadeicheva 2009). Media monitoring during 2011 revealed that Tajiks were most often associated with murder, violence, and drugs in the local press.[26]

The fact that, as a non–United Russia candidate, Roizman successfully won the election *and* successfully mobilized votes around migration issues is an interesting moment for the migration pact, which requires governors to make a populist connection with the public in order to manage any anti-migrant sentiment in a way that can be harnessed by the ruling elites. In this case, Roizman has engaged populism in a way that the governors have not. This devolution of populist responsibilities demonstrates that populism is important, but it can be politically volatile and must be balanced against any liberal voices in the region. In particular, civil society actors are an important force that must be considered, because they have the power to disrupt federally directed policies and various aspects of the patronage pact. As the following discussion will demonstrate, when civil society can interject itself into regional governance, it interrupts regional elites' ability to utilize the spoils of migration management.

Migration and Quota Allocation

Migrants in the Sverdlovsk region primarily come from Tajikistan and other Central Asian republics to work in construction, manufacturing and trade, and to a lesser extent transportation and real estate (see table 6.1) (Vandyshev et al. 2009).[27] During the years 2011–15, between 62% and 72% of foreigners entering Sverdlovsk declared that the purpose of their visit was work.[28] These percentages are high compared to other regions in Russia, where many labour migrants have traditionally entered with migration cards stating their reason for entry as "private."[29] Even with this in mind, the number of foreigners entering with the intention to work has been consistently higher than the number of migrants who received legal work documents, reaffirming the scarcity of legal labour permission (table 6.2).

Migrants in Sverdlovsk share some similar experiences with migrants across Russia in terms of access to the formal labour market, registration, etc. A 2009 survey of Tajik migrants showed that in order to prolong the period of stay in Russia (beyond 90 days), 37% of migrants completed registration through normal legal channels without the help of an intermediary, 35% used an intermediary, and 24% re-crossed the border in order to get a new migration card. Only 3% of those surveyed reported that they remained in Russia illegally. At the same time, 55%

Table 6.1. International arrivals at Kol'tsovo airport (Yekaterinburg), Sverdlovsk

	2011	2012	2013	2014	2015
Country of origin					
China	11,461	3,410	13,965	14,573	13,000
Kazakhstan	7,739	8,473	9,784	8,385	—
Kyrgyzstan	24,887	36,570	29,832	38,016	34,000
Tajikistan	47,232	66,070	74,620	72,548	52,000
Ukraine	1,526	—	4,620	2,069	720
Uzbekistan	27,833	33,288	29,832	22,924	14,000
TOTAL	145,096	186,109	203,973	180,289	144,000

Source: Sverdlovsk UFMS 2016; Sverdlovsk UFMS 2015; Sverdlovsk UFMS 2014; Sverdlovsk UFMS 2012; Sverdlovsk UFMS 2013. Years presented based on available data.

Table 6.2. Documented labour migrants, Sverdlovsk. UFMS data

	2010	2011	2012	2013	2014	2015
Work permits	51,714	45,888	30,665	29,222	23,723	3,792
Patents	—	18,923	33,425	40,345	59,633	47,759
Total documented labour migrants	51,714	64,811	64,090	69,567	83,356	51,551
Work as purpose of visit[a]	—	90,289	130,649	141,392	129,595	95,760

Source: Sverdlovsk UFMS 2016; Sverdlovsk UFMS 2015; Sverdlovsk UFMS 2013.
[a] Of foreigners entering through Kol'tsovo airport.

of migrants surveyed had no relationship with the local migration services (UFMS) (Vandyshev et al. 2009). What is particularly interesting about these survey findings is that migrants did not choose to legalize their stay by formalizing their labour status. According to the rules at that time, if migrants signed a work contract with an employer, they could extend their stay up to a year. Therefore, while many migrants found a way to retain legal registration status, they still had trouble navigating the labour market.

Once CIS migrants were added to work permit quotas in 2007, Sverdlovsk consistently maintained some of the highest quota levels in the country (see table 6.3). A number of people I spoke with in Sverdlovsk emphasized their belief that quotas and labour planning were a rational way to manage migration. In particular, those on the interdepartmental commission in charge of quotas took their job quite

Table 6.3. Quota and labour migration, Sverdlovsk. Rosstat data

	2007	2008	2009	2010	2011	2012	2013	2014
Starting quota	181,988	47,500	133,402	66,973	42,955	27,931	48,263	40,487
Year-end quota	181,988	167,486	100,693	64,700	47,024	46,464	52,263	47,974
Mid-year amendments	0	1	1	2	1	1	1	3
Work permits	81,247	109,167	111,031	82,969	34,814	26,601	25,040	20,319
(% of quota)	(44.6%)	(65.2%)	(110%)	(128%)	(74%)	(57.3%)	(47.9%)	(42.4%)
Patents	—	—	—	—	16,844	32,732	27,252	58,011
Total legal migrants	81,247	109,167	111,031	—	51,658	59,333	52,292	78,330

Source: Rosstat 2011a; Rosstat 2012c; Rosstat 2013a; Rosstat 2016c; Minzdrav/Mintrud orders defining yearly regional allocation and mid-year adjustments.

seriously and believed that the government played an essential role in regulating immigrant labour.[30] Part of this role involved an activist stance on protecting the rights of migrants, rather than the typical focus of bureaucrats on protecting the labour market. The interdepartmental commission in Sverdlovsk routinely denied employers the ability to hire a foreign worker if they found that the employer had been guilty of not paying wages to migrants in the past or violating labour laws in other ways. While violations of labour laws were officially a part of the federal government's methodology for determining quotas, they seemed to be taken more seriously in the Sverdlovsk case.[31] The interdepartmental commission also denied requests made by shell companies (those applying for quota in order to sell it).[32]

On the whole, this chapter finds that the migration situation is much better in Sverdlovsk than in many regions in Russia, though this should not be painted as an idealized picture of the region. Even in this context where the rights and well-being of migrants are considered, the Sverdlovsk migration system has not been immune to corruption and political manipulation. In fact, some scholars have found that corruption in Sverdlovsk is on par with that in Krasnodar (Dininio and Orttung 2005).[33] One scandal in 2011 provides insight into how patronage networks are constructed in the region and how they can be interrupted by a robust civil society. While the overall argument in this volume is that strong patronage networks can offer ample opportunities for regional actors to access the benefits from manipulating the migration process, the case of Sverdlovsk shows that an active migrant rights community combined with a weak patronage network can erect barriers for actors seeking to benefit from the spoils of migration management.

The interdepartmental commission in Sverdlovsk was established in 1998 to monitor the migration situation. They shifted their primary activities to quota planning in 2003 to manage newly established quotas for foreign workers requiring visas. At the time, it was led by Minister of Economics and Labour Galina Kovaleva. The mandate of the commission was to protect the rights and legal interests of both Russian citizens and foreigners living in Sverdlovsk oblast, to protect the labour market, to promote the rational use of foreign labour (through monitoring of contracts, employers, and labour law), and to ensure the epidemiological security of the region. The commission was given the right to call on regional government and non-governmental representatives to monitor their work on migration-related issues as well as the right to propose changes to current procedures.

The commission included representatives of regional executive agencies (i.e., Ministry of Economics and Labour, Ministry of Foreign Affairs, Ministry/Department of Internal Affairs, Ministry of Construction and Architecture, Ministry of Transportation, Tax Ministry, Human Rights Ombudsman, Department of Labour, etc.) as well as representatives from NGOs and trade unions. Notably, there was no representative of the regional migration services appointed to the commission in 2003.

Governor Rossel updated the commission in 2007, when CIS citizens were added to the quota system, in order to bring it in line with amendments to federal legislation. Galina Kovaleva was again named the head of the commission with responsibility for formulating quotas, while the head of the regional government, Alexei Vorobev, was tasked with coordinating the various ministries towards these efforts.[34] Rossel's update was very brief, making no reference the mandate or membership (beyond leadership) of the commission. This lack of specificity opened the door for general neglect of the commission (in terms of legally binding instructions) until 2012, when the next official changes were made to the composition of the commission.

The Sofrygin Scandal

In April 2011, Governor Misharin appointed Boston College graduate Evgenii Sofrygin to the post of minister of economics. Misharin next transferred all labour-related responsibilities (and staff) from the Ministry of Economics, including coordinating quota process, to the newly renamed Department of Labour and Employment.[35] Yet in December 2011, responsibility for quota formulation was transferred back to the Ministry of Economics.[36]

One month later, Sofrygin announced plans to change the name of the Sverdlovsk Regional Migration Centre (started by Rossel in 2004) to the United ("Single") Migration Centre or UMC (Edinyi Migratsionnyi Tsentr). This centre became a key instrument in the ensuing mismanagement of quota. Sofrygin then gave the UMC the responsibility for compiling and analysing employers' applications for quota (a role analogous to MTsTO in Moscow).[37] This move effectively replaced the role of the Department of Labour, which had formerly collected applications. Practically speaking, it meant that employers were required to submit documents to the UMC location in Yekaterinburg rather than having the option to submit applications at any of the Department of Labour's locations throughout the region.[38]

Once the responsibilities for interacting with employers had been transferred, Sofrygin, along with migration centre director Sergei Perevalov, began to sell quotas, creating a corruption racket. This was a common practice throughout Russia where migrants and employers were told that the quota was exhausted unless they paid.[39] Sofrygin and Perevalov's scheme was more sophisticated, however, because they made a practice of creating temporary shell companies in order to obtain quota through the normal procedure, which they could then sell to migrants or employers.[40]

Sofrygin was on Sverdlovsk's regional interdepartmental commission, though, in the course of a later investigation, the regional procurator deemed he was not an official member.[41] This is largely a result of Rossel's vaguely defined 2007 order on the commission. Since that order did not specify the members of the committee, the 2003 committee membership had not been updated. Any de facto changes in the intervening years were not codified and the commission thus operated in a legal grey zone.[42] Though Sofrygin was in charge of coordinating the work of various departments towards formulating the quota, according to one of the members of the interdepartmental commission, the Department of Labour and the Ministry of Economics had no contact with one another in 2011, signalling a degree of dysfunction within the commission.

The scandal that led to Sofrygin's dismissal and criminal charges occurred when he submitted a quota of 27,931 for the governor's approval, instead of the number of 32,400 as the interdepartmental commission had decided. Sofrygin misled Misharin into believing that the lower number came from the commission.[43]

On February 2, 2012, the public advisory committee of the UFMS wrote a letter to Misharin, copying the regional procurator and regional human rights ombudsman Tatiana Merzliakova. The letter expressed concern about the 2012 quota process, the unprecedentedly low overall quota (by their estimation three times lower than real labour demand), and the exclusion of the Department of Labour from the quota formulation. The letter objected to the role of the migration centre in the quota formulation process, arguing that it guaranteed a lack of transparency and the development of corrupt practices.[44] The committee requested that Misharin take measures to correct the problems created by the minister of economics. When the letter was published in an open-access journal for migration activists and experts in Russia, the editorial board posed the question: "is it possible to win against corruption if civil society competently intervenes in the fight?" (Grafova 2012).

In this case the intervention of civil society, combined with an active regional media that exposed the scandal more widely, was successful in exposing Sofrygin's activities. As Sofrygin faced the scandal, he did a number of things to save face and justify his position, including holding a roundtable that was deemed "very strange" by a local migration expert, and making public statements to the press that the quota should be increased, appealing to similar public statements by Merzliakova.[45] When I spoke with Merzliakova later that summer, she reiterated that the 2012 quotas had indeed been set too low and expressed hope that, after changes were made to the government and interdepartmental commission, the situation would improve.

The local media, which covered the scandal heavily, advanced two explanations for Sofrygin's scheme. One explanation was that Sofrygin was deliberately trying to create additional scarcity of quota. The other connected him to a suspicious company.[46] Either of these explanations is compatible with the logic of using immigration policies as a patronage resource. If Sofrygin was trying to create scarcity of quota supply, this could be accomplished directly by reducing the quota, making migrants and employers that much more susceptible to corruption schemes like the one run through the migration centre. One migration expert noted that when the news about the quota scandal broke, the price of documents through intermediary services rose from 500 rubles to 10,000–15,000 rubles almost immediately.[47]

Civil Society

Migrant advocates in Sverdlovsk have found a powerful ally in the human rights ombudsman Tatiana Merzliakova. The position of ombudsman is a political appointment, and may therefore be limited in its capacity to affect civil society and the development of human rights, depending on regional political dynamics (as we will see in chapter 7 in the case of Krasnodar). Merzliakova, however, has played an active role in mediating between state and society, and has been particularly attentive to issues of migrant rights and integration. Migrants frequently appeal directly to her office in order to request assistance with issues such as non-payment of wages or lack of access to medical care.[48] For a number of years, her office has intervened in order to help migrants with issues such as these by working directly with employers and through the courts in order to resolve labour-related problems.[49]

An example from spring 2013 demonstrates how Merzliakova also fills the role of mediator between local and migrant communities. In this case there were a number of complaints from locals in Yekaterinburg that Tajik drivers of public transportation played non-Russian music. When Merzliakova's office began to receive letters complaining about the traditional Tajik music, she contacted the transportation companies involved as well as the City Transportation Commission and worked to find a mutually agreeable solution where a mix of music would be played.[50] Later, mayor Evgenii Porunov (2010–13) decided to ban all non-Russian music, requiring drivers to play only local radio stations.[51] This decision was met with varying reactions, some supporting or denouncing the decision, though by and large the reaction of elites in various spheres of society showed a largely tolerant attitude towards migrants and their traditions as well as the need to pursue multicultural norms.[52]

It is significant in the context of the discussion on quotas that Merzliakova sits on the interdepartmental commission responsible for setting yearly figures. When I spoke with her in summer 2012, she mentioned that it is the right of the state to protect the labour market, yet she expressed concern that the quota mechanism was not without problems. In the press, Merzliakova has repeatedly expressed the need for quotas to be increased in order both to meet labour demands and allow migrants to work legally.[53]

Merzliakova is but one voice in a vibrant and dynamic community of experts working on migration-related issues in Yekaterinburg and the surrounding area.[54] Migrant civil society is made up of NGOs, migrant diaspora organizations, human rights lawyers, scholars, and some government representatives. Many activists in the region represent a specific organization that is either directly focused on migrant issues or more generally engaged in human rights advocacy. Organizations operate as migrant intermediaries, job placement services, legal assistance, migrant shelters/housing services, and analytical centres. A number of the leaders of these organizations also maintain an active online presence through LiveJournal, Facebook, and web forums that variously offer information and advice to migrants, educate the community on legal developments, raise awareness about local migration issues, and discuss the implications of these issues in a widely visible manner.

The common vein running throughout these organizations is their active participation in local and regional networks, cooperating not only with other activists and regional government representatives but also with consulates of key sending countries, in particular Tajikistan and Kyrgyzstan. Many of the leaders of the organizations are also well integrated into national and international advocacy networks, including Memorial, Migration in the 21st Century, and the International Organization for Migration. Despite difficulties in civil society throughout Russia in recent years, activists in the Sverdlovsk region have been resilient, though not completely unaffected.[55]

Diaspora groups also play an important role in migrant civil society. The work of diasporas is coordinated sometimes through consulates in Yekaterinburg and sometimes through cultural organizations. The Kyrgyz consulate is particularly active in determining the needs of its diaspora and assisting them with a variety of practical issues. The Tajik consulate is also active, as are Tajik cultural associations, which is not surprising, given the predominance of Tajiks in the migrant community. Direct assistance between Tajik migrants, however, often occurs informally: 78% of Tajiks surveyed in 2009 said that they rely on friends and family for help, though only one person out of 300 surveyed specifically cited "diaspora" as a source for help (Vandyshev et al. 2009). Of those surveyed, 10% said they had good relations with Tajik diaspora activists, but 84% said they had no relationship at all with the activists. This indicates that despite a context of active civil society, migrants themselves remain separated from activists who work to protect them by engaging with the political structure for legal and procedural change.

Key points of engagement between civil society and government actors are roundtables and other one-off events organized around a particular migration issue. More routinized participation of civil society leaders occurs through advisory committees and official government commissions (such as the interdepartmental commission for determining migration quotas, etc.). In Sverdlovsk, more civil society actors have participated through these official channels than in the other regions analysed. For example, the UFMS had a public advisory board that included a number of important civil society actors, including lawyers affiliated with Memorial, scholars, representatives of religious organizations, and NGO activists. The chairperson of this advisory board maintained an internet presence through a forum for migrants to discuss problems and procedures related to the migration process, as well as a LiveJournal page.

Furthermore, the informal community that includes the activists and government officials is a tangible reality. While conducting fieldwork, I would not infrequently encounter interviewees in the course of attending migration-related events, and in the organizations of other interviewees. And while it is important not to over-idealize civil society and its ability to impact the migration situation (e.g., the UFMS had a relatively closed relationship to civil society, according to activists in the region, despite the public advisory committee), engagement on many levels appears legitimate and real.

Aftermath of the Sofrygin Scandal

Before work on the 2013 quotas got started, Governor Misharin issued an order that reorganized the interdepartmental commission.[56] This occurred two days after the Ministry of Economics was reorganized and renamed the Ministry of Economics and Regional Development, with Dmitrii Nozhenko, not Sofrygin, as its head.[57] This chain of events follows wider patterns of political replacements in Russia; governors are more often replaced through restructuring than through being fired directly (Turovskii 2010). Yet the restructuring was one of Misharin's last actions as governor, as he applied for early retirement effective May 14. Misharin's retirement, again according to traditional patterns of cadre replacement through indirect means, is likely the result of a behind-closed-doors agreement with Kremlin officials, who were no longer willing to tolerate his ineffectiveness.

The Sofrygin scandal is a window into the Misharin administration, but is by no means the only reason that the patronage pact with the Kremlin broke down. Importantly, in the December 2011 Duma elections Sverdlovsk voters produced some of the lowest support for United Russia as well as a voter turnout of around 50%. Only 32.7% of voters in Sverdlovsk (and less than 26% in Yekaterinburg) voted for United Russia candidates. These results were interpreted as Misharin's inability to produce the loyalty and stability required of him by the Kremlin.[58] Evgenii Kuivashev was appointed acting governor to replace Misharin and was subsequently inaugurated on May 29.[59]

The new interdepartmental commission proceeded with a very public quota formulation process. Though by law the commission is not required to submit its recommendations to the Ministry of Labour in Moscow until July 10, information about 2013 quotas was published in numerous regional media outlets and official publications in early July.

News articles included explanations of how many applications were received, why certain ones were rejected, and how many in the end were accepted. While it is rare for regional governments to announce quota recommendations before they are approved by the federal level, this strategy seems to be a reaction to the Sofrygin scandal, the new government eager to resurrect the picture of a disciplined administration and the transparency demanded by civil society.

Once Sofrygin and Misharin left office in early 2012, the quota was increased substantially via the regular mid-year quota adjustment procedure. Sofrygin's quota had involved reductions across all sectors of the economy, with the exception of manufacturing and real estate, which were given an increased share (see table 6.4). The reductions particularly affected the trade sector, which was reduced by over two-thirds, and the construction industry, which was reduced by more than half.[60] Increases adopted by the new interdepartmental commission were applied relatively equally across economic sectors, with most sectors having similar percentages of the overall quota at the beginning and end of 2012. The trade and real estate sectors were an exception to this overall trend, and were adjusted towards the previous year percentages. This could indicate that some of the companies involved in Sofrygin's scheme were classified in the real estate sector and had been given an advantage during his time at the helm of the commission. A closer look at the list of companies in this sector reveals a large number of cleaning companies, with permission to hire migrants for a wide variety of jobs, including dishwashers, street cleaners (*dvorniki*), kitchen workers, and manual labourers. In other words, these companies were most likely acting as employment agencies, contracting on the work of the migrants.

Sofrygin was eventually found guilty of abuse of power, fined 300,000 rubles (around $10,000 at the time), and barred from government office for a period of two years.[61] Sergei Perevalov was also replaced as the director of the UMC in summer 2012. Despite the scandal surrounding his departure, one migration expert expressed regret that he would be leaving the migration community in Yekaterinburg, since the new director had no experience with migration issues.[62] A number of experts I interviewed in Yekaterinburg agreed that when the migration centre was opened it had been a good organization, but after Rossel left office it began using corrupt practices. Several people expressed surprise that the centre hadn't yet been closed. When I requested an interview with the new director, Semën Belkin, he refused, saying that it was no benefit

Table 6.4. Quota allocation and labour migration by sector, Sverdlovsk

	2008	2009	2010	2011	2012	2013	2014
Starting quota	47,500	133,402	66,973	42,955	27,931	48,263	40,487
Year-end quota	167,486	100,693	64,700	47,024	46,464	52,263	47,974
AGRICULTURE							
Approved quota[a]	—	3,793 (3%)	349 (0.5%)	3,405 (8%)	1,564 (6%)	1,770 (4%)	1,511 (4%)
Year-end	3,350 (2%)	—	3,163 (5%)	3,536 (8%)	2,336 (5%)	1,783 (3%)	—
Work permits issued[b]	1,610 (48%)	—	3,307 (105%)	—	—	—	—
MANUFACTURING							
Approved quota	—	18,234 (14%)	5,439 (8%)	5,533 (13%)	5,710 (20%)	8,206 (17%)	7,660 (19%)
Year-end	7,612 (5%)	—	6,522 (10%)	6,059 (13%)	9,367 (20%)	9,170 (18%)	—
Work permits issued	15,256 (200%)	—	12,623 (194%)	—	—	—	—
CONSTRUCTION							
Approved quota	—	46,232 (35%)	22,166 (33%)	14,229 (33%)	8,030 (29%)	13,305 (28%)	14,310 (35%)
Year-end	53,912 (32%)	—	18,170 (28%)	14,933 (32%)	13,685 (29%)	14,503 (28%)	—
Work permits issued	47,506 (88%)	—	21,060 (116%)	—	—	—	—
TRADE							
Approved quota	—	30,799 (23%)	26,150 (39%)	10,186 (24%)	4,335 (16%)	10,646 (22%)	5,675 (14%)
Year-end	28,585 (17%)	—	22,896 (35%)	10,970 (23%)	8,636 (19%)	10,949 (21%)	—
Work permits issued	8,321 (29%)	—	25,222 (110%)	—	—	—	—

HOSPITALITY							
Approved quota	—	3,184 (2%)	2,266 (3%)	1,009 (2%)	1,447 (5%)	3,674 (8%)	4,063 (10%)
Year-end	3,035 (2%)	—	2,294 (4%)	1,735 (4%)	2,729 (6%)	4,283 (8%)	—
TRANSPORTATION							
Approved quota	—	8,552 (6%)	2,801 (4%)	3,507 (8%)	2,587 (9%)	4,381 (9%)	3,256 (8%)
Year-end	9,149 (6%)	—	2,727 (4%)	3,683 (8%)	3,653 (8%)	4,761 (9%)	—
Work permits issued	8,321 (91%)	—	5,164 (189%)	—	—	—	—
REAL ESTATE							
Approved quota	—	8,637 (7%)	3,209 (5%)	3,390 (8%)	3,231 (12%)	3,972 (8%)	2,309 (6%)
Year-end	51,464 (31%)	—	5,298 (8%)	4,408 (9%)	4,352 (9%)	4,449 (9%)	—
SOCIAL SERVICES[c]							
Approved quota	—	7,806 (6%)	75 (0.1%)	136 (0.3%)	132 (0.5%)	199 (0.4%)	207 (0.5%)
Year-end	7,004 (4%)	—	161 (0.3%)	193 (0.4%)	197 (0.4%)	217 (0.4%)	—
SERVICES							
Approved quota	—	3,955 (3%)	4,363 (7%)	1,312 (3%)	715 (3%)	1,693 (4%)	1,254 (3%)
Year-end	3,054 (2%)	—	3,101 (5%)	1,259 (3%)	1,304 (3%)	1,741 (3%)	—

Source: Rosstat 2011a; Rosstat 2009b; Minzdrav/Mintrud orders defining yearly regional allocation and mid-year adjustments; Rostrud spreadsheets.

[a] Sectoral quota as percentage of total quota in parentheses.

[b] Number of issued work permits as percentage of sectoral quota in parentheses.

[c] Includes healthcare.

to him and that he would only meet with me for 5–7 minutes on the condition that I organize a roundtable with the UFMS director on the topic of deportation (indicating that even Belkin had difficulty accessing UFMS officials). The centre was eventually shut down, and, in a great turn of irony, the building was designated for use as a migrant detention centre.[63] Despite this, the website of the centre still portrays a functioning organization.[64]

Patent Era

Once Sofrygin was removed and Misharin resigned, the regional government was once again able to put forward a disciplined administration and resurrect the stability of the migration pact. Yet with the shift to patents, Sverdlovsk did not make a corresponding move to create a new migration centre for the one-stop issue of patents as we saw in Moscow. This is likely because the scandal of the United Migration Centre loomed like a spectre. Nevertheless, the region increased patent revenue, collecting more than 79 other regions by the first half of 2015,[65] and demonstrating "just enough" compliance with the federal push towards state capitalism. At the same time, scarcity of legal labour remains, marked by a 66% drop in legal labour migrants from 2014 to 2015 (see table 6.2), compared to an only 16% decrease in the number of registered visa-free foreigners and an 18% decrease in the number of foreign passengers arriving through Yekaterinburg's international airport (Sverdlovsk UFMS 2016).[66]

Implementation and Enforcement

When the FMS moved to a standardized web format for all regions in fall 2015, Sverdlovsk retained its old site (http://ufms-ural.ru/) in addition to creating a site on the standard format (http://www.66.fms.gov.ru/), both of which were removed when the FMS was transferred into the MVD in 2016. The new site primarily contained standardized federal information, with the exception of a few regionally specific statistics and reports. The old site contained a notice that it provided background information only and pointed to the new official site. Among the background information were a number of documents that were not transferred to the new site, including an Excel spreadsheet that listed issued and annulled patents from January 1 to October 20, 2015. This document provides unique insight into the patent process and is particularly useful because it offers the date of issue and date of annulment for those patents being revoked. Though there is no stated reason for annulment in any of these cases, the time horizon can offer some insight into nuances surrounding the requirement to submit an employment contract for patents extending beyond two months.[67]

Of the 944 annulled patents in the spreadsheet, 78 (8%) were revoked on the day of issue and 256 (27%) were revoked within two months. This indicates a procedural issue not related to the failure to submit an employment contract (since contracts must be submitted no later than two months after the patent's issue). On July 15, 2015, 527 patents (56%) were annulled, suggesting a major audit of patents on that day. Since all but five of the patents annulled had been issued more than two months prior, we can make an educated guess that the primary reason for nullification was the absence of an employment contract.[68] The more important point is that the mechanism for verifying whether migrants have an employment contract is audit-based rather than the result of real-time updates, despite the fact that contracts were submitted directly to the UFMS.[69]

The yearly UFMS statistics indicate that 20,903 employment contracts were submitted, though there is no indication that these contracts are in support of the 47,759 patents, or if contracts in support of work permits are included (nearly 4,000 in 2015). Elsewhere, the UFMS reported that they received 10,140 contracts for migrants working under the Eurasian Economic Union agreement (and thus not requiring a patent). If these contracts are included in the total of 20,903, the number of contracts submitted by migrants with patents is decreased even further. This indicates either that less than half of migrants who receive patents are working beyond two months, or that migrants simply don't submit employment contracts and hope that their patents will not be annulled.

An alternative explanation for the low number of employment contracts starts with a curious statistic recorded in the UFMS year-end figures for 2015. These data show that 31,118 patents were issued for work with private individuals and 15,641 were issued for work with companies.[70] The law *On the Legal Status of Foreign Citizens* defines an "employer" as a company, individual entrepreneur, private notary, lawyer, or any person whose professional activities are licensed by federal law. Employers can also be private Russian citizens hiring a migrant for domestic (non-commercial) purposes. However, when employment contracts are submitted to the UFMS, only contracts with companies and those registered as individual entrepreneurs are checked against national registries to verify that the employer is properly registered. Furthermore, when patents are renewed, contracts are only required for work with companies, individual entrepreneurs, private notaries, lawyers, or any person whose professional activities are licensed by federal law.

The language of the law leaves some room for interpretation on the ground, and the data suggest that in Sverdlovsk employment contracts are not required of migrants working for an individual Russian citizen. This observation is supported by a posting on the website of a reputable intermediary service: "Attention! Within two months from the day of receiving a patent, a foreign citizen signing a contract with a legal entity [company] or individual entrepreneur is required to submit to the Sverdlovsk UFMS a copy of the contract. Otherwise the patent will be annulled!"[71] Therefore if, in practice, contracts are only required for those migrants working for certain types of employers, there is some incentive for a migrant to declare that they will be working for an individual, and therefore obviate the submission of a contract.[72] Though migrants are asked to declare whether they plan to work for a company or an individual, this information is not printed on the patent.

For all practical purposes, verifying whether a migrant is working for the type of employer specified in the patent application, and enforcing the contract requirement more generally, can only be done on an auditing basis rather than in the course of real-time inspections. Law enforcement personnel who stop a migrant on the street or labour inspectors conducting workplace verifications, UFMS officials conducting migration raids, and even UFMS bureaucrats working in offices, would not have immediate access to the information from various agencies to determine whether a migrant has complied with all points of the law. Though there is a database of migrant information that purports to be comprehensive, there have been many data gaps reported, especially with respect to information sharing between different government agencies (Bahovadinova 2016). Because of these data gaps, migrants are frequently asked to produce a variety of documents to verify their status (e.g., tax receipts, employment contract), placing the burden on the migrant rather than relying on a system of coordinated and shared information between agencies.

The issue of uncoordinated enforcement provokes a further question about how likely detection of violations will be. To explore this issue, it is helpful to look at enforcement statistics, or the actual occurrences of revoking registration (shortening the valid term of stay), deportation,

Table 6.5. Enforcement compared, 2015

	Sverdlovsk	Moscow	Krasnodar
All foreigners registered	313,621	3,415,265	539,528
– at a place of stay[a]	297,400	3,386,458	514,642
Decisions to ban future entry	6,316	109,769	4,025
(% of all foreigners registered)	(2%)	(3%)	(0.8%)
Decisions to shorten valid term of stay	2,385	309	31
(% of foreigners registered at place of stay)	(0.8%)	(0.01%)	(0.01%)
Deportations	130	28	66
(% of all foreigners registered)	(0.04%)	(0.001%)	(0.01%)
Administrative violations (labour)	1,569	24,558	2,052
(% of foreigners registered at place of stay)[b]	(0.5%)	(0.7%)	(0.4%)
Administrative violations (place of stay)	2,921	16,364	5,991
(% of foreigners registered at place of stay)	(1%)	(0.5%)	(1%)
Total administrative violations[c]	37,301	146,311	56,153
Fines levied for administrative violations (rubles)	73,926	—	437,165
Migration raids	2,964	12,057	6,765
(% of all foreigners registered)	(1%)[d]	(0.4%)[e]	(1%)[f]

Source: regional UFMS data.

[a] Excludes those with permanent or temporary residence cards, who are registered at a place of residence.

[b] This figure represents the number of foreigners without permanent or temporary residence cards, as they do not need permission to work.

[c] Includes violations by employers, those who invite foreigners to Russia, as well as violations by Russian citizens of registration rules or rules related to identity documents. The latter of these two categories typically comprises the vast majority of violations.

[d] The majority of raids (1,640) were conducted at migrants' places of residence.

[e] The targets of these raids are listed as construction sites, places of consumer services, places of residence, industrial enterprises, agricultural enterprises, retail trading places, and "other." In Moscow, there were more than 2,000 raids on construction sites, and over half of all raids (6,815) are listed as "other."

[f] The vast majority of these raids (5,122) focused on migrants' places of residence.

and future re-entry bans (see table 6.5). It is particularly striking if we take Sverdlovsk in comparison to the other cases addressed in this book. Despite its reputation for tolerance, Sverdlovsk is as securitized as the others (in terms of active enforcement), if not more so. Sverdlovsk is on par with Krasnodar in terms of the number of raids in relation to foreigners registered. It is even more active in its use of entry bans and limiting migrants' period of registration.

However, these data show that enforcement of migration rules is low across all regions in question. This is especially the case because the rates of enforcement in the above estimations are based on legal migrants who have registration documents, leaving off any migrants without registration. Nevertheless, given these figures, it is reasonable to suggest that migrants can make a fairly rational calculation that if they violate migration rules they have a 1%–2% chance or less of being discovered. In this regard, Sverdlovsk demonstrates a level of enforcement that is on par with the rest of the regions. While it is not overly securitized, we cannot say that it is pursuing active implementation and enforcement of migration policies. In this aspect of migration management, Sverdlovsk again pursues a "just enough" approach to the migration pact.

Conclusion

Returning to the overall argument of the book, migration management is a multi-level balancing act requiring regional leaders to fulfil the obligations of the migration pact: make a populist connection with the public, present a coordinated political system, and produce disciplined bureaucratic activity in pursuit of legal labour scarcity. In the Sverdlovsk case, popular calls for the reduction of migration are present, but are less pointed than in other regions. Populism is largely devolved to the level of mayor, shown by Porunov's ban on non-Russian music in public transportation and Roizman's overt use of migration myths. This devolution of the populist pact allows governors to balance their approach to migration between anti-migrant sentiment and the large contingent of the population who identify with the region's history of tolerance and interethnic harmony.

The use of scarcity to capitalize on the spoils of migration management became a clear theme in the Sofrygin episode. Through this episode, the inner workings of the migration pact were revealed. Sofrygin used migration spoils in a typical way, following schemes not uncommon in other parts of Russia, but because the patronage network in Sverdlovsk was dysfunctional, his activities were exposed to the public and Misharin was unable or unwilling to insulate him from the fallout. Misharin's inability to keep his administration coordinated and disciplined disrupted the stability required as a part of his responsibility to federal elites, as well as the use of migration spoils distributed downward. Central to the breakdown of the migration pact (and likely the larger patronage pact) is the activity of civil society actors. In this case, an active migrant rights community combined with a weak patronage network erected barriers for actors seeking personal gain through the migration system, and prevented state actors from avoiding the consequences of public scandal.

After the Misharin period, there is evidence that the Sverdlovsk administration was brought back into closer alignment with the Kremlin-prefered patronage functionality. Kuivashev's administration reinvigorated the migration pact by taking great pains to present disciplined bureaucratic efforts. However, the wholesale commitment to the federal government's migration prerogatives is somewhat diminished in the Sverdlovsk case, in that regional elites provide "just enough" compliance with the rules of the patronage pact. While the number of legal labour migrants decreased and patent revenue increased, the region did not signal its commitment to the model of state capitalism by creating new migration centres to centralize the issuing of documents. This is likely because of the yet-fresh memories of Sofrygin's corruption in association with the United Migration Centre, and the lesson that civil society in Sverdlovsk is an important consideration when juggling interests in the multi-level balancing act of migration management. The repeated evidence of "just enough" compliance in the Sverdlovsk region stands as an example of how the Kremlin allows wider latitude in regions where public dissent could easily be activated.

Chapter Seven

Regional Politics of Immigration in Krasnodar

Soon after I arrived to Krasnodar in summer 2012, the city of Krymsk was largely destroyed by a flood caused by record rainfall and overflowing water reservoirs. Nearly 200 people died, more than 10,000 homes were destroyed, and roads were overrun with mud. Conversations around town quickly pointed the finger at the regional government both for the mismanagement of the reservoirs and for not adequately responding to the disaster, including the failure to warn the residents of Krymsk that the flood was imminent. Speculation was rife that Governor Alexander Tkachev (2001–15) would be fired over the débâcle. Yet within a few weeks, the events had been swept under the rug with a few token dismissals of mid-level officials sufficing for the regional government's acknowledgment of any wrongdoing. Using lower-level officials as scapegoats is common practice in Russia's political system, and in this case it signalled that Governor Tkachev was too important to be replaced because of his role in producing regional stability, including maintaining disciplined patronage networks, especially in the years immediately preceding the 2014 Sochi Winter Olympics.

Krasnodar represents a strong regional government that took an activist stance on the issue of migration management. Using a populist approach to rhetoric and a securitized policy trajectory, Tkachev's leadership demonstrates a migration system that was tightly managed and embedded in a closely administered regional government and network of elites. The illusion of control was essential for the central-regional patronage pact, but did little to actually reduce the number of migrants in the region. Further, robust and well-insulated regional corruption ensured a scarcity of legal labour that could be used to benefit

Table 7.1. Labour migration, Krasnodar

	2007	2008	2009	2010	2011	2012	2013	2014	2015
Wk permits	44,258	72,654	62,388	45,988	40,008	54,364	51,496	27,654	4,427
Patents	—	—	—	—	32,632	67,899	50,856	64,612	49,431
Total legal migrants	44,258	72,654	62,388	45,988	72,640	122,263	102,352	92,266	53,858

Source: Rostrud 2011a; Rostrud 2012b; Rostrud 2013b; Rostrud 2014b; Rostrud 2014e; Rostrud 2015d

the businesses of regional elites as well as federal interests in preparation for the Sochi Olympics.

Because of Krasnodar's location in the Caucasus region, it is a magnet for migrants coming from neighbouring regions that are politically unstable and struggling economically. Migrants coming from the regions of Chechnya, Dagestan, and Ingushetia find a comparatively stable political and security situation in Krasnodar as well as job opportunities. Krasnodar also has many migrants from Armenia. Aside from its border location, Krasnodar boasts a very liveable climate and vibrant economy, owing to favourable conditions for agriculture. I found Krasnodar an intoxicating place where one could experience the modern amenities of Starbucks and Ikea, the Soviet-era grandeur of sprawling public parks with spectacular fountains, and a suburban setting with fruit trees growing along the sidewalks.

As I spoke with various residents of Krasnodar, there was broad consensus that of course migrants would want to come there because, "just look around you, it's paradise!" These sentiments are reinforced by ratings placing Krasnodar as one of the most liveable cities in Russia.[1] A woman who struck up a conversation with me on the bus one day told me her family had relocated to Krasnodar during a brief period when the Khrushchev administration allowed greater freedom of movement, and had decided to stay because it is so idyllic. Owing to these factors, Krasnodar was a principal destination for refugees in the immediate post-Soviet period and for other migrants more generally, earning the status as the primary destination for newcomers in the 1990s (Derluguian and Cipko 1997; Malinkin 2013). During the quota period, development in preparation for the 2014 Winter Olympics in Sochi added further economic incentives for labour migrants coming to the region (see table 7.1).

In the migration literature, Krasnodar has a reputation for intolerance, and this is the primary reason I was motivated to visit and investigate the situation. Anti-migrant attitudes are often attributed to higher than average migration levels (Voronina 2006), particularly from the Caucasus (Tishkov, Zayinchkovskaya, and Vitkovskaya 2005), inducing a security dilemma and demanding a response from policymakers (Alexseev 2006a). Others point to deeper roots of ethnic intolerance. A Cossack revival, embracing a traditional militia-oriented identity, began in 1989 under glasnost and was encouraged and supported by the local leadership, which has treated Cossacks as the region's de facto indigenous group (Swerdlow 2006, 1839; Popov and Kuznetsov 2008). Cossacks see migrants and newcomers as a threat to traditional Cossack lands (Boeck 1998), and thus the revival has been advanced as a major contributing factor to the region's anti-migrant orientation (Popov and Kuznetsov 2008; Pilkington, Omelchenko, and Popov 2010).

My research revealed that the relationship between locals and migrants is nuanced and not uniformly intolerant. However, the regional government's orientation has institutionalized xenophobic messages and policies, leaving important marks on the migration context. The guiding principle of the region's migrant management strategy has focused on increasing an illusion of control while consolidating any benefits that migrant labour brings in the hands of elites. Governor Tkachev created a tightly controlled political fiefdom that channelled resources to loyal clients (in both government and economic sectors), leveraging his ability to keep the region stable and progressing towards the Sochi Olympics. The migration sphere reflects this overall situation, demonstrating how Krasnodar's strategic position, active use of regional legislation, pervasive petty corruption, and limited space for civil society has allowed the regional government to deploy migration resources both through and outside the quota system for the benefit of regional and federal elites.

The presence of a tight patronage network under Tkachev kept those involved in migrant-related corruption insulated from scandal. Even corruption experts in the region could only vaguely point to schemes surrounding the quota process, suspecting they were present but not being able to provide concrete examples, since the process was kept behind closed doors. A closely controlled patronage network also provided cover for bureaucrats and migration officials to freely engage in corruption schemes so long as they did not interfere with regional stability or reputation. During preparations for the Sochi Olympics, regional stability was of the utmost importance, as the world's eyes were on the region. After the Olympics, conflict with Ukraine raised the issue to the level of national security, given Krasnodar's proximity to the conflict zone. Ultimately, Governor Tkachev's promotion to minister of agriculture in 2015 could be interpreted as a reward for fulfilling the patronage pact.

Tkachev and Anti-Migrant Activism

Krasnodar has a history of special regional-level migration legislation that has no corollary in Sverdlovsk or Moscow, which are more deferential towards federal legislation.[2] The difference is especially stark between Sverdlovsk and Krasnodar. In Sverdlovsk, interview respondents repeatedly voiced the frustration that their hands were tied because legislation was dictated by the federal government. In Krasnodar, I encountered less of a sense that the region was constrained by federal law, and rather the attitude that there was ample room under the federal legislation to further control the migration process regionally. This attitude is borne out by active patterns of legislation and administrative orders, which, combined with anti-migrant rhetoric from officials, produces an inhospitable institutional environment for migrants.

From the beginning of his tenure as governor, Tkachev actively employed populist anti-migrant rhetoric. In 2002 he called for the deportation of all illegal migrants (including any without proper registration).[3] Tkachev further claimed it was possible to define whether a migrant was legal or illegal based on the ending of the last name, that "family names ending in 'yan,' 'dze,' 'shvili,' and 'ogly,' are illegal as are their bearers."[4] Painting broad swathes of people as illegal immigrants is an active use of the populist security myth, as it increases the perception of crime and illegal activity associated with migrants. In the same speech, Tkachev announced municipal-level goals for deporting Meskhetian Turks, and a new monthly flight from Krasnodar to Tashkent paid for out of the administration's budget.[5]

Meskhetian Turks, who had been relocated to Central Asia from Georgia during the Soviet period, formed a major immigration wave from Uzbekistan to Krasnodar starting in 1989 (Popov and Kuznetsov 2008). Because advocates for the group were able to garner international attention, Meskhetian Turks became symbolic of Krasnodar's anti-migration orientation, and solidified the region's reputation for intolerance. Meskhetian Turks encountered numerous problems with unreformed registration (or *propiska*) laws,[6] but the situation became more acute after 2002 when the regional government passed laws that increased fines, created deportation centres (or "filtration camps"), and provided for immediate deportation of illegals, causing controversy both at the national and international level (Memorial 2002).[7] These laws illustrate how the Tkachev government actively used regional legislation and administrative procedures to institutionalize an anti-migrant default position.[8]

Some claim that the 2002 laws opened the door for Cossack patrols to have a more active role in finding and deporting illegal migrants.[9] Cossack patrols operated as early as 1990 in Krasnodar, and were instrumental in seeking out Meskhetian Turks and other migrants with illegal status (Galeotti 1995; Derluguian and Cipko 1997; Osipov 2002). The role of the Cossacks is particularly important when discussing anti-migrant attitudes and activities in the region, not least because it highlights a strategic choice by the regional government to devolve migration enforcement to non-government groups as a supplement to more direct actions.[10] Many scholars recognize that the favour afforded to Cossack groups by the regional government – for example, there are Cossack representatives on migration committees at all levels – has institutionalized xenophobic attitudes in the region (Popov and Kuznetsov 2008; Pilkington, Omelchenko, and Popov 2010).

The response of the Kremlin to these new migration strategies in Krasnodar was silence. This is especially important to note because Putin's first administration (2000–4) was intensely occupied with establishing the dictatorship of the law, or legal uniformity throughout Russia. Allowing the very type of independent law-making that the dictatorship of law agenda was meant to eliminate is particularly noteworthy. Presumably, because federal migration law at the time was so underdeveloped, as discussed in the Introduction chapter, federal authorities could not provide viable policy alternatives and therefore allowed regional initiatives to proceed unhindered.

Systematic anti-migrant actions persisted throughout Tkachev's tenure, highlighted again in August 2012 when he allocated an annual 650 million rubles to employ Cossack forces as a supplement to police personnel. Tkachev actively engaged the security myth of populist rhetoric when he claimed the patrols were necessary to protect public order against increasing crime committed by migrants from neighbouring North Caucasus regions.[11] Since this decision came during my fieldwork, I was able to ask a variety of people what they thought of the development. One bureaucrat said the decision was completely justified because the government was simply using the available resources to solve an identified problem. Most others, including experts and average citizens, saw the move as populist in nature, and still others questioned the legality of the measures.

Tkachev's efforts caused a stir at the national level. The federal-level Public Chamber quickly accused Tkachev of fomenting ethnic hatred, and argued that the Cossack forces would infringe on constitutional guarantees of freedom of movement (a frequent criticism of unreformed *propiska* practices).[12] The Kremlin was again silent, even when the Moscow city government followed suit and enlisted Cossack forces several months later (Bartels 2014).[13] Putin finally came out in favour of the decision a year later, in December 2013, just before Cossack deployments in Sochi started to garner international attention, arguing that "sometimes Cossacks are much more effective than law enforcement agencies. This is because they represent the majority of people who live in the area where they work."[14]

The Cossack deployment was aimed at internal migrants (Russian citizens from neighbouring regions), yet international migrants from the CIS did not escape Tkachev's attention. In summer 2012, Tkachev made statements linking migrants from the CIS to an increase in crime of up to 30%, once again engaging the rhetoric of the security myth.[15] Some argue that the increased anti-migrant rhetoric in 2012 was an attempt to divert attention from the failure to manage the floods in Krymsk and scandals surrounding construction for the Olympics.[16] This strategy demonstrates how the populist pact can be used to correct for potential violations of the patronage pact, when public criticism could pose a threat to stability or the illusion of control (e.g., keeping corruption under wraps).

Quota Allocation in Krasnodar

The type of anti-migrant orientation that is institutionalized through regional legislative and administrative activity finds further examples in the sphere of quota allocation in Krasnodar. In contrast to Moscow and Sverdlovsk, where the regional executive devolved quota-related tasks to the interdepartmental commission, the quota process in Krasnodar was more closely managed through a series of governor's orders that outline a very detailed approach to migration planning. Three orders in particular set out the bodies responsible for coordinating the quota allocation process, the establishment of the interdepartmental commission, and a detailed set of instructions and schedule for employers and government agencies alike to adhere to.[17]

Interdepartmental Commission

Krasnodar Governor's Order (*postanovlenie*) No. 767 of August 8, 2003 defined which agency would be responsible for overseeing quotas. Originally, it gave sole responsibility to the regional Office of Migration Monitoring (renamed the Office of Interaction with Public Associations, Religious Organizations and Monitoring of Migratory Processes in 2004). When the Order was amended in 2009, it gave specific instructions for how the Office of Interaction with Public Associations (headed by Sergei Myshak) should interact with the Office of Labour Services (headed by Igor Melkikh) and the regional UFMS (headed by Igor Semeniakin). It included monthly deadlines for sharing information about the labour market and the number of invitations and work permits issued, and described how compliance should be monitored. In 2012, the Office of Interaction with Public Associations was dissolved and its responsibilities in the realm of quota definition were transferred to the Department of Labour.[18]

A second Krasnodar Governor's Order (No. 363 of April 24, 2007) set out a yearly schedule for all activities and established the membership of the interdepartmental commission. Tkachev outlined deadlines for reviewing employer applications and instructed the commission about other factors they should consider as they recommended a quota. Membership included representatives of various agencies, including the Departments of Construction, Agriculture, Industry, Consumer Sphere and Regulation of Alcohol, and Economic Development, as well as the UFMS, the Tripartite Commission on Social and Labour Relations, the Labour Inspectorate, the Tax Services, and the Council of Trade Unions.

Finally, a third Krasnodar Governor's Order (No. 298 of April 22, 2010) was in force for only a few months but contained a detailed description of the rules and schedule to be followed by employers applying for quota, and described how the interdepartmental commission would determine quota based on those applications. The order reiterated instructions and rules set out by the federal government, but went far beyond the federal directives in its level of detail, illustrating the type of micromanaging control Tkachev used to keep his administration in check. It included requirements for advertising the deadline for employer applications, posting sample applications to assist employers, and required that the list of employers granted quota be posted on the website of the Office of Interaction with Public Associations.[19] The order directed workers to answer phone calls politely, to give their full names, and to limit phone calls to 10 minutes. There were also instructions on how applications should be assembled for review by the commission, by compiling them into a journal that would be sewn together with the pages numbered in a specific way.

Comparing attention to detail in regional legislation across cases can give us a sense of government capacity and legal activism. In Krasnodar, Governor's Order No. 363 on the interdepartmental commission was amended 9 times between 2007 and 2013, primarily reflecting changes in the composition of the commission due to personnel changes in different departments. Contrast this to the commission in Sverdlovsk, which experienced a number of de facto personnel changes during the quota period but was not updated between 2003 and 2012, and then only after the Sofrygin scandal. This shows that the government in Krasnodar exercised tighter administrative coordination and control over how its agencies and committees functioned. This is further illustrated by the level of detail required of bureaucrats in Governor's Order No. 298. Despite its temporary nature, the order provides a window into the mentality of administrative control and the level of detail that both employers and bureaucrats were required to adhere to in the course of the quota process.

When I spoke with a bureaucrat who had previously held a leadership role on the interdepartmental commission, he expressed the opinion that controlling immigration through the quota was an essential part of migration management. From his perspective, the more control the government could exert over the migration process, the more controlled the situation would be in reality. His perspective not only indicated a preference for bureaucratic management over market mechanisms but also demonstrated a feeling of efficacy and capacity on the part of the bureaucracy. He explained that the regional government had gone to great lengths to inform employers about the application process for quota, and even helped employers fill out applications. He said the quota mechanism in Krasnodar was not controversial in part because the number of job vacancies was higher than the number of migrants. While this was true for 2010–11 (the two years prior to our interview), it was not true in many other years, though the number of migrants in all years *is* far lower than the unemployed population,

Table 7.2. Labour market pressures, Krasnodar

	2007	2008	2009	2010	2011	2012	2013	2014
Starting quota	113,535	27,920	48,012	25,098	43,013	28,299	28,066	22,599
Year-end		54,324	45,271	44,927	46,971	72,608	61,722	33,420
Work permits	44,258	72,654	62,388	45,988	40,008	54,364	51,496	27,654
(% of quota)	(39%)	(134%)	(138%)	(102%)	(85%)	(75%)	(83%)	(83%)
Vacancies	49,181	42,323	32,559	53,219	67,266	33,600	54,281	—
Unemployed	166,400	126,200	189,600	174,100	154,000	146,761	160,020	149,000

Source: Rostrud 2010c; Rostrud 2011a; Rostrud 2014b; Rostrud 2015b; Minzdrav/Mintrud orders defining yearly regional allocation and mid-year adjustments.

which would presumably have a similar effect of alleviating fears related to the unemployment myth (see table 7.2).

Quota Trends

Observing the quota from year to year, along with mid-year adjustments, reveals a very curious phenomenon in Krasnodar (see table 7.3). In most years, the quota starts out significantly lower than its year-end level. This is particularly interesting, considering the level of legal activism over the quota process. If all aspects of the quota process are managed so closely, why such drastic mid-year adjustments are needed is a puzzle. Within-year quota fluctuation indicates a certain disconnection between bureaucratic intent and reality. Even if we allow for some coordination foibles when a new agency (the Department of Labour) took over the quota formulation process in 2013, it does not explain within-year variation up until 2013.

One might surmise that a lower quota number at the beginning of the year, when quota numbers were more widely publicized, would be more palatable to the public.[20] The regional administration could then use mid-year quota adjustments to better meet real labour demand, maximizing the populist potential of quotas. For the most part, increases in quota within a given year were distributed equally across sectors, denoted by most sectors having a similar percentage of the regional quota at the beginning and end of each year (see table 7.4). The construction, agriculture, and manufacturing sectors consistently received the highest allocations of quota, both at the beginning of the year and throughout the mid-year adjustments.

Table 7.3. Mid-year quota adjustments, Krasnodar

	2007	2008	2009	2010	2011	2012	2013	2014
Starting quota	113,535	27,920	48,012	25,098	43,013	28,299	28,066	22,599
1st revision					43,430	52,828	50,614	
2nd revision		38,891		42,483		65,859	60,611	28,371
3rd revision			45,271	44,927			66,738	31,513
4th revision		54,324			46,971	72,608		31,728
5th revision							61,722	32,545
6th revision								32,454
7th revision								34,308
8th revision								34,267
9th revision								33,420

Source: Minzdrav/Mintrud orders defining yearly regional allocation and mid-year adjustments.
Note: number of revisions reflect federal-level activity, though individual regions did not adjust quota with every revision

The predominance of construction as an overwhelming majority of the migrant labour market is not surprising, given the massive construction and infrastructure projects undertaken in preparation for the 2014 Sochi Olympics. Russia's Olympic bid was approved in 2007, and from 2008 the state construction company Olimpstroi and the non-profit organization Orgkomitet (Organizing Committee) were allowed to hire foreign workers outside the quota.[21] Workers hired by other companies for projects such as hotels and restaurants were subject to quotas under the regular procedures. In 2011, an UFMS representative projected that, of the 28,000 work permits allotted at the beginning of 2012, 15,000 would be used for workers involved in construction in Sochi.[22] That year, 24,445 work permits were allocated for the construction industry throughout Krasnodar (see table 7.4), meaning that 61% were marked for work in Sochi (according to the official projection).

Since there is no official data on how many work permits were issued in each sector after 2010, it is difficult to verify these projections.[23] At the beginning of 2013, migration officials estimated that around 16,000 migrant workers were employed on construction sites in Sochi.[24] Other estimates from migration experts in the region, and the presidential envoy to the Southern Federal District, placed the figure closer to 50,000–70,000 foreign workers (Memorial and Grazhdanskoe Sodeistvie 2014). Workers were regularly employed through subcontractors,

Table 7.4. Quota allocation by sector, Krasnodar

	2008	2009	2010	2011	2012	2013	2014
Starting quota	27,920	48,012	25,098	43,013	28,299	28,066	22,599
Year-end quota	54,324	45,271	44,927	46,971	72,608	61,722	33,420
AGRICULTURE							
Approved quota (% total quota)	—	3,177 (7%)	2,807 (11%)	5,324 (12%)	2,213 (8%)	2,050 (7%)	3,876 (12%)
Year-end	3,533 (7%)	—	5,050 (11%)	5,033 (11%)	4,493 (6%)	4,603 (7%)	4,060 (13%)
Work permits issued (% quota)	5,098 (144%)	—	4,346 (86%)	—	—	—	—
MANUFACTURING							
Approved quota (% total quota)	—	1,917 (4%)	789 (3%)	1,648 (4%)	919 (3%)	766 (3%)	3,079 (10%)
Year-end	1,487 (3%)	—	1,504 (3%)	1,768 (4%)	1,561 (2%)	2,740 (4%)	3,109 (10%)
Work permits issued (% quota)	3,811 (256%)	—	3,543 (236%)	—	—	—	—
CONSTRUCTION							
Approved quota (% total quota)	—	41,405 (86%)	20,082 (80%)	33,347 (78%)	24,445 (86%)	24,121 (86%)	20,441 (64%)
Year-end	43,332 (80%)	—	36,043 (80%)	37,292 (79%)	64,355 (86%)	47,397 (77%)	20,721 (64%)
Work permits issued (% quota)	39,778 (92%)	—	28,864 (80%)	—	—	—	—
TRADE							
Approved quota (% total quota)	—	335 (0.7%)	332 (1%)	691 (2%)	59 (0.2%)	280 (1%)	298 (1%)
Year-end	1,409 (3%)	—	412 (1%)	693 (2%)	167 (0.2%)	356 (0.5%)	314 (1%)
Work permits issued (% quota)	640 (45%)	—	2,076 (504%)	—	—	—	—

HOSPITALITY							
Approved quota (% total quota)	—	292 (1%)	356 (1%)	872 (2%)	313 (1%)	518 (2%)	2,142 (7%)
Year-end	460 (1%)	—	871 (2%)	894 (2%)	1,421 (2%)	4,145 (7%)	2,187 (7%)
TRANSPORTATION							
Approved quota (% total quota)	—	62 (0.1%)	51 (0.2%)	181 (0.4%)	1 (0.004%)	23 (0.08%)	308 (1%)
Year-end	88 (0.2%)	—	180 (0.4%)	185 (0.4%)	9 (0.01%)	563 (0.9%)	339 (1%)
Work permits issued (% quota)	640 (727%)	—	460 (256%)	—	—	—	—
REAL ESTATE							
Approved quota (% total quota)	—	529 (1%)	98 (0.4%)	421 (1%)	70 (0.3%)	90 (0.3%)	750 (2%)
Year-end	3,278 (6%)	—	168 (0.4%)	524 (1%)	130 (0.2%)	1,233 (2%)	750 (2%)
SERVICES							
Approved quota (% total quota)	—	63 (0.1%)	143 (0.6%)	302 (0.7%)	174 (0.6%)	178 (0.6%)	659 (2%)
Year-end	411 (1%)	—	310 (0.7%)	317 (0.7%)	358 (0.5%)	358 (0.6%)	799 (3%)

Source: Rosstat 2011a; Rosstat 2009b; Minzdrav/Mintrud orders defining yearly regional allocation and mid-year adjustments; Rostrud spreadsheets

leaving several layers between the contracting and construction companies and migrant workers. Often these subcontractors did not give migrants a contract or proper work documents (e.g., producing a patent instead of a work permit, or not providing any work documents at all). CIS migrants who could theoretically obtain a work permit on their own were frequently told the quota had already been exhausted.

After December 31, 2013, all migrant labourers working on projects deemed necessary by Olimpstroi or the Krasnodar administration were exempted from quotas.[25] This exemption, along with the expectation that most Olympic-related projects would be finished by February 2014, explains the significant decrease in quota allotment for the construction sector from around 80% of total regional quota to just over 60% in 2014 (see table 7.4).

Even though construction companies received far higher shares of the overall quota than other industries across all years, it is important to highlight migrant agricultural workers as a key feature of the Krasnodar economy and labour market. During the quota period, the entire labour force for the construction industry in Krasnodar (migrant and local workers combined) was between 160,000 and 200,000 per year, according to Rosstat data. The agricultural sector dwarfs this labour force, employing around 400,000 workers per year. Nevertheless, agricultural companies received only 6%–13% of Krasnodar's regional quota (see table 7.4).

One of the most consistent recipients of quota was the company Agrokompleks, which received larger quotas than any other business in the agricultural sector. Governor Tkachev's father is on the board of directors of the company, demonstrating how elites close to the governor benefit disproportionately from the migration sector (Shahnazarian 2011).[26] Furthermore, while general trends show decreasing quota, quota for Agrokompleks grew robustly: 80 in 2008 and 2009, 220 in 2010, 240 in 2011 and 2012 (increased to 270 by the end of 2012), 386 (increased to 471) in 2013, and 354 (increased to 425) in 2014.[27] In other words, Agrokompleks received from 2% to 19% of the total agricultural quota during these years and far exceeded the average number of workers allotted per company (see appendix to chapter 7 for more detailed data on quota allocation by sector).

Despite their secondary position in quota allocation, migrant agricultural workers have been a lightning rod for public attention and populist campaigning on the part of the regional government. After 2011, controversy centred on Chinese migrants. The government actively worked to manage public opinion through populism and a variety of migration myths. Yet the persistent presence of Chinese workers demonstrates relative importance of symbolic control measures over and above actual government control.

Chinese Agricultural Workers

Though this book has focused primarily on the policies governing CIS workers, the example of Chinese migrants in Krasnodar is relevant on a number of levels. First, Chinese workers, along with all workers from visa countries, have been under a quota since 2003. During the period 2007–14, when CIS workers were also included in quotas, migrants from visa countries were governed by a sub-quota as discussed in chapter 3. Second, in all periods, visa migrants were under more restrictions than CIS migrants, and were especially dependent on employers not only for work permits but also for visas. Nevertheless, a variety of strategies to bypass government regulations evolved, including entering Russia on a tourist visa and then working without a work permit.

In November 2011, after meeting with the regional Security Council on the issue of migration, Tkachev announced that Chinese migrant workers would not be allowed to work in agriculture as of January 1, 2012. Despite dramatically increased requests by employers for Chinese workers (from zero to 10,000) for 2012, Tkachev announced that "we have denied them quota and I demand strict control of the situation."[28] The justification for the ban was based on investigations of the working and living conditions of the migrant workers as well as questionable agricultural practices.[29]

The timing of Tkachev's announcement is curious. According to federal and regional laws, regional quota recommendations must be submitted to the federal authorities by July 15 each year. This means that any decisions made about Chinese farm workers for 2012 had been made months before Tkachev's announcement. On July 14, in response to an exposé in *Rossiiskaia Gazeta* about Chinese workers in Krasnodar, UFMS head Semeniakin tried to allay public fears by stating that Chinese citizens had only received 502 work permits in 2009, 697 in 2010, and 1,389 in 2011. He made no mention that a ban would be enacted in the following year, even though his statement came only one day before the interdepartmental commission (of which he is a part) were to submit their quota requests to the federal level. If a ban had been enacted by the commission, Semeniakin would have been able to verify it at the time of his statements. His silence on this detail could reflect a desire to be aligned with the centre and keep any potential conflict or negotiation between regional and federal authorities out of the public eye. Therefore if the ban had already been approved at the regional level, it was announced only after federal authorities issued projected regional quota allocations on November 3. In all other years, Krasnodar kept to a similar pattern of waiting until the end to announce the following year's quota allocations. Contrast this pattern to Sverdlovsk's early July announcement in 2013 (after the Sofrygin scandal, when the government was concerned with transparency), when officials discussed the 2014 quota in great detail, including specifying companies that were denied quota for various reasons. This announcement came before Sverdlovsk's quota request was even submitted to federal authorities.

Another potential explanation is that the commission did not pass a ban on Chinese workers, as such, and it was more of populist strategy of Tkachev than an actual policy. Despite his resolute pronouncement, the mechanism of how a ban like this would work is unclear. There was no specific document declaring an official ban on Chinese workers, and at the time the quota distribution did not specify a migrant's country of origin. According to federal instructions, quota could be allocated according to profession, region, and country of origin, yet how country of origin should factor into quota distribution remained unclear. Federal regulations specified that employer applications could be rejected for a variety of reasons, none of which included country of origin; yet at the same time regional governments were directed to consider country of origin in the overall quota estimation. From 2007, when the forms for employer applications were adopted, there were blanks for workers' countries of origin, though until 2014 this information did not appear in the Rostrud spreadsheets specifying quota allocation. In 2014, six companies in Krasnodar received permission to hire a total of 24 Chinese workers as chefs, sports instructors, and massage therapists, but no agricultural workers.

Even before federal authorities included country of origin information in quota allocation, country of origin could conceivably be used at the regional level to decide which companies would be assigned quota. It is therefore possible that the interdepartmental commission could enforce a zero quota simply by not granting quota to employers who requested Chinese workers, even in the absence of an official published ban. This seems to be the mechanism the Krasnodar government pursued, given a 2013 statement by UFMS head Semeniakin claiming that for the previous two years the interdepartmental commission had not allocated any quota for Chinese agricultural workers.[30] What is surprising about this statement is that it comes from the UFMS, which in other regions adheres only loosely to the commission's quota recommendations, as discussed in chapter 3 and indicated in many regions by a higher number of work permits issued than quota allocated. Semeniakin's statements point to a much more highly coordinated administration than in either Moscow or Sverdlovsk. However, Krasnodar also issued more work permits than quota allocation in some years, indicating that the projection of coordination was more important than its actual fact. This is powerful evidence that the symbolic control produced by populist politicians is far more important than actual control through enforcement.

A variety of reports indicate that whatever ban on Chinese workers was in place did not have the promised effect. In 2012 there were rumours that the use of illegal Chinese agricultural workers was widespread throughout Russia, especially in Krasnodar and regions in the Urals and Siberia.[31] In 2013, the issue became even more visible in Krasnodar when 23 Chinese citizens were arrested for having work permits issued in the neighbouring region of Karachay-Cherkessia.[32] Also in 2013, an audit was announced on the Chinese company Lun Fei, which had received quota in the December 2011 amendment to the 2011 quota, clearing them to hire 87 foreign workers, including one commercial director, 81 vegetable workers, 3 translators, and 2 chefs. This means Lun Fei was granted quota after the ban on Chinese workers for 2012 was announced by Tkachev in November 2011. Since quota allocations at the time (outlined in the Rostrud spreadsheets) did not specify a worker's country of origin, it is possible that Lun Fei could have applied for workers from other countries. Nevertheless, that they were not allocated quota in 2012 or any year following is a telling indicator that the workers they intended to hire were indeed Chinese.

From November 2012 to November 2013, 82 separate court cases were opened against Lun Fei or its workers. Sixty cases were against individual Chinese citizens, specifying immigration or work document violations. In all of the cases, the defendants pled guilty and were given a fine of 2,000 rubles along with deportation orders.[33] A number of cases were against the company itself, either for violations of sanitary norms or for employment of illegal foreign workers. In the cases against the company, the penalty levied was a suspension of selected activities for a period of 60–90 days rather than the hefty fines outlined in migration law.

In May 2013, an illegal Chinese farm was discovered in the Dinskoi district approximately 40 kilometres from the capital city of Krasnodar. Inspectors found a number of sanitary violations and 85 workers without proper work permits. In response, UFMS head Semeniakin stated that all Chinese workers in Krasnodar were illegal because of the ban. Plans were announced to deport the workers after they paid a 2,000-ruble fine and were given a 5-year re-entry ban. The media reported that fines were also planned for the owners of the business (which was not named), to be decided by the courts.[34] In July 2013, over 200 Chinese agricultural workers were arrested in Dinskoi, and the UFMS announced fines for the (again unnamed) employers in the sum of 250,000–800,000 rubles per illegal worker (Krasnodar UFMS 2013). In August 2013, more than 30 additional illegal Chinese agricultural workers were arrested in Dinskoi.[35] Court records in the Dinskoi district from April to August 2013 show 333 new cases related to immigration violations by individuals in the Dinskoi district, all of which concluded with rulings of administrative violations.[36] No cases were opened against any employers for immigration-related violations during this period.

Tkachev again promised in 2013 that "next year [2014] there will not even be one Chinese person in the region!" Yet in 2014, he decried "shocking" Chinese agricultural practices in the region, warning that "if we don't stop this flow [of Chinese migrants] today, tomorrow it may be too late."[37] His statements indicate that the problem was ongoing, and despite repeated immigration raids and prosecutions, the ban on Chinese agricultural workers had not reached its goal.[38]

The issue of Chinese migrants illustrates that, despite having a coordinated administration, where the interdepartmental commission planning quotas and the UFMS distributing quotas claimed to work towards the same end, the quota mechanism did not actualize migration control. As long as economic demand persisted, workers were willing to work without proper documents, and employers were willing to hire undocumented workers, illegal migration continued. The events further illustrate a pattern of a populist rhetoric backed up by a securitized immigration approach, yet little actual progress in implementing policy promises, primarily due to the type of corruption that is pervasive in the region.

The Socio-Political Context of Migration

Corruption

Despite a lack of direct evidence for quota-related schemes, examples of migration-related corruption schemes in Krasnodar are ample, which is a symptom of widespread regional corruption. A variety of sources have consistently ranked Krasnodar as having one of the highest levels of corruption in Russia (Derluguian and Cipko 1997; Shahnazarian 2011; Transparency International Russia 2002).[39] Numerous exposés about corruption connected to the development of Sochi for the Olympic Games reveal a regional climate ripe for a variety of schemes (Nemtsov and Martyniuk 2013).

In addition to the typical bribe-related schemes, I heard of a particular case in Krasnodar of a migrant who had false identification documents but avoided arrest by doing renovation projects at the house of a police investigator, using his labour as a bribe so that he could remain in Russia.[40] Police and labour inspectors are also frequently bribed to overlook employment violations, such as cases when employers confiscate the documents of migrants and restrict their movements.

Another scheme involved the fairly common practice of crossing the nearest border, getting a new migration card, and returning to Russia. Until 2013, a new migration card would reset a CIS migrant's period of legal stay for another 90 days. There was nothing illegal about this practice, though a number of informal practices evolved in support of it. One was that migrants would send their passports across the border with a friend or family member so that they could receive a new migration card without actually leaving their work and life in Russia. While this practice was risky from the perspective of migrants because they were left without documents for a period of time, the bigger issue was that border officials were complicit in the scheme if they issued migration cards for people who were not physically present. There was also a corruption scheme in Krasnodar where migrants were bussed to the port of Kavkaz, near the Ukrainian border, and given new documents while they remained on the bus, though they never actually crossed the border. This type of scheme again necessarily involved state agents (border officials) because they must stamp/validate the migration card.

Finally, the migration sector was full of intermediaries that arranged paperwork for migrants. Often intermediaries had concrete links to bureaucratic officials and were able to use those connections to obtain work permits. One such organization is the Krasnodar Intergovernmental Migration Centre (Krasnodarskii Mezhgosudarstvennyi Migratsionnyi Tsentr, or KMMTs). KMMTs is a private for-profit business run by the wives of migration officials and located next door to the UFMS.[41] There is nothing illegal or corrupt about offering fee-based services to facilitate migration documents. In this case, however, corruption comes from the benefits that come from from personal relationships with the UFMS and because the migration officials who help their wives process the documents share in the profits. To migrants, the benefit of using this type of organization is that the documents are official and real. As an alternative, there are numerous schemes that provide false documents for migrants.[42]

The type of petty corruption present in Krasnodar is a sign of a robust internal patronage network. It is common for spoils to be paid up the chain of command, and sometimes higher officials give informal "quotas" for how much should be collected in proceeds. Therefore, officials from the lower levels of bureaucracy up to the governor's office are complicit in keeping corrupt practices functioning *and* insulating participants from being discovered or held accountable for their actions. Even the director of an anti-corruption NGO in Krasnodar admitted that it is often difficult to uncover the specific mechanisms of corruption in the region because they are intricately woven into norms of reciprocity and patterns of mutual benefit.[43] In this context it is not only difficult for civil society to discover corruption schemes but also nearly impossible to produce any real accountability because government actors at all levels have a vested interest in keeping the system closed and seamlessly functioning.

Civil Society

I found the community of migrant experts in Krasnodar very different from those in Moscow or Sverdlovsk. It was smaller and more diffuse, consisting of just a few lawyers, scholars, and human rights activists. In only a few cases did these individuals work for an NGO with full-time staff members. While activists were well connected to counterparts in Moscow through networks such as Memorial, their ability to engage the regional government was extremely limited. In several cases, people I had hoped to contact had recently moved out of the region to avoid pressure from regional authorities. Several of those who stayed endured arrests and interrogations on several occasions.

In this context, less institutionalized diaspora organizations played a bigger, though sometimes reluctant, role in migrant affairs. One diaspora leader, after discussing the migration situation in Krasnodar, told me that his organization was not engaged in migration issues. He emphasized that, as a diaspora organization, its focus was on the preservation of culture and traditions, though it tried to help migrants if they came to the group with complaints. While there are numerous formal and informal diaspora groups in Krasnodar, being listed as an officially registered national-cultural association requires a group to focus its activities on promotion of cultural traditions as its primary purpose (Savva and Tishkov 2011). Having a program that includes cultural activities such as the celebration of holidays, language lessons for children, etc. is important for these organizations to be able to secure and retain government funding, which is usually allocated through grant competitions. Given the close control that Tkachev's government exercises over administrative affairs, it is likely that grant applications are heavily scrutinized, and if a group strays outside the narrowest definition of acceptable activities, its funding would be threatened. As we will see shortly, this type of strategy by the regional government is consistent with its attempts to limit activities that are related to human rights and advocacy.

While I was in Krasnodar, I attended a roundtable that brought together diaspora leaders, civil society actors, and government representatives from the migration services and police as well as a representative from the migration service of Tajikistan. My impression, both from the tenor of the meeting and from the news coverage, was that this type of meeting was not a frequent occurrence.[44] The roundtable seemed to reflect true engagement between government and civil society actors, because officials from the UFMS and the Office of Interaction with Public Associations stayed for the entire meeting and even attended a reception hosted by diaspora leaders afterward. Through the contacts I made at this roundtable, I was able to meet with representatives of various government agencies, including the UFMS. This demonstrates that in a smaller system (i.e., compared with Moscow), there is a greater chance for people in government and civil society to know one another, and have personal ties. Yet in the Krasnodar case, close acquaintance is not necessarily always positive, since active migrant advocates can come under greater scrutiny from the authorities. For example, an activist I met in the Sochi area had numerous encounters with police in the course of advocating primarily for Central Asian citizens.

The most severe example of government pressure on migration activists is the case of Professor Mikhail Savva.[45] Savva was an active researcher and member of the academic community in the city of Krasnodar, focusing on interethnic relations and the integration of migrants. From 2001 he was the director of the Southern Regional Resource Centre and in this capacity conducted research projects and organized roundtables. He regularly engaged both regional and federal government organs to advocate for migrant rights, human rights more generally, and anti-corruption measures. Towards these goals, from 2005 Savva served on a variety of Public Councils (i.e., the Governor's Council for Human Rights, and the Advisory Committee to the Ministry of Internal Affairs). In the course of his work, he became an outspoken critic of the Tkachev administration.

Savva was arrested on the eve of a trip to Moscow in April 2013. He was scheduled to speak at a Public Chamber hearing on politically motivated inspections of NGOs. He was charged with embezzlement of public funds related to the grants received by the Southern Regional Resource Centre and held in pre-trial detention for 8 months. After a further 4 months of house arrest, a guilty verdict was passed down along with a conditional sentence of 3 years, with 2 years of probation and a fine of 70,000 rubles ($2,000 at the time), a sentence that was upheld upon appeal. After being released from house arrest, Savva resumed his normal activities until it became clear that the regional government planned to bring new charges, at which point he fled Russia and applied for refugee status through the United Nations High Commissioner for Refugees.

Though Savva was supported by the human rights community within Russia and abroad, he had little support from the regional ombudsman. Considering the positive and active role played by the regional ombudsman in Sverdlovsk, this makes for an interesting comparison. At the time, the ombudsman was Alexander Kozitskii, who declined to comment on the issue.[46] Kozitskii was replaced in June 2013 by Sergei Myshak, formerly of the Office of Interaction with Public Associations, which had no human rights duties but was actively involved in migration issues, as discussed earlier in the chapter. Myshak also took an aloof stance. When questioned about the Savva case, he said he would not want to challenge the court's decision because "first of all, the office of the ombudsman is a government agency …" indicating he did not believe it was his place to contradict court officials, regardless of any violations of human rights.[47] He went on to say that Savva had access to the appellate process both within Russia and through the European Court of Human Rights, but did not acknowledge any responsibility for assisting in this process. The federal ombudsman's office, by contrast, had advocated for Savva receiving a reduced sentence.

As an insider (having held a variety of positions throughout the region, all of which depended on the appointment of the governor and/or regional legislature), Myshak was unwilling to challenge the authorities prosecuting Savva. In his previous position as the head of the Office of Interaction with Public Associations, Myshak developed a reputation for being tough on opposition and protest movements. Many speculate that he was given the position of ombudsman simply because of his loyalty to Tkachev (who frequently rotated his cadre of loyal supporters to various positions throughout the region).[48] Myshak's orientation towards the Savva case demonstrates the limits of insiders' ability to criticize the regional government and the importance of producing loyalty to the patronage system over justice or the protection of rights.

In the context of the Sochi Olympics, there was increased international scrutiny of both the migration situation and corruption. It tended to focus either on the micro-level (i.e., violations of migrant rights by unnamed employers or bureaucrats) or on the involvement of federal-level elites, rather than on implicating specific regional actors. Therefore, even when the world's eyes were on Russia, media and human rights activists were not able to penetrate or expose the corrupt patronage networks active in Krasnodar.

Public Opinion and the Populist Potential of Migration Management

Given the documented pattern of discrimination against minorities, I was surprised to find that the public attitude towards migrants from Central Asia was more or less calm in Krasnodar. A leader of the Tajik diaspora reported that in the preceding 10 years, relations between migrants, law enforcement, and the population had been quite good, and negative incidents were rare.[49] During my fieldwork, I found the orientation towards foreigners more complex than simply a generalized intolerance.

One dynamic I noticed is that public ill-will often focused on internal migrants and minorities (i.e., those from Chechnya and Dagestan) rather than on migrants from Central Asia. There are also complex relationships between the Russian majority and minorities from the Southern Caucasus (i.e., Armenia, Azerbaijan, and Georgia). The primary difference between migrants from Central Asia and those from Armenia, for example, is that the former are temporary labour migrants (and therefore have an impact on patent and quota numbers), whereas the latter are generally long-term migrants who eventually stay and get citizenship. Most locals and experts I interviewed acknowledged and accepted the multiethnic character of Krasnodar that is readily apparent on the streets, providing a stark contrast to the region's reputation for intolerance.

A group of university-aged Russian locals I spoke with expressed the idea that though they had latent negative feelings towards minority groups, they struggled to reconcile traditional attitudes with their experiences and their more progressive beliefs that all people have equal value.[50] Latent negativities are often transmitted through families, the school system, and the media, which demonstrates the power of elites to form public opinion both through the media and through official statements.

Though the quota mechanism had some populist utility in Krasnodar, as argued earlier in this chapter, the public was not as informed about the details of quota formulation as in Moscow or Sverdlovsk. Because of the closed nature in Krasnodar of politics generally and the quota formulation process specifically, the public was given a very imprecise impression of the quota process, which the regional leaders could use to their advantage.[51] On the whole, there is very little to indicate that the public was aware of fluctuations in the quota, especially within each year. This could have to do with a more passive attitude towards politics, or it could be a result of the fact that there is very little publicity about quota numbers in the local media.[52] Though the media often reports on migrant-related issues, coverage rarely discusses the mechanisms that are used to control migration (i.e., quota or patents). When more technical information is included, it is often based on an imprecise conception of migration data that furthers the anti-migrant tenor of the reporting. One extreme example is a report that in 2013 there were 1.3 million labour migrants in Krasnodar, a figure that does not correspond to any official migration figures from 2013.[53] This type of data reporting is a common strategy of populists, who use imprecise and sometimes completely false data to make an emotional appeal to the public. Often the veracity of the data is secondary, or even irrelevant, to the populist goals of the message.

Through vague or imprecise data, regional officials can capitalize on the public's lack of awareness about quotas for populist purposes.

Examples of anti-migrant populism linking migrants to increasing crime rates, health risks, and upsets to the local labour markets are numerous in the region, evoking the full bevy of security and unemployment migration myths.[54] While the rhetoric and the mechanisms of migration control often do not match, as seen in the example of the Chinese agricultural workers, the power of populism comes from its emotional appeal rather than its grounding in reality. This is powerfully illustrated by the fact that of our case studies, the region that exercises the greatest bureaucratic controls is no better able to manage the actual migration process. However, the efforts of the regional government to use populist anti-migrant rhetoric to appeal to the public are an important part of constructing a sense of regional stability. Evidence for the thesis of this book is ample in Krasnodar: as long as stability is preserved, regional actors can use migration resources however they choose. Through the mechanisms of a highly coordinated and controlled administration stocked with loyal insiders, and a civil society kept weak by various forms of subtle or overt pressure, the regional government both allows corruption to flourish and insulates its members from accountability.

Patents

The shift to patents in Krasnodar was marked by a surprising level of neglect on the part of regional officials. There were no efforts to create state-affiliated migration centres or coordinate the patent process in any way. In its annual report for 2015, the UFMS acknowledged that there was no official list of testing facilities for the language exams because the regional Ministry of Education was still deliberating over the issue (Krasnodar UFMS 2016). Given the tendency of the regional government to micromanage administrative coordination, this delay is out of character. By not moving to maximize patent revenues, the regional government shows some resistance to the federal government's project of state capitalism.

In fact, Krasnodar demonstrated a fairly dramatic inability to adapt to new patent procedures, which garnered the attention of federal elites. In April, the President's Council for Human Rights (Sovet pri Prezidente Rossiiskoi Federatsii po razvitiiu grazhdanskogo obshchestva i pravam cheloveka) penned a letter to FMS director Konstantin Romodanovskii in response to a video posted on YouTube, which showed migrants in Krasnodar being "rudely ejected from the premises."[55] The FMS acknowledged in turn that the Krasnodar UFMS did not have the facilities to serve all of the migrants seeking patents. They noted that the nearly 70,000 patents issued in 2014 were expiring between January and April of 2015, and in addition 27,000 migrants who had received work permits in 2014 would also need to transfer over to patents. This was a surprising admission that labour demand in Krasnodar had not decreased, despite the completion of Olympic preparations. The FMS response went on to detail several changes that would be made by the Krasnodar UFMS, including delegating the issuing of patents to 7 branches throughout the region.[56]

That patents would be issued at 7 locations, instead of one, highlights a very important point, made more poignant in the words of an UFMS official in Sochi in response to the changes: "This is beneficial because it means people will not have to go from Sochi to Krasnodar (city), 300 kilometres there, 300 kilometres back, stand in line, return, and go back once again to pick up the documents."[57] Up until March 2015, all patents were issued through one office in Krasnodar (city). Though prior to 2015 patents were issued in various locations throughout the region, operations were consolidated at the end of 2014.[58] This likely reflects a desire to increase control over the migration process alongside an assumption that foreign labour would decrease after the 2014 Olympics. It does not, however, show an effort to maximize patent revenues.

The regional government, in an effort to balance migration interests, found itself in a difficult spot once the Olympics ended and patents were expanded. In many ways it was stuck between federal prerogatives of state capitalism and populist promises to reduce immigration. The regional government made lofty promises about the decrease in migrant workers after the Olympics, much akin to the type of control rhetoric used in regard to Chinese agricultural workers. Yet again we see that populist rhetoric combined with increasingly strict policy and enforcement does not produce actual immigration control. It is clear from official statistics that once other regional offices started issuing patents, the numbers rose substantially (see table 7.5), and therefore reports of long lines at migration offices continued.[59]

Nearly 50,000 patents were issued by the end of 2015, representing an almost 50% decrease in total documented labour migrants compared to 2014 (see table 7.1). Though there is no official data reporting how much tax revenue was earned from patents in 2014, based on UFMS reports of the number of patents issued monthly, the maximum possible revenue was 445 million rubles for 2014. This sum is based on what

Table 7.5. Patents issued by month, 2015, Krasnodar

	January	February	March	April	May	June
Patents (cumulative)	1,804 (1,804)	744 (2,548)	4,857 (7,405)	9,590 (16,995)	9,293 (26,288)	5,134 (31,422)
	July	August	September	October	November	December
Patents (cumulative)	4,363 (35,785)	2,883 (38,668)	2,599 (41,267)	2,426 (43,693)	2,346 (46,039)	3,392 (49,431)

Source: UFMS regional statistics.

migrants would have paid if they kept their patents paid and valid from the time of issue until the end of the year. The actual revenue is likely lower, accounting for seasonal workers and those who did not pay the monthly taxes.

For 2015, an official of the Krasnodar UFMS stated that around 900 million rubles had been collected in taxes from patents, showing a substantial increase in revenues over 2014, consistent with national-level trends.[60] Yet the figure of 900 million rubles is slightly suspicious, given that earlier statements by officials claimed that around 600 million rubles was collected from patents issued from January to September 2015 (Krasnodar UFMS 2015).[61] If the maximum possible revenue from the final three months of 2015 is added to the figure of 600 million cited by the UFMS, actual revenues would be nearer 650 million rubles.[62] However, if *all* migrants remained in Krasnodar from the time they received their patents until the end of the year and remained fully tax compliant, the maximum revenue would total 956 million rubles. This maximum revenue would only be possible if migrants submitted a contract in order to prolong their stay beyond two months. Since only 32,314 migrants submitted contracts in 2015, the maximum revenue is not possible.[63] Even if all of these contracts were submitted early in the year, with the corresponding migrants remaining in Russia and fully tax compliant for the rest of the year, the maximum possible revenue would be 877 million rubles.[64] Though this figure corresponds with the reported "around 900 million rubles," it is highly unlikely that this picture of full and maximum compliance (i.e., a high rate of contract submission, and practically no tax evasion) corresponds with reality. Because the 900 million ruble figure was announced in February 2016 but not included in the 2015 annual report, it suggests some retroactive massaging of the numbers to demonstrate maximum compliance with the federal prerogative of state capitalism. Again we see that in Krasnodar, the façade of control and implementation is more important than its actual fact. Data manipulation like this is not uncommon in Russia, often motivated by the need to meet the expectations and goals of higher-level officials (Kalgin 2016).

The case for data misrepresentation and lax enforcement is strengthened when we consider the number of patents that were annulled or employment contracts terminated. The UFMS reported that in 2015, 28 patents were annulled and 8,903 employment contracts were terminated. If all 28 annulments resulted from not submitting an employment contract, all of the migrants who did not submit a contract (around

17,000) either left the region within two months or continued working on their original patent but remained undetected by audits like those that occurred in the Sverdlovsk case. Likewise, the 8,903 migrants whose contracts were terminated either had to submit a new contract (since working for a third party is grounds for annulment of a patent),[65] leave the country, or continue working on their original patent and hope they could avoid detection. Both of these data points dramatically reduce the number of patent-receiving migrants who remained legally compliant.

The picture is even more stark when the number of patents is compared to registrations. In 2015, 514,642 foreigners registered at temporary locations (places of stay) in Krasnodar (compared to 484,061 in 2014). Of these, 454,939 (88%) came without a visa (compared with 405,095, or 84%, in 2014). It is important to take into account that some of these foreigners could be in Russia for the purpose of tourism (Russia allows visa-free travel for tourists from a select few countries), or in the context of the Eurasian Economic Union (which allows free movement and work for citizens of Belarus, Kazakhstan, Kyrgyzstan, and Armenia), though exact data for these subsets is not available.[66] Nevertheless, the broader point should not be overlooked: *more* foreigners went to Krasnodar in 2015 than in 2014, despite the Olympics in 2014 and the end of Olympic-related construction, yet we see a nearly 50% drop in the number of documented labour migrants. This is despite the fact that 34% of foreigners (174,978) in 2015 declared their purpose of visit as work (Krasnodar UFMS 2016). In other words, only 28% of those foreigners entering Krasnodar with intent to work received a patent.

Low numbers of documented labour migrants, coupled with a comparatively undeveloped infrastructure for issuing and monitoring patents, indicate a continuation of Krasnodar's heavy-handed migration management that is interested first and foremost in the appearance of control and compliance with the federal government's priorities, but does not produce real results. This strategy produces the on-paper administrative discipline required of the migration pact, and actively utilizes the spoils of migration management to meet regional goals. While this tactic worked relatively well during the quota era, it produces lacklustre adherence to the Kremlin's state capitalism project. While patent revenues have indeed increased in 2015, there has been no effort to either marginalize or institutionalize the intermediary market by bringing it closer to the state. The KMMTs carried on its activities and made little effort to expand operations by offering one-stop services akin to the Moscow Multifunctional Migration Centre. The end result is that scarcity of legal labour has increased substantially, though the revenue brought in by patents required padding in order to meet with federal approval.

Conclusion

In Krasnodar we see a closely controlled administrative structure under Governor Tkachev, who not only had a wide-reaching patronage network but also produced the stability that was of paramount importance to the Kremlin, especially around the time of the Sochi Olympics in 2014. These factors allowed for migration management that could be used to suit the needs of regional elites. However, the end of the Sochi Olympics brought migration fatigue, and the issue received less attention. Part of this is owing to a new administration, which has been silent on any issue related to migration, choosing to discontinue Tkachev's patterns of flagrant anti-migration populism.

When Tkachev was moved to Moscow to take up the position of minister of agriculture in April 2015, he was replaced by Krasnodar insider Veniamin Kondrat'ev. Kondrat'ev spent the majority of his career in the regional administration, including a long stint as the deputy governor in charge of property relations, where he maintained a low public profile. In January 2014, he moved to Moscow to take up an appointment as deputy head of the Department of Federal Property Management of the President of the Russian Federation. He was appointed to head of that department a year later. After a further promotion to deputy manager of presidential affairs in March 2015, he was appointed acting governor of Krasnodar in April until the time of his election to the post in September, which he secured with 83% of the vote.[67] The appointment of Kondrat'ev signals the Kremlin's need for a loyal insider who is well connected to regional networks. Not only had Kondrat'ev built up his own networks and proved useful to the regional elite in Krasnodar, but he also proved loyal to the Kremlin's aims during the delicate task of managing property related to the Sochi Olympics.

The Tkachev period demonstrated a well-functioning migration pact that benefited both federal patrons and regional clients. The use of populism is particularly evident, and shows how rhetoric can be used both to justify policies (in the case of Chinese agricultural workers) and to manage public opinion. Yet populist rhetoric need not be related to demonstrable results in the migration arena, shown by the fact that the public remained largely unaware of implementation gaps that persisted. The projection of control (i.e., reduced immigration), rather than control itself, is the more important goal of populism. Tkachev also presented a coordinated political system, and implemented federal prerogatives by creating legal labour scarcity first through quotas and then through patents. Not only did regional elites close to Tkachev benefit from the management of these scarce resources, but the federal government was able to utilize the comparative advantage of cheap illegal labour to build the infrastructure necessary for the 2014 Sochi Olympics. In this case, the spoils of migration management came not only from corruption schemes associated with the distribution of documents but also from the widespread use of illegal labour itself by state-associated elites and businesses.

Conclusion

In March 2016, newswires erupted with the story of an Uzbek nanny standing at a busy Moscow metro station waving the severed head of a child and shouting, "I am a terrorist!" Giul'chekhra Bobokulova was an illegal migrant from Uzbekistan. She claimed that her actions had been ordered by Allah in retaliation for Muslims killed by Russian air strikes in Syria. As the mother of small children, I read the news coverage with repulsion and empathy for the child's parents. As a scholar of immigration politics in Russia, my dread was only increased as I feared that the actions of one mentally unstable woman would be used to mobilize a rash of anti-migrant sentiment. This type of event could easily be used to evoke a number of migration myths at once, and indeed nationalist voices were quick to place blame on Islam, make links to terrorism, and call for increased immigration controls.[1]

Anti-immigration populism reached a new peak globally in 2016, becoming an increasingly salient factor in the domestic politics of many major immigrant-receiving countries, stoking fear and justifying strict policies. Fear-based media framings of immigration fuelled anti-immigrant populists, and populist rhetoric became an essential feature of the electoral process. In the UK and the US, populism created a perfect storm, leading to shocking political outcomes such as the Brexit referendum and the election of Donald Trump. Right-wing and mainstream media alike were quick to portend the potential effect of these developments for elections, including the possibility that outsiders such as Norbert Hofer in Austria, Marine Le Pen in France, and Geert Wilders in the Netherlands might be elected. Mainstream media became increasingly sensitized to (and at the same time reinforced) the spectre of the looming right-wing threat, running headlines such as "Angela Merkel's party beaten by right-wing populists in German elections."[2]

While mainstream media stoked fears of right-wing trends sweeping Europe, it was not neutral in its framings of migrants. An alarming case in point was the 2016 coverage of New Year's Eve events in Cologne, Germany. Mainstream international media sources were quick to link a rash of sexual attacks on women to the influx of refugees: "As Germany welcomes migrants, sexual attacks in Cologne point to a new reality."[3] "Reports of attacks on women in Germany heighten tension over migrants,"[4] and "Cologne attacks show Germany unprepared for migration challenge."[5] Several news sources that did not link the attacks to migrants in Germany were criticized for covering up the ethnic background of attackers (of North African and Arab descent).[6]

After a number of other highly publicized incidents of migrant-related crime (some of which were based on "fake news"), German Chancellor Angela Merkel made an appeal to citizens to "stick to the known facts."[7] Government data did not demonstrate a surge of crime after Germany's decision to accept over 1 million refugees. But the different sides interpreted the facts in vastly different ways by focusing on different data points. For example, using government data, one side claimed that "non-Germans" were overrepresented in criminal activities (based on their percentage in the population), while the other side claimed that migrants were less likely to commit crimes than Germans.[8] Notwithstanding the limits of even the best data to present an objectively constructed assessment (Merry 2016; Andreas and Greenhill 2011), in an era of post-truth populism, the seemingly rational basis of government data is no match for subjective interpretations filtered through fear and ideological preconceptions on all sides of the spectrum.[9]

The politics of fear frames the question of "why control immigration?" as an urgent matter of security and survival, and renders a decision not to increase control an utter anathema. Yet anti-immigrant populism is not a new trend, even if it intensified and became more globally visible in 2016. In fact, scholars noticed an increasing convergence of immigration policies towards stricter control well before the recent wave of populism (Cornelius et al. 2004), as a result of public demands for lower immigration (Hollifield, Martin, and Orrenius 2014). The current reaction, then, is not a response to too-liberal migration policies, but rather to the inevitable failure of strict policies to actually reduce immigration. The vicious cycle of immigration control is that strict policies produce more illegal immigration, which produces more public fear and backlash; more populism ensues as anti-immigration rhetoric becomes a sure-fire way to mobilize political support; stricter policy responses are adopted when populist agendas succeed because state legitimacy is at stake, which produce more illegal immigration, ad infinitum. This vicious cycle is not only palpable in the Russian case, as I have demonstrated in the preceding chapters, but also relevant at the theoretical level.

The underlying argument of this book is that competing interests, or "structural contradictions" (Calavita 1992), between economic demand for workers and political demand to limit immigrants have led the Russian government to choose strict policies that produce a scarcity of legal labour. I have argued that migration management is a multi-level balancing act, which uses formal and informal strategies in an attempt to produce stable, prosperous, and legitimate governance. Producing an equilibrium, where the public, employers, and state actors at all levels are relatively satisfied with the status quo, relies on a mix of pacts and privileges that signal the obligations and latitudes actors can take as they pursue official and personal interests. This strategy relies on producing a scarcity of documented legal labour, giving wide latitude to employers who hire illegal migrants, and managing public opinion through populist messages. Of these strategies, this book has focused its attention on how the state produces a scarcity of legal labour by creating rigid and often complicated policies and then sending signals to bureaucrats and regional executives as to the appropriate level of scarcity.

The period of 2007–15 covered by this book reflects a period of active policy attention in Russia. In particular, two key mechanisms regulated the labour migration process for citizens of CIS countries. Even though work permit quotas and labour patents employed different economic logics, they were both used to ensure the scarcity of legal labour, which was the most valuable tool for producing spoils from migration management. When legal documents for migrants are scarce, they are valuable. A variety of actors throughout the political system can use scarcity strategically by granting documents preferentially to close associates, increasing the spoils that can be collected through corruption schemes, and increasing the pool of undocumented workers who can be a cheaper or lower-commitment alternative to domestic workers or documented migrants.

Migration management in Russia is a constantly moving target. Laws, policies, and institutions change rapidly in an effort to chase new problems and imbalances in the system's equilibrium. Yet the underlying logic of migration management and the characteristics of the migration situation remain the same. After the analysis for this book was completed, a major restructuring of security and migration institutions was announced. A presidential decree by Putin in April 2016 dissolved the FMS and moved its functions into the Ministry of Internal Affairs under the newly created General Directorate for Migration (Glavnoe Upravlenie po Voprosam Migratsii, or GUVM). While the impact of these changes remains to be seen, the underlying mechanisms of migration management are likely to stay. The fundamental elements of the multi-level balancing act of migration management in Russia remain a foundation of populist rhetoric, symbolic control, the scarcity of documented labour, and dependence on patronage and informal practices.

In many ways, the developments in the Russian case should ring familiar to those who have watched the cyclical patterns of immigration control unfold in other contexts. While the depth and breadth of the informal mechanisms that are described in this book (management through patronage ties and related opportunities for corruption) set Russia apart from the typical governance practices laid out in migration theory, informal mechanisms are integral for managing migration in most contexts. Further, the most unexpected conclusion of assessing Russia in comparative perspective is that the outcomes of migration management (illegal immigration in response to strict policies) are not markedly different from what we see in other major migrant-receiving countries. In numerous cases we see competing interests leading to strict policies that increase illegal immigration and demand informal management solutions. This finding has important implications for the theoretical frameworks that guide many assumptions of the migration literature as well as those driving the literature on Russian politics. For the migration literature, whose puzzles are driven by the "liberal paradox," Russia demonstrates that regime type does not produce any significant variation in the outcomes of immigration control. The study of Russian politics is also marked by an incessant fervour to classify the system according to its regime type. The finding that a major area of governance (migration management) has comparative implications that do not fit neatly into frameworks dominated by regime calls us to rethink fundamental assumptions in our approach to Russia and its politics.

How the Liberal Paradox Has Become a Straw Man

Because the migration literature is dominated by studies of Western democratic immigrant-receiving states, theoretical assumptions about how migration works are intertwined with assumptions about how politics in democratic regimes function. Many of the major puzzles identified in the literature are driven by the "liberal paradox," or the idea that democratic states often adopt migration policies that contradict liberal principles (Hollifield 1992). The liberal paradox, in its original formulation, pits the forces of economic liberalism and globalization (including freedom of movement as a fundamental human right and increasing demand for mobile labour) against democratic publics that call for fewer immigrants (Hollifield 2004).[10] It is further paradoxical that states are unable to control a subset of the population that is least politically protected (Hollifield 1992).

The liberal paradox has driven a foundationally important body of work on migration, and represents a common thread in much of the literature. The identification of the liberal paradox ushered in a wave of migration literature that paralleled a larger discussion about the limits of state sovereignty and capacity in the face of globalization (Sassen 1996; Mann 1997; Keck and Sikkink 1999; Strange 1996). The consensus of early work was that states indeed have the capacity to control immigration, but they choose not to because of the pressures that liberalism poses, including demands for human rights and the influence of interest groups operating through democratic institutions, all of which lead to gaps between policy goals and outcomes (Cornelius, Martin, and Hollifield 1994; Freeman 1994; Joppke 1998). Though these studies acknowledge the role of anti-migrant impulses of native populations, public sentiments are not seen as the main force driving migration policies (Cornelius and Tsuda 2004).

More than 20 years after the introduction of the liberal paradox (and the ensuing gap hypothesis), scholars are still puzzled by its contradictions. Up to a certain point, the liberal paradox was driven by an inexplicable convergence towards permissive immigration policies despite anti-immigrant public opinion (Boswell 2007). Recently, however, the paradox has shifted to something like: if "accepting unwanted immigration is inherent in the liberalness of liberal states" (Joppke 1998), why do we see increasingly strict policies in these very same states (Triadafilopoulos 2011; Goodman 2011; Hollifield, Martin, and Orrenius 2014)? In other words, though the policy trajectory of liberal states has shifted, the paradox remains. While we would expect illiberal policies in non-democracies, we seem continually surprised (despite overwhelming evidence) that countries we call liberal would choose similar policy courses.

After considering the Russian case, I would like to suggest that the expectation that liberal states will choose liberal policies is actually a straw man obscuring a more fundamental set of causes and effects that have nothing to do with regime type. The migration literature has walled itself off analytically by only considering immigration in democratic states, reinforcing its conclusions while making them inaccessible for wider theoretical application. An analytical focus on only democratic receiving states also ignores the realities of the migration world, where tens of millions of migrants choose non-democracies as their destinations. When we expand our case pool to include a more representative view of immigration management, the puzzles driven by the liberal paradox fail to travel. If liberal states (despite being liberal) still choose illiberal policies, regime type fails to be a valid explanatory variable. Furthermore, the explanatory value of regime type is not helpful when the dependent variable (strict policies that produce increased illegal immigration) does not vary.[11]

The migration literature is correct when it explains that immigration policies and outcomes are a result of politics (Tichenor 2009; Hollifield, Martin, and Orrenius 2014), but it would be incorrect to suggest that politics do not occur in non-democracies. Parties and elections may not be the location of competition in non-democratic polities, yet the struggle for decision-making power and control exists and has a robust impact on how policies are adopted and implemented. Russia demonstrates fundamental components of political struggle that are not tied to regime type: interministerial struggles, the dynamics of federal relations, the government's keen sense that public opinion is a vital component of legitimacy, and the need for the state to produce conditions for economic prosperity. The informal mechanisms of politics in a non-democracy, relying on patronage and giving ample opportunity for corruption, are far more pronounced than in democracies and are not disciplined by the rule of law or given rigorous debate in the public sphere. Nevertheless, the driving importance of political struggles in producing and implementing policies remains.

As in the Russian case, many immigrant-receiving countries experience the vicious cycle of immigration control, where politics drives the adoption of unsustainable policies that then must be managed through informal efforts to balance the system. Evoking the vicious cycle are the structural contradictions or competing interests that first make it impossible to please all constituents with any one immigration policy, and second lead to policy gaps as strict policies work against economic prosperity and must be continually corrected for. Many countries use informal solutions to balance immigration control problems. When we discuss informal solutions in democratic contexts, we often use phrases such as "bureaucratic discretion," "selective" or "lax enforcement," and "stop-gap procedures," yet the parallels to the Russian system are germane for this discussion. In many states that rely on informal solutions there is a strong rhetoric opposing illegal immigration, but a variety of practices that either encourage or ignore illegal immigration, or channel illegal migrants into more desirable categories.

The latter situation was a major strategy of the US Immigration and Naturalization Service (INS) during the bracero guestworker program (1942–64). The INS used a number of strategies to encourage farmers to hire Mexican workers through the bracero program, including allowing them to select favoured illegal immigrants to channel into the program (Calavita 1992). Furthermore, offering farmers ample access to bracero workers (i.e., liberalizing immigration) helped keep illegal immigration under control.[12] The end of the bracero program came amid various political pressures, including interministerial conflicts (Durand 2007), and left Mexican workers with few legal options to immigrate. In a context where employer sanctions were weakly enforced (an informal signal that hiring undocumented workers would be tolerated), illegal immigration quickly increased, creating an equilibrium where employers got the cheap labour they needed while the government deployed just enough resources to convince the public that border control was being taken seriously (but not seriously enough to cut off the flow of illegal workers) (Massey, Durand, and Malone 2002; Orrenius 2001). As with many informal solutions, "the de facto way has proved to be the most feasible one, since all parties remain paradoxically content, although no one can say it aloud" (Durand 2007).

The Italian case is one where we might expect to find even more informal solutions at play, in addition to more structural similarities with Russia, including a history of weak institutions, systemic corruption, and a large underground economy. As in the Russian case, bureaucratic rigidity and contradictory immigration policy effectively guarantee that many immigrants will be unable to achieve legal status in Italy (Calavita 2005). Many aspects of procedures for legal entry are controlled at the administrative level, leading to uneven implementation of laws and arbitrary treatment of immigrants, manifesting in discrimination against some migrants and favouritism for those with personal connections (Veikou and Triandafyllidou 2001; Triandafyllidou 2003). One of the key mechanisms reinforcing illegality is frequent amnesty programs, which create a situation where many migrants bide their time in the shadows as they wait for a chance to legalize their status (Triandafyllidou and Ambrosini 2011). Despite the active involvement of far-right anti-migrant parties in government, leading to increasingly securitized policies (Perlmutter 2014), there is widespread acknowledgment that migrant workers are necessary to fill key labour gaps. As in Russia, a large informal economy offers a space for these immigrants to work without obtaining the necessary legal documents (Finotelli and Sciortino 2008).

In contrast to Italy, the UK is an example of a state with strong institutions and rule of law. However, the UK's heavily bureaucratic approach can produce a surge of immigrants who seek to slip through the cracks. A shift to strict entry requirements in the UK began in 1997 under Tony Blair's Labour government, in part to stave off criticism from the right (Somerville and Goodman 2010; Geddes 2005), and continued under the Cameron government (2005–10) (Bale 2013). The UK's reputation for a tightly controlled immigration system and focus on state capacity in delivering immigration policy notwithstanding, illegal migrants occupy jobs in sectors where enforcement is lax (Geddes 2005). Lax enforcement (as in the US case) acts as an informal signal that these migrants will be tolerated by the government. Even within the legal labour sphere, low-wage migrants from EU member states can act "as a hidden 'subsidy' to hard-pressed employers," despite the potential for these jobs to be filled by domestic labour (Geddes and Scott 2010).

We could draw parallels with myriad other cases in which increased immigration control leads to illegal immigration and other "unintended" consequences, and requires informal solutions to balance disparate interests: Japan and Korea have experienced increased illegal immigration as a result of restrictive policies (Chung 2014); in the European Union many asylum seekers become illegal immigrants because EU member states engage in "an exercise in evading responsibility" (Schuster 2011), making it difficult for refugees to complete bureaucratic procedures. In many cases, stop-gap policies are adopted to address the further by-products of immigration, such as banning hijabs, minarets, or halal food production, often framed as issues of integration. Also common to many of these cases is a public discourse on migrants that employs fear-based and inflammatory anti-immigration rhetoric. The frames may be different, focusing on terrorist threats, "bogus" asylum seekers, cultural threats, or criminality, but sensationalism is a constant that runs throughout (Geddes 2005; Mudde 2007; Wodak 2015).

The important conclusion of this discussion is that there is less variation across regimes than one might expect. If regime type cannot explain variation (or its absence) in outcomes (i.e., informal solutions including the tacit acceptance of a certain level of illegal immigration), then there is no liberal paradox, since it is not democracy (liberalism) or its absence that is producing the outcomes in the first place. In this light, the findings of this book are a powerful critique of the migration literature that calls scholars to rethink the puzzles that drive the normative framing of their inquiry and the assumptions underlying their explanations. As an example, many studies in the migration literature focus on problems related to migrant rights, in particular the violation or absence of rights owing to state policies or legal status. This is a framework driven by regime mentalities and associated values, setting out liberal or democratic values as an ideal all states should uphold. Yet research shows that variable access to rights exists even within democratic regimes as a result of political struggles and policy trade-offs (Ruhs 2013). Therefore, it is not regime type (or embedded regime values) that drives the extension of rights (or lack thereof) to migrants. Furthermore, reframing the field without a normative focus would allow more space for discussions of migrant agency, or the ability to solve problems and cope with the realities of migrant life.

For migrants, vulnerability and agency are two sides of the same coin. Cases of exploitation can be found in virtually every migration context, and those who seek stories of rights violation will surely not be disappointed by a lack of evidence. Yet a focus on exploitation without giving due weight to migrant agency creates a picture of poor, bedraggled migrants who are disadvantaged in the host state, but driven to migrate for work because of even more disadvantaged status at home. This picture is one of desperation and a lack of agency that contributes to a picture of migrants as victims. While the discourse intends to humanize migrants, instead it essentializes and objectifies them. The rights discourse fails to appreciate how, in non-democratic systems that lack a robust rule of law, the same mechanisms that fail to produce rights in fact produce opportunities for migrant agency. In Russia, migrants have agency not least because of the opportunities provided by corruption. Yet because of our normative frameworks, we rarely move beyond framing Russia's corrupt institutions and lack of rule of law as examples of poor governance because they do not meet Western standards. This discourse has concrete policy effects, because when regime-related ideals are held out as standards to be met by all states, yet are not upheld even in democracies, policymakers in authoritarian states are unlikely to be motivated to put migrant rights high on the list of priorities.

Reframing Russia

The political science literature more generally often treats governance in non-democracies as various manifestations of pathology, or degradations of democratic ideals.[13] The democratization literature of the 1990s coincided with Russia's transition from communism and a resilient optimism that it would become democratic (Evans 2011). Pronouncements that democracy had become a "universal value" (Sen 1999) and that there had been a "total exhaustion of viable systematic alternatives to Western liberalism" (Fukuyama 1989) left a normative mark on the field, in which scholars regularly admit a preference for democracy. The residue of these research agendas remains, and, in many cases, research puzzles driving the study of authoritarianism (in Russia and beyond) are based on reified assumptions of the constitutive contents of regimes, producing questions such as "why do authoritarian countries use 'democratic' institutions?"

This type of question is based on the assumption that certain institutions (i.e., elections, parties) are fundamentally democratic, and analyses based on such questions are at great pains to explain how non-democracies subvert democratic institutions. Furthermore, as "democratic" institutions have become more widely used around the world (regardless of regime type), analysis takes the components of democracy as a state of nature rather than a relatively short blip in the much longer history of authoritarian governance worldwide. Inquiry proceeding from these assumptions is driven by the desire to explain how leaders subvert nature (i.e., civil society and public participation) in their quest for authoritarian control. Yet such inquiries fail to question whether particular institutions (e.g., elections, parliaments) remain the domain of democracy, or if they have simply become accepted as more basic components of the state. I suggest that by taking the discussion of regime type off the table and moving up Sartori's ladder of abstraction or generality (Collier and Levitsky 1997), we will be able to make more meaningful comparisons that identify commonalities across regimes and allow lessons and critiques about public policy to travel in both directions.

Comparative political scientists certainly must compare, and *any* exercise in comparison necessarily involves a move up the ladder of generality, decreasing differentiation and nuance in order to create a basis for comparison, or valid root concept, that is not stretched beyond its original meaning (Collier and Levitsky 1997). Yet political science in too many cases defaults to democratic norms, institutions, and values as its main point of reference (Goode and Ahram 2016; Sen 1999; McFaul 2004). When the basis for comparison becomes entangled with the normative assumptions and preferences of democracy itself, political systems are framed not as what they are (Levitsky and Way 2002), but rather as what they fail to be (e.g., Evans 2011; Fish 2005; Gill 2002; Svolik 2012).[14] If democracy becomes an epistemological default, the "propensity to downplay democratic shortfalls" (Ahram and Goode 2016) skews analysis because comparisons fail to acknowledge that not only do authoritarian regimes not meet democratic ideals but also there are deep contradictions present in modern democracies that make any ideal of democracy unachievable (Dahl 1998; Sandel 1984). Further, many phenomena that are associated with a particular regime type (i.e., political participation or corruption) are observable in a wide variety of political systems (Howard and Walters 2014). Such a state of affairs prevents us from making a whole array of insights if non-democracies are relegated to unrelatable, authoritarian "others," because little basis then remains for constructing provocative critiques not only of democratic systems but more fundamentally of the way we construct comparative frameworks.

The categorization of regime types is not only analytical but is also often politically constructed and reinforced (Steiner 2014; Mainwaring, Brinks, and Pérez-Liñán 2001). The political bias introduced, along with corresponding efforts of "democracy promotion," makes authoritarian polities hypersensitive to any contradiction present in democratic states. Tensions or paradoxes in democracy, though unavoidable in even the most developed polities, are seen as hypocritical by the leaders of authoritarian regimes. This has been particularly apparent in Putin's statements on the refugee crisis in Europe. Never in any public discourse is he more critical of migration issues than in his statements of how Europe is failing to manage the integration of refugees (Schenk forthcoming). While such statements are often dismissed as anti-Western rhetoric,[15] the critiques should be taken seriously, and should certainly be evaluated by scholars with no normative defaults in mind as we construct our analytical frames of reference.[16]

This book has offered powerful evidence that Russia is indeed an authoritarian regime plagued by corruption. As such, its framing is not unique in the study of Russian politics. However, I seek to move beyond the normative entanglements of critiquing Russia on the basis of what it is not. Rather, by including an analysis of micropolitics, recognizing governance practices as they are, and shifting the level of analysis from regime to state, this book offers a fresh perspective that, if taken to heart, can change not only how we see Russia but also how we approach the study of politics irrespective of regime type.

Many analyses of Russian politics focus on big power politics (i.e., parties, electoral performance, etc.), which tend to provide macro-level explanations. In particular, these explanations reinforce the idea that individual actors are constrained by the increasingly authoritarian nature of Russian politics, which emanates directly from the Kremlin and often as the personal whims of Vladimir Putin. When framed in this way, micropolitics in Russia are turned into something unknowable, and actors below the Kremlin are rendered powerless. This study of migration politics and governance shows that the individual behaviour of state, economic, and societal actors differs markedly based on their position, connections, and a number of regional-level variables, but that actors at all levels have agency. The microfoundations of politics are embedded both in the institutional framework of patronage and in the structural contradictions of economic and political demands surrounding migration, defining interests and latitudes for the exercise of agency. Demonstrating the complexity and contingency that functions across the Russian system shows that the machine of politics portrayed in the literature and the vertical of power advertised by the administration are not so sacrosanct as they appear.

Russia certainly suffers from a number of governance pathologies. Nevertheless, *governance occurs*. Lawmakers make laws. Bureaucrats create and follow procedures with great (and even mind-numbing) regularity and precision. The state provides services to citizens and migrants through government agencies. These functions of governance should not be underestimated simply because Russia is authoritarian. Nor should values constraining Western bureaucrats be cast as the logical opposite to corruption. Rather, the opportunity costs and structures provided by patronage in Russia are a result of institutions, not values or regimes. Institutions are entwined with governance practices at the executive and administrative levels, which are firmly in the domain of the state. In illustration, Russia shares many aspects of governance that persist across regime types, including interministerial competition for power over policy areas, and various dysfunctions of public administration.

Chapters 2–4 demonstrated the interministerial struggle to control migration policy. This type of struggle between different administrative bodies over control of decision-making functions is not unique to authoritarian regimes (Allison 1971). The adage "Where you stand depends on where you sit" is an apt explanation of the different policy preferences of Mintrud and the FMS. Mintrud is responsible for the labour market, and thus their preferred policy of quotas for foreign workers gave them direct control over migrant access to the labour market. The FMS, in charge of most other migration-related issues, wanted to maximize control and profit, and thus advocated for the pay-as-you-go patent system. These perspectives are not directly related to corruption at the uppermost levels, though certainly control over policy areas gives a particular ministry's administrative workers both formal and informal levers of control (including the potential spoils of corruption schemes). At the upper levels, struggling for control over policy areas is also related to demonstrating agency, competence, and utility, which often results in increased budgets, and can produce career rewards for successful ministers. These struggles and rewards are not unique to authoritarian regimes (Etzioni-Halevy 2013; Calavita 1992; Cox and Shmerling 1979; Wilson 1989; Bradley 2014).

Administrative capacity (or dysfunction) is also not a product of regime type. In fact, unintended consequences and gaps in performance are hallmarks of modern public policy (Hood, Margetts, and Perri 6 2010). Furthermore, public administration across regime types tends to be myopic. Agencies focus on meeting certain targets or performance measures, which often become the sole driving force of administrative activity (Hood 2006). These measures necessarily reduce complex human activities and interactions into quantitatively accessible measurements, embedding subjective judgments into outputs that are taken to reflect rational assessments (Best 2012; Merry 2016). Across a variety of regimes, the incentive to manipulate data in order to meet targets comes from a desire to avoid blame from the public or other government agencies (Hood 2010; Kalgin 2016).

The more fundamental point is that public administration, bureaucracy, and the executive functions of ministers are seen as a part of essential state function. While regime values may have an effect on how administration functions, when we are discussing migration *governance* or management, this is fundamentally the realm of the state rather than the regime. Immigration governance does not "fail" because of values (the domain of regimes), it rather fails because of the interaction of state institutions with politics. While politics occur in both more democratic and less democratic systems, it is the power struggle rather than values that creates gaps in migration governance.

Questions of state capacity, policy effectiveness, and strategic uses of migration management are crucial for all migrant-receiving countries. The idea that managing migration can be accomplished through a technocratic approach that designs and implements the correct type of policy has been repeatedly debunked in the literature (Castles 2004). Rather, migration policy and the associated discursive, implementation, and efficacy gaps are a result of politics. In all states, decision makers seek to balance a variety of inputs in a way that produces some sort of equilibrium of satisfied actors. Russia is no different in this endeavour. Though the location of political power, relations between power holders, and thus the methods for exercising power stem from its nature as an authoritarian regime, the underlying need to produce social, economic, and political stability is the same.

What is different about Russia is the degree of flexibility that is present in adapting to changes in the migration system. Because power is concentrated in the upper echelons of elites, decision making can proceed quite rapidly, and adjustments can be easily made to correct for any problems that threaten to tip the equilibrium out of balance. Decision making that focuses on addressing the immediate demands of elites at the top of the political system often produces policy that does not correspond to how migration implementation works at the street level. Nevertheless, flexibility is interjected into the system by the widespread availability of informal strategies. State actors at all levels benefit from these strategies, as do employers and migrants.

When migration in Russia is framed in terms of its pathologies, whether corruption or human rights, the agency of actors (including migrants) is neglected. Though problems are created when policies are disconnected from migration realities, actors have myriad options for solving problems that would simply not be available in a rule-of-law system. It can certainly not be ignored that there are negative consequences of corruption and informal practices, particularly for those without access to informal networks or the capital necessary to pay bribes and arbitrarily applied fines. Yet to focus only on vulnerabilities is to underemphasize the resourcefulness of actors in the migration system and the utility of informal mechanisms.

Conclusion

In light of these major critiques of the literatures on migration and Russian politics, where do we go next? If structural contradictions produce similar outcomes across all regime types and across different types of state institutions (i.e., meritocratic vs patronage based, corrupt vs non-corrupt), the explanation for outcomes is embedded in initial conditions. Across all immigrant-receiving countries, policy responses reinforce the vicious cycle of immigration control because increased illegal immigration produces fear and more populism, which provoke stricter policy responses, and then more illegal immigration. For policy solutions to work, economic demand for cheap labour must be satisfied without provoking a political backlash. In the wake of the Brexit referendum in the UK and the election of Donald Trump in the US, this seems unlikely, since the populist politics of fear is actively being used to mobilize voters and solidify anti-immigrant political power. Fear makes for great (sensational, heated, and contentious) politics, but its policies only solidify vicious circles of unintended consequences.

In seeking a way out of the vicious circle, there is a policy way forward, which involves liberalizing policies as the *only* viable solution to illegal immigration, and there is a political way forward, which is populism. These solutions are in fundamental conflict with one another, and the tragedy of modern immigration control is that populism is increasingly supplanting sound policy. The greatest power of states in migration management is the ability to decide what proportion of the immigrant population will be legal. Strict policies based on control will inevitably lead not only to increasing illegality but also to a more permanent (less mobile) migrant population. As Dauvergne (2008) reminds us, "illegality is a creation of the law." Reflecting on migration patterns throughout the world, she concludes that "each extension of the law regulating migration increases illegal migration through defining increasingly larger categories as being outside the law" (Dauvergne 2008). It is political demand that erects immigration laws in the first place, meaning that anti-immigration demands in fact create illegal immigration. It is also political demand that makes it difficult to reduce illegal immigration because the impulse to increase control is never reduced. Other migration scholars remind us that:

> No set of border controls has ever worked to contain fully people's desire and need to move. In this sense, national borders are a dystopian/utopian project. No state, however powerful and well resourced, will manage to control migration and ensure that only those with the right motivation, values, and plans cross the border in the right direction. (Anderson 2013)

> As long as there is a strong, stable demand for foreign labour in advanced industrial economies, resourceful immigrants in pursuit of abundant and high-paying jobs (and the smugglers and labour brokers who assist them) will always find a way to circumvent a government's immigration laws, border controls, and any other obstacle placed in their path. Indeed, the more restrictive the immigration policy, the greater the number of migrants who will simply find ways to enter the country illegally in response to employer demand, and the larger the immigration control gap. (Cornelius et al. 2004)

By casting the Russian case in comparative context, we see that the populist politics of fear produces a vicious cycle of immigration control across all regime types. This realization problematizes our normative assumptions about the uniquely pathological impact of authoritarian politics. It also highlights the key role that publics play in the policy process (i.e., creating public demand for policies), even in authoritarian regimes and outside electoral accountability. This study confirms the theoretical findings in the migration literature that strict immigration control leads to increased proportions of illegal immigration and will likely lead to a more permanent immigrant population. The only hope of breaking the vicious cycle of immigration control is to reframe migration not as a threat, but as a source of many and various benefits for society at large, which in turn can provide concrete incentives for constructive political movement towards more open immigration systems.

Appendixes

Appendix to Chapter 3

Table A3.a. Mid-year quota adjustments

	Total	Distributed to regions	Reserve	Issued by Minzdrav/ Mintrud Order:
2007	6,000,000	5,795,678	–	No. 185 of March 22, 2007
2008	1,828,245	1,335,657	492,588	No. 73n of February 18, 2008
	1,828,245	1,568,671	259,574	No. 251n of June 2, 2008
	1,828,245	1,828,245	0	No. 299n of June 30, 2008
	3,384,129	2,516,950	867,179	No. 567n of October 16, 2008
	3,384,129	2,536,134	847,995	No. 776n of December 26, 2008
2009	3,976,747	1,988,374	1,988,373	No. 777n of December 26, 2008
	3,976,747	1,981,669	1,995,078	No. 139n of March 30, 2009
	3,976,747	1,934,648	2,042,099	No. 312n of June 15, 2009
	3,976,747	1,802,724	2,174,023	No. 813n of October 6, 2009
2010	1,944,356	1,361,049	583,307	No. 1008n of December 22, 2009
	1,944,356	1,361,471	582,885	No. 182n of March 24, 2010
	1,944,356	1,379,192	565,164	No. 455n of June 18, 2010
	1,944,356	1,398,593	545,763	No. 727n of August 26, 2010
	1,944,356	1,417,549	526,807	No. 811n of September 20, 2010
2011	1,745,584	1,221,833	523,751	No. 1080n of December 8, 2010
	1,745,584	1,237,788[a]	505,798	No. 223n of March 22, 2011
	1,745,584	1,274,069	471,515	No. 432n of May 27, 2011
	1,745,584	1,322,941	422,643	No. 883n of August 4, 2011
	1,745,584	1,368,143	377,441	No. 1135n of October 6, 2011
	1,745,584	1,383,353	362,231	No. 1540n of December 14, 2011

(*Continued*)

Table A3.a. Mid-year quota adjustments (Continued)

	Total	Distributed to regions	Reserve	Issued by Minzdrav/ Mintrud Order:
2012	1,745,584	1,267,978	477,606	No. 1434n of November 30, 2011
	1,745,584	1,317,689	427,895	No. 257n of March 26, 2012
	1,745,584	1,338,533	407,051	No. 531n of May 14, 2012
	1,745,584	1,410,578	335,006	No. 23n of July 16, 2012
	1,745,584	1,476,888	268,696	No. 75n of August 24, 2012
	1,745,584	1,489,390	256,194	No. 582n of December 11, 2012
2013	1,745,584	1,224,185	521,399	No. 556n of November 30, 2012
	1,745,584	1,295,549	450,035	No. 168n of April 29, 2013
	1,745,584	1,320,054	425,530	No. 273n of June 19, 2013
	1,745,584	1,410,469	335,115	No. 309n of July 16, 2013
	1,745,584	1,444,308	301,276	No. 426n of September 3, 2013
	1,745,584	1,448,715	296,869	No. 548n of October 21, 2013
2014	1,631,586	1,142,110	489,476	No. 739n of December 16, 2013
	1,631,586	1,142,709	488,877	No. 268n of April 21, 2014
	1,631,586	1,151,178	480,408	No. 330n of May 20, 2014
	1,631,586	1,177,306	454,280	No. 422n of June 30, 2014
	1,631,586	1,261,921	369,665	No. 471n of July 17, 2014
	1,631,586	1,269,400[b]	361,929	No. 557n of August 20, 2014
	1,631,586	1,312,566	319,020	No. 633n of September 8, 2014
	1,631,586	1,347,405	284,181	No. 683n of October 9, 2014
	1,631,586	1,358,542	273,044	No. 871n of November 10, 2014
	1,631,586	1,368,299	263,287	No. 955n of November 28, 2014

[a] Due to errors in the document, where regional subtotals do not reflect actual allocation to the regions, the total quota minus reserve does not equal quota distributed to the regions. Specifically, Order No. 223n states the regional subtotal in the Central Federal District is 383,764, though the actual sum of quota in these regions is 383,092; in the Volga Federal District the stated subtotal is 121,853, though the actual sum of all regions is 120,527.

[b] Order No. 557n states the regional subtotal in the Central Federal District is 398,800, though the actual sum of quota in these regions is 398,452; in the Southern Federal District the stated subtotal is 93,893, though the actual sum of all regions is 93,984.

Table A3.b. Schedule of quota formulation (Government Order No. 783)

Deadline:	
01-May	Employers submit their applications to hire a foreign worker in the following year. Applications are submitted to an agency designated by the regional governor as coordinator of the quota process.
01-Jun	Regional coordinator distributes employer applications to relevant regional ministries (dealing with economics, education, employment, etc.), UFMS, Labour and Employment services, and tripartite commission on social-labour relations.[a]
15-Jun	Estimates of effective use of foreign labour for the previous year are completed by regional ministries and submitted to quota coordinator, who summarizes the results.
15-Jun	Ministries submit their recommendations on the feasibility of the quota based on employer applications.[b] Recommendations should also consider: • Demographic development • Possible changes in the local labour market due to national projects, investment projects, development programs, etc. • Labour potential of the local workforce (i.e., prognosis of unemployed workers and layoffs) • Potential to fill labour needs (as specified in employer applications) with local resources (i.e., through job retraining programs for the unemployed) • Possibility of redistributing labour resources within the region or attracting labour from other Russian regions • Graduates who can fill labour needs • Allowable shares of migrants[c] • Participation in the compatriot program • Ability of housing and social infrastructure to absorb migrants • Estimates of effective use of foreign labour in the previous year
15-Jun	UFMS, taking into account employer applications, must submit • Use of previous and current year's quota • Compliance with allowable shares • Any violations by employers of the rules for using foreign workers (and the resolution of any violations) • Countries of origin (of migrants)[d]
15-Jun	Labour and Employment Service gives quota coordinator information about any labour-related violations of specific employers.
25-Jun	Quota coordinator sends the following to the interdepartmental committee • Information about labour needs of employers (from applications • Reports from the ministries, UFMS, and Labour and Employment Service (submitted June 15) • Results of the effective use of labour (submitted June 15)

(Continued)

Table A3.b. Schedule of quota formulation (Government Order No. 783) (Continued)

Deadline:	
10-Jul	Interdepartmental commission gives its report about the feasibility of employer applications and decides to approve in part or in whole, or to reject, individual employer applications. The commission can reduce the overall quota or reject applications if any of the following apply: • Possibility of filling jobs with local labour resources or internal migration from other Russian regions • Violations of the rules of employing foreign workers • Labour violations • Inability to provide migrants with housing
Within 10 days	Quota coordinator informs employers in writing if their application was rejected in whole or in part. Employers can appeal.
Within one month	Quota coordinator informs employers
15-Jul	Quota coordinator submits a formal recommendation for the regions' quota, breakdown by profession, and report on the effective use of foreign workers to Minzdrav (later Mintrud), which will analyse regional reports in light of the labour market (prioritizing Russian citizens), demographic situation, and reports on effective use of foreign workers and request additional information as needed.
15-Aug	Federal Service for Labour and Employment gathers information from the regions on work vacancies and those registered for employment service assistance and makes recommendations for how local workers can be used instead of foreign workers, suggesting quota reductions and changes to regional allocations.
15-Oct	Minzdrav (Mintrud) prepares three draft orders along with the Ministry of Economic Development, Ministry of Regional Development, and Federal Migration Service • On the demand for foreign workers in general and by professional category • Quota for invitations • Quota for work permits
Within two weeks	Minzdrav (Mintrud) and Ministry of Economic Development determines demand for highly qualified specialists and approves a list of professions approved for quota-free entry.
Within three weeks	Federal Service of Labour and Employment confirms the professional positions for which migrants can be hired and informs the FMS, Ministry of Economic Development, Ministry of Internal Affairs, and regional quota coordinators.
Within one month	Minzdrav (Mintrud), Ministry of Economic Development, and FMS approve regional allocations of quota (for invitations), including a reserve of no more than 50% of overall quota for corrections within the year.

Table A3.b. Schedule of quota formulation (Government Order No. 783) (Continued)

Deadline:	
Within one month	Minzdrav (Mintrud), Ministry of Economic Development, and FMS approve regional allocations of quota (for work permits) according to profession, specialty, qualification, country of origin, and "other economic and/or social criteria," including a reserve of no more than 50% of overall quota for corrections within the year.
Timeline/rules for corrections and amendments	
01-May	Employers submit applications for increases in quota.[e] Interdepartmental commission considers applications by the same criteria as those in the regular quota application process.
15-Jul	Regions submit a proposal to Minzdrav (Mintrud) for increases/ decreases.
15-Jul	Federal ministries, in consultation with regional ministries, can make a proposal to Mintrud for increases/decreases in quota at the regional level in order to accomplish national projects.
15-Aug	Mintrud makes decisions about granting increases/decreases in quotas. Any increases are deducted from the reserve.

[a] The tripartite commission is not given a deadline for submitting their recommendations.

[b] These recommendations are for overall quota number and the professional breakdown of requests, not necessarily a line-item approval or rejection of individual employer applications. Some of these recommendations come from agencies who have also submitted "estimates of effective use," but others do not. The ministries involved in submitting data for the estimates of effective use do not see the summarized information before they must submit their recommendations.

[c] See chapter 4, table 4.2.

[d] The document does not specify if it is country of origin of current migrants or those requested in the applications that should be submitted.

[e] There is no procedure for an employer to apply for a decreased quota allocation (or release their unneeded quota).

Table A3.c. Replicating the government methodology

Considerations to be made by commissions	Data, variable names, and methodological notes
Government Order No. 783[a]	
Prospects for demographic development, expected migration (especially internal migration)	These projections are done at the regional level, but are not available in a compiled cross-regional format. Mintrud issues a prognosis every year, but only give aggregated federal-level data.
Prospects for changing labour demand, including job creation owing to various projects and programs at the local, regional, and federal levels	***vacancyrt*** (*vacancy rate*) number of recorded workplace vacancies (used to measure labour market demand) as a percentage of the economically active (employed plus unemployed) population. Data available 2006–13 (Rosstat 2010d; Rosstat 2015b) ***ile*** (*internal labour emigrants*) Data available 2006–12 (Rosstat 2011b; Rosstat 2013b) In terms of labour demand from projects and programs, these considerations would take into account projects such as infrastructure and construction development for events like the Sochi Olympics in Krasnodar and the APEC summit in Vladivostok. Nevertheless, there is no comprehensive document detailing these projects by year or by region.
Labour potential (including projected number of unemployed and lay-offs)	***unemprt*** (*unemployment rate*), unemployed persons as a percentage of the total economically active population of the region, when unemployed persons are determined by the International Labour Organization methodology. Data available 2006–14 (Rosstat 2010d; Rosstat 2015b)
Possibility of filling labour needs with local workers (including job retraining programs, etc.)	There is no data published by the government that specifically addresses this issue; however, by considering domestic labour migration, unemployment, and graduates entering the labour market, the future labour potential is addressed.
Possibility of filling labour needs with workers from other Russian regions	***ili*** (*internal labour immigrants*) Data available 2006–12 (Rosstat 2011b; Rosstat 2013b)
Expected number of graduates that could fill labour needs	***grad*** (*number of graduates at all levels of post-secondary education*), the sum of students graduating from vocational programs, or with bachelors, masters, or specialist degrees. Data available 2006–13 (Rosstat 2013b; Rosstat 2014d)

Table A3.c. Replicating the government methodology (Continued)

Considerations to be made by commissions	Data, variable names, and methodological notes
Government Order No. 783[a]	
Allowable share of foreign workers in different sectors of the economy	This issue would be a factor regional bureaucrats should consider when approving or denying specific employer applications. However, since data from original applications is not available, this is not reproducible on a large scale. The issue is addressed to some degree by looking at data on work permits issued in the previous year.
Participation of the region in the compatriots (ethnic repatriation) program	***compatriot*** number of people arriving to a region through the government program. Data available 2008–14 (Rosstat 2015a)
Ability of the region's housing and social infrastructure to absorb foreign workers	***housingdens*** (*housing density*) area of living space per capita in square metres Data available 2006–13 (Rosstat 2007a; Rosstat 2008a; Rosstat 2009a; Rosstat 2010d; Rosstat 2014c) ***hospbed*** (*hospital beds*) number of hospital beds per 1,000 people Data available 2006–13 (Rosstat 2010d; Rosstat 2014c) ***school*** number of schools, including preschools Data available 2006–13 (Rosstat 2008a; Rosstat 2010d; Rosstat 2012c; Rosstat 2014c)
Estimate of the effective/efficient use of the foreign labour force (determined by Minzdrav Order 604)	No formal document with the results of these estimates (see below for approximation).
Use of previous year's quota and compliance with limits on the use of foreign workers in certain economic sectors	***quota1*** (*quota at the beginning of the year*) ***quota10*** (*quota at the end of the year*) Data available 2007–14; see table A3.a for sources ***wkptperc*** (*number of work permits issued to foreign workers as a percentage of quota*)
Employer violations of the procedures for hiring foreign workers	This is typically a consideration used when assessing individual applications, not overall regional quota numbers.
Foreign workers' countries of origin	While this information is indicated on employer applications, there is no indication here of how the data should influence quota process. Presumably it is more useful for determining the balance between overall quota and the subquota for visa invitations for foreign workers from non-CIS countries.

(*Continued*)

Table A3.c. Replicating the government methodology (Continued)

Considerations to be made by commissions	Data, variable names, and methodological notes
Minzdrav Order No. 604[b]	
Contribution of foreign workers to regional economic development as a whole and by sector for the previous three years using the following metrics: • gross regional product • turnover by sector, shipment of goods and services • number of workers by sector • number of foreign workers in general • number of foreign workers by sector	***wkpt*** (*number of work permits issued to foreign workers*) Data available 2006–14 (by sector, available only for 2006, 2008, and 2010) (Rosstat 2007b; Rosstat 2009b; Rosstat 2011a; Rosstat 2014c) ***patent*** (*number of patents issued to foreign workers*) Data available 2011–14 (Rosstat 2012c; Rosstat 2013a; Rosstat 2014d; Rosstat 2015c) ***migcont*** (*migrant contribution to GRP*) migrant intensity (migrants as a portion of the working population) multiplied by GRP GRP data available 2006–13 (Rosstat 2011a; Rosstat 2014c; Rosstat 2015b) ***migint*** (*migrant intensity*) foreign workers as a percentage of the employed population Employed population data available 2006–14 (Rosstat 2013b; Rosstat 2015d)
Contribution vs expenditures related to attraction/use of foreign workers for the previous three years using the following metrics: • number of foreign nationals receiving emergency medical care • cost of such medical care • number of children of foreigners in schools and kindergartens • cost of such education • cost of maintenance of infrastructure used by foreign nationals (hostels, transportation, communications, utilities, etc.) • cost of administrative detention and expulsion/deportation of foreigners	***migcont*** (*migrant contribution to GRP*) Other categories of data are not available.

Table A3.c. Replicating the government methodology (Continued)

Considerations to be made by commissions	Data, variable names, and methodological notes
Minzdrav Order No. 604[b]	
• other expenses (from federal and municipal budgets) • foreign workers' contribution to revenue • taxes paid by foreign workers, by sector • salaries paid to foreign workers	
Engagement of foreign workers in labour market by sector and skill for the previous three years using the following metrics: • number of foreign workers • number of foreign workers by sector • number of foreign workers by skill level • internal migrants by sector and skill level • quota of foreign workers	***wkpt*** (*number of work permits issued to foreign workers*) ***ili*** (*internal labour immigrants*) ***quota1*** (*quota at the beginning of the year*) ***quota10*** (*quota at the end of the year*)
Foreign workers as a proportion of the total labour force for the previous three years using the following metrics: • average percentage of foreign workers in the total work • average percentage of foreign workers in the total work by sector • average percentage of foreign workers in the total work by skill level	***migint*** (*migrant intensity*)

(*Continued*)

Table A3.c. Replicating the government methodology (Continued)

Considerations to be made by commissions	Data, variable names, and methodological notes
Minzdrav Order No. 604[b]	
Labour market trends since 2005 using the following metrics: • yearly growth in the numbers of foreign workers since 2005 • changes in the annual percentage of foreign workers in the total work force since 2005	***wkpt*** (*number of work permits issued to foreign workers*) ***migint*** (*migrant intensity*)
Foreign workers' impact on the intensity (pressure) of the labour market for the past three years using the following metrics: • average ratio of unemployed people to number of foreign workers (in general, by sector, and by skill level) • average ratio of foreign workers to number of reported job vacancies (in general, by sector, and by skill level) • annual changes in the qualification structure of the unemployed, reported vacancies, and foreign workers	***wkpt*** (*number of work permits issued to foreign workers*) ***unemppl*** (*number of unemployed persons*) ***vacancy*** (*vacancies*) number of recorded workplace vacancies
Impact of foreign workers on wages in industries with a high proportion of foreign labour for the past three years using the following metrics: • ratio of average monthly wages/salaries of foreign workers to Russian citizens (or all employees if data on the Russian-only population is not available) (in general, by sector, and by skill level)	***avewag*** (*average wage*) average monthly nominal wages across all professions and sectors of the economy for all workers Data available 2006–14 (Rosstat 2013b; Rosstat 2015d) No data for migrant wages

Table A3.c. Replicating the government methodology (Continued)

Considerations to be made by commissions	Data, variable names, and methodological notes
Minzdrav Order No. 604[b]	
Involvement of foreign workers in informal economic relations for the past three years using the following metrics: • ratio of foreigners registered at a place of stay to number of work permits issued to foreign citizens • ratio of foreign workers granted work permits to the number of notifications received from employers	Data not available As a proxy, a variable for the size of informal sector in general ***infwkrperc*** (*number of informal workers as a percentage of the economically active population*) Data available 2007, 2009, 2012, and 2013 (Rosstat 2008b; Rosstat 2010b; Rosstat 2012b; Rosstat 2014b I have filled in missing data for intervening years using the average of surrounding years.
Working conditions of foreign workers for the past three years using the following metrics: • rates of injury and death among foreign workers (per 1,000 foreign workers), including type of activity	Data not available
"Other" indicators: • number of crimes committed by foreigners against foreigners, by type of crime, and the share of these crimes in the total number of offences in the region • crime rate among foreigners compared to average crime rates • number of administrative offences committed by foreigners, by type of offence, and their share in total number of regional offences	***crmrt*** (*crime rate*) number of crimes committed per 10,000 people Data available 2009–13 (General'naia Prokuratura Rossiiskoi Federatsii) ***immshcrm*** (*share of crimes committed by immigrants*) percentage of total crimes committed by foreign citizens Data available 2009–13 (General'naia Prokuratura Rossiiskoi Federatsii)

(*Continued*)

Table A3.c. Replicating the government methodology (Continued)

Considerations to be made by commissions	Data, variable names, and methodological notes
Minzdrav Order No. 604[b]	
• number of violations of labour laws by foreign citizens compared to those committed by local workers • number of NGOs and aid workers in the region and availability of funding	

[a] Replaced by Government Order No. 800 of September 12, 2013.
[b] Went out of force July 29, 2014 according to Mintrud Order No. 214n of April 7, 2014. Though the order was passed in April, it did not enter into force until July. The reason for the delay is not indicated in the document.

LABOUR MARKET

To measure labour market dynamics, I include a number of indicators that assess both the domestic workforce and the impact of migrants. Labour supply of domestic workers (unemployment,[1] graduates entering the labour market, domestic workers moving to the region) is expected to have a negative relationship with quota, whereas indicators of labour market demand (workplace vacancies, workers leaving the region) and of migrant supply (work permits) should have a positive relationship.[2] Migrant intensity in the labour market (*migint*) and migrant contribution to GDP (*migcont*) could plausibly be expected to have either a positive or negative relationship with quota. Regions whose labour markets use a larger proportion of migration workers could signal deficits of local labour resources and thus be an indicator of demand for foreign workers. On the other hand, from a labour protectionist perspective, regions that have a high degree of migrant labour might signal a need to reduce dependency on foreign labour resources, thereby producing a lagged effect of depressing demand. Likewise in the migration literature, scholars have hypothesized that higher numbers of migrants in a receiving country can lead to more restrictive immigration policies (Givens and Luedtke 2005).

As a proxy for migrants working in the informal economy,[3] I include a variable that assesses the number of workers in the informal sector (*infwkrperc*).[4] Though the government methodology directs regional commissions to take into consideration the number of migrants working in the informal labour market, it does not indicate a particular expected or directed relationship.[5] Nevertheless, we can reason that, if the government wants to legalize workers that are engaged in informal activities, there should be a positive relationship between informal workers and quotas (as a method of legalization).

SOCIO-ECONOMIC

The government methodology calls for bureaucrats to consider measures of migrant criminality (*immshcrm*) as well as labour-related violations.[6] A negative relationship is expected between quota and the crime variables. Though not included in the government methodology, the data set also includes a measure on confirmed instances of hate crimes (*htcrm*) as a measure of the level of intolerance towards migrants in the region.[7] An additional measure that targets potential intolerance is the percentage of regional population that is ethnic Russian (*ethRus*).[8] For both the hate crimes and percentage of ethnic Russian variables, any effects of intolerance are expected to produce negative coefficients.

To measure the impact of infrastructure capacity on quota, I include variables that assess the education (*school*), health care (*hospbed*), and housing (*housingdens*) sectors. I expect that greater capacity in each of these sectors will produce reduced downward pressure on quotas, indicated by positive coefficients for *school* and *hospbed*, and negative coefficients for *housingdens*.

RESULTS

The panel data set constructed of the above variables is the basis of several time series regression models. In order to analyse the decision making of bureaucrats within each region over time, I use fixed effects estimators (table 3.5), which control for geographic and other time invariant factors (which are regionally specific and constant over time) that could bias results.[9] In order to control for these factors, fixed effects models only assess within-region variation from year to year, while ignoring variation across regions. The added benefit of this type of modelling is that it is especially appropriate for testing regional decision making, because it isolates within-region processes. Because bureaucrats are unlikely to give factors outside their region (other than federal cues) more than passing consideration, fixed effects estimation will mimic the logic of regional decision makers.[10]

Fixed effects modelling does not account for exogenous influences, since it only assesses within-region variation. The crucial exogenous factor in the quota formulation is the impact of Putin's 2008 pronouncement that quotas should be decreased because of economic crisis. To assess the impact of these factors, I include year dummies.[11] I lag all of the independent variables by one year to replicate the realistic delay of information various bureaucratic offices are using.[12] In addition to assessing individual explanatory factors, these models seek to compare the impact of macroeconomic and labour market indicators on the quota at the beginning and end of year (as adjusted throughout the year) and on the number of work permits issued in a given year. This will serve to demonstrate whether Minzdrav/Mintrud and the interdepartmental commissions follow a consistent logic within each region when setting and adjusting quota, and whether regional UFMS branches follow a similar logic when issuing work permits.[13]

Table A3.d. OLS model[a]

DV: quota1 (log)	2007–14[b]	
migcont	0.00	(0.00)
unemprt	–5.01***	(1.66)
avewag (log)	–0.10	(0.15)
infwkrperc	–1.23*	(0.72)
vacancyrt	5.43*	(3.57)
grad (log)	0.07	(0.10)
migint	0.84	(3.08)
wkpt (log)	0.74***	(0.08)
housingdens	–0.004	(.004)
school	0.00	(0.00)
hospbed	0.00	(0.00)
Constant	3.49*	(1.84)
Observations	664	
R^2	0.8338	

[a] All independent variables are lagged by one year. Robust standard errors in parentheses. * = p < .10, ** = p < .05, *** = p < .01.

[b] Includes year dummies. Coefficients for dummy variables not reported. Dummies for 2007–11 are statistically significant. 2007 has a positive coefficient (also 2012 and 2013), and 2008–11 have negative coefficients.

Appendix to Chapter 5

The Rostrud spreadsheets give extremely detailed information on companies granted quota each year from 2008 to 2014, providing employer information (name, address, and sometimes tax ID numbers) and information on the migrants being hired (job title, number of migrants, wages, what type of housing they would be provided, and in 2014, migrants' countries of origin). The spreadsheets were issued 17 times over the 7 years, and included a separate document for each region, for a total of over 1,400 documents. The documents were not always issued (by Rostrud Order) in a timely manner, nor for every mid-year change in the quota allocation (issued by Minzdrav or Mintrud Order), and there are many inconsistencies across the documents (see table A5.a).

Table A5.a. Mid-year quota allocations and adjustments, Moscow

	Moscow quota	Issued by Minzdrav/ Mintrud Order:	Spreadsheets issued as attachment to Department of Labour Order No. ___:
2007	750,000	No. 185 of March 22, 2007	–
2008	300,000	No. 73n of February 18, 2008a	–
	359,103	No. 299n of June 30, 2008	–
	594,886	No. 567n of October 16, 2008	No. 61 of March 24, 2008 and No. 239 of November 18, 2008
2009	392,157	No. 777n of December 26, 2008	No. 45 of February 20, 2009
2010	250,000	No. 1008n of December 22, 2009	No. 34 of February 5, 2010
2011	128,803	No. 1080n of December 8, 2010	No. 9 of January 21, 2011
	126,623	No. 223n of March 22, 2011	No. 102 of May 17, 2011
	135,351	No. 432n of May 27, 2011	No. 150 of July 12, 2011
	181,336	No. 883n of August 4, 2011	No. 214 of September 23, 2011
	199,778	No. 1540n of December 14, 2011	No. 313 of December 27, 2011
2012	136,384	No. 1434n of November 30, 2011	No. 215 of December 28, 2011
	153,383	No. 257n of March 26, 2012	No. 90 of April 23, 2012
	196,802	No. 23n of July 16, 2012	No. 190 of August 22, 2012
	199,755	No. 75n of August 24, 2012	No. 218 of October 5, 2012
	209,513	No. 582n of December 11, 2012	No. 285 of December 29, 2012
2013	101,546	No. 556n of November 30, 2012	No. 279 of December 24, 2012
	120,784	No. 168n of April 29, 2012	–
	200,765	No. 309n of July 16, 2012	–
	215,479	No. 548n of October 21, 2012	No. 245 of November 26, 2013
2014	95,020	No. 739n of December 16, 2013	–

(*Continued*)

Table A5.a. Mid-year quota allocations and adjustments, Moscow (Continued)

Moscow quota	Issued by Minzdrav/ Mintrud Order:	Spreadsheets issued as attachment to Department of Labour Order No. ___:
161,252	No. 471n of July 17, 2014	(Ministry of Labour Order) No. 502 of July 30, 2014 and (Ministry of Labour Order) No. 595 of September 1, 2014
172,535	No. 633n of September 8, 2014	–
181,659	No. 683n of October 9, 2014	
188,225	No. 871n of November 10, 2014	–

[a] One version of this order (Ministry of Labour and Social Protection of the Chuvash Republic, accessed July 22, 2017, http://gov.cap.ru/laws.aspx?gov_id=31&id=53463.) cites the beginning of the year quota at 244,309. However, this figure is not found in other versions of the order.

No spreadsheet was issued for 2007, which is not surprising considering that the initial year of quota allocation was decided on the basis of expert estimates rather than employer applications. In 2008, spreadsheets were issued in March and November. However, in the three regions analysed for this study (Moscow, Sverdlovsk, and Krasnodar), both spreadsheets are identical and use the year-end quota numbers, which in the case of Moscow were issued only in October. From 2009 to 2012, the spreadsheets are roughly in sync with the Ministerial Orders. However, in 2013 and 2014 there seems to be some bureaucratic fatigue, since more than half of the quota adjustments are not met with revised spreadsheets. This is particularly apparent in 2014 when there are no spreadsheets issued that correspond to the beginning or end of year quota. Rather, the spreadsheets issued reflect mid-year quota numbers (e.g., in 2014 Moscow's quota began at 95,020 and ended at 188,225, but the only spreadsheet available for this region in 2014 reflects the July quota amendment of 161,252).

In order to get an overall sense of what types of employers are granted quota, I organized the data by economic sector according to the Russian Classification of Economic Activities (Obsherossiiskii Klassifikator Vidov Ekonomicheskoi Deiatel'nosti, or OKVED), which divides the economy into 15 sectors: agriculture, fishing, mining and resource extraction, manufacturing, utilities, construction, trade, hospitality, transportation and communication, finance, real estate, government, education, health and social services, and services (communal, social, and personal).[14] These categories match up with the migration statistics reported Rosstat and therefore are a useful check on the official data, where available.[15] For each OKVED sector, I calculated the total number of migrants (i.e., quota granted), and number of companies (see table A5.b).[16] I also include a measure of the number of times a company is entered into the spreadsheet as a measure of bureaucratic burden. For example, in some cases, a company's quota is divided into separate entries (i.e., lines of data) based on the professions of the workers, type of housing provided, country of origin, etc. My assumption is that each entry represents a separate request made by the employer, and therefore bureaucratic burden is higher when an employer is required to complete separate applications for migrant workers with different characteristics.

Table A5.b. Bureaucratic output of quota, Moscow

	2008	2009	2010	2011	2012	2013	2014
Starting quota	300,000	392,157	250,000	128,803	136,384	101,546	161,252[a]
Year-end quota	594,886	392,157	250,000	199,778	209,513	215,479	
MANUFACTURING							
Approved quota	—	26,581	11,531	33,392	8,765	3,736	13,458
	25,925	—	19,066	13,355	11,375	12,023	
– % of regional	—	7%	5%	26%	6%	4%	8%
quota	4%	—	7%	7%	5%	6%	—
Companies	—	462	662	663	131	114	420
	590	—	872	275	267	432	—
– average workers	—	58	17	50	67	33	32
per co.	44	—	22	49	43	28	—
Entries	—	1,710	2,267	5,946	1,213	924	3,449
	2,227	—	4,673	2,232	2,192	3,543	—
– average entries	—	3.7	3.4	9.0	9.3	8.1	8.2
per co.	3.8	—	5.4	8.1	8.2	8.2	—
CONSTRUCTION							
Approved quota	—	153,133	62,258	27,584	29,856	27,281	41,321
	192,068	—	79,065	19,846	59,461	58,241	—
– % of regional	—	39%	25%	21%	22%	27%	26%
quota	32%	—	32%	10%	28%	27%	—
Companies	—	612	804	226	311	203	545
	903	—	1,073	174	534	654	—
– average workers	—	250	78	122	96	134	76
per co.	213	—	74	114	111	89	—
Entries	—	4,932	5,054	3,167	4,416	3,457	7,341
	6,825	—	9,490	2,198	7,649	8,625	—
– average entries	—	8.1	6.3	14.0	14.2	17.0	13.5
per co.	7.6	—	8.8	12.6	14.3	13.2	—

(Continued)

Table A5.b. Bureaucratic output of quota, Moscow (Continued)

	2008	2009	2010	2011	2012	2013	2014
TRADE							
Approved quota	—	116,602	36,258	18,974	34,780	32,035	54,088
	138,355	—	61,032	132,474	50,094	71,153	
– % of regional	—	30%	15%	15%	26%	32%	34%
quota	23%	—	24%	66%	24%	33%	—
Companies	—	2,232	2,513	1,092	1,246	744	1,474
	2,958	—	2,990	4,373	1,802	2,633	—
– average workers	—	52	14	17	28	43	37
per co.	47	—	20	30	28	27	—
Entries	—	11,663	7,992	4,369	5,050	3,767	10,889
	13,553	—	13,561	24,731	7,656	16,532	—
– average entries	—	5.2	3.2	4	4.1	5.1	7.4
per co.	4.6	—	4.5	5.7	4.3	6.3	—
HOSPITALITY							
Approved quota	—	19,198	7,928	3,356	6,492	3,904	5,680
	13,514	—	10,605	2,863	10,564	8,927	—
– % of regional	—	5%	3%	3%	5%	4%	4%
quota	2%	—	4%	1%	5%	4%	—
Companies	—	332	360	221	338	197	262
	392	—	500	124	534	412	—
– average workers	—	58	22	15	19	20	22
per co.	35	—	21	23	20	22	—
Entries	—	1,348	1,370	1,036	1,519	926	1,689
	1,492	—	2,830	692	2,529	2,766	—
– average entries	—	4.1	3.8	4.7	4.5	4.7	6.5
per co.	3.8	—	5.7	5.6	4.7	6.7	—
TRANSPORTATION							
Approved quota	—	18,187	10,354	7,668	10,087	11,437	12,223
	30,336	—	12,917	6,154	12,759	13,413	—
– % of regional	—	5%	4%	6%	7%	11%	8%
quota	5%	—	5%	3%	6%	6%	—
Companies	—	213	276	198	160	110	265
	295	—	359	79	252	397	—
– average workers	—	85	38	39	63	104	46
per co.	103	—	36	78	51	34	—
Entries	—	510	755	741	705	527	1,574
	703		1,349	329	1,117	2,222	—
– average entries	—	2.4	2.7	3.7	4.4	4.8	5.9
per co.	2.4	—	3.6	4.2	4.4	5.6	—

Table A5.b. Bureaucratic output of quota, Moscow (Continued)

	2008	2009	2010	2011	2012	2013	2014
REAL ESTATE							
Approved quota	—	39,143	27,832	23,643	30,790	20,538	25,404
	116,637	—	40,002	15,754	44,793	35,307	—
– % of regional	—	10%	11%	18%	23%	20%	16%
quota	20%	—	16%	8%	21%	16%	—
Companies	—	1,197	1,773	1,407	1,058	667	666
	1,520	—	2,112	917	1,473	1,273	—
– average workers	—	33	16	17	29	31	38
per co.	77	—	19	17	30	28	—
Entries	—	3,326	4,690	7,376	6,125	3,932	4,498
	4,402	—	9,859	4,983	8,780	8,788	—
– average entries	—	2.8	2.7	5.2	5.8	5.9	6.8
per co.	2.9	—	4.7	5.4	6	6.9	—
GOVERNMENT							
Approved quota	—	0	80,033	0	0	0	0
	29,257	—	8,383	0	155	0	—
– % of regional	—	0	32%	0	0	0	0
quota	5%	—	3%	0	0.07%	0	—
Companies	—	0	4	0	0	0	0
	6	—	4	0	1	0	—
– average workers	—	0	20,008	0	0	0	0
per co.	4,876	—	2,096	0	155	0	—
Entries	—	0	18	0	0	0	0
	24	—	23	0	24	0	—
– average entries	—	0	4.5	0	0	0	0
per co.	4	—	5.8	0	24	0	—
SERVICES							
Approved quota	—	9,850	6,197	2,795	9,452	4,742	4,582
	20,884	—	8,627	3,773	12,403	7,672	—
– % of regional	—	3%	3%	2%	7%	5%	3%
quota	4%	—	4%	2%	6%	4%	—
Companies	—	221	262	188	238	141	148
	311	—	347	147	349	278	—
– average workers	—	45	24	15	40	34	31
per co.	67	—	25	26	36	28	—
Entries	—	780	684	913	1,324	835	904
	58	—	1,684	822	1,913	1,656	—
– average entries	—	3.5	2.6	4.9	5.6	5.9	6.1
per co.	0.2	—	4.9	5.6	5.5	6	—

[a] Does not reflect beginning of the year figures, but is the first spreadsheet issued for the year.

The spreadsheets give great insight into what bureaucrats require of employers in order to successfully submit an application and receive quota. In many cases, companies receive multiple entries in the spreadsheet, specifying different aspects of their foreign labour force's jobs, housing conditions, countries of origin, etc. In different years, and even within a given year, different categories of information are included, resulting in a company's allocation being divided into fewer or greater entries. Though the forms employers must fill out are standard, the information contained in the applications is not treated equally. For example, employers are required to list the wages they will pay workers, yet in many cases in Moscow (though not in the other regions) the wage information is missing, or not realistic (e.g., 1 ruble per month). This highlights the discretion regional interdepartmental commissions use when processing employer applications.

While this administrative discretion can lead to missing categories of information, it can also lead to the opposite situation where applications are not processed until full information is provided, leading to a comparatively increased bureaucratic burden. Often in these circumstances, bureaucrats can refuse to process documents until they are satisfied that all necessary information has been provided. For example, in 2010 the overall number of entries nearly doubles during the mid-year quota redistributions, from 24,298 at the beginning of the year to 47,313 at the end, even though the overall quota for Moscow remained the same. The major reason for this is that the spreadsheets underwent a dramatic reformatting during 2010, providing more detailed information about housing, required work experience, and level of social insurance provided. There was also an increased specificity in job titles. For example, the number of unique job titles increased from 1,154 at the beginning of the year to 1,570 at the end of the year. The quota of 250,000 was also redistributed from 7,080 companies at the beginning of the year to 8,745 companies at the end.

Inconsistencies in data and data processing show a lack of standardized systems, allowing for the possibility that individuals will process data how they see fit and therefore data outputs will vary not only from region to region but from bureaucrat to bureaucrat. For example, the first spreadsheet issued in 2011 reflects the quota allocation at the beginning of the year (128,803 for all of Moscow), and allocates quota for 1,092 companies to hire 18,974 workers in the sector of trade. A revised spreadsheet was issued in September (reflecting the year-end quota allocation of 199,778) that gave permission to 4,373 companies in the trade sector to hire 132,474 workers. All other sectors with the exception of the service sector experienced reductions, both in numbers of companies and workers, across these two spreadsheets. This raises serious questions about why quota was reallocated so significantly within the span of just a few months, and why so many companies lost quota (388 in the manufacturing sector and 52 in the construction sector). However, on further analysis, a number of those jobs merely reflect a reclassification according to OKVED categories by the person compiling the spreadsheet. A search of unique companies across the quota allocations reveals that only 55 companies distributed across all economic sectors lost their quota allocation from the beginning to the end of 2011.

The analysis of quota allocation at the sectoral level highlights an onerous bureaucratic process that lacks consistency across years and across regions. While some of these idiosyncrasies may not have an overall impact on quota allocation or the migration process, they open an interesting window into bureaucratic function. However, in some cases, bureaucratic discretion, especially of the type that refuses applications for not following detailed whims of the personnel accepting documents, can serve to decrease the availability of an already scarce quota.

Appendix to Chapter 6

Table A6.a. Bureaucratic output of quota, Sverdlovsk

	2006	2007	2008	2009	2010	2011	2012	2013	2014
Starting quota		181,988	47,500	133,402	66,973	42,955	27,931	48,263	40,487
(Year-end quota)		—	167,486	100,693	64,700	47,024	46,464	52,263	47,974
AGRICULTURE									
Approved quota	—	—	—	3,793	349	3,405	1,564	1,770	1,511
	—	—	3,350	—	3,163	3,536	2,336	1,783	—
– % of regional quota	—	—	—	3%	0.50%	8%	6%	4%	4%
	—	—	2%	—	5%	8%	5%	3%	—
Companies	—	—	—	70	12	59	41	43	39
	—	—	89	—	73	61	66	45	—
– average workers per co.	—	—	—	54	29	58	38	41	39
	—	—	38	—	43	58	35	40	—
Entries	—	—	—	91	26	168	113	152	92
	—	—	127	—	195	178	174	154	—
– average entries per co.	—	—	—	1.3	2.2	2.9	2.8	3.5	2.4
	—	—	1.4	—	2.7	2.9	2.6	3.4	—
Work permits	248	—	1,610	—	3,307	—	—	—	—
% of (year-end) quota used	—	—	48%	—	105%	—	—	—	—
MANUFACTURING									
Approved quota	—	—	—	18,234	5,439	5,533	5,710	8,206	7,660
	—	—	7,612	—	6,522	6,059	9,367	9,170	—
– % of regional quota	—	—	—	14%	8%	13%	20%	17%	19%
	—	—	5%	—	10%	13%	20%	18%	—
Companies	—	—	—	262	127	138	182	263	189
	—	—	296	—	172	144	306	278	—

– average workers per co.	—	—	—	70	43	40	31	31	41
	—	—	26	—	38	42	31	33	—
Entries	—	—	—	806	351	537	696	949	784
	—	—	806	—	567	562	1,120	1,045	—
– average entries per co.	—	—	—	3.1	2.8	3.9	3.8	3.6	4.2
	—	—	2.7	—	3.3	3.9	3.7	3.8	—
Work permits	4,635	—	15,256	—	12,623	—	—	—	—
% of (year-end) quota used	—	—	200%	—	194%	—	—	—	—
CONSTRUCTION									
Approved quota	—	—	—	46,232	22,166	14,229	8,030	13,305	14,310
	—	—	53,912	—	18,170	14,933	13,685	14,503	—
– % of regional quota	—	—	32%	35%	33%	33%	29%	28%	35%
	—	—	—	—	28%	32%	29%	28%	—
Companies	—	—	—	356	150	134	145	191	206
	—	—	422	—	183	140	233	199	—
– average workers per co.	—	—	—	130	148	106	55	70	70
	—	—	128	—	99	107	59	73	—
Entries	—	—	—	1,173	544	707	722	1,040	974
	—	—	1,280	—	862	752	1,186	1,073	—
– average entries per co.	—	—	—	3.3	3.6	5.3	5.0	5.5	4.7
	—	—	3.0	—	4.7	5.4	5.1	5.4	—
Work permits	18,990	—	47,506	—	21,060	—	—	—	—
% of (year-end) quota used	—	—	88%	—	116%	—	—	—	—
TRADE									
Approved quota	—	—	—	30,799	26,150	10,186	4,335	10,646	5,675
	—	—	28,585	—	22,896	10,970	8,636	10,949	—
– % of regional quota	—	—	—	23%	39%	24%	16%	22%	14%
	—	—	17%	—	35%	23%	19%	21%	—
Companies	—	—	—	441	291	199	164	297	215
	—	—	390	—	385	233	294	317	—

(*Continued*)

Table A6.a. Bureaucratic output of quota, Sverdlovsk (Continued)

	2006	2007	2008	2009	2010	2011	2012	2013	2014
– average workers per co.	—	—	—	70	90	51	26	36	26
	—	—	73	—	60	47	29	35	—
Entries	—	—	—	1,045	672	770	530	1,025	526
	—	—	814	—	1,255	911	998	1,083	—
– average entries per co.	—	—	—	2.4	2.3	3.9	3.2	3.5	2.5
	—	—	2.1	—	3.3	3.9	3.4	3.4	—
Work permits	24,104	—	8,321	—	25,222	—	—	—	—
% of (year-end) quota used	—	—	29%	—	110%	—	—	—	—
HOSPITALITY									
Approved quota	—	—	—	3,184	2,266	1,009	1,447	3,674	4,063
	—	—	3,035	—	2,294	1,735	2,729	4,283	—
– % of regional quota	—	—	—	2%	3%	2%	5%	8%	10%
	—	—	2%	—	4%	4%	6%	8%	—
Companies	—	—	—	93	90	94	65	179	154
	—	—	116	—	124	120	122	191	—
– average workers per co.	—	—	—	34	25	11	22	21	26
	—	—	26	—	19	15	22	22	—
Entries	—	—	—	281	256	285	299	799	592
	—	—	301	—	406	421	554	856	—
– average entries per co.	—	—	—	3.0	2.8	3.0	4.6	4.5	3.8
	—	—	2.6	—	3.3	3.5	4.5	4.5	—
Work permits	—	—	—	—	—	—	—	—	—
% of (year-end) quota used	—	—	—	—	—	—	—	—	—
TRANSPORTATION									
Approved quota	—	—	—	8,552	2,801	3,507	2,587	4,381	3,256
	—	—	9,149	—	2,727	3,683	3,653	4,761	—
– % of regional quota	—	—	—	6%	4%	8%	9%	9%	8%
	—	—	6%	—	4%	8%	8%	9%	—

Companies	—	—	—	72	27	41	76	121	79
	—	—	83	—	44	45	113	125	—
– average workers per co.	—	—	—	119	104	86	34	36	41
	—	—	110	—	62	82	32	38	—
Entries	—	—	—	139	53	212	298	295	230
	—	—	147	—	152	229	388	316	—
– average entries per co.	—	—	—	1.9	2.0	5.2	3.9	2.4	2.9
	—	—	1.8	—	3.5	5.1	3.4	2.5	—
Work permits	2,191	—	8,321	—	5,164	—	—	—	—
% of (year-end) quota used	—	—	91%	—	189%	—	—	—	—
REAL ESTATE									
Approved quota	—	—	—	8,637	3,209	3,390	3,231	3,972	2,309
	—	—	51,464	—	5,298	4,408	4,352	4,449	—
– % of regional quota	—	—	—	7%	5%	8%	12%	8%	6%
	—	—	31%	—	8%	9%	9%	9%	—
Companies	—	—	—	59	46	81	96	124	69
	—	—	148	—	87	89	130	128	—
– average workers per co.	—	—	—	146	70	42	34	32	34
	—	—	348	—	61	50	34	35	—
Entries	—	—	—	171	116	333	387	460	226
	—	—	406	—	393	412	536	473	—
– average entries per co.	—	—	—	2.9	2.5	4.1	4.0	3.7	3.3
	—	—	2.7	—	4.5	4.6	4.1	3.7	—
Work permits	—	—	—	—	—	—	—	—	—
% of (year-end) quota used	—	—	—	—	—	—	—	—	—
HEALTH/SOCIAL SERVICES									
Approved quota	—	—	—	7,806	75	136	132	199	207
	—	—	7,004	—	161	193	197	217	—
– % of regional quota	—	—	—	6%	0.1%	0.3%	0.5%	0.4%	0.5%
	—	—	4%	—	0.3%	0.4%	0.4%	0.4%	—

(Continued)

Table A6.a. Bureaucratic output of quota, Sverdlovsk (Continued)

	2006	2007	2008	2009	2010	2011	2012	2013	2014
Companies	—	—	—	19	12	30	22	26	30
	—	—	36	—	35	32	34	32	—
– average workers per co.	—	—	—	411	6	5	6	8	7
	—	—	195	—	5	6	6	7	—
Entries	—	—	—	50	17	43	43	54	78
	—	—	67	—	60	60	68	63	—
– average entries per co.	—	—	—	2.6	1.4	1.4	2	2.1	2.6
	—	—	1.7	—	1.7	1.9	2	2	—
Work permits	—	—	—	—	—	—	—	—	—
% of (year-end) quota used	—	—	—	—	—	—	—	—	—
SERVICES									
Approved quota	—	—	—	3,955	4,363	1,312	715	1,693	1,254
	—	—	3,054	—	3,101	1,259	1,304	1,741	—
– % of regional quota	—	—	—	3%	7%	3%	3%	4%	3%
	—	—	2%	—	5%	3%	3%	3%	—
Companies	—	—	—	32	35	86	46	61	55
	—	—	43	—	72	59	75	63	—
– average workers per co.	—	—	—	124	125	15	16	28	23
	—	—	71	—	43	21	17	28	—
Entries	—	—	—	93	41	219	157	61	153
	—	—	76	—	272	183	266	322	—
– average entries per co.	—	—	—	2.9	2.9	2.5	3.4	5.1	2.8
	—	—	1.8	—	3.8	3.1	3.5	5.1	—
Work permits	—	—	—	—	—	—	—	—	—
% of (year-end) quota used	—	—	—	—	—	—	—	—	—

Appendix to Chapter 7

Table A7.a. Bureaucratic output of quota, Krasnodar

	2006	2007	2008	2009	2010	2011	2012	2013	2014
Starting quota	—	113,535	27,920	48,012	25,098	43,013	28,299	28,066	22,599
(Year-end quota)	—	—	54,324	45,271	44,927	46,971	72,608	61,722	33,420
AGRICULTURE									
Approved quota	—	—	—	3,177	2,807	5,324	2,213	2,050	3,876
	—	—	3,533	—	5,050	5,033	4,493	4,603	4,060
– % of regional quota	—	—	—	7%	11%	12%	8%	7%	12%
	—	—	7%	—	11%	11%	6%	7%	13%
Companies	—	—	—	48	47	86	42	41	49
	—	—	59	—	96	88	75	74	51
– average workers per co.	—	—	—	66	60	62	53	50	79
	—	—	60	—	53	57	60	62	80
Entries	—	—	—	81	68	160	72	75	88
	—	—	102	—	179	160	144	170	91
– average entries per co.	—	—	—	1.7	1.5	1.9	1.7	1.8	1.8
	—	—	1.7	—	1.9	1.8	1.9	2.3	1.8
Work permits	2,546	—	5,098	—	4,346	—	—	—	—
% of (year-end) quota used	—	—	144%	—	86%	—	—	—	—
MANUFACTURING									
Approved quota	—	—	—	1,917	789	1,648	919	766	3,079
	—	—	1,487	—	1,504	1,768	1,561	2,740	3,109
– % of regional quota	—	—	—	4%	3%	4%	3%	3%	10%
	—	—	3%	—	3%	4%	2%	4%	10%
Companies	—	—	—	67	48	81	51	42	70
	—	—	93	—	85	87	92	92	72

(Continued)

Table A7.a. Bureaucratic output of quota, Krasnodar (Continued)

	2006	2007	2008	2009	2010	2011	2012	2013	2014
– average workers per co.	—	—	—	29	16	20	18	18	44
	—	—	16	—	18	20	17	30	43
Entries	—	—	—	173	136	238	160	120	262
	—	—	272	—	281	253	261	283	265
– average entries per co.	—	—	—	2.6	2.8	2.9	3.1	2.9	3.7
	—	—	2.9	—	3.3	2.9	2.8	3.1	3.7
Work permits	61	—	3,811	—	3,543	—	—	—	—
% of (year-end) quota used	—	—	256%	—	236%	—	—	—	—
CONSTRUCTION									
Approved quota	—	—	—	41,405	20,082	33,347	24,445	24,121	20,441
	—	—	43,332	—	36,043	37,292	64,355	47,397	20,721
– % of regional quota	—	—	—	86%	80%	78%	86%	86%	64%
	—	—	80%	—	80%	79%	89%	77%	64%
Companies	—	—	—	195	99	251	114	94	130
	—	—	239	—	270	279	224	203	134
– average workers per co.	—	—	—	212	203	133	214	257	157
	—	—	181	—	134	134	287	234	155
Entries	—	—	—	1,363	1,125	2614	1,476	1,282	1,638
	—	—	1,303	—	3,134	2830	3,086	2,768	1,651
– average entries per co.	—	—	—	7.0	11.4	10.4	13.0	13.6	12.6
	—	—	5.5	—	11.6	10.1	13.7	13.6	12.3
Work permits	12,005	—	39,778	—	28,864	—	—	—	—
% of (year-end) quota used	—	—	92%	—	80%	—	—	—	—
TRADE									
Approved quota	—	—	—	335	332	691	59	280	298
	—	—	1,409	—	412	693	167	356	314
– % of regional quota	—	—	—	0.7%	1%	2%	0.2%	1%	1%
	—	—	3%	—	1%	2%	0.2%	0.5%	1%

Companies	—	—	—	71	41	69	12	16	30
	—	—	166	—	62	69	24	26	33
– average workers per co.	—	—	—	5	8	10	5	18	10
	—	—	9	—	7	10	7	14	10
Entries	—	—	—	129	98	213	37	48	85
	—	—	312	—	154	214	50	64	88
– average entries per co.	—	—	—	1.8	2.4	3.1	3.1	3.0	2.8
	—	—	1.9	—	2.5	3.1	2.1	2.5	2.7
Work permits	2,085	—	640	—	2,076	—	—	—	—
% of (year-end) quota used	—	—	45%	—	504%	—	—	—	—
HOSPITALITY									
Approved quota	—	—	—	292	356	872	313	518	2,142
	—	—	460	—	871	894	1,421	4,145	2,187
– % of regional quota	—	—	—	1%	1%	2%	1%	2%	7%
	—	—	1%	—	2%	2%	2%	7%	7%
Companies	—	—	—	28	28	83	26	34	60
	—	—	61	—	59	89	78	73	65
– average workers per co.	—	—	—	10	13	11	12	15	36
	—	—	8	—	15	10	18	57	34
Entries	—	—	—	53	74	243	55	85	305
	—	—	103	—	199	252	210	342	314
– average entries per co.	—	—	—	1.9	2.6	2.9	2.1	2.5	5.1
	—	—	1.7	—	3.4	2.8	2.7	4.7	4.8
Work permits	—	—	—	—	—	—	—	—	—
% of (year-end) quota used	—	—	—	—	—	—	—	—	—
TRANSPORTATION									
Approved quota	—	—	—	62	51	181	1	23	308
	—	—	88	—	180	185	9	563	339
– % of regional quota	—	—	—	0.10%	0.20%	0.40%	0.00%	0.08%	1%
	—	—	0.20%	—	0.40%	0.40%	0.01%	0.90%	1%

(Continued)

Table A7.a. Bureaucratic output of quota, Krasnodar (Continued)

	2006	2007	2008	2009	2010	2011	2012	2013	2014
Companies	—	—	—	16	10	10	1	3	17
	—	—	25	—	17	11	3	25	18
– average workers per co.	—	—	—	4	5	18	1	8	18
	—	—	4	—	11	17	3	23	19
Entries	—	—	—	21	12	41	1	7	37
	—	—	36	—	50	45	3	111	49
– average entries per co.	—	—	—	1.3	1.2	4.1	1	2.3	2.2
	—	—	1.4	—	2.9	4.1	1	4.4	2.7
Work permits	70	—	640	—	460	—	—	—	—
% of (year-end) quota used	—	—	727%	—	256%	—	—	—	—
REAL ESTATE									
Approved quota	—	—	—	529	98	421	70	90	750
	—	—	3278	—	168	524	130	1,233	750
– % of regional quota	—	—	—	1%	0.4%	1%	0.3%	0.3%	2%
	—	—	6%	—	0.4%	1%	0.2%	2%	2%
Companies	—	—	—	15	14	23	12	10	22
	—	—	21	—	19	24	17	26	22
– average workers per co.	—	—	—	35	7	18	6	9	34
	—	—	156	—	9	22	8	47	—
Entries	—	—	—	32	38	108	27	41	127
	—	—	70	—	73	116	35	107	127
– average entries per co.	—	—	—	2.1	2.7	4.7	2.3	4.1	5.8
	—	—	3.3	—	3.8	4.8	2.1	4.1	5.8
Work permits	—	—	—	—	—	—	—	—	—
% of (year-end) quota used	—	—	—	—	—	—	—	—	—

SERVICES									
Approved quota	—	—	—	63	143	302	174	178	659
	—	—	411	—	310	317	358	358	799
– % of regional quota	—	—	—	0.1%	0.6%	0.7%	0.6%	0.6%	2%
	—	—	1%	—	0.7%	0.7%	0.5%	0.6%	3%
Companies	—	—	—	10	14	24	10	12	34
	—	—	21	—	33	27	22	31	34
– average workers per co.	—	—	—	6	10	13	17	15	19
	—	—	20	—	9	12	16	12	24
Entries	—	—	—	23	32	128	100	69	148
	—	—	35	—	131	137	133	111	167
– average entries per co.	—	—	—	2.3	2.4	5.3	10.0	5.8	4.6
	—	—	1.7	—	4.0	5.1	6.0	3.6	4.9
Work permits	—	—	—	—	—	—	—	—	—
% of (year-end) quota used	—	—	—	—	—	—	—	—	—

Notes

Introduction

1 CIS countries include Armenia, Azerbaijan, Belarus, Moldova, Kazakhstan, Kyrgyzstan, Tajikistan, and Uzbekistan.
2 Ukrainian citizens are also extended the same entry and work privileges, though Ukraine is not an official member of the CIS. They are also counted in the statistics of CIS migrants.
3 The methodology for estimating the US foreign-born population, for example, includes an estimate of illegal immigrants (Hoefer, Rytina, and Baker 2012)
4 *Concept of State Migration Policy* to 2025 (Presidential Decree (*ukaz*) of June 13, 2012).
5 The trend has slowed, though in the second decade after the collapse of the Soviet Union, the ethnic Russian population grew from 111 million to nearly 116 million (measured from the 2002 to 2010 censuses).
6 Federal Law No. 115 of July 25, 2002.
7 Federal Law No. 62 of May 31 2002. Until 2000, citizens of the former Soviet Union had been able to gain Russian citizenship relatively easily regardless of their place of birth. The situation did not change for citizens of Kyrgyzstan, Belarus, and Kazakhstan according to the terms of a 1999 agreement that offered former Soviet citizens born or permanently living within any of the four countries at the time of the Soviet Union's collapse reciprocal access to citizenship within three months (International Treaty of February 26, 1999).
8 It is interesting that the law (both then and now) has never specified that non-visa immigrants are CIS citizens. The law simply distinguishes between those immigrants who need a visa and those who don't. The details of

which countries' citizens qualify for non-visa entry are determined by bilateral and multilateral agreements. In practice, while citizens of some countries may have visa-free access to Russia for tourist or business purposes (e.g., Serbia, South Korea, Turkey), only citizens of CIS countries are afforded the labour market benefits specified in the law for non-visa immigrants.

9 Presidential Decree (*ukaz*) No. 928 of July 19, 2004.

10 Zhanna Zaionchkovskaia, interview by Ogoniok, *Kvoti s potolka* [*Quotas from the ceiling*], August 20, 2007.

1. Why Control Immigration?

1 While "migration" refers to the movement of people both across borders and within countries, "immigration" refers to those migrants who are entering a particular country. There is no standard time horizon for either category, and therefore temporary or permanent travellers can be referred to either as migrant or immigrant. From the state's perspective, while there are different dynamics and policies for temporary vs permanent immigrants, the temporal aspect of migration is secondary to the more immediate concerns of managing movement and labour. I use the terms migrant and immigrant interchangeably as appropriate.

2 Illegal migrants are those without the full legal recognition of the receiving state, either because of entering unlawfully or staying past the legally prescribed period of time, lacking residence registration documents (for countries that require them), working in the informal sector, or working in the formal sector either without proper documents (e.g., a work permit) or with falsified documents. The literature uses a range of terms to refer to migrants whose status is in question. At times, the distinction is one of fully illegal vs partially illegal (irregular migrants may have some, but not all, of their paperwork completed, or may have legal status but work illegally) (Jandl 2007). Some scholars include categories of "semi-compliance" (Ruhs and Anderson 2010) or "semi-legality" (Kubal 2013) to highlight the grey zone between fully legal and illegal statuses. In many cases labels are a semantic choice meant to cast migrants in a particular light, with "irregular" focusing on exclusion and vulnerability (Paspalanova 2008). I use the term "illegal" migrant synonymously with "undocumented" and "informal" migrant. Using "illegal" to describe migrants is provocative; some might even call it politically incorrect. Yet it brings into sharp relief the relationship between legal frameworks and the migrants those frameworks intend to cover, especially the idea that

it is the law (and nothing else) that allows for the possibility of illegal migrants (Dauvergne 2008). By deciding what proportion of the immigrant population has access to legal status, entry policies by default have an impact on the integration potential of immigrants (i.e., how fully they will integrate, learn the host country language, participate in the labour market, naturalize, etc.).

3 Though the general assumption in the migration literature is that states work to limit illegal immigration, several studies have found that it is sometimes beneficial to politicians to allow illegal entry or residence. For example, Sadiq (2005) shows that the government in Malaysia allows and encourages illegal immigration in order to create a more ethnically homogeneous population, and (through the use of false documents) to increase electoral support for certain parties. Other studies suggest that selective enforcement of immigration policies may result from a desire to channel illegal migrants into certain economic sectors (Hillman and Weiss 1999), or to gain votes by promising strict immigration enforcement that is then deliberately underfunded (Facchini and Testa 2014).

4 There is ample evidence from France (Hollifield 2014), Germany (Martin 2014), and the US (Massey and Pren 2012) that when migration policy becomes more strict, migration flows that had previously been circular or temporary become more permanent. Evidence from the US case shows that while a tightening of border controls has led migrants to shift their entry points, it has not led to a decrease in overall entries, and further has led to the unfortunate consequence of increased deaths of migrants attempting border crossings (Massey, Durand, and Malone 2002; Cornelius 2001).There is a greater theoretical point here, that so long as the macroeconomic and other structural factors attracting migrants to host countries remain, migrants will continue to come, regardless of state policies.

5 See, for example, Benhabib (2004) and Walzer (1983) for normative arguments on immigration control, and Carens (1987) and Caplan (2012) for justifications of open border policies.

6 While there are notable examples of migration research on non-democratic countries, these cases are not well integrated into migration theory or into current efforts to build migration indices.

7 Decreasing numbers of permanent migrants starting in the 2000s are partially a result of more difficult procedures for obtaining registration documents as a result of the laws *On Citizenship* and *On the Legal Status of Foreign Citizens*, both passed in 2002 (Zaionchkovskaia, Mkrtchyn, and Tyuryukanova 2009).

8 While CIS migrants are the main focus of this analysis because of their scale and separate legal regime, I include several examples of labour migrants from other countries (and occasionally internal labour migrants who are Russian citizens) in order to offer further evidence of the book's argument.

9 The reality of Russia's immigration system is complex and nuanced with many overlapping categories. Studies that focus on citizenship (permanent migration), refugees, compatriot or return migration, or labour migration capture only a subset of the overall picture, while still capturing some of the important overlapping themes. It is not easy to draw a concrete line between different categories of migrants. For the migrants this book focuses on, the choice of status (e.g., refugee, compatriot, temporary labour migrant, temporary resident, permanent resident, citizen) has less to do with the desire to remain in Russia and integrate into society than it does with the exigencies of obtaining the documents that will provide the most secure status enabling work and travel between Russia and the home country. Therefore, low-skilled migrant workers as a group share a great deal in common, whether they are illegal, documented as temporary workers, or have permanent residence or even citizenship. Nevertheless, the vast majority of economic migrants are temporary and either undocumented or working as labour migrants, and so I use terms like labour migrants and temporary migrants as shorthand, knowing full well the nuances and overlaps involved.

10 Catherine Putz, "Tough times ahead in Tajikistan," *Diplomat*, May 27, 2015, accessed March 11, 2016. http://thediplomat.com/2015/05/tough-times-ahead-in-tajikistan/.

11 Some estimates place the number of immigrants from Uzbekistan, Kyrgyzstan, and Tajikistan alone at over 5 million (Anichkova 2012), and the total number of migrants at 10 million, of which no more than 2.5 million are legal (Malashenko 2012). Other experts dismiss such high figures as unsubstantiated (Zaionchkovskaya 2013). Illegal migrants do not only come from CIS countries, as there is evidence of migrants from China and African countries entering on tourist visas or as asylum seekers and allowing their status to lapse or working without a work permit.

12 While some experts observe that Russians who occupy low-skilled jobs demand higher wages than migrants (Mukomel 2006), this should not be taken as evidence that migrants produce downward pressure on wages or that, if the labour market were protected from immigrants, unemployment in the local population would decrease. Rather, migrants represent a much more flexible and mobile workforce than local workers, who consider a

wide range of social factors (over and above income) when making labour market decisions (Piore 1979).

13 Similar trends can be observed with the number of entries into Russia (table 1.3) and the number of documented labour migrants (table 1.1), though documented labour migration was slower to recover than either remittances or entries into Russia.

14 Migrant advocate, interview by the author, Moscow, June 2016.

15 Predictions even in the 1970s indicated a decline of working-age population especially in Slavic areas of the USSR. Experts foresaw the need to import a labour force of as many as 9 million people from Central Asia and the Caucasus (Lewis and Rowland 1979). Therefore, the current trend can be seen not only as a continuation of Soviet trends but also one that the government has long been well aware of, as it was acknowledged by Soviet experts (Manevich 1968).

16 Presidential Decree (*ukaz*) No. 1351 of October 9, 2007.

17 Lyudmila Nazdracheva, "How former Soviet countrymen resettle in Russia," *Russia beyond the Headlines*, September 26, 2013, accessed December 11, 2014.

18 Margarita Alekhina, "'Trudosposobnoe naselenie Rossii sokrashchaetcia po millionu v god' Demograf Zhanna Zaionchkovskaia ['Working age population in Russia is shrinking by one million per year' says demographer Zhanna Zaionchkovskaia]," *Novye Izvestiia*, May 22, 2012, accessed January 26, 2015. http://www.newizv.ru/society/2012-05-22/163781-demograf-zhanna-zajonchkovskaja.html. The *Demographic Policy Concept to 2025* (Presidential Decree (*ukaz*) No. 1351 of October 9, 2007) gives targets of migration growth of "more than 300,000" per year. The *Concept of State Migration Policy to 2025* does not give specific numerical targets.

19 Temporary and permanent residence permits are not disaggregated in FMS data, but the quota for temporary residence permits in 2013 was 105,000, meaning that of 350,000 *no more than* 105,000 were temporary residence permits.

20 "Inflow of migrants to Russia a necessity – migration service," *Russia beyond the Headlines*, November 3, 2012, accessed June 18, 2014. http://rbth.com/articles/2012/11/03/inflow_of_migrants_to_russia_a_necessity_-_migration_service_19740.html; Craig Oliphant, *Russia's Role and Interests in Central Asia*. 2013, accessed June 19, 2014. saferworld.org.uk.

21 I focus in particular on the policies that affect temporary CIS migrants who do not qualify as highly qualified specialists, seek temporary or permanent residence permits (which allow them to work without additional documents), or work in the free labour zone among Eurasian Economic Union

countries (Armenia, Belarus, Kazakhstan, Kyrgyzstan, and Russia) as of 2015.

22 Though some studies extend migration concepts to industrialized countries regardless of regime type (Castles 2004), or give a cursory nod to principles that hold true "particularly in democratic states," but "even in authoritarian states" (Czaika and de Haas 2013), the systematic integration of non-democratic cases into the literature is still at the early stages. This gap is reinforced by the current focus on index building, which relies on information from the best-studied cases (Gest et al. 2014; Beine et al. 2013; Bjerre et al. 2014), reinforcing the insular focus on Western immigrant recipients and limiting the generalizability of migration theory.

23 I have elaborated some of these nuances as they pertain to Russia's migration situation in greater detail elsewhere (Schenk forthcoming).

24 The ruling elite's use of patriotic and nationalist ideas has ebbed and flowed since the fall of the Soviet Union. Yeltsin typically avoided any reference to ethnic nationalism and preferred to focus on a civic idea of Russian national identity, marked by the use of *rossiiskii* (a non-exclusive term for "Russian" that denotes citizenship rather than ethnicity). In the Putin era, the traditionally ethnic demarcation of "Russian" (*russkii*) became conflated with the more inclusive *rossiiskii*, creating an ambiguous idea of national identity (Shevel 2011; Tolz and Harding 2015; Casula 2013).

25 In Russia, all foreigners and citizens must be registered at a specific location (called a place of stay for temporary visitors such as labour migrants, and a place of residence for those with temporary or permanent residence permits or citizenship). Rubber apartments are places where numerous foreigners are registered. In some cases, migrants live on premises, which causes concerns about the spread of infection due to close living quarters. In other cases, the registrations are fictitious and have no relationship to the physical place where migrants actually live. In this latter case, apartment owners, intermediaries, or government officials sell registrations to (sometimes numerous) migrants.

26 Definitions of populism are diffuse and debated. Populism has been most intensively studied in relation to the activities of parties competing in electoral systems, and as a result many discussions focus on anti-systemic or anti-elite solutions to political problems (Canovan 1999; Mudde 2004). Yet populism can also be used by political insiders and by actors across the ideological spectrum (Canovan 2004). Populist strategies can be used by the right (Betz and Immerfall 1998) or the left (Acemoglu, Egorov, and Sonin 2013), by democrats or authoritarians (Dix 1985), and can be

exclusionary (as in Europe) or inclusionary (as in Latin America) (Mudde and Rovira Kaltwasser 2013).

27 Because the state-owned and/or -controlled media is the main transmission mechanism for anti-migrant sentiment, it can be argued that the state directs nationalist sentiment at some level (Schenk 2012). However, the media does not always follow the cues from the regime (i.e., public speeches of Putin), and editorial prerogatives can take on their own agendas (Tolz and Harding 2015). Anti-migrant attitudes and framings are also associated with nationalist groups and social movements that are weakly linked to the state (Tipaldou and Uba 2014; Markowitz and Peshkova 2016; Laruelle 2009). The construction of national identity, then, is not a unidirectional or top-down phenomenon, but is rather mobilized at certain points by socially embedded state actors as they interact with the public in various ways and for various purposes.

28 Another set of nationwide surveys, which found similar support for the idea of "Russia for Russians" (59% in 2013 and 2014), reported a slight increase in the proportion of respondents who "fully agree" with the sentiment from 2013 (25.2%) to 2014 (31.2%) (Neoruss Project 2014). Thirty-nine per cent of respondents restrict "Russians" to only ethnic Russians (instead of to all Russian citizens regardless of ethnicity). These data are informative because they provide more nuance than the Levada surveys, though the Levada surveys provide the opportunity to assess results over a longer time period.

29 The Neoruss survey findings are similar: 28–9% of respondents were opposed to easing the restrictions on migrant employment.

30 TNS Opinion and Social, 2012, Awareness of Home Affairs, Special Eurobarometer 380, European Commission, accessed January 28, 2015. http://ec.europa.eu/public_opinion/archives/ebs/ebs_380_en.pdf.

31 "Immigration," 2014, accessed January 28, 2015. http://www.gallup.com/poll/1660/immigration.aspx.

32 Benjamin Dodman, "Far-right leaders vow to 'save Europe' at French gathering," *France 24*, December 1, 2014, accessed January 28, 2015. http://www.france24.com/en/20141130-france-national-front-europe-far-right-leaders-marine-le-pen-wilders-russia/; Jacob Heilbrunn,"Charlie Hebdo fallout: Specter of Fascist past haunts European nationalism," *Reuters*, January 13, 2015, accessed January 28, 2015. http://blogs.reuters.com/great-debate/2015/01/13/charlie-hebdo-fallout-specters-of-fascist-past-haunt-europes-new-nationalism/.

33 Andrew Porter, "Migrants 'take the jobs from young Britons,'" *Telegraph*, June 30, 2011, accessed January 28, 2015. http://www.telegraph.co.uk/

news/uknews/immigration/8609827/UK-jobs-Migrants-take-the-jobs-from-young-Britons.html.

34 Though economic theory has long predicted that immigrants will pose a threat to both the wages and the employment of certain native workers (Borjas 2013), these predictions have not been borne out by empirical analysis (Orrenius and Zavodny 2012). The consensus among economists, rather, is that any impact of immigration on the labour market is quite small (Kleinman 2003). Many factors contribute to the degree of labour impact, including skills, geographical distribution, and sectoral aspects of the economy (Brücker and Jahn 2011; Borjas 1999), and therefore it is difficult to make broad generalizations even within one country, let alone at a theoretical level. Evidence demonstrates that immigrants rarely compete directly with native workers and that they have a very small impact on wages, in large part because they fill jobs that are undesirable to native workers (Somerville and Sumption 2009).

35 "Vladimir Putin: Kvota na gastarbaiterov dolzhna byt umenshena bole chem vdvoe [Vladimir Putin: Quota for guest workers should be reduced by more than half]," *Russkii Obozrevatel'*, December 4, 2009, accessed June 24, 2013. http://www.rus-obr.ru/days/1331.

36 Further, Tolz and Harding (2015) identify a shift towards less inflammatory coverage of migrant issues beginning in 2013 because the government recognized that anti-migrant media reporting created concrete dangers of increasing conflict and violence in society. In reality, 2015 saw a complex web of inputs that could explain shifts in both public opinion and elite framing of issues related to national identity and migration, including Russia's involvement in Ukraine and increasingly poor relations with the West, the latter of which became a focal point for xenophobia.

37 Director of an anti-trafficking organization, interview by the author, Moscow, June 2009. This is despite the fact that until 2013, when obtaining false registration was added to the criminal code, migration-related violations were all administrative, not criminal, offences.

38 Tat'iana Lysova, Bela Liauv, and Mariia Zheleznova, "Interv'iu – Sergei Sobyanin, brio mera Moskvy [Interview: Sergei Sobyanin, acting mayor of Moscow]," *Vedomosti*, August 6, 2013, accessed June 27, 2014. http://www.vedomosti.ru/library/news/14969351/intervyu-sergej-sobyanin-vrio-mera-moskvy. Because of a relic of the Soviet Union, which required citizens to have residence registration (*propiska*), it is possible for internal migrants to also have nebulous legal status if they are physically present in one location but their registration is in a different region, which limits their ability to access some social services.

39 Viktor Polevoi, "Chtoby ne boltalis' [So that they don't slack off]," *Moskovskaia Pravda*, December 19, 2008; Yevgeny Zubchenko, "Nezvanye Gosti [Uninvited guests]," *Novye Izvestiia*, October 14, 2009, accessed December 5, 2009. http://www.newizv.ru/news/2009-10-14/115845/.

40 "V Ekaterinburge produkty dlia shkol proizvodilis' nelegal'nymi migrantami v usloviiakh antisanitarii [In Yekaterinburg produce for schools was produced by illegal migrants in unsanitary conditions]," October 22, 2012, accessed January 23, 2015. http://www.1tv.ru/news/social/218206.

41 "Trudovye migranty dolzhny imet' obiazatel'nuiu medstrakhovku, polagaet Onishchenko [Labour migrants should have obligatory medical insurance, suggests Onishchenko]," February 7, 2010, accessed January 23, 2015. http://www.newsru.com/russia/07feb2010/srtr.html; "Onishchenko: gastarbaitery zarazhaiut rossiian SPIDom i tuberkulezom [Onishchenko: Guest workers infect Russians with AIDS and tuberculosis]," *Russkii Obozrevatel'*, October 12, 2011, accessed January 23, 2015. http://www.rus-obr.ru/days/14049; "Trudovye migranty v Rossii – 'politicheskie trupy' – Onishchenko [Labour migrants in Russia – 'political corpses' – Onishchenko]," October 12, 2012, accessed January 23, 2015. http://nbnews.com.ua/news/59732/.

42 Rospotrebnadzor Order (*prikaz*) No. 336 of September 14, 2010. Declaring migrants undesirable was not a new idea at the time of Onishchenko's comments, as the concept was a part of the original law *On the Order of Exit and Entry* of 1996, and was added to *On the Legal Status of Foreign Citizens* in 2008. The authority for declaring a migrant undesirable is delegated to key agencies, who use their own internal criteria for decision making. See Schenk (2016) for further discussion.

43 Sixty-five per cent of respondents to Levada's yearly opinion polls would like to restrict internal migrants from other parts of Russia from settling in their region, compared with 70% who believe that immigration should be restricted (Levada Center 2013).

44 "No price hikes after ban on foreign traders – official," *RIA Novosti*, April 2, 2007, accessed January 26, 2015. http://sputniknews.com/russia/20070402/62950443.html.

45 The publication was produced by the St Petersburg city government's program on tolerance, available at http://spbtolerance.ru/wp-content/uploads/2012/09/vostok-zapad-rus.pdf, accessed December 20, 2014.

46 "Novyi uchebnik znakomit migrantov s traditsionnymi tsennostiami, shchami i blinami [New textbook acquaints migrants with traditional values, soup and pancakes]," December 11, 2014, accessed January 31, 2015. http://www.newsru.com/religy/11dec2014/lehrbuch.html.

47 "Moscow warns Muslims against animal sacrifice on eve of major holiday," *Russia Today*, September 30, 2013, accessed January 31, 2015. http://rt.com/politics/moscow-muslim-sacrifice-holiday-528/.

48 "Prodazhu i zaboi zhertvennykh zhivotnykh na Kurban-bairam zapretiat v Mosvke [Sale and slaughter of sacrificial animals on Kurban-bairam is prohibited in Moscow]," *Mir 24*, September 30, 2014, accessed February 1, 2015. http://mir24.tv/news/society/11310433.

49 "S Sobyanin: Ne fakt, chto Moskve nuzhny eshche mecheti [S Sobyanin: It's not a fact, that Moscow needs more mosques]," *RBK*, October 11, 2012, accessed February 1, 2015. http://top.rbc.ru/society/11/10/2012/673938.shtml.

50 Though other categories of migrants (i.e., those from China, Vietnam, etc., all of whom come through the visa regime) are also important in Russia's migration processes, their numbers are far fewer. Nevertheless, they will be considered peripherally throughout this study.

51 Funding for field research was provided by the American Councils for International Education, the Fulbright Scholar Program, and a seed grant from Nazarbayev University. In addition to field research, this book was informed tremendously by several projects. In 2014, I worked with an international group of scholars to produce a report on trafficking and slavery for an Australian NGO called Walk Free. The team interviewed NGOs across Russia that work with victims of human trafficking and labour slavery. In 2015, I took part in the Eurasia Foundation's Social Expertise Exchange, where I contributed to a project assessing Russian NGOs' ability to assist migrants.

52 An additional complication with fieldwork is that approaching government officials may bring scrutiny of the researcher's immigration status, leading to deportation. In my personal research notes, I have documented several cases of researchers being deported, and have written more generally about the legal mechanisms used for expelling researchers from Russia (Schenk 2016); four of these cases were a direct result of trying to engage migration officials for the purpose of migration research.

53 There is a major caveat to this observation, concerning the temporary nature of some documents' availability. Laws and most of their amendments are reliably available through sources like consultant.ru and *Rossiiskaia Gazeta*'s online databases, and federal-level statistics are available through the state statistical services at gks.ru. However, regional and ministerial documents can be more difficult to find, and are often online only for short periods of time. There is tremendous regional variation in terms of what documents and other information are available online (e.g.,

government orders, regional legislation, migration reports and statistics, etc.). The two major government agencies that I analyse in this book, the Ministry of Labour and the Federal Migration Service, have undergone major restructuring during the period of my research. As websites transitioned, large amounts of data were taken down. While the internet-based data collection strategy I use has its limitations, it is an informative test of public data availability.

54 Other technologies, such as social media, also allow for "ethnographic sensibility" (Schatz 2009) to continually inform the development of the research project. I interact regularly with a number of experts and activists I met during fieldwork. The simple process of observing what news stories people post on Facebook allows me to continually assess how people frame migration governance over time. This new era of "virtual fieldwork" is embedded in relationships that are initially formed in a spatial context, but do not remain bound by distance.

2. The Multi-Level Balancing Act of Migration Management

1 A pseudonym.

2 Also see the work of Reeves (2013) on this topic.

3 Often discussions of mechanisms are dominated by considerations of causality, and the role of mechanisms is to link together a chain of events (Gerring 2010; Hedström and Swedberg 1998; Opp 2005). In the example of a corruption scheme as a mechanism, a causal scenario could be elaborated: restrictive laws cause increased informal or illegal behaviour (a claim made in the literature by Johnson et al. 1997; Loayza, Oviedo, and Servén 2005; Schneider 1997; and De Soto 1989). Corruption schemes such as bribes or the sale of documents are the means by which the causal link is made. However, this type of causal story is not the most interesting thing about the mechanisms in the present case. What is more interesting is what new possibilities mechanisms allow, or the types of flexibility they interject into the system that would otherwise not be available. The story of immigration in Russia is less about discrete causes and effects, and more about how strategic managers, through the use of a variety of mechanisms, are able to juggle a cacophony of causes and effects in a way that brings about points of equilibrium (fleeting though they may be).

4 Mechanisms are component parts of processes (Machamer, Darden, and Craver 2000; Tilly 2001; Gerring 2008), and the increasing focus on mechanisms in the social sciences has led to the development of process tracing as a methodological approach (Steel 2004).

5 A notable exception is Ledeneva (2006), who separates practices from institutions in a similar logic to the one used here. I prefer the term "mechanism" to "practice" because, evoking Weber, it implies a machine at work (Hedström and Swedberg 1998). While a machine can be harnessed to achieve an actor's aims, it requires effort on the part of the actor to direct activity and always has the potential to spin out of control.

6 It is also possible that formal laws may *not* be institutions in the sense of presenting constraints on behaviour if there are reliable mechanisms to circumnavigate legal procedures, or if in the course of practice additional (non-written) requirements can be imposed (i.e., if it is the officials who are not constrained by law).

7 These are at least organized formally, according to the law, though their function may rely substantially on informal principles.

8 Informal practices more generally are an important part of the analysis of post-Soviet politics. A number of scholars have traced the persistence and adaptation of informal processes in the post-Soviet period, both on the level of patron-client ties (DeBardeleben and Zherebtsov 2010) and on the level of informal elite networks that link political and economic actors (Sharafutdinova 2010a). Approaches focus variously on personalistic networks (Ledeneva 2013) and institutions such as the party system (Reuter 2013; Panov and Ross 2013). More generally, there is a large literature that demonstrates the centrality of informal practices across all spheres of society in the post-Soviet period, from the labour market (Tartakovskaya and Ashwin 2006) to health care (Gordeev, Pavlova, and Groot 2014) to access to education (Williams, Round, and Rodgers 2013).

9 For a discussion of the range of terms and their nuances, see Hale (2014) and Gel'man (2016).

10 These patterns produce markedly different outcomes from Freeman's "client politics" framework in the migration literature, which argues that there are interest groups within immigrant-receiving states lobbying for increasingly open immigration (Freeman 1995). Though, both in Freeman's work and in Russia, immigration policies are elite-driven and interest-based (Freeman 2002), the clients in the Russian case are not expressly in the private sector, and can even be state actors themselves who push for their favoured immigration policies (sometimes more open, sometimes more closed) in order to take advantage of the scarcity of legal labour. Furthermore, the mechanisms used for advocating interests are vastly different in the Russian case. The explicitly stated assumption in the existing migration literature is that interest groups use democratic procedures to pursue policies that benefit them and the groups they lobby for (Joppke 1998; Givens

and Luedtke 2005). This assumption cannot be extended to the Russian political system because of its reliance on informal politics and network ties *in lieu of* democratic procedures.

11 Exceptions to this general pattern could be made for situations in which patrons use their clients as scapegoats or to make an example of their capacity to punish. Even in these cases, clients who are significantly contributing to the priorities of stability, economic growth, and legitimacy are less likely to fall victim to political theatre.

12 This does not preclude the existence of multiple simultaneous patronage pacts. In fact it is quite likely that bureaucrats may be in pacts with their superiors and with other important elites (i.e., governors, mayors, local business elites, etc.). Ledeneva (2013) says that "networks are neither vertical nor horizontal" and that "the necessity of informal governance is linked to the crisscrossing and overlapping hierarchies ... associated with the non-hierarchical negotiation process." These comments highlight the importance of the larger web of networks within which the individual patron-client pacts (which are necessarily vertical) function.

13 Here I am using "Putin administration" as a demarcation of time more than as a statement of a personalistic power. Though politics in Russia is dominated by elites close to Putin, it should not be inferred that all of Russian politics is controlled by Putin. In general, I elide the terms Kremlin, executive, and Putin/Putin administration, acknowledging that the government is not only Putin, but rather relies on a closely knit team of political elites that coalesces in the public image of Putin.

14 Petrov, Lipman, and Hale (2014) give an alternative version of the social contract, which they call a "non-intrusion pact": a public that remains politically passive and tolerant of corruption so long as the government provides economic growth, stability, global strength, a strong leader, and the space for people to pursue their own private interests without the intrusion of the state.

15 A number of scholars equate breakdowns of this type as a signal of state and/or regime weakness (Krastev and Holmes 2012; Petrov, Lipman, and Hale 2014). While this perspective correctly highlights the difference between institution-bound and network-driven decision making, it measures politics against an ideal picture of the state, rather than demonstrating the continued resilience of both the state and regime despite factors that might predict their demise. Rather than framing Russia as a weak state scrambling to compensate for its institutional pathologies, this study presents the Russian political system as an entity with agency that actively creates and manages policy spheres with a variety of interests in mind.

16 "Putin khochet sazhat' khozyaev 'rezinovykh kvartir' [Putin wants to jail owners of 'rubber apartments']," BBC Russian Service, January 26, 2012, accessed June 27, 2014. http://www.bbc.co.uk/russian/russia/2012/01/120126_migration_criminal_putin.shtml.
17 Presidential Decree (*ukaz*) No. 602 of May 7, 2012.
18 It is not entirely clear who is included in the "top political leadership." Discussions of elite-driven politics in Russia typically focus on those closest to Putin (Kryshtanovskaya and White 2005). While the core of this group has been quite resilient, those outside the top dozen or so elites are more in flux and therefore difficult to define concretely.
19 "Profsoiuzy vystupili protiv patentov dlia gastarbaiterov i predlozhili strane voobshche oboitis' bez migrantov [Trade unions oppose patents for guest workers and recommended the country do without migrants]," December 8, 2009, accessed March 2, 2015. http://www.newsru.com/russia/08dec2009/migrants.html.
20 Marina Gritsiuk, "Gosudarstvo vziatok ne beret [The state does not take bribes]," *Rossiiskaia Gazeta*, December 8, 2009, accessed March 2, 2015. http://www.rg.ru/2009/12/08/migranty.html.
21 "Popolneniia v biudzhet RF za schet vvedeniia trudovykh patentov migrantov za dva goda sostavili 8.3 mlrd rub [Replenishment of the Russian budget as a result of the introduction of patents for migrants accounted for 8.3 billion rubles for two years]," September 20, 2012, accessed March 2, 2015. https://news.mail.ru/economics/10309536/.
22 Interministerial conflict among Russia's bureaucratic agencies is variously seen as a result of legacies of Soviet and imperial logics of patrimonial administration (Sakwa 2010), a specific peculiarity of the post-Soviet system (Gel'man 2016), or as the routine conflict that occurs in Weberian systems of rational-legal bureaucracy (i.e., through the lenses of Allison's bureaucratic politics model) (Taylor 2011).
23 Presidential Decree (*ukaz*) No. 636 of May 21, 2012. Presidential Decree (*ukaz*) No. 30 of January 15, 2013.
24 These observations are in relation to the interdepartmental work towards the drafting of the *Concept of State Migration Policy to 2025*, which was adopted in 2012.
25 Steven Erlanger, "Tatar area in Russia votes on sovereignty today," *New York Times*, March 21, 1992, accessed February 7, 2017. http://www.nytimes.com/1992/03/21/world/tatar-area-in-russia-votes-on-sovereignty-today.html.
26 Key reforms included the establishment of federal districts under the leadership of presidential envoys, reconfiguration of the Federation Council,

amendments to electoral policies making regional parties obsolete and moving to an entirely proportional representation system, and rescinding the election of governors.

27 A recent trend in the literature on Russian federalism has preferred to conceptualize centre-periphery dynamics in terms of principal-agent rather than patron-client relations (Sharafutdinova 2010a; Gel'man and Ryzhenkov 2011; Reuter and Remington 2009), though the concepts are not entirely mutually exclusive (Gel'man 2010). In fact, the components of these relations are essentially the same, yet I prefer the patronage frame because it highlights the spoils of the system (i.e., the proceeds of corruption exploited by regional actors) not as an unfortunate by-product of incomplete monitoring or coordination, but rather as essential to the system's function.

28 Surprisingly, economic performance seems to be less crucial for maintaining the pact (Slider 2011; Baranov et al. 2015; Petrov 2010).

29 In this sense, the populist pact is a part of the migration pact; however, it can also function on its own when populism is mobilized around non-migration issues.

30 The state itself recognizes the scope and depth of corruption. Putin's (2012) article *Russia: The National Question* mentions corruption several times in the context of migration. Nevertheless, this does not mean that every bureaucrat engages in corrupt activity or that engagement is uniform across agencies or regions.

31 "Kvoty tolkaiut migrantov v 'ten'' [Quotas are pushing migrants into the 'shadows']," *Rosbalt*, September 22, 2011, accessed July 16, 2017. http://www.rosbalt.ru/moscow/2011/09/22/892898.html.

32 "Za Evgeniem Sofryginym prishli iz prokuratury [People from the prosecutor's office came for Evgenii Sofrygin]," *Eduard Crane: Kanva i kommenty pot katom (korruptsiia kak ona est') [Outline and comments under the cut (corruption how it is)]*, March 28, 2012, accessed October 21, 2012. http://eduardcrane.livejournal.com/466422.html.

33 The UFMS official I spoke with, for example, eventually moved into agribusiness with government committee work on the side. The state-business nexus is well analysed in the literature on Russian politics, but is largely outside the scope of this book.

34 Sometimes auditors from anti-corruption agencies or tax inspectors themselves demand bribes in the course of audits (Schulze, Sjahrir, and Zakharov 2016; Mokhtari and Grafova 2007).

35 Migration expert, interview by the author, Krasnodar, August 2012.

36 The most frequently cited gift among my interview subjects was bottles of liquor.

37 Migration expert, interview by the author, Irkutsk, March 2015.
38 These bureaucrats who come in regular and direct contact with the public are often labelled street-level bureaucrats, based on the work of Lipsky (1980).
39 Street-level UFMS officials may also participate in migrant raids and as a result may have a different set of opportunities and incentives. However, this did not come up as a major theme in the interviews I conducted. This may be in part because migrant raids were not conducted as frequently during the periods of field research as they were in subsequent years.
40 Based on interview data. Bribes are given to police and labour inspectors (also street-level bureaucrats) much more frequently, though this was not a systematic focus of my analysis.
41 This type of quota mentality was reported a number of times, though not by officials themselves, in the interviews I conducted.
42 Migration expert, interview by the author, Moscow, July 2009.
43 Research on informal economies generally finds that the overregulation of economic actors through high taxes, cumbersome regulations, and complicated processes of licensing and permits, etc. encourages enterprises to opt out of the formal economy in order to avoid the associated costs (Schneider 1997; De Soto 1989). Given high levels of regulation and/or taxation, actors can either choose the route of corruption or informality, paying bribes to officials in lieu of paying taxes or adhering to other legal regulations, or evading detection altogether by exiting the formal economy (Johnson et al. 1997, 170). Research shows that, as overall regulation increases, the informal economy grows to comprise an increasingly greater portion of the GDP (Loayza, Oviedo, and Servén 2005).
44 Representative of international organization for the protection of migrants, interview by the author, Moscow, July 2009.
45 The migration literature tends to focus on the vulnerability that illegal migration entails. Anderson (2013) writes about the "migrant dilemma," where migrants must choose between being exploited in liberal democracies and remaining at home where they suffer from all of the conditions that motivate them to migrate in the first place. A number of studies frame migrants across Europe and North America as "precarious workers," or those who are vulnerable owing to legal status or labour conditions (Faraday 2014; Fudge 2012; Porthé, et al. 2010; Anderson 2010; Taran 2011). While not ignoring the risks migrants face, this narrative seeks to elucidate the agency migrants have and the choices available to them.
46 These economic principles hold true whether workers are foreign or native, and thus there are parallels between the informal economy in general and the economy of illegal immigration.

47 Representative of international organization for the protection of workers, interview by the author, Moscow, July 2009.

48 Some say even a Russian citizen would have difficulty navigating the bureaucratic procedures required of migrants. Anton Filimonov, "Patenty vmesto razreshenii na rabotu: chego zhdat' ot novykh pravil privlecheniia 'bezvizovykh' inotstrantsev [Patents in place of work permits: What to expect from the new rules for attracting 'visa-free' foreigners]," December 30, 2014, accessed February 7, 2017. http://www.garant.ru/article/592407/.

49 Yekaterina Sinelschikova, "Changes to migration regulations aim to legalize shadow workers," *Russia beyond the Headlines*, December 5, 2014, accessed April 6, 2016. http://rbth.com/arts/2014/12/05/changes_to_migration_regulations_aim_to_legalize_shadow_workers_42011.html.

50 "Komitet GD odobril popravki o postrednikakh pri uchete trudovykh migrantov [Duma committee endorses amendments about intermediaries registering migrants]," *RIA Novosti*, November 6, 2014, accessed July 17, 2017. http://ria.ru/society/20141106/1031997369.html.

51 Interviews were conducted by a group of scholars, including the author, for a project on human trafficking and slavery funded by the Australian NGO Walk Free.

52 The company's primary site is http://www.migraciya.com, with another site devoted to avoiding FMS fines, http://www.anti-fms.com/. The company previously had another site, http://www.reg-ooo.biz, for registering companies as legal entities.

53 As the website explains, these work permits can be drawn up in the name of their company or the actual employer's company. The company was indeed on the list of approved employers (receiving quota allocation) for some years, though it did not receive quota allocation every year and in no year has it received an allocation of more than a few dozen.

54 According to the 2007 legislation, employers can be fined from 250,000 to 800,000 rubles for hiring an illegal migrant. In 2015, around 8.8 billion rubles were collected as a result of 2,250,000 violations. According to these figures, the average fine (4,000 rubles) was far less than the minimum charge of the services of Slavic Right.

55 Before CIS migrants were limited to a 90-day stay within every 180-day period (as of December 2013), travelling to the border was a relatively easy way to reset the period of validity of their legal stay. With the advent of the new patent policies as of 2015, whereby migrants must complete all exams and paperwork within 30 days of their arrival in Russia, going to the border to receive a new migration card again became an important strategy to allow migrants to reset the clock so they could finish their paperwork.

56 Aleksandr Gavrilenko, Marina Gritsiuk, Svetlana Dobrynina, Ol'ga Zhurman, Nikita Zaikov, Vera Chereneva, Elena Shulepova, "Popali v istroiiu [Going down in history]," *Rossiiskaia Gazeta*, February 5, 2015, accessed July 17, 2017. http://www.rg.ru/2015/02/06/migranty.html.

57 Mikhail Shmakov, interview by Rustam Arifdzhanov, *Rabochii moment*, May 16, 2008.

58 Representatives of international organizations for the protection of workers and migrants, interviews by the author, Moscow, July 2009.

59 Director of an anti-trafficking organization, interview by the author, Moscow, June 2009.

60 Statements of public officials involved in the policy process acknowledging the numbers of illegal immigrants and the presence of corruption schemes are ample in the press. See, for example, Elena Mukhametshina, Ol'ga Churakova, and Bela Liauv, "Gosduma podderzhit otmenu posrednikov pri prodazhe trudovykh patentov migrantam i otmenit regional'nye kvoty na migratsiiu [State Duma supports the abolition of intermediaries in the sale of patents and the abolition of the regional migration quota]," November 7, 2014, accessed February 13, 2017. http://www.vedomosti.ru/politics/articles/2014/11/07/patenty-tolko-v-roznicu.

3. Scarcity Mechanism #1

1 "No price hikes," *RIA Novosti*.

2 For comparison, the US sets limits separately for different categories of visas, but an analogous category would be for temporary non-agricultural workers, which is set at 66,000 per year. A number of countries use quotas to manage certain categories of immigrants, including the United States, United Kingdom, Norway, Korea, Portugal, Spain, Austria, Estonia, Hungary, Slovenia, and Italy (Chaloff 2014). Of these countries, some use mathematical functions, such as Austria, which sets a quota of 7% of the total dependent labour supply, Slovenia, which designates a limit of 5% of the actively working national population (though a specific number is set annually on the recommendation of the Ministry of Labour based on labour market analysis), and Estonia, which uses 0.1% of the permanent population as its limit (though the quota is typically set lower by the government) (European Migration Network 2013). In Hungary, the quota is determined based on the monthly average of labour requests filed in the previous year. Like Russia, Italy uses a procedure that starts with applications from employers, which are then filtered and adjusted by state agencies (Calavita 2004; Estruch and Zupi 2009).

3 In 2007, the quotas for visa migrants and non-visa migrants were set separately. The quota for visa citizens was 308,842, whereas the quota for non-visa migrants was 6 million. After 2007, the quota for visa invitations was set as a sub-quota within the overall quota, and no separate quota for non-visa migrants was specified.
4 In the Soviet period, quotas referred to production output targets, whereas, in the current period, migration quotas refer to upper limits.
5 Because management of the labour market in the USSR was restricted to available domestic labour resources, the issue at hand is internal rather than international migration, and especially the process of rural-urban migration.
6 Control mechanisms compelling citizens to move were more frequently used during the Stalin period, whereas market-style inducements and incentives dominated labour allocation after the 1950s (Grossman 1979). Even the assignment of graduates to work sites in needed areas and industries in practice could be considered "semicompulsary," and on the whole, only 10–12% of migration was a result of planned and organized government movement (Lewis and Rowland 1979).
7 Shortages varied by region and by industry. Whereas there were labour surpluses in agriculture, particularly in Central Asia and the Caucasus, shortages were particularly acute in industrial production in Siberia and the Far East (Grandstaff 1980; Rutland 1985). These shortages have been explained as a result of infinite demand due to an artificially low cost of labour (Buckley 1991), the exhaustion of new sources of labour (particularly by the 1960s) (Rutland 1985; Grandstaff 1980), and/or the rapid growth of the industrial sector to an extent that continually outstripped labour supply (Brown 1957).
8 State planners set limits on the population size of larger cities, with complementary limits on industrial enterprises and educational institutions (Lewis and Rowland 1979). Administrative controls, in particular residence permits (*propiska*) that were issued only by permission from the state, limited the ability of many people to live legally in urban centres (Rutland 1985; Buckley 1991).
9 Managers could increase the wage fund allotted by central planners by requesting larger numbers of workers from central planners (Lane 1987). It was also common to falsify financial records, and to sell goods deemed defective in order to raise funds outside the plan (Belova 2001).
10 Government Order No. 682 of November 15, 2006.
11 The procedure for considering employer applications was established by Government Order (*postanovlenie*) No. 783 of December 22, 2006.

12 Government Order (*postanovlenie*) No. 737 of October 3, 2008.
13 Marina Gritsiuk,"Inostrantsev urezali: Kvota na migrantov snizhena vdvoe [Foreigners cut: Quota for migrants halved]," *Rossiiskaia Gazeta*, December 12, 2008, accessed December 15, 2009. http://www.rg.ru/2008/12/12/migrant.html.
14 Spain reduced its work permit quotas by an even greater factor in response to the financial crisis, from 15,000 in 2008 to only 1,000 in 2009 (Ruhs 2013).
15 The concept of a reserve has a precedent in the Soviet labour market, when workers who were no longer needed by particular factories or offices (as a result of new technology, etc.) were nonetheless retained as a "manpower reserve" to hedge against changes in central plans and possible labour shortages (Manevich 1968). Whereas the Soviet era reserve was kept in the hands of the employer, the reserve in this situation was controlled by the federal government.
16 For 2007, the reserve was officially limited to 10% of the overall quota. However, when quotas were issued via Government Order No. 682 of November 15, 2006, no reserve was specified. Nevertheless, not all of the quota was distributed to the regions, in effect leaving a certain amount in reserve (see table 3.2), which should not have exceeded 600,000. The maximum possible reserve was increased to 30% in November 2007, and to 50% in December 2008. The implication of this is that at the beginning of 2008, the maximum reserve was 548,473.5 (though the actual reserve was 548,483). When the quota was established for 2009, the maximum reserve was 1,988,373.5 (actual reserve 1,988,373). Beginning in 2010 the maximum allowable reserve was far above the actual reserve.
17 While most regions reduced their quota during 2009, several regions saw increases, including Briansk, Kaluga, Murmansk, Nenets, Adygeya, Astrakhan, Volgograd, Kabardino-Balkaria, Perm, Kurgan, Zabaikalski, Omsk, Khakasia, and Sakhalin.
18 Regional leaders were also vocal in their requests for reduced quota, for example in Volgograd, Krasnoyarsk, and Tatarstan. "V Volgogradskoi oblast pochti na tysiachu uvelichili 'trudovye' kvoty dlia inostrantsev [In Volgograd oblast 'labour' quota for foreigners increased by nearly a thousand]," *Komsomol'skaia Pravda*, December 7, 2009, accessed December 22, 2009. http://volgograd.kp.ru/online/news/582818/; "V Krasnoyarskom krai umen'shat kvotu na inostrannykh rabotnikov [In Krasnoyarsk the quota for foreign workers will be decreased]," December 21, 2009, accessed December 22, 2009. http://www.newslab.ru/news/298249; "Tatarstan pochti vdvoe umen'shil kvoti na inostrannuiu rabochuiu silu [Tatarstan

reduced quota for foreign labour force by nearly half]," December 18, 2009, accessed December 22, 2009. http://www.regions.ru/news/2259883/.

19 "Putin sokratil kvoty na trudovykh migrantov [Putin has reduced quota on migrant workers]," December 24, 2009, accessed November 30, 2015. http://lenta.ru/news/2009/12/24/migrants/.

20 "Rossiia priglashaet na rabotu v 2010 godu 1.3 mln trudovykh migrantov [Russia invites 1.3 million labour migrants to work in 2010]," RIA Novosti, January 1, 2010, accessed December 31, 2009. http://www.rian.ru/economy/20100101/202498551.html.

21 Increases were recorded in Voronezh, Smolensk, Kaliningrad, St Petersburg, Astrakhan, Volgograd, Kalmykia, Rostov, Dagestan, Ingushetia, Stavropol, Tyumen, Yamalo Nenets, Irkutsk, Jewish Autonomous Oblast, Kamchatka, and Magadan.

22 Bureaucrats could further justify reduced quota on the basis that they were roughly in line with the number of migrants who had chosen to take advantage of the legal procedures (by obtaining work permits) even when quotas were at their highest (see table 3.3).

23 Though the data shows lower remittances and fewer entries in the years following the 2008 global financial crisis, both recovered by 2012.

24 Government Order (*postanovlenie*) No. 783 of December 22, 2006.

25 Minzdrav Order (*prikaz*) No. 603 of September 17, 2007.

26 *On the Legal Status of Foreign Citizens* directs the government to set quotas in line with national security priorities and prioritizing local workers. Government Order No. 783 gives much more specific criteria (see appendix table A3.c.).

27 When Government Order No. 783 was passed on December 22, 2006, it directed Minzdrav to clarify how the rules set by the government would be applied, and to work with the Ministry of Economic Development and Trade to establish a methodology by March 1, 2007 that would be used to estimate the efficiency and effectiveness of the current foreign labour force. Minzdrav Order (*prikaz*) No. 604 was finally passed six months after the deadline on September 17, 2007.

28 Presidential Decree (*ukaz*) No. 636 of May 21, 2012.

29 Three levels of rules are important for understanding this shift: federal law, government orders, and ministerial orders. When work permit quotas were introduced, *On the Legal Status of Foreign Citizens* specified the government as the responsible agency. Government Order No. 783 then named Minzdrav as the federal body responsible for coordinating the quota process and set out the schedule for employers and government agencies. Minzdrav in turn issued orders (*prikazy*) defining the procedures

and forms to be used by both employers and interdepartmental commissions. After Mintrud was made the responsible federal body in 2012, elites in the ministry pushed for changes to *On the Legal Status of Foreign Citizens* (codifying their position as the responsible agency at the level of federal law) and for a new Government Order (No. 800, to replace No. 783) that removed any reference to employer applications, regional interdepartmental commissions, and any specific criteria or priorities that should be used in setting quotas. Government Order No. 800 of September 12, 2013 gave Mintrud the sole authority (on the *recommendation* of regional governments) to define quotas. In 2014 Mintrud issued orders specifying the role of employer applications and regional interdepartmental commissions. These procedures were never used for CIS work permit quotas, though they remain in force for visa invitation quotas.

30 A regional bureaucrat in Krasnodar who had previously held a high position within the interdepartmental commission described to me how the regional authorities worked closely with employers to train them how to use the online portal. Regional bureaucrat, interview by the author, Krasnodar, August 2012.

31 A number of other aspects of the process are not transparent unless individual regions choose to publicize them, including which employers apply for quota, which employers are denied quota, what quota regional leaders submit to federal authorities, which companies actually use quota (which companies are able to get letters of invitations and work permits), which companies employ migrants from CIS working within their first 90 days, and if those companies received quota.

32 Vishnevsky (2013) notes that while up to 200,000 ethnic repatriates were expected to come as a result of the compatriot initiative between 2007 and 2009, only 16,000 people participated in the program. The situation changed to some degree in 2014 when many Ukrainian refugees were funnelled into the compatriot program (Schenk 2016).

33 In a very careful cross-national assessment of migration policies and rights in Europe, Ruhs (2013) argues that it is not objectively possible to assess relative differences of this nature, absent convincing explanations as to why some indicators might matter more than others. For this reason, his study weighs all indicators equally. Though the purpose of his study is different from the analysis to follow, weighing factors equally across cases has methodological precedent.

34 Several regions were merged in 2008, reducing the number from 89 to 83. In those cases, data for 2006–7 is merged to reflect the post-2008 divisions. As of 2014, Russia reports data for 85 regions, including Crimea and the

federal city of Simferopol. However, because they were added only in the final year of the quota system, they are not included in this analysis.

35 One might say their work was never done in the sense that once quota was set, the task of amending the quota (also based on employer applications) began.

36 Feruza Dzhani, "Kletka dlia migrantov, ili Kak poluchit' rasreshenie na rabotu [A cage for migrants, or how to obtain a work permit]," April 29, 2013, accessed January 26, 2017. http://www.fergananews.com/articles/7708.

37 NGO representative, interview by the author, Moscow (via skype), June 2016.

38 Marina Gritsiuk, "Delo malen'koe. No svoe [The business is small. But it's ours]," *Rossiiskaia Gazeta*, March 2, 2010, accessed July 28, 2017. http://www.rg.ru/2010/03/02/rabota.html. Moscow UFMS, accessed August 27, 2015. http://www.fmsmoscow.ru/pr/news/52.html.

39 FMS Order (*prikaz*) No. 36 of February 26, 2009.

40 The procedure for extending the period of stay by submitting an employment contract was added to *On the Legal Status of Foreign Citizens* only in 2010.

41 According to a labour expert in Moscow, around 50% of migrants in 2008 were counted multiple times in the statistics on foreign workers, based on the number of work permits issued (interview by the author, July 2009). If 50% of the 1.5 million migrants given work permits in 2008 were counted twice, it means only 750,000 were allowed to legalize. As a result, if Russia had an estimated 6 million migrants (legal and illegal) at the time, only 12% of them would have been working legally. Multiple counting is a problem for registration as well, since migrants are fairly mobile and might register a number of times in one year. Migration expert, interview by the author, Moscow, June 2009.

42 The forms and instructions were codified through Government Order (*postanovlenie*) No. 798 of December 23, 2006, and replaced by Government Order (*postanovlenie*) No. 183 of March 18, 2008, before being taken out of force in 2010 with the issue of FMS Order (*prikaz*) No. 147 of June 28, 2010.

43 Gritsiuk, "Delo malen'koe. No svoe [The business is small. But it's ours]."

44 Oftentimes international companies hiring expatriate or highly skilled workers from the West are more fully compliant (though not entirely without informal resources and practices) because in many cases they must receive a quota allocation in order to get visas for their employees. These cases are in the minority, however, managed by the sub-quota for foreign workers from visa countries.

45 Sinelschikova, "Changes to migration regulations."

46 Moscow UFMS, accessed August 27, 2015. http://www.fmsmoscow.ru/pr/news/52.html.

47 Sean Guillory, "Corruption, not migrants, is Russia's problem," *Nation*, August 20, 2013, accessed June 19, 2014. http://m.thenation.com/article/175815-corruption-not-migrants-russias-problem; Lyubov Kura-chyova and Olya Chizhova, "Behind Russia's migrant raids, a vast network of bribes and opportunism," *Atlantic*, August 8, 2013, accessed June 19, 2014. http://www.theatlantic.com/international/archive/2013/08/behind-russias-migrant-raids-a-vast-network-of-bribes-and-opportunism/278481/.

4. Scarcity Mechanism #2

1 Job codes are defined by the Russian Classification of Economic Activities (Obsherossiiskii Klassifikator Vidov Ekonomicheskoi Deiatel'nosti, or OKVED). OKVED job code 95 is for provision of household services, including maids, cooks, waiters, servants, butlers, laundry attendants, gardeners, gatekeepers, grooms, chauffeurs, watchmen, governesses, babysitters, home teachers, secretaries, etc. Patents are defined in a slightly different way by *On the Legal Status of Foreign Citizens*, specifying only that they can be used for personal, domestic, or similar needs not connected with entrepreneurial activity. A more direct way to distinguish between employers who are individuals vs corporations would be through tax-ID code (Individual'nyi Identifikatsionnyi Nomer, or IIN), which is 12 digits for individuals and 10 digits for companies. However, the Rostrud spreadsheets only began including tax-ID numbers of employers mid-way through 2010, once patents were already instituted and therefore cannot help determine the pre-patent demand for domestic workers by individuals.

2 Patents were adopted in May and went into effect in July of 2010, but there are no official statistics of the number of patents issued for the remainder of 2010. Reports of patents issued in 2010 are typically combined with those issued in the first months of 2011. For example, the FMS reported that 208,500 patents were issued between July 1, 2010 and April 1, 2011. Mariia Selivanova, "Migrantam patent ne nuzhen [Migrants don't need patents]," *RIA Novosti*, May 19, 2011, accessed January 26, 2017. https://ria.ru/analytics/20110519/377157673.html.

3 It was also fairly easy to purchase a new migration card from an intermediary without actually crossing the border.

4 "Profsoiuzy vystupili protiv patentov dlia gastarbaiterov i predlozhili strane voobshche oboitis' bez migrantov [Trade unions oppose patents for guest workers and recommended the country do without migrants]"; "Poluchit' patent teper' eshche proshche [Receiving a patent is now even easier]," September 27, 2010, accessed January 25, 2016. https://64.mvd.ru/news/item/647362/?print=1.

5 Marina Gritsiuk, "Gosudarstvo vziatok ne beret [The state does not take bribes]," *Rossiiskaia Gazeta*, December 8, 2009, accessed March 2, 2015.

6 The same amendment also introduced a new mechanism for highly qualified specialists (a category defined by a minimum yearly income of 1 million rubles) to obtain legal work documents outside the quota system.

7 Kseniia Babich, "Minzdravsotsrazvitiia Rossii protiv otmeny kvot na inostrannuiu rabochuiu silu [Minzdrav is opposed to cancelling quotas for foreign workers]," *Trud*, May 12, 2011, accessed March 16, 2015. http://www.trud.ru/article/12-05-2011/262797_minzdravsotsrazvitija_rossii_protiv_otmeny_kvot_na_inostrannuju_rabochuju_silu.html; "Minzdravsotsrazvitiia vystupaet protiv otmeny trudovykh kvot na migrantov [Minzdrav acts in opposition to cancelling labour quotas on migrants]," *RIA Novosti*, May 11, 2011, accessed July 20, 2017. http://ria.ru/society/20110511/372919932.html.

8 "Popolneniia v biudzhet RF za schet vvedeniia trudovykh patentov migrantov za dva goda sostavili 8.3 mlrd rub [Replenishment of the Russian budget as a result of the introduction of patents for migrants accounted for 8.3 billion rubles for two years]."

9 There is some speculation that Putin did not write the article himself. After the article was published, journalists advanced the argument that Putin's ghost writers borrowed heavily from a 2010 document published by the Ministry of Education, http://lenta.ru/news/2012/01/23/source/, accessed December 6, 2015.

10 Presidential Decrees (*ukazy*) Nos. 594, 596–606.

11 Presidential Decree (*ukaz*) No. 602 of May 7, 2012.

12 Presidential Decree (*ukaz*) No. 1304 of September 19, 2012; "'Nechego lichnogo': Putin oserchal na trekh medvedevskikh ministrov, kotorye ne ispolniaiut ego ukazov ['It's nothing personal': Putin enraged at three of Medvedev's ministers who won't fulfil his decrees]," September 18, 2012, accessed January 29, 2016. http://www.newsru.com/russia/18sep2012/nothingpersonal.html.

13 Presidential Decree (*ukaz*) No. 754 of September 30, 2013; Anatoly Medetsky, "Putin stays firm on fulfilling promises," *Moscow Times*, December 5, 2013, accessed January 29, 2016. http://www.themoscowtimes.com/

business/article/putin-stays-firm-on-fulfilling-promises/490997.html. "Putin demands implementation of May decrees despite regional finance problems," *Tass*, March 27, 2014, accessed January 29, 2016. http://tass.ru/en/russia/725571.

14 The commission was initially chaired by FMS director Konstantin Romodanovskii until 2011, when Vice-Premier Igor Shuvalov took over the leadership. The bulk of the commission comprised representatives of government ministries and regional executives. However, it also included business representatives such as OPORA (the national organization of small and medium enterprises), civil society actors, and migrant advocates such as Svetlanna Gannushkina (2009–), Ella Pamfilova (2009–10), and Lidiia Grafova (2009–10), and the scholarly perspectives of Irina Ivakhnyuk (2009–) and Yaroslav Kuzminov (2012–). Additionally, a number of experts and organizations were consulted for their input on drafts.

15 "Kvoty dlia inostrannykh migrantov otmeniat [Quota for foreign workers to be cancelled]," April 11, 2011, accessed March 16, 2015. http://deita.ru/news/society/08.04.2011/165420-kvoty-dlja-inostrannykh-migrantov-otmenjat/.

16 "Topilin: kvota na rabotu dlia inostrantsev otmeniat' nel'zia [Topilin: We can't cancel the quota for foreigners]," July 4, 2013, accessed March 16, 2015. http://actualcomment.ru/topilin_kvoty_na_rabotu_dlya_inostrantsev_otmenyat_nelzya.html.

17 Within the span of two paragraphs, Putin danced around three of the migration myths identified in chapter 1: criminality, cultural incompatibility, and migrants as a drain on education and social services. Putin himself rarely engages in inflammatory anti-immigrant rhetoric, and even in this case his language is measured and policy-focused. As he does in many cases, Putin put the blame for migration problems squarely on the policy context, rather than on migrants themselves (Schenk forthcoming).

18 "Putin demands implementation of May decrees despite regional finance problems," *Tass*, March 27, 2014, accessed January 29, 2016. http://tass.ru/en/russia/725571.

19 Elena Mukhametshina, "Migrantov khvatit na vsekh [There are enough migrants for everyone]," *Gazeta*, March 4, 2014, accessed March 2, 2015. http://www.gazeta.ru/social/2014/03/04/5935597.shtml.

20 "Mintrud gotovit predlozheniia ob izmenenii podkhodov k trudu migrantov [Mintrud prepares recommendations for changes in the approach to labour migrants]," *RIA Novosti*, December 20, 2013, accessed July 20, 2017. http://wap.ria.ru/society/20131220/985539041.html.

21 Marina Gritsiuk, "Shtatnyi otvet [Standard response]," *Rossiiskaia Gazeta*, January 25, 2015, accessed July 20, 2017. http://www.rg.ru/2015/01/26/mintrud.html. As of 2012, according to the law *On Compulsory Pension Insurance*, foreign workers with a contract of more than six months have been included in the federal pension scheme, though the mechanism for foreigners drawing the pension benefits has yet to be worked out.

22 Tat'iana Shirmanova and Pavel Chernyshov, "Pravitel'stvo otmenit kvoty na gastarbaiterov [Government abolishes quota on guest workers]," *Izvestiia*, March 31, 2014, accessed July 20, 2017. http://izvestia.ru/news/568283; "Kvoty i razresheniia na rabotu dlia 'bezvizovykh' inostrannykh rabotnikov planiruetsiia otmenit' [Plans to cancel quota and work permits for 'visa-free' foreign workers]," April 4, 2014, accessed July 20, 2017. http://www.garant.ru/news/535036/.

23 Elena Nekrasova, "V sluchae bezrabotitsy inostrantsam pridetcia pokinut' Rossiiskie regiony [In case of unemployment foreigners have to leave Russian regions]," February 9, 2015, accessed July 20, 2017. http://www.innov.ru/news/other/v-sluchae-bezrabotitsy-in-0902/.

24 Gritsiuk, "Shtatnyi otvet [Standard response]."

25 As before, the quota for non-CIS workers is actually a quota on visa invitations, which must be procured by employers before work permits can be obtained (also by the employer).

26 When exams were instituted, there were only five approved institutions that could conduct exams (three in Moscow, one in St Petersburg, and one in Tyumen). All other testing centres must have an affiliation with one of these in order to produce valid certificates. In some cases, as in the Samara region, migrants have been required to take courses before being eligible to sit for the exams. In some regions, free courses are available, but other courses may cost upwards of 10,000 rubles in addition to the cost of the exams, which also varies by region. Gavrilenko et al., "Popali v istroiiu [Going down in history]."

27 For example, Government Order (*postanovlenie*) No. 574 of September 21, 2005 allowed citizens of Russia and Tajikistan to travel between the two countries with only an internal passport. In June 2014, Government Order No. 574 was taken out of force (by Government Order No. 555), returning citizens of Tajikistan to the conditions named in an international treaty (of November 30, 2000) between Belarus, Kazakhstan, Kyrgyzstan, Russia, and Tajikistan, which required international passports for border crossings. "Grazhdane Tadzhikistana bol'she ne smogut v"ekhat' v Rossiiu po vnutrennim pasportam svoei strany [Citizens of Tajikistan can no longer enter Russia on the internal passport of their country]," June 23, 2014, accessed March 4, 2015. http://www.garant.ru/news/549395/. Only later in 2014

were similar procedures adopted for citizens of Kyrgyzstan. "S 2015 goda pri peresechenii granits Rossii grazhdane Kyrgyzstana dolzhny pred"iavit' zagranichnyi pasport [From 2015 citizens of Kyrgyzstan must present an international passport to cross Russia's borders]," October 29, 2014, accessed March 4, 2015. http://kabarlar.org/news/34141-s-2015-goda-pri-peresechenii-granic-rossii-grazhdane-kyrgyzstana-dolzhny-predyavit-zagranichnyy-pasport-grs.html.

28 Matthew Luxmoore, "Ruble ripple: New Russian laws make life difficult for migrant workers," *Aljazeera*, February 27, 2015, accessed March 4, 2015. http://america.aljazeera.com/articles/2015/2/27/new-russian-laws-make-life-difficult-for-migrant-workers.html.

29 From the time the patent law was enacted (November 24, 2014) to the end of 2015, the law *On the Legal Status of Foreign Citizens* changed 17 times.

30 For example, Federal Law No. 2487-1 of March 11, 1991.

31 In Russian, colloquial references include *chernyi spisok* (blacklist) and *zapret na v"ezd* (prohibited entry). As a legal concept, *zapret na v"ezd* currently refers *only* to US citizens who are prohibited from entering Russia (Schenk 2016). Previously it was a more general category used in *On the Legal Status of Foreign Citizens*, and though it was removed in the 2013 amendments, it remains a widely used term.

32 Since 2008, according to *On the Legal Status of Foreign Citizens*, temporary residence could be denied or revoked if a foreigner is deemed undesirable.

33 The figure 3.5% is based on FMS data. Using Rosstat border entry data for 2015, the percentage of foreigners affected is even smaller, only 1.8%.

34 The base price for a patent is set at 1,200 rubles by the Tax Code. Patent prices in the regions are a product of this base price multiplied by a yearly coefficient set by the Ministry of Economic Development, and a regional coefficient set by regional governments.

35 FMS data differs substantially in some cases from the data available from Rosstat. This is particularly stark for the numbers of foreign citizens entering Russia, and in this case provides a more conservative estimate of border entries (Rosstat does not show the decreasing trend discussed here). Rosstat data comes from the border agency (a division of the FSB), whereas FMS relies on their own internal data.

36 "Sobyanin: Prodazha patentov migrantam prinosit v biudzhet bol'she dokhodov, chem neftianye kompanii [Sobyanin: The sale of patents brought more income to the budget than oil companies]," February 2, 2016, accessed January 27, 2017. https://mc.mos.ru/presscenter/news/detail/2483728.html.

37 Government Order (*rasporiazhenie*) No. 1638-r of November 5, 2009.

38 All official PVS branch websites are accessible through the main website www.pvsmvd.ru. The United Migration Centre's website, which is in the Russian, Tajik, and Uzbek languages, is www.migrantcenter.ru.

39 All legal entities in Russia are classified according to the Unified Classification of the Legal Forms of Organizations (*obshcherossiiskii klassifikator organizatsionno-pravovykh form,* or OKOPF). State unitary enterprises are regulated both by the Civil Code and by the law on state and municipal unitary enterprises, Federal Law No. 161 of November 14, 2002.

40 Federal Law No. 210 of July 27, 2010.

41 My Document locations are standardized in the sense that they are all designated Multifunctional Centres, and are therefore governed by the Federal Law No. 210 (see previous note). And while all of the centres are unified by the same logo and similar websites, they are not administered through a central organization, nor are the websites aggregated through one federal-level site as we see with PVS. Further, My Documents locations have various legal forms. For example, the Moscow affiliate is a state budget institution (*gosudarstvennoe biudzhetnoe uchrezhdenie)* whereas the affiliate in Yakutia is an autonomous state institution (*gosudarstvennoe avtonomnoe uchrezhdenie*).

42 Federal Migration Service, accessed February 12, 2016. http://www.fms.gov.ru/press/news/item/57126/.

43 "V Iuzhno-Sakhalinske otkrylcia otdel 'MFTs' po rabote s migrantami [In South Sakhalin a department of the 'MFC' opens to work with migrants]," October 5, 2015, accessed January 31, 2016. http://mfc.admsakhalin.ru/news/?ELEMENT_ID=924.

44 The Tula and St Petersburg centres are not a part of the My Documents network. In some of these centres, the migration services are provided in the same location as other services.

45 Government Order (*postanovlenie*) No. 72 of February 5, 2016.

46 "V Voronezhe otkrylcia Edinyi migratsionnyi Tsentr – EMTS. Ego rol' otsenivaetsia po-raznomu [In Voronezh the United Migration Centre – UMC – is opened. Its role is evaluated variously]," October 19, 2015, accessed July 21, 2017. http://migrant.ru/v-voronezhe-otkrylsya-edinyj-migracionnyj-cent-emc-ego-rol-ocenivaetsya-po-raznomu/; "Edinyi migratsionnyi tsentr otkrylcia v Tomske [United Migration Centre opens in Tomsk]," *Lenta Novostei,* March 18, 2015, accessed July 21, 2017. http://tomsk-novosti.ru/edinyj-migratsionnyj-tsentr-otkrylsya-v-tomske/.

47 The difference in attitudes outside of Moscow is palpable. During field research I found people in Sverdlovsk, Krasnodar, and Irkutsk to be generally much more open to migrants from Central Asia (e.g., willing to hire

them to do renovations on their house), and more attached to ideas of Russia as a multicultural or multinational country.

5. Local Politics of Immigration in Moscow

1 "Sobyanin: Prodazha patentov migrantam prinosit v biudzhet bol'she dokhodov, chem neftianye kompanii [Sobyanin: The sale of patents brought more income to the budget than oil companies]," February 2, 2016, accessed January 27, 2017. https://mc.mos.ru/presscenter/news/detail/2483728.html.

2 Moscow Mayoral Order (*rasporiazhenie*) No. 243 of May 24, 1994.

3 Yuri Luzhkov, "Migratsiya Zdravogo Smysla [Common sense migration]," *Rossiiskaia Gazeta*, November 10, 2006.

4 "Litsom ne vyshli [Their faces aren't good enough (i.e. did not pass face control)]," *Vedomosti*, December 18, 2009, accessed March 10, 2016. http://demoscope.ru/weekly/2009/0403/gazeta04.php.

5 Moscow Central Administative District web portal, March 2, 2010, accessed 14 March 2010. http://cao.mos.ru/document/2010/03/02/d19440/.

6 Georgii Belenev, "Moskva otdana migrantam [Moscow is given to migrants]," *Nezavisimaia Gazeta*, December 18, 2009, accessed March 13, 2010. http://demoscope.ru/weekly/2009/0403/gazeta04.php.

7 Tat'iana Shirmanova, "Zhivite, gde khotite [Live where you like]," *Trud*, February 4, 2009.

8 Brian Whitmore, "The Luzhkov phenomenon," *RFE/RL*. May 12, 2010, accessed July 14, 2010. http://www.rferl.org/content/The_Luzhkov_Paradox/2040348.html.

9 "ZAO 'Inteko'. Spravka [Closed joint-stock company 'Inteko'. Spravka]," *RIA Novosti*, September 6, 2011, accessed January 30, 2017. https://ria.ru/spravka/20110906/431275060.html; "VTB takes over Bank of Moscow," *Russia beyond the Headlines*, April 29, 2011, accessed January 27, 2017. http://rbth.com/articles/2011/04/29/vtb_takes_over_bank_of_moscow_12824.html; "Sud vnov' prodlil na polgoda protseduru bankrotstva ZAO 'Prem'er Esteit' [Court extents bankruptcy of ZAO 'Premier Estate' for another six months]," *Russian Agency for Legal and Court Information*, October 1, 2014, accessed January 27, 2017. http://rapsinews.ru/judicial_news/20141001/272257123.html.

10 Iulia Petrova, "Baturina prodala 'Inteko' [Baturina sells Inteko]," *Vedomosti*, September 7, 2011, accessed January 27, 2017. http://www.vedomosti.ru/realty/articles/2011/09/07/sberbankinvesticii_kupil; Olga Sichkar,

"Russian police raid firm of ex-Moscow mayor's wife," *Reuters*, February 17, 2011, accessed January 27, 2017. http://www.reuters.com/article/us-russia-raid-inteko-idUSTRE71G6QP20110217.

11 It is immediately clear that these estimates are derived from official sources. If migrants comprised 13% of 5 million total construction workers (or 650,000 migrants), the total migrant population (if 40% work in construction) would be 1.6 million migrants, which is substantially lower than the estimated 6–7 million total migrants in Russia at the time (Tyuryukanova 2009a).

12 "100 Bogateishikh Biznesmenov Rossii: Reitingi [100 richest businessmen in Russia: Ratings]," 2009, accessed January 27, 2017. http://www.forbes.ru/rating/100-bogateishih-biznesmenov-rossii/2009#all_rating.

13 Olga Grekova, "Rynok. Cherkizovskii dobazarilcia [Market. Cherkizovskii bargained itself into trouble]," *Moskovskii Komsomolets*, August 31, 2006; Igor Kalinovskii, and Elena Vladimirova. "Konchai bazar! [Quit the chit-chat!]" *Rossiiskaia Gazeta*, April 3, 2008.

14 Sergei Zubrin, "Khronika ChP [Chronicle of emergencies]," *Moskovskaia Pravda*, July 29, 2008; "Cherkizovskii poka ne zakryvaiut [Cherkizovskii will not close yet]," *Vecherniaia Moskva*, April 15, 2009.

15 Sergei Kanev, "Taina Cherkizovskogo rynka [The mystery of Cherkizovskii market]," *Novaia Gazeta*, June 2, 2008.

16 Mark Franchetti, "Vladimir Putin 'furious' over flaunting oligarch Telman Ismailov," *Times Online*, June 28, 2009, accessed March 15, 2010. http://www.timesonline.co.uk/tol/news/world/europe/article6591398.ece.

17 In this case, migration policy was formulated in order to justify a "clean sweep" of markets, which had become a haven for counterfeit drugs and retail merchandise, alcohol, and other criminal practices (Vitkovskaya 2009). Though the ban was instituted effective April 1, 2007, the category of wholesale and retail trade remained a part of the migration statistics collected by the FMS and Rosstat and continued to grow after the ban. According to Rosstat, the number of migrant workers employed in wholesale and retail trade (which also includes auto and general household repair services) increased from 270,944 in 2006 to 330,000 in 2007 and 411,800 in 2008.

18 Mikhail Moshkin, "Sovetskikh prosiat ne bespokoitsia [Soviets, please don't worry]," *Vremia Novosti*, July 1, 2009.

19 Maria Antonova, "100 detained around Cherkizovsky Market," *Moscow Times*, July 6, 2009.

20 Though there was frequent debate during the Medvedev presidency about whether he represented an independent power base or was subservient to

Putin, any arguments that Medvedev was anything more than a place-holder were laid to rest after Putin's return to the presidency in 2012.

21 Brian Whitmore, "Medvedev fires Moscow mayor for 'losing president's trust,'" *RFE/RL*, September 28, 2010, accessed July 21, 2017. http://www.rferl.org/content/Medvedev_Fires_Moscow_Mayor/2169987.html.

22 "Putin loyalist Sobyanin appointed new Moscow mayor," *Sputnik*, October 21, 2010, accessed June 19, 2015. http://sputniknews.com/russia/20101021/161035971.html

23 Elina Bilevskaya, "Moscow: Interregnum," *Nezavisimaia Gazeta*, accessed June 19, 2015. http://archive.premier.gov.ru/eng/premier/press/ru/5220/.

24 Resin's changes to the commission were minor, but included the appointment of Sergei Nikolaevich Kochengin, who represented the Guild of Construction Industry Organizations. Given Resin's connections to the construction industry, this type of appointment can be interepreted as a move towards installing his own patronage networks. However, Kochengin was not retained in the following iteration of the commission conferred by Sobyanin in 2011.

25 "Sobyanin: v Moskve rabotaiut 2 mln nelegal'nykh migrantov [Sobyanin: 2 million illegal migrants work in Moscow]," *BBC Russian Service*, November 23, 2010, accessed July 4, 2015. http://www.bbc.com/russian/russia/2010/11/101123_moscow_migrants_sobyanin.shtml.

26 Sobyanin's statements are based on claims that crime in Moscow (half of which he says is committed by migrants – both internal and international) had decreased by 25%. "Sergei Sobyanin: V Moskve dva milliona vakansii, bez migrantov ne oboitis' [Sergei Sobyanin: In Moscow there are two million vacancies, we can't get by without migrants]," March 2, 2012, accessed January 27, 2017. http://www.fergananews.com/news.php?id=18276. "Kudeneev: Gastarbaiterov v Moskve men'she ne stanovitsia [Kudeneev: Guest workers in Moscow have not decreased]," *Rosbalt*, February 3, 2012, accessed January 27, 2017. http://www.rosbalt.ru/moscow/2012/02/03/941324.html.

27 "Sergei Sobyanin: V Moskve dva milliona vakansii, bez migrantov ne oboitis' [Sergei Sobyanin: In Moscow there are two million vacancies, we can't get by without migrants]."

28 "Sobyanin otritsaet dannye ob uvelichenii vdvoe kvoty na migrantov [Sobyanin denies data about the doubling of quotas for migrants]," *Rosbalt*, December 13, 2012, accessed July 4 2015. http://www.rosbalt.ru/moscow/2012/12/13/1070899.html.

29 "S. Sobyanin: Moskva oboidetsia bez dvornikov-migrantov [S. Sobyanin: Moscow gets by without migrant street cleaners]," *RBK*, June 14,

2013, accessed July 6, 2015. http://top.rbc.ru/economics/14/06/2013/861906.shtml; Lidiia Glazko and Anna Baidakova, "Sobyanin vstretil spetsnaz s lopatami [Sobyanin met special forces with a shovel]," February 11, 2013, accessed July 6, 2015. http://www.mn.ru/moscow/20130211/337370404.html.

30 "S. Sobyanin: Moskva oboidetsia bez dvornikov-migrantov [S. Sobyanin: Moscow gets by without migrant street cleaners]."

31 Alexei Navalny, interview by Aleksei Venediktov, *Ekho Moskvy*, August 23, 2013, accessed July 5, 2015. http://echo.msk.ru/programs/beseda/1139878-echo/. Because Navalny was the opposition candidate and campaigned on an anti-corruption and anti-Kremlin platform, he was often labelled "liberal" by commentators. However, he was in no way liberal on the immigration issue. Rather, he supported the idea of introducing a visa regime with countries in Central Asia and the Caucasus (not all CIS countries, such as Ukraine and Belarus). Both the Moscow mayoral race and the Yekaterinburg race, where the opposition candidate (Roizman) won, demonstrate that the nationalist or populist views held by so-called liberal or opposition candidates find traction in the migration sphere.

32 Separate searches using each candidate's name, along with various terms denoting migrants (migrants, guest workers, foreigners), in the Eastview Database of Russian Newspapers turned up 167 articles associated with Sobyanin and 86 articles with Navalny.

33 Alec Luhn, "Russia detains immigrants in 'concentration camps,'" *Guardian*, August 6, 2013, accessed July 4, 2015. http://www.theguardian.com/world/2013/aug/06/russia-immigrants-concentration-camps.

34 Oleg Garmanov, "Imitatsiia bor'by s nelegal'nymi migrantami," *Spravedlivaia Rossiia*, August 13, 2013, accessed July 5, 2015. http://188.127.236.217/files/pf55/053666.pdf.

35 Tom Balmforth, "Moscow police arrest 1,200 migrant workers after murder of ethnic Russian," October 14, 2013, accessed July 5, 2015. http://www.theguardian.com/world/2013/oct/14/russia-police-arrest-migrants-nationalist-rioting.

36 "More Moscow officials sacked after anti-migrant protests," *RIA Novosti*, November 1, 2013, accessed November 18, 2013. en.ria.ru/russia/20131101/184470023/More-Moscow-Officials-Sacked-After-Anti-Migrant-Protests.html.

37 Both in 2003 and 2007, changes made to the commission show a tendency towards ad hoc decision making. In 2003, the commission was established on July 29 despite the August 1 deadline for regional governments (i.e., the commission) to submit quota estimates to the Ministry of Labour. In 2007,

the new commission was established only in October, well after the July 15 deadline for regional committees to submit their recommendations to the Ministry of Health for the following year's quota. Whether this measure was taken to correct problems encountered in planning for the 2008 quota or whether it retroactively codifies a composition that participated in the 2008 quota formulation is not clear.

38 These organizations are designated as state institutions of Moscow city (Gosudarstvennogo uchrezhdeniia goroda Moskvy), which are a special classification of non-profit organization that is specifically tasked with providing services that help to realize state/municipal legislation.

39 For example, Alina Olegovna Kondrashova has been the commission secretary from 2007 to the present, as a representative first of the Committee on Interregional Connections and National Politics of the city of Moscow, then of the city Department of Labour and Employment, and finally as a consultant for the Department of Labour. Vladimir Mikhailovich Romanov was also retained from 2007 to the present, first as a representative of the Committee on Social Connections of the city of Moscow, and then as the head of the state institution Moscow City Centre for Labour Conditions and Protection (Moskovskogo gorodskogo tsentra uslovii i okhrany truda). Through both of these positions, he also acted as the head of the Secretariat of Moscow Trilateral Commission for Regulating Social-Labour Relations, which brings together representatives of the government, trade unions, and employers.

40 It is possible that this working group existed prior to 2012, but since it was established by Department of Labour orders, which are not kept in any standardized or comprehensive way either on their own website or in the typical legal databases such as Garant or consultant.ru, it is difficult to verify.

41 The South East Prefecture of Moscow has a similar sub-commission in charge of coordinating migration issues in that region of the city. The presence of these sub-commission groups illustrates the intricacy of the bureaucratic process as well as the importance of the micro-level actors in creating the information required to operate a complex bureaucratic machine.

42 Including 5,300 painters, 3,500 *dvorniki*, 2,550 asphalt layers, 4,700 drivers of various types, 850 dishwashers, and a number of various other low-skilled mostly manual labour positions.

43 Including 16,000 managers, 12,000 specialists, 10,000 chefs, and a number of low-skilled and manual labourers.

44 "Kvota na inostrannykh rabotnikov: ot politiki k nauke [Quota on foreign workers: From politics to science]," accessed July 22, 2017. http://www.hr-portal.ru/article/kvota-na-inostrannyh-rabotnikov-ot-politiki-k-nauke.

45 "Kvota na inostrannuiu rabochuiu silu sostavit v Moskve 200 tysiach chelovek [Quota on foreign workers in Moscow is 200,000]," *RIA Novosti*, June 24, 2010, accessed October 7, 2010. http://www.rian.ru/moscow/20100624/249912263.html.

46 The number of employer applications considered each year is not a part of official reports, though it is reported for some years in the media.

47 In 2015, when the quota system returned to covering only migrants from visa countries, these spreadsheets were removed from the website.

48 One might expect shifts in the construction labour market owing to the after-effects of the 2008 financial crisis to impact the quota allocations. However, during this period, the overall labour force in the construction industry remained resilient, and therefore any reductions in quota were not owing to reduced labour demand. In Moscow, the total construction labour force was 749,400 in 2005, 757,100 in 2006, 774,900 in 2007, 815,700 in 2008, 764,300 in 2009, 817,400 in 2010, and 828,000 in 2011 (Rosstat 2007a; Rosstat 2008a; Rosstat 2009a; Rosstat 2011a; Rosstat 2012c).

49 "ZAO 'Inteko'. Spravka [Closed joint-stock company 'Inteko'. Spravka]." *RIA Novosti*.

50 "Bashniu 'Rossiia' v 'Moskva-siti' postroiat turki [Turks will construct the tower 'Russia' in 'Moscow-city']," March 28, 2013, accessed July 22, 2017. http://realty.newsru.com/article/28mar2013/renaissance; "Bashniu 'Evoliutsiia' v 'Moskva-Siti' vvedut v ekspluatatsiiu v blizhaishee vremia ['Evolution' tower in 'Moscow-City' will be put into operation in the near future]," December 5, 2014, accessed July 22, 2017. https://riarealty.ru/news_cre/20141205/403972262.html; "Kiprskii sud arestoval aktivy Aleksandra Chigirinskogo [Cypriot court seizes the assets of Aleksandr Chigirinskii]," December 15, 2016, accessed July 22, 2017. http://www.rbc.ru/business/15/12/2016/585169bb9a79475b8f041c1c.

51 Belenev, "Moskva otdana migrantam [Moscow is given to migrants]."

52 Navalny, interview by Aleksei Venediktov.

53 There are a number of different types of subsidiary institutions including state budget institutions (*gosudarstvennoe biudzhetnoe uchrezhdenie*), state public institutions (*gosudarstvennoe kazennoe uchrezhdenie*), and state unitary enterprises (*gosudarstvennoe unitarnoe predpriiatie*). While the vast majority of subsidiaries are public, in some cases open joint stock companies are also used.

54 "Subordinate Organizations," Moscow Department of Housing and Communal Services, accessed July 22, 2017. http://dgkh.mos.ru/about/subordinate/.

55 There has been some negative coverage of Mosgortrans; for example, an article that declares "Every sixth driver of Mosgortrans is a migrant

[Kazhdyi shestoi voditel' 'Mosgortransa' migrant]," December 3, 2014, accessed January 30, 2017. https://life.ru/805278. However, this type of coverage is relatively isolated; this article was not picked up by any major news outlets.

56 "Sobyanin: Prodazha patentov migrantam prinosit v biudzhet bol'she dokhodov, chem neftianye kompanii [Sobyanin: The sale of patents brought more income to the budget than oil companies]."

57 Ibid. "Sergei Sobyanin: V Moskve otkryli samyi krupnyi v strane migratsionnyi tsentr [Sergei Sobyanin: The biggest migration centre in the country has opened in Moscow]," January 29, 2016, accessed July 22, 2017. https://www.mos.ru/news/item/6513073.

58 Multifunctional Migration Centre, accessed February 15, 2016. http://mc.mos.ru/.

59 3,500 rubles for the patent service fee, 400 rubles for the translation and notarization of passport, and 500 rubles for the language test are to be paid directly to the Moscow city Department of Finance. "Cost of a patent," Multifunctional Migration Centre, accessed September 11, 2015. http://mc.mos.ru/migrantam/the-value-of-the-patent/. The cost of medical insurance is paid directly to the insurance companies.

60 Most migrants cannot afford to pay a full year of taxes when initially applying for the patent, and must therefore pay on a monthly basis. Typical of the move towards advanced technology, such as middlemen who interact with migrants primarily through mobile apps, the automation of the tax payment system makes it relatively easy to pay, either via kiosk or bank transfer. It is possible to fill out a receipt online through the Federal Tax Service website, which can be submitted in person to a bank or electronically. It is not clear whether the taxes stay at the federal level or whether they are distributed to the city/regional budgets as intended by the legislation. The FMS website shows statistics on money contributed to the budget from the proceeds of patents. It is unclear, however, if these figures refer to the federal budget, the FMS budget, or some other fund.

61 There is some evidence that registration has not been required at all of patent holders, and that a patent is seen as sufficient to stand in place of registration documents (Kubal 2016b).

62 The law states that patents are automatically extended (i.e., without a visit to the UFMS) with the monthly payment of taxes, and are likewise terminated if taxes are not paid (*On the Legal Status of Foreign Citizens*, Article 13.3.5). Termination of patents is a different legal category from annulment of patents, which occurs when migrants violate the law or do not submit an employment contract.

63 Some regional-level data is available from UFMS websites.
64 "Pravila oplaty naloga po patentu [Rules for paying taxes on patents]," June 11, 2015, accessed February 17, 2016. http://migrant.ru/pravila-oplaty-naloga-po-patentu/. Diaspora leader and migrant-rights activist, interviews by the author, Kazan and Moscow, June 2016.
65 "Memo to the foreign citizen," Multifunctional Migration Centre, accessed February 17, 2016. http://mc.mos.ru/about-the-patent/memo-to-the-foreign-citizen/.
66 "Competitions and tenders," Multifunctional Migration Centre, accessed September 11, 2015. http://mc.mos.ru/auctions-and-tenders/.
67 "GBU 'Migratsionnyi tsentr' narushilo antimonopol'noe zakonodatel'stvo [SBI 'migration centre' violated antimonopoly legislation]," December 24, 2015, accessed February 15, 2016. http://fas.gov.ru/press-center/news/detail.html?id=39970.
68 "Migratsionnyi Tsentr ob obvineniiakh FAS: tekhnicheskaia oshibka [Migration Centre on FAS charges: It was a technical mistake]," December 25, 2015, accessed February 15, 2016. http://ria.ru/society/20151225/1349025043.html.
69 "S 15 fevralia trudovye migranty dolzhny oformliat' medspravki tol'ko v Migratsionnom tsentre v Sakharovo [From 15 February labour migrants must get medical checks only in the migration centre in Sakharov]," February 12, 2016, accessed February 15, 2016. http://mc.mos.ru/presscenter/news/detail/2514392.html.
70 "Mnogofunktsional'nyi migratsionnyi tsentr v Sakharovo. Osobennosti polucheniia patenta na rabotu [Multifunctional migration centre in Sakarov. Particulars of getting a patent]," Confidence Group, accessed February 20, 2016. http://www.confidencegroup.ru/default.aspx?did=153&sid=183.
71 Facebook post, Svetlanna Gannushkina, February 21, 2016; Migrant advocate, interview by the author, Moscow, June 2016.
72 The twofold increase of foreigners coming from visa-free countries includes people coming for tourism, short business visits, or other reasons.
73 Migrant advocate, interview by the author, Moscow, June 2016.

6. Regional Politics of Immigration in Sverdlovsk

1 Within nine months of Rossel's removal, other regional heavyweights resigned or were removed, including Shamiyev (Tatarstan), Rakhimov (Bashkortostan), and Luzhkov (Moscow). Misharin was among a sweep of governors that included no less than 20 replacements (Blakkisrud 2015).

2 Tadzhiki mogut zapolonit' Sverdlovskuiu oblast' [Tajiks could flood Sverdlovsk oblast], February 12, 2004, accessed July 24, 2017. http://politsovet.ru/7850-.html.

3 "V Yekaterinburg ne pustiat gastarbaiterov [Guest workers will not be allowed in Yekaterinburg]," *Komsomol'skaia Pravda*, January 28, 2009, accessed July 23, 2017. http://www.kp.ru/daily/24234/434714/. "Gastarbeiter" is a German term for a foreign guest worker that is frequently used in the Russian discourse.

4 Al'bina Nigmatzianova, and Aliia Akhtarieva, "Gastarbaitery: zagranitsa nam pomozhet?! [Guest workers: Will the foreigners help us?!], January 29, 2009, accessed September 3, 2015. http://ufa1.ru/text/news/63903-print.html.

5 Anatolii Gorlov, "Eduard Rossel': Na stroikakh oblasti vmesto migrantov budut rabotat' ural'tsy [Eduard Rossel: On construction sites locals will work instead of migrants]," *Rossiiskaia Gazeta*, December 17, 2008, accessed July 23, 2017. http://www.rg.ru/2008/12/17/reg-ural/migranti-anons.html.

6 Artem Kovalenko, "Ne bei po rukam [Don't beat on the hands]," *Expert Ural*, April 6, 2009, accessed February 19, 2017. http://expert.ru/ural/2009/13/migratsiya/.

7 "Governor Misharin's example of how to create regional chaos in Medvedev's Russia," May 17, 2010, accessed July 23, 2017. http://www.rusbiznews.com/news/n798.html.

8 Mariia Pliusnina, "Preemnik vtoroi ocheredi [Successor of the second order]," *Kommersant Daily*, August 2, 2012.

9 A list of potential candidates available to replace officials removed by the Kremlin (Ross 2012).

10 "New report names and shames Russia's worst regional governors," *Moscow Times*, March 30, 2015, accessed February 29, 2016. http://www.themoscowtimes.com/news/article/new-report-names-and-shames-russias-worst-regional-governors/518223.html.

11 "Evgenii Kuivashev: natsional'no-kul'turnye ob"edineniia dolzhny pomoch' v adaptatsii migrantov [Evgenii Kuivashev: National-cultural associations should help in the adaptation of migrants]," October 28, 2015, accessed February 29, 2016. http://www.apiural.ru/news/politics/117569/; "Gubernator Kuivashev vstupilcia za geev, migrantov i stalinistov [Governor Kuivashev stands up for gays, migrants and Stalinists]," June 4, 2014, accessed February 29, 2016. http://glagolurfo.com/newsitems/2014/6/4/kujvashev-vstupilsia-za-geev-migrantov/; "Na soveshchanii v Tyumeni Evgenii Kuivashev rasskazal ob opyte regiona po realizatsii strategii gosudarstvennoi natsional'noi politiki [At a meeting

in Tyumen Evgenii Kuivashev described the experience of the region in realizing the strategy of state nationality policy]," May 28, 2015, accessed February 29, 2016. http://gubernator96.ru/news/show/id/3319.

12 "Evgenii Kuivashev vystupil za uvelichenie srokov polucheniia patentov dlia migrantov [Evgenii Kuivashev speaks up for increasing the period for migrants receiving a patent]," May 28, 2015, accessed February 29, 2016. http://www.obltv.ru/news/society/jevgenij_kujvashev_vystupil_za_uvelichenije_srokov_poluchenija_patentov_dla_migrantov/.

13 At the time Roizman was a regional representative of a single-member district before electoral laws were changed, eliminating independent candidates. Patrick Jackson, "No room at the Duma," *BBC News*, November 30, 2007, accessed July 23, 2017. http://news.bbc.co.uk/2/hi/europe/7120863.stm.

14 Evgenii Roizman, interview by Ksenia Sobchak and Ksenia Sokalova, *GQ*, February 8, 2012, accessed July 23, 2017. http://www.gq.ru/lifestyle/sobchak-sokolova-i-evgenij-rojzman.

15 Yekaterinburg local, interview by the author, Yekaterinburg, July 2012. When I called to request an interview with Roizman, he said he was categorically not doing interviews at the time.

16 "Publications on 'the Tajik problem,'" Foundation "City without Drugs," accessed April 5, 2015. http://www.nobf.ru/publik/tadzhik.

17 Roizman, interview by Ksenia Sobchak and Ksenia Sokalova.

18 "E. Roizman: 'Gorod bez narkotikov' i 'Gorod bez tadzhikov' – eto dve bol'shie raznitsy? [E. Roizman: 'City without drugs' and 'City without Tajiks' – are these two different things?]," May 13, 2004, accessed July 23, 2017. http://www.centrasia.ru/newsA.php?st=1084405140.

19 Jackson, "No room at the Duma."

20 Roizman, interview by Ksenia Sobchak and Ksenia Sokalova.

21 Ibid.

22 "Evgenii Roizman: Im nuzhny nashi baby, im nuzhna rabota [Evgenii Roizman: They want our women, they want our jobs]," August 1, 2013, accessed July 23, 2013. http://www.snob.ru/selected/entry/63338.

23 Ibid.

24 Svetlana Basharova, and Natal'ia Korchmarek, "Migrantov perestali testirovat' na narkotiki i alkogol' [Migrants no longer tested for narcotics and alcohol]," *Izvestiia*, August 27, 2013, accessed July 23, 2017. http://izvestia.ru/news/555944.

25 Evgenii Roizman, "Gde-to podvokh [There is a trick somewhere]," *Sila v pravde* [*Power in truth*], August 27, 2013, http://roizman.livejournal.com/1606765.html.

26 "Natsional'naia tema v SMI Yekaterinburga [National themes in the Yekaterinburg mass media]," accessed July 23, 2017. http://www.ethnoinfo.ru/nacionalnye-nko-v-publichnom-prostranstve/778-nacionalnaja-tema-v-smi-Yekaterinburga.

27 Aleksei Starostin, "Prichiny migrantofobii na Urale: terpenie lopnulo, zhurnalisty ubedili ili politiki spekuliruiut? [Reasons for migrantophobia in the Urals: Patience exhausted, journalists convinced, or politicians speculating?]," August 31, 2013, accessed July 23, 2017. http://www.fergananews.com/articles/7842; "Analiticheskii obzor, kharakterizuiushchii migratsionnuiu situatsiiu i deiatel'nost' UFMS Rossii po Sverdlovskoi oblasti po realizatsii gosudarstvennoe migratsionnoi politiki v regione za 2012 god [Analytical review, characterizing the migration situation and activities of the UFMS in Sverdlovsk oblast for the implementation of state migration policies in the region for 2012]," accessed July 23, 2017. http://www.pandia.ru/text/78/145/68583.php.

28 Prior to 2015, neither the federal FMS nor Rosstat released data on how many migration cards specified work as the purpose of entry, though some regions like Sverdlovsk publicized such figures.

29 For the years recorded in table 6.1, 17–24% of entries were recorded as private. In Krasnodar, for 2013–15, 80% of entries were classified as private, and 10–15% as work. In Moscow the proportions have shifted systematically over time from 33% work and 36% private in 2011 to 69% work and 14% private in 2015 (reflecting the legal change in 2015 requiring a migration card with work specified in order to work legally, i.e. get a patent).

30 Human Rights Ombudsman, interview by the author, Sverdlovsk, July 2012; bureaucrat, interview by the author, Sverdlovsk, July 2012.

31 "'Tadzhikskikh melodii' v marshrutkakh stanet men'she. Merzliakova poprosila [Merzliakova asked there there would be fewer 'Tajik melodies' in marshrutkas]," February 5, 2013, accessed May 7, 2015. http://66.ru/news/society/131582/.

32 "Ia odnoznachno znaiu, Chto za etim delom stoit … [I definitely know what this business is …]," September 13, 2013, accessed May 17, 2015. https://www.znak.com/2013-09-13/osuzhdennyy_segodnia_eks_chlen_sverdlovskogo_kabmina_sofrygin___o_zakaznom_haraktere_svoego_dela_i_p.

33 The study cited compares residents' *perceptions* of corruption in various regions across Russia. One potential explanation for high levels of perceived corruption is that, with a more open political orientation, Sverdlovsk is more critical of governance problems. Another explanation is that during the Rossel period there were significant elements of mafia rule in the region, even to the point that the state was captured by business interests.

34 Sverdlovsk Governor's Decree (*ukaz*) No. 402 of May 7, 2007.

35 Sverdlovsk Governor's Decree (*ukaz*) No. 467 of May 30, 2011; Sverdlovsk Government Order (*postanovlenie*) No. 674 of June 1, 2011.

36 These changes were made in the course of government orders that specified the working tasks of the Ministry of Economics and Department of Labour. There was no comprehensive order or decree during this time changing the composition or tasks of the interdepartmental commission. Sverdlovsk Government Order (*postanovlenie*) No. 126 of February 2, 2010; Sverdlovsk Government Order (*postanovlenie*) No. 674 of June 1, 2011.

37 "On the beginning of the 2013 quota campaign in Sverdlovsk oblast," Ministry of Economics Sverdlovsk oblast, January 16, 2012, accessed October 11, 2012..http://econom.midural.ru/trud/rynoktruda/628/.

38 "I soberut ikh v 'Edinom migratsionnom tsentre' [And bring them to the 'United Migration Centre']," *URFO Pravda*, January 26, 2012, accessed September 5, 2015. http://pravdaurfo.ru/news/66/migrantam-urezhut-kvoty. It was also possible to submit applications online.

39 Zhanna Zaionchkovskaia, interview by Dar'ia Mironova, *Rosbalt*, September 22, 2011, accessed July 23, 2017. http://www.rosbalt.ru/moscow/2011/09/22/892898.html.

40 Former employee of the United Migration Centre, Interview by the author, Yekaterinburg, July 2012.

41 "Proverka v sfere migratsionnoi politiki privela k vozbuzhdeniiu ugolovnogo dela [Inspection in sphere of migration politics leads to a criminal case]," April 27, 2012, accessed February 26, 2016. http://prokurat-so.ru/news.php?id=6626.

42 In the 2003 commission, the director of a local NGO and active member of civil society was included as a member. At some point, there was a shift in the composition, however, and this person was removed, though it is unclear when. One of the migration experts in Yekaterinburg told me that productive work on migration policies was easier when the NGO leader was on the committee.

43 "Proverka v svere migratsionnoi politiki privela k vozbuzhdeniiu ugolovnogo dela [Inspection in sphere of migration politics leads to a criminal case]"; "Ministerskaia kvota na ugolovnoe delo [There is a ministerial quota on criminal affairs]," *Kommersant*, March 29, 2012, accessed February 29, 2016. http://www.kommersant.ru/doc/1903221; "Ministerskaia kvota [Ministerial quota]," March 29, 2012, accessed February 29, 2016. http://aktualno.ru/news/view/ministerskaia-kvota-4794; "Kvoty vne zakona [Quotas are outlawed]," May 4, 2012, accessed February 29, 2016. http://www.interfax-russia.ru/Ural/view.asp?id=312681.

44 On this logic, the activity of MTsTO should also be viewed with suspicion, though there were no analogous efforts to expose potential corruption in the Moscow case, or any success in doing so.

45 Migration expert, interview by the author, Sverdlovsk, July 2012; "Kvota na privlechenie trudovykh migrantov v Sverdlovskoi oblasti budet uvelichena [Quota for attracting labour migrants to Sverdlovsk oblast will be increased]," April 20, 2012, accessed July 23, 2017. https://news.mail.ru/economics/8718617/.

46 "Evgenii Sofrygin navlek gnev Aleksandra Misharina [Evgenii Sofrygin incurs the wrath of Aleksandr Misharin]," March 28, 2012, accessed February 29, 2016. http://uralpolit.ru/news/polit_vlast/news_polit/evgenii-sofrygin-navlek-gnev-aleksandra-misharina.

47 Migration expert, interview by the author, Sverdlovsk, July 2012; "Ministerskaia kvota na ugolovnoe delo [Ministerial quota becomes a criminal affair]"; Iurii Ovodov, "Odin pishem – a v ume? [Writing one – but minding? (i.e., minding the informal, not the official)]," *Uralskii Rabochii*, April 10, 2012, accessed July 17, 2017. http://xn-----6kcabbhjttpdjeip1d1agp-py8h0e.xn--p1ai/society/4347/.

48 Marina Kolchina,"Pora bit' trevogu [It's time to sound the alarm]," May 2, 2013, accessed February 2, 2017. http://aktualno.ru/news/view/pora-bit-trevogu-11864; "'Tadzhikskikh melodii' v marshrutkakh stanet men'she ["Tajik melodies" in marshrutka become fewer]."

49 Ol'ga Melkozerova, "Kvotoi v nebo [Quotas in the sky]," *Rossiiskaia Gazeta*, August 12, 2008, accessed February 2, 2017. https://rg.ru/2008/08/12/reg-ural/migranty.html.

50 Andrei Gorbunov, "Na Urale voditelei-migrantov poprosili vkliuchat' v marshrutkakh russkie pesni [In the Urals migrant drivers asked to turn on Russian songs in marshrutkas]," *Komsomol'skaia Pravda*, February 6, 2013, accessed February 2, 2017. http://www.kp.ru/online/news/1359800; "'Tadzhikskikh melodii' v marshrutkakh stanet men'she. ["Tajik melodies" in marshrutka become fewer]."

51 Andrei Gorbunov, "Meriia Yekaterinburga zapretila voditeliam-gastarbaiteram vkliuchat' v marshrutkakh pesni na natsional'nom iazyke [Mayor of Yekaterinburg prohibits migrant drivers from playing songs in national language]," *Komsomol'skaia Pravda*, March 25, 2013, accessed February 2, 2017. http://www.ural.kp.ru/daily/26051/2963305/.

52 "V marshrutkakh Yekaterinburga zapretili 'nerusskuiu muzyku' [In the marshrutkas of Yekaterinburg 'non-Russian music' is banned]," accessed July 23, 2017. http://www.ethnoinfo.ru/nacionalnaja-kultura-v-publichnom-prostranstve.

53 "Defitsit kvot na trudovykh migrantov mozhet vozniknut' v Sverdlovskoi oblasti [There could be a deficit of quota for labour migrants in Sverdlovsk oblast]," March 28, 2008, accessed July 24, 2017. http://eanews.ru/news/society/i103405/; "Kvota na privlechenie trudovykh migrantov v Sverdlovskoi oblasti budet uvelichena [Quota for attracting labour migrants to Sverdlovsk oblast will be increased]."

54 Sundstrom (2006) notes that support for civil society has not been uniform across Sverdlovsk, NGOs typically finding more support from the municipal level (in Yekaterinburg) than from the regional government. For the migration sector, the concentration of civil society groups in Yekaterinburg is also a factor of more migrants being located in the capital city than elsewhere in the region.

55 Beginning in 2006, when heavy reporting requirements were introduced for any organizations accepting foreign funding, restrictions on both foreign and domestic civil society organizations have become increasingly draconian. With the introduction of the "foreign agents law" in 2012 and the extension of scrutiny to international organizations through a new law in 2015 that gives government officials the authority to ban the activities of foreign organizations deemed "undesirable," the scope of work for migration activists has become circumscribed both by decreasing access to funding (outside of government grants) and opening activists to scrutiny, and possible prosecution, freezing of assets, or being barred from re-entry to Russia (for foreigners). It is interesting to note that the label "undesirable" is rooted in migration law, extending the group of undesirable entities from individuals to entire organizations. Being dubbed undesirable comes with concrete restrictions on entry to and exit from Russia (Schenk 2016). My fieldwork in the region commenced as the foreign agents' law was introduced, leading one activist to repeatedly wonder during the course of our interview whether he would encounter trouble as a result of meeting with me. However, in the ensuing years, I have heard many reports by NGOs and migration-related organizations in Russia that while being labelled a foreign agent limits their work in some ways, it is absolutely possible to continue many of their activities until the label can be removed. Many of my colleauges in Russia, therefore, see the foreign agents legislation as a political and bureaucratic irritation more than an absolute limitation on their ability to work.

56 Sverdlovsk Governor's Decree (*ukaz*) No. 285 of April 28, 2012.

57 "Sverdlovskim ministrom ekonomiki ne stali ni Maksimov, ni Sofrygin [Sverdlovsk minister of economics is neither Maksimov nor Sofrygin],"

April 26, 2012, accessed July 23, 2017. http://www.e1.ru/news/spool/news_id-367868.

58 Biography of Aleksandr Misharin, accessed July 23, 2017. http://lenta.ru/lib/14199847/.

59 Mariia Pliusnina, "Preemnik vtoroi ocheredi [Successor of the second order]." Misharin eventually went on to be vice-president of Russian Railways after a period out of the public eye.

60 See appendix table A6.a for the full picture of sectoral quota allocation.

61 "Vinoven: byvshii ministr ekonomiki Evgenii Sofrygin oshtrafovan na 300 tysiach rublei [Guilty: Former minister of economics Evgenii Sofrygin fined 300 thousand rubles]," *Argumenti i Fakti*, September 13, 2013, accessed February 2, 2017. http://www.ural.aif.ru/incidents/criminal/827310.

62 Migration expert, interview by the author, Yekaterinburg, July 2012; "V Sverdlovskom migratsionnom tsentre – kadrovye perestanovki. Davaite znakomit'sia s ego novym rukovoditelem [In the Svedlovsk migration centre – a personnel reshuffle. Let's meet the new head]," August 9, 2011, accessed July 23, 2017. http://www.ura.ru/content/svrd/09-08-2011/news/1052132474.html.

63 Migration expert, interview by the author, Yekaterinburg (via skype), July 2014.

64 United Migration Centre, accessed July 24, 2017. http://www.migraciaural.ru/.

65 Maksim Solopov and Stepan Opalev, "Rassledovanie RBK: kto zarabatyvaet na migrantakh [RBK investigation: who earns from migrants]," *RBK*, July 20, 2015, accessed February 2, 2017. http://www.rbc.ru/politics/20/07/2015/55a269449a7947fa0ba06593.

66 Entries and registrations increased in both Moscow and Krasnodar. A decrease in Sverdlovsk indicates that either the region was more affected by the economic crisis, that migrants were deterred by new legal procedures, or that migrants opted to remain instead of visiting home.

67 Patents can be annulled if migrants commit certain criminal acts or administrative violations, if they fail to submit an employment contract, or if they work for a third party. Non-payment of taxes, on the other hand, terminates the validity of a patent, but is not grounds for annulment. The number of administrative violations for migration-related issues (see table 6.5) far exceeds the number of patents annulled, and is therefore not likely reflected in these figures, especially given the patterns of timing of annulments revealed in the spreadsheet. The most likely cause of annulment reflected in the spreadsheet is not submitting an employment contract.

68 Of these patents, 43 had been issued in February, 146 in March, 331 in April, and 7 in May.

69 Verifying other aspects of patent validity, such as tax payments, requires interministerial cooperation and information sharing.

70 Compare this with a more equal distribution of patents for private (22,924) and commercial (26,507) purposes in Krasnodar. Moscow does not release figures for private vs commercial patents.

71 "Pervichnoe oformlenie patenta dlia migranta [Initial patent application for a migrant]," Migratika, accessed July 24, 2017. http://migratika.ru/patent/. Contrast this organization's instructions to the wording on the Moscow MMTs website: "Within two months after receiving a patent, a foreign citizen should submit to the Moscow UFMS a copy of their employment contract."

72 The applications both for an initial patent and for renewals ask where work is *planned*.

7. Regional Politics of Immigration in Krasnodar

1 "Krasnodar is the best city to live in," November 2, 2012, accessed July 24, 2017. http://www.euroasia-uclg.ru/en/news/novosti-partnerov-i-chlenov-ogmv/krasnodar-luchshiy-gorod-dlya-zhizni/.

2 Early legislation was indicative of Yeltsin-era asymmetrical federalism, where regions had much more latitude to make laws even if they contradicted federal laws (Voronina 2006; Andrienko and Guriev 2005; Rubins 1998; Katanian 1998). Krasnodar's activism extended well into the Putin period, despite the push towards legal uniformity across the federal system. Examples of legislation include Governor's Order (*postanovlenie*) No. 826 of July 25, 2002 (establishing a department for migration monitoring), Krasnodar Law No. 460 of April 11, 2002 (establishing registration procedures), Krasnodar Law No. 735 of July 2, 2004 (on procedures to fight against illegal immigration), and Governor's Order (*postanovlenie*) No. 1094 of November 22, 2005 (specifying how government agencies should coordinate their migration-related activities).

3 Ararat Petrosian, "Profamil'naia zachistka [Surname sweep]," *Izvestia*, March 19, 2002.

4 Igor Bederov, "Hezakonnaia Familiia [Illegal surnames]," *Novaia Gazeta*, July 11, 2002, accessed February 26, 2014. http://2002.novayagazeta.ru/nomer/2002/49n/n49n-s00.shtml. *Yan* and *dze* are typical endings for Armenian names, whereas *shvili* is Georgian and *ogli* has Turkish roots.

5 Petrosian, "Profamil'naia zachistka [Surname sweep]."

6 Though formally the Soviet *propiska* system was dismantled in 1993, even into the 2000s a number of regional governments retained registration rules that were restrictive in nature, and it was not uncommon for ethnic minorities to encounter barriers to proper registration (Federal Law No. 5242-1 of June 25, 1993; Russian Constitution 1993; Voronina 2006; Katanian 1998; Schaible 2001). Meskhetian Turks in Krasnodar were systematically denied registration, leaving them without legal rights such as access to legal employment, property ownership, passports and other legal documents, health care, etc. (Swerdlow 2006). The problem was further compounded when regional legislation was passed in 1996 requiring "migrants" (an undefined category, and therefore subject to interpretation) to reside in the region for 10 years before they could receive permanent registration (Popov and Kuznetsov 2008).

7 Though the 2002 immigration laws did not single out Meskhetian Turks, some claimed that their enforcement was disproportionately focused on the group. Susan B. Glasser, "Immigrants feeling Russians' wrath: Paramilitary groups aid crackdown by nationalist governor," *Washington Post*, June 12, 2002; Ararat Petrosian, "S Kubani deportiruiut nezakonnykh migrantov [Kuban deports illegal migrants]," *Izvestia*, March 27, 2002, accessed July 17, 2017. http://iz.ru/news/260013; Ararat Petrosian, "Etnicheskie chistki po-Kubanski [Ethnic cleansing in Kuban]," *Izvestia*, March 29, 2002.

8 Krasnodar Law No. 460 of April 11, 2002 elaborated regionally specific *propiska* procedures and remained in force until July 21, 2004. The accompanying Krasnodar Legislative Order No. 1381-P of March 27, 2002 dealt with procedures for increasing control over illegal immigration, though it went out of force a few months later on August 1, 2002.

9 Susan B. Glasser, "More racism in Russia," *Washington Post*, June 13, 2002.

10 Cossack groups, though not officially government entities, have been supported and given authority by the regional government in a variety of ways. In 1996, the federal government guaranteed social benefits for Cossack groups performing public service (Presidential Decree (*ukaz*) No. 564 of April 16, 1996), a benefit that was confirmed by regional legislation in Krasnodar in 2000 (Krasnodar Law No. 247 of March 13, 2000). In May 2002, Cossack forces were specifically tasked with maintaining public order in Krasnodar and working to reduce illegal immigration (Krasnodar Legislative Order No. 1532-P of May 29, 2002). This order directs Cossack forces to make monthly raids in order to find those "without registration or *propiska*." This is a further regional legislative confirmation of *propiska*, though the *propiska* regime officially ended a decade earlier. Prior to this, the Cossack patrols worked on the basis of agreements with various

government entities, for example exchanging benefits like tax breaks for their services in patrolling borders and doing various security tasks. Eduard Aslanov, "Cossacks menace Krasnodar minorities," *Institute for War and Peace Reporting*, January 18, 2002, accessed March 6, 2014. http://iwpr.net/report-news/cossacks-menace-krasnodar-minorities. Often these volunteer patrols themselves violated the law and acted without representation of police forces, using extortion and sometimes even violence (Popov and Kuznetsov 2008).

11 Tkachev's rhetoric and the surrounding discourse are an example of how internal and international migration are conflated in Russia. This particular decision focused on internal migrants, who are sometimes considered illegal if their registration documents are not in order. "Gubernator Krasnodarskogo kraia Aleksandr Tkachev otvergaet obvineniia v natsionalizme [Krasnodar Governor Alexander Tkachev rejects accusations of nationalism]," *Kavkazskii Uzel*, August 4, 2012, accessed July 17, 2017. http://www.kavkaz-uzel.eu/articles/210722/; Natal'ia Kostenko, "Obshchestvennaia palata nashla kriminal v prizyve Tkacheva ogranichit' migratsiiu kavkaztsev [The Public Chamber finds Tkachev's limitation of Caucasian migrants criminal]," *Vedomosti*, August 6, 2012, accessed February 17, 2015. http://www.vedomosti.ru/politics/articles/2012/08/06/filtry_tkacheva; Sergei Smirnov, Ol'ga Kuz'menkova, and Ekaterina Vinokurova, "Tkachev fil'truet Kuban' [Tkachev filters the Kuban]," *Gazeta*, August 3, 2012.

12 Cossack units went to the streets beginning September 1, 2012 in all 44 of Krasnodar's municipalities, accompanying police personnel. They are required to wear traditional Cossack attire and may not carry weapons, but have the authority to check documents and hand suspects over to internal affairs officials. In this capacity they detained 100 "troublemakers" on their first day of service. Tat'iana Kuznetsova, "Kazach'i druzhiny v pervyi den' sluzhby zaderzhali bolee 100 narushitelei [In the first day of service Cossack patrols arrest more than 100 violators]," *RIA Novosti*, September 3, 2012, accessed February 3, 2017. https://ria.ru/incidents/20120903/742131108.html; Anastasiia Laukkanen, "Medvedev, migranty i 'umerennyi aparteid' [Medvedev, migrants, and 'moderate apartheid']," August 11, 2012, accessed February 3, 2017. http://inosmi.ru/russia/20120811/196465640.html; Kostenko, "Obshchestvennaia palata nashla kriminal v prizyve Tkacheva ogranichit' migratsiiu kavkaztsev [The Public Chamber finds Tkachev's limitation of Caucasian migrants criminal]."

13 "Cossack vigilantes start patrolling Moscow streets," November 27, 2012, accessed July 27, 2017. https://www.rt.com/politics/watch-starts-patrolling-streets-672/. Cossack deployments have been used in various

places (especially in border regions) since 1990 (Galeotti 1995; Toje 2006), including St Petersburg (Shenfield 2001), and the Primorski region (Petkov and Shklyar 1999).

14 "Putin: kazach'i druzhiny chasto effektivnee pravookhranitel'nykh organov [Putin: Cossack brigades are often more effective than law enforcement agencies]," *RIA Novosti*, December 19, 2013, accessed August 13, 2015. http://ria.ru/society/20131219/985137741.html; Alec Luhn, "The Cossacks Ride Again," January 31, 2014, accessed August 13, 2015. http://www.slate.com/articles/news_and_politics/roads/2014/01/cossacks_will_patrol_the_sochi_olympics_vladimir_putin_is_drafting_these.html.

15 Nikita Serebriannikov, "V Krasnodarskom krae vyiavleno bolee 36 tysiach narushenii migratsionnogo zakonodatel'stva [More than 36,000 violations of migration law have been discovered in the Krasnodar region]," *Kavkazskii Uzel*, July 7, 2012, accessed July 27, 2017. http://www.kavkaz-uzel.ru/articles/209340/.

16 "Ugolovnye rekordy Olimpiady v Sochi [Criminal records of the Olympics in Sochi]," *Skandaly. Intrigi. Rassledovania* [*Scandals. Intrigues. Investigation*], September 11, 2012, accessed February 17, 2016. http://intrigi-spletni.blogspot.co.il/2012/09/blog-post_6422.html#.UI6zv8Up-B8. This type of diversionary politics has a number of applications in Russia (see, for example, Marten 2014), showing that diversions can create a complex web of simultaneous actions used to manage public opinion.

17 In Moscow and Sverdlovsk, typically both the agency in charge and the membership of the interdepartmental commission are addressed within the scope of one executive order.

18 I contacted Igor Melkikh, head of the Department of Labour, in August 2012 just months after he was promoted from a regular member to vice-chair of the commission. With his promotion, the Department of Labour was put in charge of the quota formulation process. Nevertheless, he refused an interview, saying he had nothing to do with migration management.

19 This requirement was never fulfilled. Despite checking the site numerous times across several years, I found that the website had no information about quotas at all.

20 Quota corrections (increases in this case) are reported in the media only occasionally. Across all of the regions analysed they are not widely or systematically reported.

21 Government Order (*postanovlenie*) No. 758 of October 13, 2008. Similar exemptions are made for construction on other state projects, such as the World Cup (Federal Law No. 108 of June 7, 2013). This exemption is part of a body of legislation specific to the development of Sochi, i.e. Federal Law

No. 310 of December 1, 2007, Government Order (*postanovlenie*) No. 991 of December 29, 2007, Presidential Decree (*ukaz*) No. 686 of August 19, 2013.

22 Oleg Riabov, "Kubanskii khleb gastarbaiterov [Kuban bread of guest workers]," *Kubanskiie Novosti*, November 29, 2011.

23 Migration data by economic sector was issued biannually until 2010; in 2012 reports shifted to categorizing migrants by professional qualifications.

24 "EU afraid of switching to visa-free travel by Sochi Games – Federal Migration Service," *Russia beyond the Headlines*, January 21, 2013, accessed August 31, 2015. http://rbth.com/news/2013/01/21/eu_afraid_of_switching_to_visa-free_travel_by_sochi_games_-_federal_migr_22056.html.

25 FMS Order (*prikaz*) No. 387 of September 23, 2013.

26 Biography of Aleksandr Tkachev, accessed August 19, 2015. http://lenta.ru/lib/14173927/full.htm.

27 Several companies in the region were similarly connected to Tkachev, but only one other (Chateau de Taliu) received a quota allotment. Irina Zhavoronkova, Anfisa Voronina, and Elena Likhomanova, "Glava Minsel'khoza Tkachev rasskazal ob agrobiznese svoei sem'i [Head of the Ministry of Agriculture Tkachev discusses agroholdings of his family]," RBK, June 22, 2015, accessed July 26, 2017. http://top.rbc.ru/business/22/06/2015/5587d8e89a7947815378a3ff.

28 Aleksei Esikov, "Na Kuban 'osedaet' vse bol'she inostrannykh migrantov [More and more foreign migrants 'settle' in the Kuban]," November 16, 2011, accessed July 26, 2017. http://93.ru/text/news/456943.html.

29 Riabov, "Kubanskii khleb gastarbaiterov [Kuban bread of guest workers]"; "Kitaitsam zapretiat vyrashchivat' ovoshchi na territorii RF [Chinese are prohibited from growing vegetables on Russia's territory]," September 27, 2011, accessed July 18, 2017. www.foodmarkets.ru/news/topic/6323.

30 Vera Cherepnina, "Kitaiskaia otrava [Chinese poison]," April 30, 2013, accessed February 17, 2016. http://kuban.mk.ru/articles/2013/04/30/849532-kitayskaya-otrava.html; "Bolee 80 kitaitsev-nelegalov vydvoriat iz Krasnodara za predely Rossii [More than 80 illegal Chinese migrants will be expelled from Krasnodar and Russia]," *Interfax*, May 21, 2013, accessed February 17, 2016. http://www.interfax-russia.ru/South/news.asp?id=402800&sec=1671.

31 Kris Aversman, "RF stolknulac' s agrarnoi kolonizatsiei so storony KNR [RF faces agrarian colonization by PRC]," August 19, 2012, accessed November 7, 2013. newsland.com/news/detail/id/1019358/.

32 Work permits are non-transferrable, and are valid only in the region of issue.

33 According to a migration expert, actual deportations (as opposed to the court orders on deportation) were relatively rare at the time because there was no budget allocated to send migrants home.
34 "V Dinskom Raione raspustili nelegal'nyi Kitaiskii 'kolkhoz' [In Dinskii region illegal Chinese farms have been dissolved]," May 25, 2013, accessed November 6, 2013. 9tv.ru/news/item/38445.
35 "V Dinskom Raione zaderzhali bol'she 30 nelegal'nykh migrantov [In Dinskii region more than 30 illegal migrants were arrested]," August 14, 2013, accessed November 6, 2013. http://9tv.ru/news/item/40755.
36 Court documents accessed through https://rospravosudie.com
37 "Tkachev: Migranty iz Kitaia redko pokidaiut Kuban' [Tkachev: Migrants from China rarely leave the Kuban]," June 20, 2014, accessed February 20, 2016. https://news.mail.ru/politics/18618380/.
38 "A. Tkachev: 'Na sleduiushchii god chtoby ni odnogo kitaitsa v krae ne bylo!' [A. Tkachev: 'Next year there will not be a single Chinese person in the region']," June 5, 2013, accessed July 26, 2017. http://krasnodar.rusplt.ru/index/news_11405.html.
39 "Rostovskaia oblast' i Kuban' voshli v TOP-5 regionov Rossii po urovniu korruptsii [Rostov oblast and Kuban found in the top 5 regions of Russia by level of corruption]," September 19, 2014, accessed February 3, 2017. http://www.yugopolis.ru/news/social/2014/09/19/73582/korrupciya-vzyatki.
40 Migration expert, interview by the author, Krasnodar, August 2012.
41 Ibid.
42 Migration and corruption expert, interview by the author, Krasnodar, August 2012.
43 Ibid.
44 The roundtable was covered in the local press, though it was represented variously. Headlines read: "Trudovye migranty chasto stradaiut ot nechestnykh rabotodatelei i chinovnikov, zaiavili uchastniki vstrechi v Krasnodare [Migrant workers often suffer from dishonest employers and officials, stated participants of a meeting in Krasnodar]," *Kavkazskii Uzel*, August 3, 2012, accessed February 4, 2017. http://www.kavkaz-uzel.eu/articles/210665/ and "Kak kubanskie chinovniki i politseiskie 'razvodiat' migrantov [How Kuban officials and police conned migrants]," August 23, 2012, accessed February 4, 2017. http://fedpress.ru/news/society/reviews/kak-kubanskie-chinovniki-i-politseiskie-razvodyat-migrantov. And from the UFMS press centre: "A discussion in Krasnodar about the issues of protecting the rights of foreign workers in relation to representatives of authorities."

45 As a matter of research ethics, I have chosen not to include the names of civil society actors who are still working in Russia in order to protect their identities and future ability to work effectively in an increasingly closed environment. In the case of Professor Savva, however, I believe it is important to include the details of events to show the depth of the regional administration's commitment to control. All of these events are well documented on Savva's website (http://mvsavva.ru/) and therefore already part of the public record, yet I also asked for his express permission to write about the case here. Professor Savva has left Russia to seek asylum abroad, and is neither active in migrant advocacy in Krasnodar nor under further pressure from the regional government.

46 Anna Davydova, "'Neugoden na vsiakii sluchai': na Kubani budut sudit' uchenogo Mikhaila Savvu ['Objectionable just in case': Scholar Mikhail Savva will be tried in the Kuban]," *Argumenty i Fakty*, October 31, 2013, accessed July 26, 2017. http://www.aif.ru/politics/russia/1012365.

47 Sergei Myshak, interview by Novaia Gazeta Kuban, April 23, 2014, accessed July 29, 2017. http://ngkub.ru/online-intervyu/myshak-sergej-valentinovich.

48 "Kubanskomu ombudsmenu pozelali publichnosti [The ombudsman to Kuban wanted publicity]," July 13, 2013, accessed September 1, 2015. http://kavpolit.com/kubanskomu-ombudsmenu-pozhelali-publichnosti/.

49 Tajik diaspora leader, interview by the author, Krasnodar, August 2012.

50 Focus group, Krasnodar, August 2012.

51 The lack of transparency is evidenced by surveying official documents on government agency websites, announcements of quota in media, press conferences, etc. Though in Krasnodar there are many advertisements instructing employers how they should go about applying for quota, the initial estimates made by the interdepartmental commission in the summer are not announced in the regional media. It is only once quota numbers have been confirmed at the federal level and the official documents have been released in the fall that quota numbers may appear in the press, and even so it is rare to find articles in the regional press devoted to the issue of quotas. For example, a search of the local government newspaper *Kubanskie Novosti* for quota-related articles turned up only 6 articles mentioning regional quota numbers, compared with 13 articles announcing relevant legislation for quotas and 9 articles announcing the procedure for employers to participate in the annual quota formulation. This relatively high emphasis on announcements to employers reinforces the point made in the interview that the government makes a serious effort to involve employers in the yearly quota campaign.

52 There is a general difference in attitude between the populations of Krasnodar and Sverdlovsk. Sverdlovsk tends to be quite activist. For example, there were a number of large protests surrounding the 2011 federal Duma elections. In contrast, when I asked a Russian girl in Krasnodar if there had been protests she said, "Well, I don't think so."

53 Vera Cherepnina, "1.3 mln gastarbaiterov dlia Kubani [1.3 million guest workers for the Kuban]," March 27, 2013, accessed September 1, 2015. http://kuban.mk.ru/articles/2013/03/27/831954-13-mln-gastarbayterov-dlya-kubani.html.

54 For example "Aleksandr Tkachev: 'Mery po presecheniiu pravonarushenii v migratsionnoi sfere dolzhny byt' bolee zhestkimi' [Aleksandr Tkachev: 'Measures to prevent offences in the migration sphere should be more stringent']," October 22, 2013, accessed July 26, 2017. http://kubantv.ru/kuban/51189-aleksandr-tkachev-mery-po-presecheniju-pravonarushenijj-v-migratsionnojj-sfere-dolzhny-byt-bolee-zhestkimi/; "A. Tkachev: 'Na sleduiushchii god chtoby ni odnogo kitaitsa v krae ne bylo!' [A. Tkachev: 'Next year there will not be a single Chinese person in the region']."

55 "'Barany!!!!!' – imenno tak nazyvali migrantov v UFMS Krasnodar [Sheep!!!!! This is what migrants are called in the UFMS of Krasnodar]," March 13, 2015, accessed February 18, 2016. https://www.youtube.com/watch?v=eBUcR_hlIYw; "FMS ob"iasnila, kak reorganizovala rabotu po vydache patentov v Krasnodarskom krae posle rosta obrashchenii migrantov [The FMS explains how they reorganized the issuance of patents in Krasnodar after the growth of appeals by migrants]," April 27, 2015, accessed February 18, 2016. http://president-sovet.ru/presscenter/news/read/2393/.

56 The decision to delegate responsibilities to UFMS offices throughout the region was made through several UFMS orders (*prikazy*) that are not publically available.

57 Denis Sidorov, "Na Kubani vyroslo chislo zhelaiushchikh poluchit' trudovoi patent [The number of those seeking labour patents has risen in the Kuban]," April 6, 2015, accessed February 18, 2016. http://kuban24.tv/item/na-kubani-vyiroslo-chislo-jelayuschih-poluchit-trudovoy-patent-117468.

58 Lina Lavrova, "V Sochi prekratili vydachu patentov dlia migrantov [Sochi has stopped issuing patents for migrants]," December 3, 2014, accessed February 18, 2016. http://www.sochi-express.ru/sochi/news/sochi/73172.

59 "Trud inostranta [Labour of foreigners]," Pravo na Biznes, accessed February 20, 2016. http://правонабизнес.рф/index.php/zakoni2/150-trud-inostrantsa.

60 "Okolo 900 mln rublei postupilo v biudzhet Kubani za vydachu patentov migrantam [The issuing of patents to migrants has brought around 900 million rubles to the budget of the Kuban]," *Kubanskie Novosti*, February 15, 2016, accessed March 10, 2016. http://kubnews.ru/news/35830/. Regional income from patents is not included on the standard statistics form issued by UFMS branches. Information is limited to press releases and statements by officials.

61 The maximum possible revenue for January–September would have been over 900 million rubles if migrants were fully tax compliant, submitted employments after two months, *and* stayed from the issue of their patent until the end of September.

62 If the total revenue for 2015 were 650 million rubles, it would signify 232,046 individual monthly payments by migrants (or an average of 4.7 months of tax payments per migrant). A total revenue of 900 million rubles would reflect 321,296 individual monthly payments (or an average of 6.5 months).

63 The receipt of 32,314 contracts represents a 65% submission rate, which is higher than the rate in Sverdlovsk (44%). Data on the number of contracts submitted are not recorded in Moscow or federal reports.

64 In this scenario, the first 32,314 migrants to receive patents (those who arrived January–June, and a portion of migrants in July) would have paid taxes from the receipt of their patent until the end of the year. The remainder of patent recipients would submit no more than two months of tax payments.

65 In which case they would be counted twice in the 32,314 figure of contracts received.

66 Data from 2014 show that Armenian citizens received 20% of patents and Kyrgyz citizens received 2%, indicating that their absence in the 2015 figures cannot account for as precipitous a drop as is indicated. Those who have temporary refugee status (including 15,000 Ukrainians in 2014 and 20,000 in 2015) also do not need permission to work (i.e. a patent).

67 Biography of Veniamin Ivanovich Kondrat'ev, Kavkazskii Uzel, August 8, 2016, accessed February 20, 2016. http://www.kavkaz-uzel.ru/articles/267535/.

Conclusion

1 Marina Karpova, "Russian bloggers react to the nanny that decapitated a child," *Russia beyond the Headlines*, March 7, 2016, accessed January 13, 2017. http://rbth.com/politics_and_society/2016/03/07/russian-bloggers-react-to-the-nanny-that-decapitated-a-child_573629; Anna Nemtsova, "The head-chopping nanny from hell becomes a political symbol in Moscow," *Daily*

Beast, March 3, 2016, accessed January 13, 2017. http://www.thedailybeast.com/articles/2016/03/02/the-head-chopping-nanny-from-hell-becomes-a-political-symbol-in-moscow.html.

2 Philip Oltermann, "Angela Merkel's party beaten by rightwing populists in German elections," *Guardian*, September 6, 2016, accessed January 13, 2017. https://www.theguardian.com/world/2016/sep/04/mecklenburg-vorpommern-german-anti-immigrant-party-strong-regional-election-exit-polls-merkel.

3 Alison Smale, "As Germany welcomes migrants, sexual attacks in Cologne point to a new reality," *New York Times*, January 14, 2016, accessed January 13, 2017. https://www.nytimes.com/2016/01/15/world/europe/as-germany-welcomes-migrantssexual-attacks-in-cologne-point-to-a-new-reality.html?_r=2.

4 Melissa Eddy, "Reports of attacks on women in Germany heighten tension over migrants," *New York Times*, January 5, 2016, accessed January 13, 2017. https://www.nytimes.com/2016/01/06/world/europe/coordinated-attacks-on-women-in-cologne-were-unprecedented-germany-says.html.

5 Michelle Martin, "Cologne attacks show Germany unprepared for migration challenge," *Reuters*, January 28, 2016, accessed January 13, 2017. http://www.reuters.com/article/us-europe-migrants-germany-challenges-in-idUSKCN0V6173.

6 Kate Connolly, "Tensions rise in Germany over handling of mass sexual assaults in Cologne," *Guardian*, January 7, 2016, accessed January 13, 2017. https://www.theguardian.com/world/2016/jan/06/tensions-rise-in-germany-over-handling-of-mass-sexual-assaults-in-cologne; Nick Ferrari, "Cologne migrant attacks cover-up shames the BBC, blasts Nick Ferrari," *Express*, January 10, 2016, accessed January 13, 2017. http://www.express.co.uk/comment/columnists/nick-ferrari/633179/migrant-attacks-cover-up-shamed-Cologne-Jeremy-Corbyn-North-Korea-Alzhemiers; Matthew Karnitschnig, "Cologne puts Germany's 'lying press' on defensive," *Politico*, January 20, 2016, accessed January 13, 2017. http://www.politico.eu/article/cologne-puts-germany-lying-media-press-on-defensive-migration-refugees-attacks-sex-assault-nye/.

7 "Merkel urges Germans to stick to facts on refugee crime," *Local*, December 7, 2016, accessed January 13, 2017. https://www.thelocal.de/20161207/merkel-urges-germans-to-stick-to-facts-on-refugee-crime.

8 Eugene C. Emery, Jr, "Donald Trump says Germany now riddled with crime thanks to refugees," *Politifact*, May 11, 2016, accessed January 13, 2017. http://www.politifact.com/truth-o-meter/statements/2016/may/11/donald-trump/donald-trump-says-germany-now-riddled-crime-thanks/;

Raheem Kassam, and Chris Tomlinson, "REPORT: Migrants committing disproportionately high crime in Germany while media and govt focus on 'far right' thought crimes," *Breitbart*, May 23, 2016, accessed January 13, 2017. http://www.breitbart.com/london/2016/05/23/germany-registers-surge-crimes-right-wing-radicals/.

9 Oxford dictionaries define post-truth as "relating to or denoting circumstances in which objective facts are less influential in shaping public opinion than appeals to emotion and personal belief," and named it the 2016 word of the year because of the upsurge in usage surrounding the UK Brexit vote and US presidential election. https://en.oxforddictionaries.com/word-of-the-year/word-of-the-year-2016, accessed December 8, 2016.

10 In this sense it is the liberal principle of allowing citizens a voice in their governance that conflicts with the seemingly illiberal decisions that participatory governance produces. Drawing boundaries around the state, within which rights and equality prevail, is the communitarian version of liberalism (Walzer 1983), as opposed to a cosmopolitan liberalism that maintains that the borders of states and citizenship do not justify barriers to freedom of movement as a universal human right (Jacobson 1996; Soysal 1994; Sassen 1998; Carens 1987).

11 This claim is not meant to imply that policies are the same everywhere, or that there aren't outliers (states that produce open immigration policies). Rather, it is simply a statement that if there is a pool of countries that adopt increasingly strict policies and experience the almost certain increase in illegal immigration, a common convergence cannot be explained by varying regime types among the cases.

12 Because migrants were concretely tied to specific employers through contracts, employers had a great deal of control over workers, including the ability to retain them for only part-time work, resulting in scores of under-employed migrants (Calavita 1992). Some criticize the contract system as "semi-slavery" and "feudalism" (Durand 2007). The US experience should be carefully considered in light of Russian reforms to delink work permits from a specific employer in 2007, and the subsequent requirement of contracts for extension of work permits, patents, and work in the context of the Eurasian Economic Union.

13 Though there has been significant work on the development of hybrid regimes, the concept and sub-concepts remain fuzzy, difficult to apply to systems that often change rapidly, and without overarching consensus on key features.

14 Svolik (2012), for example, calls dictatorship a "residual category that contains all countries that do not meet established criteria for democracy."

The trend towards characterizing Russia in terms of its failures is not new. As Howard and Walters (2014) argue, even prior to the fall of the Soviet Union, the region was interpreted as backward, using the lenses of modernization theory. Running through both periods is a tendency to use the experience of Western states as a benchmark for comparison.

15 In the US intelligence report assessing the evidence for Russian hacking of the Democratic National Convention and its impact on the 2016 presidential elections, concern was raised over Russian reporting on government and corporate corruption, allegations of electoral fraud, and "shortcomings in democracy and civil liberty" (Office of the Director of National Intelligence 2017). Yet as Russia analyst Kevin Rothrock aptly points out, demonstrating the double standard by which critiques of the US are dismissed, "the intelligence assessment sounds the alarm over RT news reports about the Occupy Wall Street movement, and segments highlighting 'a lack of democracy' in America, excessive surveillance, police brutality, and other injustices. Not only are these perfectly legitimate subjects for journalism, but these are also the mainstay themes of American reporting on Russia." Kevin Rothrock, "American unintelligence on Russia (op-ed)," *Moscow Times*, January 7, 2017, accessed February 19, 2017. https://themoscowtimes.com/articles/american-unintelligence-on-russia-op-ed-56746.

16 A rare but promising example is a critique of the 2016 US elections using the framework of competitive authoritarian regimes (Slater and Way 2017). I would suggest this type of critical approach creates a more equal playing field for the discussion of regimes.

Appendixes

1 In the migration literature, there is mixed evidence for the relationship between unemployment and immigration restrictions. Some studies have argued that higher levels of unemployment will lead to increasing immigration restrictions, which is certainly in line with popular political rhetoric about the need to protect domestic labour markets from immigrant workers. However, other studies have found little support for the impact of unemployment on immigration restrictions (Givens and Luedtke 2005). Studies on internal migration in the Russian context show evidence that low unemployment rates tend to attract migrants to a particular region (Andrienko and Guriev 2004; Gerber 2006). Therefore both decreased labour market demand and increased labour protectionism should produce lower quotas as unemployment increases.

2 Though a number of additional variables are included in the government methodology, inclusion in the models produced collinearity. The Variance Inflation Factors (VIF) of the full set of indicators (i.e., GRP, population) were assessed in order to select the final set of independent variables.
3 Neither estimates nor the data needed to create estimates are disaggregated to the regional level. The difference between border entries (number of migration cards issued) and registrations is a key piece of data used by the FMS to determine estimates of illegal migrants, as explained to me by a representative of the Krasnodar UFMS. There are major flaws with this method of estimating illegal migrants, due to the gap between time of entry and registration, which varies depending on a foreigner's country of citizenship. Furthermore, migration cards are issued at the first point of entry, which may not in the end be the place a foreigner registers. For example, if the foreigner took a connecting flight through Moscow to another city in Russia, the migration card would be issued in Moscow. Also because foreigners are required to reregister each time they travel to a different region of Russia for more than 7 days (in most cases), it frequently happens that one person will register multiple times while holding the same migration card. It would be useful to include these estimates in the dataset because it is the data that would be used by regional governments in their quota considerations. Yet because this information is not available in a comprehensive regionally disaggregated form, it is not possible to even replicate the data the government might use.
4 Rosstat's methodology for determining estimates of the informal sector is based on surveys and includes not only traditional categories of informal workers, such as domestic and household workers and those entrepreneurs who are not officially registered with the government and tax services, but also those who are registered as individual entrepreneurs. Individual entrepreneurs comprise a category of economic actors, both citizen and foreigner, who are registered and pay taxes and social insurance payments.
5 The definition of informal labour migrants is based on the proportion of migrants who have registered in the region who do not have a work permit, as well as the proportion of work permits issued that have not been registered with the tax services.
6 Because data on labour violations is not available, this analysis considers only criminality.
7 Data is from SOVA centre monitoring on hate crimes, most of which are targeted at migrants and ethnic minorities.
8 The data is taken from the 2010 census and is used as a regional score across all years.

9 Fixed effects modelling helps control for omitted variables that differ across cases.

10 Andrienko and Guriev (2004) and Gerber (2006), when using similar panel data from Russia's regions, encountered problems with heteroskedasticity (or standard errors that are not uniform, but are rather correlated with one or more independent variables), endogeneity as a result of autocorrelation, and omitted variable bias, which occurs because not all of the potential factors causing regional differences are considered in the cross-regional comparison. Fixed effects is a strategy that can correct for these types of problems, and produce more reliable significance tests for the independent variables. The issue of autocorrelation is a typical problem in time-series data sets where previous year's effects are highly correlated with current year's indicators, and correcting for it warrants a few words of discussion. The way the government methodology is constructed practically guarantees and at the very least reinforces autocorrelation, because it directs bureaucrats to consider the prior three years, and in some cases all the way back to 2005. Therefore expecting bureaucrats to correct for problems related to autocorrelation is a bit dubious. Nevertheless, in order to properly assess what indicators are truly driving quota numbers, we must produce as reliable a model as possible.

11 To look at the impact of individual years, I ran regular OLS models subsetted by year (see table A3.d.). Each year, when taken in isolation, maintains a certain level of internal consistency, producing r-squared values between 87% and 94%. A similar effect is produced through the use of dummy variables for year. When dummies are included for every year, the r-squared is not dramatically increased over models using a dummy for 2007 only. This indicates that most of the increased explanatory power produced by the use of year dummies can be explained by a "2007 effect." This effect is not surprising, given the dramatic difference between the quotas set by experts in 2007 and those set in the following years by the government methodology.

12 Additional models that included independent variables for *compatriot*, *crmrt*, and *immshcrm* produced no added explanatory value (additional indicators were not statistically significant).

13 While the fixed effects models are corrective and produce more reliable coefficients, this estimation technique is not particularly good at accounting for exogenous shocks, such as the signal by Putin in 2008 that quota should not be increased. Fixed effects models also cannot assess whether the methodology is being used consistently across the country, which is important if we are to make any claims about the vertical of power and robustness of feder-

ally defined laws across the expanse of Russia. Though a random effects model might get at these between-region variations, the Hausman test shows that the errors are highly correlated with IVs, procuring endogeneity, and thus that random effects is not appropriate. Therefore an OLS model is included below (shown in table A3.d) in order to assess overall and within-year variation, which is important to establish whether quota procedures are being implemented more or less uniformly across Russia. Even if the coefficients are not unbiased or efficient, the r-squared value is informative in showing the indicators included in the government methodology are fairly consistently explaining quota allocation across Russia. This finding indicates that the federal-level approval of quota allocation (by Minzdrav or Mintrud) followed the same methodological underpinnings as regional quota requests.

14 Each of these categories is further subdivided so that jobs are assigned a relatively specific classification. All 15 categories and their subcategories are defined by the Federal Agency for Technical Regulation and Metrology (*Gosstandart* Order No. 454-st of November 6, 2001, which is an extremely detailed 261 pages long).

15 Quotas are variously divided into OKVED sectors and by professional qualifications. Each year, in addition to overall allocation by region, Minzdrav/Mintrud specified how each region's quota should be divided by professional qualifications. After 2010, official labour migration statistics are issued according to professional qualifications instead of by economic sector. However, these professional qualification groupings are not indicated in the spreadsheets, nor do they correspond to any set classification such as the OKVED or OKPDTR (Obshcherossiiskii klassifikator professii rabochikh, dolzhnostei sluzhashchikh i tarifnykh razriadov, Russian Classification of Professions, Positions of Civil Servants, and Wage Categories). For these reasons, they are not included in the analysis.

16 For the sake of brevity, only the first and last iteration of each year are reported.

Works Cited

Publications

Abashin, Sergey. 2017. "Migration Policies in Russia: Laws and Debates." In *Migrant Workers in Russia: Global Challenges of the Shadow Economy in Societal Transformation*, ed. Anna-Liisa Heusala and Kaarina Aitamurto, 16–34. New York: Routledge.

Acemoglu, Daron, Georg Egorov, and Konstantin Sonin. 2013. "A Political Theory of Populism." *Quarterly Journal of Economics* 128 (2): 771–805. https://doi.org/10.1093/qje/qjs077.

Ahram, Ariel I., and J. Paul Goode. 2016. "Researching Authoritarianism in the Discipline of Democracy." *Social Science Quarterly* 97 (4): 834–49. https://doi.org/10.1111/ssqu.12340.

Alexseev, Mikhail. 2006a. "Fortress Russia: An Overview of the 2005 Russian Federation Survey on Immigration Attitudes and Ethnic Relations." May. Accessed August 6, 2010. http://www.ccis-ucsd.org/PUBLICATIONS/wrkg139.pdf.

Alexseev, Mikhail. 2006b. *Immigration Phobia and the Security Dilemma: Russia, Europe and the United States*. New York: Cambridge University Press.

Alekseeva, Liudmila, and Catherine A. Fitzpatrick. 1990. *Nyeformaly: Civil Society in the USSR*. Helsinki Watch.

Allison, Graham. 1971. *Essence of Decision: Explaining the Cuban Missile Crisis*. Boston: Little Brown.

Anderson, Bridget. 2010. "Migration, Immigration Controls and the Fashioning of Precarious Workers." *Work, Employment and Society* 24 (2): 300–17. https://doi.org/10.1177/0950017010362141.

Anderson, Bridget. 2013. *Us and Them? The Dangerous Politics of Immigration Control*. Oxford: Oxford University Press.

Anderson, Bridget, Nandita Sharma, and Cynthia Wright. 2009. "Editorial: Why No Borders?" *Refuge: Canada's Periodical on Refugees* 26 (2): 5–18.

Andreas, Peter, and Kelly M. Greenhill. 2011. *Sex, Drugs, and Body Counts: The Politics of Numbers in Global Crime and Conflict*. Ithaca: Cornell University Press.

Andrienko, Yuri, and Sergei Guriev. 2004. "Determinants of Interregional Mobility in Russia: Evidence from Panel Data." *Economics of Transition* 12 (1): 1–27. https://doi.org/10.1111/j.0967-0750.2004.00170.x.

Andrienko, Yuri, and Sergei Guriev. 2005. "Understanding Migration in Russia." *CEFIR Policy Paper 23*. Accessed December 18, 2006. http://www.nes.ru/~sguriev/papers/UnderstandingMigration2005.

Anichkova, Daria. 2012. "Central Asia's Migrant Headache." *Carnegie Endowment for International Peace*. June 21. Accessed May 29, 2014. http://carnegieendowment.org/2012/06/21/central-asia-s-migrant-headache/c41a.

Åslund, Anders. 2005. "Russian Resources: Curse or Rents?" *Eurasian Geography and Economics* 46 (8): 610–17. https://doi.org/10.2747/1538-7216.46.8.610.

Awad, Ibrahim. 2009. *The Global Economic Crisis and Migrant Workers: Impact and Response. International Migration Program*. Geneva: International Labour Office.

Bahovadinova, Malika B. 2016. "Ideologies of Labour: The Bureaucratic Management of Migration in Post-Soviet Tajikistan." PhD dissertation, Indiana University.

Bale, Tim. 2013. "More and More Restrictive – but Not Always Populist: Explaining Variation in the British Conservative Party's Stance on Immigration and Asylum." *Journal of Contemporary European Studies* 21 (1): 25–37. https://doi.org/10.1080/14782804.2013.766474.

Baranov, Alexey, Egor Malkov, Leonid Polishchuk, Michael Rochlitz, and Georgiy Syunyaev. 2015. "How (Not) to Measure Russian Regional Institutions." *Russian Journal of Economics* 1 (2): 154–81. https://doi.org/10.1016/j.ruje.2015.11.005.

Bartels, Elizabeth C. 2014. *Volunteer Police in the United States: Programs, Challenges, and Legal Aspects*. New York: Springer. https://doi.org/10.1007/978-3-319-02365-6.

Basch, Linda, Nina Glick-Schiller, and Christina Szanton-Blanc. 1994. *Nations Unbound: Transnational Projects, Postcolonial Predicaments, and Deterritorialized Nation-States*. London, New York: Routledge.

Beine, Michel, Brian Burgoon, Mary Crock, Justin Gest, Michael Hiscox, Patrick McGovern, Hillel Rapaport, and Eiko Thielemann. 2013. "Dilemmas in Measuring Immigration Policies and the IMPALA Database." *Migration and Citizenship: Newsletter of the American Political Science Association Organized Section on Migration and Citizenship* 1 (2): 15–22.

Belova, Eugenia. 2001. "Economic Crime and Punishment." In *Behind the Façade of Stalin's Command Economy: Evidence from the Soviet State and Party Archives*, ed. Paul R. Gregory, 131–58. Stanford: Hoover Institution Press.

Benhabib, Seyla. 2004. *The Rights of Others*. New York: Cambridge University Press. https://doi.org/10.1017/CBO9780511790799.

Betz, Hans-Georg, and Stefan Immerfall. 1998. *The New Politics of the Right: Neo-Populist Parties and Movements in Established Democracies*. New York: St Martin's Press.

Best, Jacqueline. 2012. "Bureaucratic Ambiguity." *Economy and Society* 41 (1): 84–106. https://doi.org/10.1080/03085147.2011.637333.

Bhagwati, Jagdish. 2003. "Borders beyond Control." *Foreign Affairs* 82 (1): 98–104. https://doi.org/10.2307/20033431.

Bianchi, Milo, Paolo Buonanno, and Paolo Pinotti. 2012. "Do Immigrants Cause Crime?" *Journal of the European Economic Association* 10 (6): 1318–47. https://doi.org/10.1111/j.1542-4774.2012.01085.x.

Bjerre, Liv, Marc Helbling, Friederike Romer, and Malisa Zobel. 2014. "Conceptualizing and Measuring Immigration Policies. A Comparative Perspective." *International Migration Review* 49 (3): 555–600. https://doi.org/10.1111/imre.12100.

Blakkisrud, Helge. 2015. "Governing the Governors: Legitimacy vs. Control in the Reform of the Russian Regional Executive." *East European Politics* 31 (1): 104–21. https://doi.org/10.1080/21599165.2014.956925.

Boeck, Brian J. 1998. "The Kuban' Cossack Revival (1989–1993): The Beginnings of a Cossack National Movement in the North Caucasus Region." *Nationalities Papers* 26 (4): 633–57. http://dx.doi.org/10.1080/00905999808408592.

Bonjour, Saskia. 2011. "The Power and Morals of Policy Makers: Reassessing the Control Gap Debate." *International Migration Review* 45 (1): 89–122. https://doi.org/10.1111/j.1747-7379.2010.00840.x.

Borjas, George J. 1999. *Heaven's Door: Immigration Policy and the American Economy*. Princeton: Princeton University Press.

Borjas, George J. 2013. "The Analytics of the Wage Effect of Immigration." *IZA Journal of Migration* 2 (22). https://doi.org/10.1186/2193-9039-2-22.

Boswell, Christina. 2007. "Theorizing Migration Policy: Is There a Third Way?" *International Migration Review* 41 (1): 75–100. https://doi.org/10.1111/j.1747-7379.2007.00057.x.

Boucher, Anna, and Justin Gest. 2015. "Migration Studies at a Crossroads: A Critique of Immigration Regime Typologies." *Migration Studies* 3 (2): 182–98. https://doi.org/10.1093/migration/mnu035.

Bradley, Katharine W.V. 2014. "Who Lobbies the Lobbyists? Bureaucratic Influence on State Medicaid Legislation." PhD dissertation, University of Michigan.

Bremmer, Ian, and Samuel Charap. 2007. "The Siloviki in Putin's Russia: Who They Are and What They Want." *Washington Quarterly* 30 (1): 83–92. https://doi.org/10.1162/wash.2006-07.30.1.83.

Brettell, Caroline B. 2008. "Theorizing Migration in Anthropology: The Social Construction of Networks, Identities, Communities, and Globalscapes." In *Migration Theory: Talking across Disciplines*, ed. Caroline B. Brettell and James F. Hollifield, 113–59. New York: Routledge.

Breunig, Christian, Xun Cao, and Adam Luedtke. 2012. "Global Migration and Political Regime Type: A Democratic Disadvantage." *British Journal of Political Science* 42 (4): 825–54. https://doi.org/10.1017/S0007123412000051.

Brochmann, Grete, and Tomas Hammer. 1999. *Mechanisms of Immigration Control: A Comparative Analysis of European Regulation Policies*. New York: Oxford International Publishers.

Brodersen, Arvid. 1966. *The Soviet Worker: Labor and Government in Soviet Society*. New York: Random House.

Brown, Emily Clark. 1957. "The Soviet Labor Market." *Industrial & Labor Relations Review* 10 (2): 179–200. https://doi.org/10.1177/001979395701000201.

Brücker, Herbert, and Elke J. Jahn. 2011. "Migration and Wage-Setting: Reassessing the Labour Market Effects of Migration." *Scandinavian Journal of Economics* 113 (2): 286–317. https://doi.org/10.1111/j.1467-9442.2010.01634.x.

Buckley, Cynthia. 1991. "Rural-Urban Migration in a Centrally Planned Economy: The Case of the Soviet Union." PhD dissertation, University of Michigan.

Buckley, Cynthia. 1995. "The Myth of Managed Migration: Migration Control and Market in the Soviet Period." *Slavic Review* 54 (4): 896–916. https://doi.org/10.2307/2501398.

Buonfino, Alessandra. 2004. "Between Unity and Plurality: The Politicization and Securitization of the Discourse of Immigration in Europe." *New Political Science* 26 (1): 23–49. https://doi.org/10.1080/0739314042000185111.

Burgess, Michael. 2009. "Between a Rock and a Hard Place: The Russian Federation in Comparative Perspective." In *Federalism and Local Politics in Russia*, ed. Cameron Ross and Adrian Campbell, 25–54. New York: Routledge.

Calavita, Kitty. 1992. *Inside the State: The Bracero Program, Immigration, and the INS*. New York: Routledge.
Calavita, Kitty. 2004. "Italy: Economic Realities, Political Fictions, and Policy Failures." In *Controlling Immigration: A Global Perspective*, ed. Wayne A. Cornelius, Takeyuki Tsuda, Philip L. Martin, and James F. Hollifield, 345–81. Stanford: Stanford University Press.
Calavita, Kitty. 2005. *Immigrants at the Margins: Law, Race, and Exclusion in Southern Europe*. New York: Cambridge University Press.
Camarota, Steven A., and Karen Zeigler. 2009. *Jobs Americans Won't Do? A Detailed Look at Immigrant Employment by Occupation*. August. Accessed January 28, 2015. http://cis.org/illegalImmigration-employment.
Canovan, Margaret. 1999. "Trust the People! Populism and the Two Faces of Democracy." *Political Studies* 47 (1): 2–16. https://doi.org/10.1111/1467-9248.00184.
Canovan, Margaret. 2004. "Populism for Political Theorists?" *Journal of Political Ideologies* 9 (3): 241–52. https://doi.org/10.1080/1356931042000263500.
Caplan, Bryan. 2012. "Why Should We Restrict Immigration?" *Cato Journal* 32 (1): 5–24.
Cappelen, Ådne, and Terje Skjerpen. 2014. "The Effect on Immigration of Changes in Regulations and Policies: A Case Study." *Journal of Common Market Studies* 52 (4): 810–25. https://doi.org/10.1111/jcms.12118.
Carens, Joseph. 1987. "Aliens and Citizens: The Case for Open Borders." *Review of Politics* 49 (2): 251–73. https://doi.org/10.1017/S0034670500033817.
Castles, Stephen. 2004. "Why Migration Policies Fail." *Ethnic and Racial Studies* 27 (2): 205–27. https://doi.org/10.1080/0141987042000177306.
Castles, Stephen, and Mark J. Miller. 2009. *The Age of Migration: International Population Movements in the Modern World*. New York: Palgrave Macmillan.
Casula, Philipp. 2013. "Sovereign Democracy, Populism, and Depoliticization in Russia." *Problems of Post-Communism* 60 (3): 3–15. https://doi.org/10.2753/PPC1075-8216600301.
Chaloff, Jonathan. 2014. "Evidence-Based Regulation of Labour Migration in OECD Countries: Setting Quotas, Selection Criteria, and Shortage Lists." *Migration Letters* 11 (1): 11–22.
Chebankova, Elena. 2010. *Russia's Federal Relations: Putin's Reforms and Management of the Regions*. New York: Routledge.
Cheloukhine, Serguei, and Joseph King. 2007. "Corruption Networks as a Sphere of Investment Activities in Modern Russia." *Communist and Post-Communist Studies* 40 (1): 107–22. https://doi.org/10.1016/j.postcomstud.2006.12.005.

Chung, Erin Aeran. 2014. "Japan and South Korea: Immigration Control and Immigrant Incorporation. " In *Controlling Immigration: A Global Perspective*, ed. James Hollifield, Philip Martin, and Pia Orrenius, 399–421. Stanford: Stanford University Press.

Cohen, Edward. 2001. "Globalization and the Boundaries of the State: A Framework for Analyzing the Changing Practice of Sovereignty." *Governance: An International Journal of Policy, Administration and Institutions* 14 (1): 75–97. https://doi.org/10.1111/0952-1895.00152.

Collier, David, and Steven Levitsky. 1997. "Democracy with Adjectives: Conceptual Innovation in Comparative Research." *World Politics* 49 (3): 430–51. https://doi.org/10.1353/wp.1997.0009.

Cornelius, Wayne A. 2001. *Death at the Border: The Efficacy and "Unintended" Consequences of U.S. Immigration Control Policy 1993–2000*. Working Paper 27, San Diego: The Center for Comparative Immigration Studies.

Cornelius, Wayne A. 2005. "Controlling 'Unwanted' Immigration: Lessons from the United States, 1993–2004." *Journal of Ethnic and Migration Studies* 31 (4): 775–94. https://doi.org/10.1080/13691830500110017.

Cornelius, Wayne A., David Scott FitzGerald, Pedro Lewin Fischer, and Leah Muse-Orlinoff, eds. 2010. *Mexican Migration and the US Economic Crisis: A Transnational Perspective*. Boulder, CO: Lynne Rienner.

Cornelius, Wayne, Philip Martin, and James Hollifield. 1994. "Introduction." In *Controlling Immigration: A Global Perspective*, ed. Wayne Cornelius, Philip Martin, and James Hollifield, 3–41. Stanford: Stanford University Press.

Cornelius, Wayne A., and Mark R. Rosenblum. 2005. "Immigration and Politics." *Annual Review of Political Science* 8 (1): 99–119. https://doi.org/10.1146/annurev.polisci.8.082103.104854.

Cornelius, Wayne, and Takeyuki Tsuda. 2004. "Controlling Immigration: The Limits to Government Intervention." In *Controlling Immigration: A Global Perspective*, ed. Wayne Cornelius, Takeyuki Tsuda, Philip Martin and James Hollifield, 3–48. Stanford: Stanford University Press.

Cornelius, Wayne A., Takeyuki Tsuda, Philip L. Martin, and James F. Hollifield, eds. 2004. *Controlling Immigration: A Global Perspective*. Stanford: Stanford University Press.

Cox, Betsy C., and Gary Shmerling. 1979. "Interagency Conflict: A Model for Analysis." *Georgia Journal of International and Comparative Law* 9:241–85.

Czaika, Mathias, and Hein de Haas. 2013. "The Effectiveness of Immigration Policies." *Population and Development Review* 39 (3): 487–508. https://doi.org/10.1111/j.1728-4457.2013.00613.x.

Dahl, Robert A. 1998. *On Democracy*. New Haven: Yale University Press.

Dauvergne, Catherine. 2008. *Making People Illegal: What Globalization Means for Migration and Law*. New York: Cambridge University Press. https://doi.org/10.1017/CBO9780511810473.

Dawisha, Karen. 2015. *Putin's Kleptocracy: Who Owns Russia?* New York: Simon and Schuster.

DeBardeleben, Joan, and Mikhail Zherebtsov. 2010. "The Transition to Managerial Patronage in Russia's Regions." In *The Politics of Sub-National Authoritarianism in Russia*, ed. Vladimir Gel'man and Cameron Ross, 85–106. Burlington, VA: Ashgate.

Derluguian, Georgi M., and Serge Cipko. 1997. "The Politics of Identity in a Russian Borderland Province: The Kuban Neo-Cossack Movement, 1989–1996." *Europe-Asia Studies* 49 (8): 1485–1500. https://doi.org/10.1080/09668139708412511.

De Soto, Hernando. 1989. *The Other Path: The Invisible Revolution in the Third World*. New York: Basic Books.

Di Bartolomeo, Anna, Shushanik Makaryan, and Agnieszka Weinar. 2014. *Regional Migration Report: Russia and Central Asia*. CARIM-East Project of the Migration Policy Centre of the European University Institute, San Domenico di Fiesole. European University Institute.

Dininio, Phyllis, and Robert Orttung. 2005. "Explaining Patterns of Corruption in the Russian Regions." *World Politics* 57 (4): 500–29. https://doi.org/10.1353/wp.2006.0008.

Dix, Robert H. 1985. "Populism: Authoritarian and Democratic." *Latin American Research Review* 20 (2): 29–52.

Dmitriev, Anatolii, and Grigorii Piadukhov. 2009. "Tenevaia posrednicheskaia deiatel'nost' v trudovoi migratsii: modeli, tendentsii, perspektiva [Shadow intermedary activities in labour migration: models, tendencies, perspectives]." In *Novoe Migratsionnoe Zakonodatel'stvo Rossiiskoi Federatsii: Pravoprimenitel'naia Praktika* [*New Migration Legislation in the Russian Federation: Enforcement Practices*], ed. Galina Vitkovskaya, Anna Platonova, and Vladimir Shkolnikov, 277–303. Moscow: International Organization for Migration, Federal Migration Service of Russia, Organization for Security and Cooperation in Europe.

Doomernik, Jeroen, and Michael Jandl, eds. 2008. *Modes of Migration Regulation and Control in Europe*. Amsterdam: Amsterdam University Press. https://doi.org/10.5117/9789053566893.

Durand, Jorge. 2007. "El programa bracero (1942–1964). Un balance crítico [The Bracero Program (1942–1964): A Critical Appraisal]." *Migración y Desarrollo* 9: 27–43.

Düvell, Franck. 2011. "Paths into Irregularity: The Legal and Political Construction of Irregular Migration." *European Journal of Migration and Law* 13 (3): 275–95. https://doi.org/10.1163/157181611X587856.

Ediev, Dalkhat. 2001. "Application of the Demographic Potential Concept to Understanding the Russian Population History and Prospects: 1897–2100." *Demographic Research* 4 (9): 289–336. https://doi.org/10.4054/DemRes.2001.4.9.

Estruch, Elisenda, and Marco Zupi. 2009. "Italian and Spanish Experience on Practical Methods for Assessing and Forecasting Labour Market Requirements for Migrant Workers." In *Review of Approaches in Measuring the Need for Migrant Workers and Labour Migration Planning, Russian Federation and International Experience*, ed. ILO Subregional Office for Eastern Europe and Central Asia, 39–116. Moscow: International Labour Organization.

Etzioni-Halevy, Eva. 2013. *Bureaucracy and Democracy*. Routledge Library Editions: Political Science Volume 7. New York: Routledge.

European Migration Network. 2013. *The Application of Quotas in EU Member States as a Measure for Managing Labour Migration from Third Countries*. EMN Inform, EMN. Accessed September 29, 2014. http://www.emnbelgium.be/publication/application-quotas-managing-labour-migration-emn-inform.

Evans, Alfred B. 2011. "The Failure of Democratization in Russia: A Comparative Perspective." *Journal of Eurasian Studies* 2 (1): 40–51. https://doi.org/10.1016/j.euras.2010.10.001.

Facchini, Giovanni, and Cecelia Testa. 2014. "The Rhetoric of Closed Borders: Quotas, Lax Enforcement and Illegal Migration." IZA Discussion Paper No. 8457.

Fadeicheva, Marianna A. 2009. "Rezul'taty monitoringa osveshchenia migratsionnoi temy v regional'nykh SMI Sverdlovskoi oblasti [Results of monitoring the coverage of migration themes in the regional mass media of Sverdlosvk oblast]." In *Obshchestvennyi monitoring i analiz protsessov trudovoi migratsii iz Respubliki Tadzhikistan v Sverdlovskuiu oblast'* [*Public monitoring and analysis of the process of labour migration from the Republic of Tajikistan to Sverdlovsk oblast*]. A publication of Otdelenie mezhdunarodnoi organizatsii Institut "Otkrytoe Obshchestvo" – Fond sodeistviia v Tadzhikistane i Nekommercheskoe partnerstvo "Mezhnatsional'nyi informatsionnyi tsentr" [Branch office of the International Organization of Open Society Institute – Assistance Foundation in Tajikistan and the non-profit partnership "Interethnic information centre"]. Yekaterinburg.

Faraday, Fay. 2014. *Profiting from the Precarious: How Recruitment Practices Exploit Migrant Workers*. Toronto: Metcalf Foundation. Accessed October

12, 2015. http://metcalffoundation.com/wp-content/uploads/2014/04/Profiting-from-the-Precarious.pdf.

Federation for American Immigration Reform. 2013. *Illegal Aliens Taking U.S. Jobs*. Accessed January 28, 2015. http://www.fairus.org/issue/illegal-aliens-taking-u-s-jobs.

Feklyunina, Valentina, and Stephen White. 2011. "Discourses of 'Krisis': Economic Crisis in Russia and Regime Legitimacy." *Journal of Communist Studies and Transition Politics* 27 (3–4): 385–406. https://doi.org/10.1080/13523279.2011.595154.

Fetzer, Joel S. 2012. "Public Opinion and Populism." In *Oxford Handbook of the Politics of International Migration*, ed. Marc R. Rosenblum and Daniel J. Tichenor, 301–23. New York: Oxford University Press. https://doi.org/10.1093/oxfordhb/9780195337228.013.0013.

Filippov, Pyotr. 2011. "Is Corruption in Russia's DNA?" *openDemocracy*. November 16. Accessed June 19, 2014. http://www.opendemocracy.net/od-russia/pyotr-filippov/is-corruption-in-russias-dna.

Finotelli, Claudia, and Giuseppe Sciortino. 2008. "New Trends in Italian Immigration Policies: 'To Change Everything in Order to Keep Everything the Same." *Real Instituto Elcano*. Accessed January 16, 2010. http://www.realinstitutoelcano.org/wps/wcm/connect/0eb458004f018b40b1fcf53170baead1/ARI161-2008_Finotelli-Sciortino_New_Trends_Italian_Immigration_Policies.pdf?MOD=AJPERES&CACHEID=0eb458004f018b40b1fcf53170baead1.

Fish, M. Steven. 1995. *Democracy from Scratch: Opposition and Regime in the New Russian Revolution*. Princeton: Princeton University Press.

Fish, Steven. 2005. *Democracy Derailed in Russia: The Failure of Open Politics*. New York: Cambridge University Press. https://doi.org/10.1017/CBO9780511791062.

Flynn, Moya. 2004. *Migrant Resettlement in the Russian Federation: Reconstructing Homes and Homelands*. London: Anthem Press.

Freeman, Gary P. 1994. "Can Liberal States Control Unwanted Immigration." *Annals of the American Academy* 534 (1): 17–30. https://doi.org/10.1177/0002716294534001002.

Freeman, Gary P. 1995. "Modes of Immigration Politics in Liberal Democratic States." *International Migration Review* 29 (4): 881–902. https://doi.org/10.2307/2547729.

Freeman, Gary P. 2002. "Winners and Losers: Politics and the Costs and Benefits of Migration." *West European Immigration and Immigrant Policy in the New Century*, 77–96.

Freeman, Gary P. 2011. "Comparative Analysis of Immigration Politics: A Retrospective." *American Behavioral Scientist* 55 (12): 1541–60. https://doi.org/10.1177/0002764211409386.

Fudge, Judy. 2012. "Precarious Migrant Status and Precarious Employment: The Paradox of International Rights for Migrant Workers." *Comparative Labour Law & Policy Journal* 34 (1): 95–132.

Fukuyama, Francis. 1989. "The End of History?" *National Interest* 16: 3–18.

Galeotti, Mark. 1995. "The Cossacks: A Cross-Border Complication to Post-Soviet Eurasia." *IBRU Boundary and Security Bulletin* Summer: 55–60.

Gavrilova, Irina. 2001. "Migration Policy in Modern Russia: To Be or Not to Be." *Perspectives on European Politics and Society* 2 (2): 261–87. https://doi.org/10.1080/1570585018458762.

Geddes, Andrew. 2005. "Chronicle of a Crisis Foretold: The Politics of Irregular Migration, Human Trafficking and People Smuggling in the UK." *British Journal of Politics and International Relations* 7 (3): 324–39. https://doi.org/10.1111/j.1467-856X.2005.00192.x.

Geddes, Andrew, and Sam Scott. 2010. "UK Food Businesses' Reliance on Low-Wage Migrant Labour: A Case of Choice or Constraint." In *Who Needs Migrant Workers?: Labour Shortages, Immigration, and Public Policy*, ed. Martin Ruhs and Bridget Anderson, 193–223. Oxford: Oxford University Press. https://doi.org/10.1093/acprof:oso/9780199580590.003.0007.

Gellner, Ernest. 1983. *Nations and Nationalism*. Ithaca: Cornell University Press.

Gel'man, Vladimir. 2004. "The Unrule of Law in the Making: The Politics of Informal Institution Building in Russia." *Europe-Asia Studies* 56 (7): 1021–40. https://doi.org/10.1080/1465342042000294347.

Gel'man, Vladimir. 2010. "The Dynamics of Sub-National Authoritarianism: Russia in Comparative Perspective." In *The Politics of Sub-National Authoritarianism in Russia*, ed. Vladimir Gel'man and Cameron Ross, 1–18. Burlington, VT: Ashgate.

Gel'man, Vladimir. 2016. "The Vicious Circle of Post-Soviet Neopatrimonialism in Russia." *Post-Soviet Affairs* 32 (5): 455–73. http://dx.doi.org/10.1080/1060586X.2015.1071014.

Gel'man, Vladimir, and Sergei Ryzhenkov. 2011. "Local Regimes, Sub-National Governance and the 'Power Vertical' in Contemporary Russia." *Europe-Asia Studies* 63 (3): 449–65. https://doi.org/10.1080/09668136.2011.557538.

Gerber, Theodore P. 2006. "Regional Economic Performance and Net Migration Rates in Russia, 1993–2002." *International Migration Review* 40 (3): 661–97. https://doi.org/10.1111/j.1747-7379.2006.00037.x.

Gerber, Theodore P. 2014. "Beyond Putin? Nationalism and Xenophobia in Russian Public Opinion." *Washington Quarterly* 37 (3): 113–34. https://doi.org/10.1080/0163660X.2014.978439.

Gerring, John. 2008. "The Mechanismic Worldview: Thinking inside the Box." *British Journal of Political Science* 38 (1): 161–79. https://doi.org/10.1017/S0007123408000082.

Gerring, John. 2010. "Causal Mechanisms: Yes, But …" *Comparative Political Studies* 43 (11): 1499–1526. https://doi.org/10.1177/0010414010376911.

Gest, Justin, Anna Boucher, Suzanna Challen, Brian Burgoon, Eiko Thielemann, Michel Beine, Patrick McGovern, Mary Crock, Hillel Rapoport, and Michael Hiscox. 2014. "Measuring and Comparing Immigration, Asylum and Naturalization Policies across Countries: Challenges and Solutions." *Global Policy* 5 (3): 261–74. https://doi.org/10.1111/1758-5899.12132.

Gill, Graeme. 2002. "The Failure of Democracy in Russia." *Perspectives on European Politics and Society* 3 (2): 169–97. https://doi.org/10.1080/15705850208438833.

Gill, Graeme, ed. 2007. *Politics in the Russian Regions*. New York: Palgrave Macmillan. https://doi.org/10.1057/9780230597280.

Givens, Terri, and Adam Luedtke. 2005. "European Immigration Policies in Comparative Perspective: Issue Salience, Partisanship and Immigrant Rights." *Comparative European Politics* 3 (1): 1–22. https://doi.org/10.1057/palgrave.cep.6110051.

Gontmakher, Evgeny. 2015. "Russian Federalism: Reality or Myth?" In *Putin's Russia: How It Rose, How It Is Maintained, and How It Might End*, ed. Leon Aron, kindle version. Washington, DC: American Enterprise Institute.

Goode, J. Paul. 2007. "The Puzzle of Putin's Gubernatorial Appointments." *Europe-Asia Studies* 59 (3): 365–99. https://doi.org/10.1080/09668130701239799.

Goode, J. Paul. 2010. "Redefining Russia: Hybrid Regimes, Fieldwork, and Russian Politics." *Perspectives on Politics* 8 (4): 1055–75. https://doi.org/10.1017/S153759271000318X.

Goode, J. Paul, and Ariel I. Ahram. 2016. "Special Issue Editors' Introduction: Observing Autocracies from the Ground Floor." *Social Science Quarterly* 97 (4): 823–33. https://doi.org/10.1111/ssqu.12339.

Goode, J. Paul, and David R. Stroup. 2015. "Everyday Nationalism: Constructivism for the Masses." *Social Science Quarterly* 96 (3): 717–39. https://doi.org/10.1111/ssqu.12188.

Goodman, Sara Wallace. 2011. "Controlling Immigration through Language and Country Knowledge Requirements." *West European Politics* 34 (2): 235–55. https://doi.org/10.1080/01402382.2011.546569.

Gordeev, Vladimir S., Milena Pavlova, and Wim Groot. 2014. "Informal Payments for Health Care Services in Russia: Old Issue in New Realities." *Health Economics, Policy and Law* 9 (1): 25–48. https://doi.org/10.1017/S1744133113000212.

Gorenburg, Dmitry. 2010. "Center-Periphery Relations after Ten Years of Centralization." *Russian Politics and Law* 48 (1): 3–7. https://doi.org/10.2753/RUP1061-1940480100.

Grafova, Lidiia. 2006. "Pod flagom nenavisti [Under the flag of hatred]." *polit.ru*, December 7. Accessed February 9, 2015. http://polit.ru/article/2006/12/07/migration/.

Grafova, Lidiia. 2012. "Ural'skii pretsedent [The Ural precedent]." *Migratsiia XXI Vek* 1 (10): 46.

Grandstaff, Peter J. 1980. *Interregional Migration in the USSR: Economic Aspects, 1959–1970*. Durham, NC: Duke University Press.

Greene, Samuel A. 2012. "Citizenship and the Social Contract in Post-Soviet Russia. Twenty Years Late?" *Demokratizatisya: The Journal of Post-Soviet Democratization*, 133–40.

Gregory, Paul. 2001. "The Dictator's Orders." In *Behind the Façade of Stalin's Command Economy: Evidence from the Soviet State and Party Archives*, ed. Paul Gregory, 11–33. Stanford: Hoover Institution Press.

Gregory, Paul. 2004. *The Political Economy of Stalinism*. New York: Cambridge University Press.

Grossman, Gregory. 1977. "The Second Economy in the USSR." *Problems of Communism*, 25–40.

Grossman, Philip. 1979. "The Soviet Government's Role in Allocating Industrial Labor." In *Industrial Labor in the U.S.S.R.*, ed. Arcadius Kahan and Blair Ruble, 42–58. New York: Pergamon Press.

Grzymala-Busse, Anna. 2010. "The Best Laid Plans: The Impact of Informal Rules on Formal Institutions in Transitional Regimes." *St Comp Int Dev*, 311–33. https://doi.org/10.1007/s12116-010-9071-y.

Guriev, Sergei. 2004. "Red Tape and Corruption." *Journal of Development Economics* 73 (2): 489–504. https://doi.org/10.1016/j.jdeveco.2003.06.001.

Hale, Henry E. 2014. *Patronal Politics: Eurasian Regime Dynamics in Comparative Perspective*. New York: Cambridge University Press. https://doi.org/10.1017/CBO9781139683524.

Hardwick, Susan W. 2008. "Place, Space, and Pattern: Geographical Theories in International Migration." In *Migration Theory: Talking across Disciplines*, ed. Caroline B. Brettell and James F. Hollifield, 161–82. New York: Routledge.

Harrison, Mark, and Byung-Yeon Kim. 2006. "Plans, Prices, and Corruption: The Soviet Firm under Partial Centralization, 1930 to 1990." *Journal of Economic History* 66 (1): 1–41. https://doi.org/10.1017/S0022050706000015.

Hedström, Peter, and Richard Swedberg. 1998. "Social Mechanisms: An Introductory Essay." In *Social Mechanisms: An Analytical Approach to Social Theory*, ed. Peter Hedström and Richard Swedberg, 1–31. Cambridge: Cambridge University Press.

Heleniak, Timothy. 2003. "Geographic Aspects of Population Aging in the Russian Federation." *Eurasian Geography and Economics* 44 (5): 325–47. https://doi.org/10.2747/1538-7216.44.5.325.

Heleniak, Timothy. 2008. "An Overview of Migration in the Post-Soviet Space." In *Migration, Homeland, and Belonging*, ed. Cynthia J. Buckley, Blair A. Ruble, and Erin Trouth Hofmann, 29–67. Baltimore: Johns Hopkins University Press.

Helmke, Grechen, and Steven Levitsky. 2004. "Informal Institutions and Comparative Politics: A Research Agenda." *Perspectives on Politics* 2 (4): 725–40. https://doi.org/10.1017/S1537592704040472.

Hill, Fiona, and Clifford Gaddy. 2013. *Mr. Putin: Operative in the Kremlin*. Washington, DC: Brookings Institute Press.

Hillman, Arye L., and Avi Weiss. 1999. "A Theory of Permissible Illegal Immigration." *European Journal of Political Economy* 15 (4): 585–604. https://doi.org/10.1016/S0176-2680(99)00039-7.

Hoefer, Michael, Nancy Rytina, and Bryan Baker. 2012. *Estimates of the Unauthorized Immigrant Population Residing in the United States: January 2011*. Population Estimates, Department of Homeland Security, Office of Immigration Statistics. Accessed December 20, 2014. http://www.dhs.gov/xlibrary/assets/statistics/publications/ois_ill_pe_2011.pdf.

Hollifield, James F.. 1992. *Immigrants, Markets, and States: The Political Economy of Postwar Europe*. Cambridge, MA: Harvard University Press.

Hollifield, James F. 2000. "The Politics of International Migration: How Can We 'Bring the State Back.'" In *Migration Theory: Talking across Disciplines*, ed. Caroline B. Brettell and James F. Hollifield, 183–237. New York: Routledge.

Hollifield, James F. 2004. "The Emerging Migration State." *International Migration Review* 38 (3): 885–912. https://doi.org/10.1111/j.1747-7379.2004.tb00223.x.

Hollifield, James F. 2014. "France: Immigration and the Republican Tradition in France." In *Controlling Immigration: A Global Perspective* (third edition), ed. James F. Hollifield, Philip L. Martin, and Pia M. Orrenius. Stanford: Stanford University Press.

Hollifield, James F., Philip L. Martin, and Pia M. Orrenius. 2014. "The Dilemmas of Immigration Control." In *Controlling Immigration: A Global Perspective* (third edition), ed. James F. Hollifield, Philip L. Martin and Pia M. Orrenius, kindle version. Stanford: Stanford University Press.

Hood, Christopher. 2006. "Gaming in Targetworld: The Targets Approach to Managing British Public Services." *Public Administration Review* 66 (4): 515–21. https://doi.org/10.1111/j.1540-6210.2006.00612.x.

Hood, Christopher. 2010. *The Blame Game: Spin, Bureaucracy, and Self-Preservation in Government*. Princeton: Princeton University Press.

Hood, Christopher, Helen Margetts, and Perri 6. 2010. "A Drive to Modernize. A World of Surprises?" In *Paradoxes of Modernization: Unintended Consequences of Public Policy Reform*, ed. Perri 6, Christopher Hood, and Helen Margetts, 3–16. Oxford: Oxford University Press. https://doi.org/10.1093/acprof:oso/9780199573547.003.0001.

Hough, Jerry F. 1979. "Policy-Making and the Worker." In *Industrial Labor in the U.S.S.R.*, ed. Arcadius Kahan and Blair Ruble, 373–87. New York: Pergamon.

Howard, Marc Morjé, and Meir R. Walters. 2014. "Explaining the Unexpected: Political Science and the Surprises of 1989 and 2011." *Perspectives on Politics* 12 (2): 394–408. https://doi.org/10.1017/S1537592714000899.

Huskey, Eugene. 2011. "The Bureaucracy." In *Routledge Handbook of Russian Politics and Society*, ed. Graeme Gill and James Young, 175–85. New York: Routledge.

Ibrahim, Maggie. 2005. "The Securitization of Migration: A Racial Discourse." *International Migration* 43 (5): 163–87. https://doi.org/10.1111/j.1468-2435.2005.00345.x.

International Crisis Group. 2010. "Central Asia: Migrants and the Economic Crisis." Asia Report #183.

International Labour Organization. 2009. *Preventing Forced Labour Exploitation and Promoting Good Labour Practices in the Russian Construction Industry.* Geneva: International Labour Organization and European Bank for Reconstruction and Development, 2009a. Accessed May 13, 2010. http://www.ilo.org/wcmsp5/groups/public/---ed_norm/---declaration/documents/publication/wcm_041904.pdf.

Ioffe, Grigory, and Zhanna Zayonchkovskaya. 2010. *Immigration to Russia: Why It Is Inevitable, and How Large It May Have to Be to Provide the Workforce Russia Needs.* NCEEER Working Paper. Seattle: The National Council for Eurasian and East European Research.

Isakova, Irina. 2001. "Regionalism in Russia: From Disintegration to Centralization." *Whitehall Papers* 53 (1).

Ivakhnenko, G.A. 2013. "Zdorov'e trudovykh migrantov v Rossii [Health of labour migrants in Russia]." *Sotsiologiia meditsiny* (2): 48–51. Accessed January 23, 2015. http://demoscope.ru/weekly/2014/0599/analit04.php.

Ivakhnyuk, Irina. 2006. *Migration in the CIS Region: Common Problems and Mutual Benefits.* International Symposium on International Migration and

Development, Turin: United Nations Department of Economic and Social Affairs, Population Division.

Ivakhnyuk, Irina. 2009a. *The Impact of the Economic Crisis on Migration Trends and Migration Policy in the Russian Federation and the Eastern European and Central Asian Area. Analytical Report*. Moscow: International Organization for Migration.

Ivakhnyuk, Irina. 2009b. *The Russian Migration Policy and Its Impact on Human Development: The Historical Perspective*. United Nations Human Development Research Paper 2009/14, United Nations Development Programme.

Ivakhnyuk, Irina. 2013a. "2008 Global Crisis and Migration." In *Migration in Russia 2000–2013*, ed. Igor Ivanov, 107–25. Moscow: Russian International Affairs Council.

Ivakhnyuk, Irina. 2013b. "Conceptualizing Migration Policy in Russia." In *Migration in Russia 2000–2013*, ed. Igor Ivanov, 78–91. Moscow: Russian International Affairs Council.

Ivanov, Igor. 2013. *Migration in Russia 2000–2013*. Moscow: Russian International Affairs Council in collaboration with the Federal Migration Service of the Rusian Federation and sponsored by "EUROCEMENT Group."

Jacobson, David. 1996. *Rights across Borders: Immigration and the Decline of Citizenship*. Baltimore: Johns Hopkins University Press.

Jahn, Andreas, and Thomas Straubhaar. 1999. "A Survey of the Economics of Illegal Migration." In *Immigrants and the Informal Economy in Southern Europe*, ed. Martin Baldwin-Edwards and Joaquin Arango, 16–42. Portland, OR: Frank Cass Publishers.

Jandl, Michael. 2007. "Irregular Migration, Human Smuggling, and the Eastern Enlargement of the European Union." *International Migration Review* 41 (2): 291–315.

Johnson, Simon, Daniel Kaufmann, Andrei Shleifer, Marshall I. Goldman, and Martin L. Weitzman. 1997. "The Unofficial Economy in Transition." Brookings Institution. *Brookings Papers on Economic Activity* (2): 159–239. https://doi.org/10.2307/2534688.

Jones, Larisa, Richard Black, and Ronald Skeldon. 2007. *Migration and Poverty Reduction in Tajikistan*. Working Paper C11. Brighton, UK: Development Research Centre on Migration, Globalisation and Poverty.

Joppke, Christian. 1998. "Why Liberal States Accept Unwanted Immigration." *World Politics* 50 (2): 266–93. https://doi.org/10.1017/S004388710000811X.

Kalgin, Alexander. 2016. "Implementation of Performance Management in Regional Government in Russia: Evidence of Data Manipulation." *Public Management Review* 18 (1): 110–38. https://doi.org/10.1080/14719037.2014.965271.

Karachurina, Liliya. 2013. "Migration in Post-Soviet Countries." In *Migration in Russia: 2000–2013*, ed. Igor Ivanov, 125–47. Moscow: Russia International Affairs Council.

Karapetyan, Lili, and Liana Harutyunyan. 2013. *The Development and the Side Effects of Remittances in CIS Countries:the Case of Armenia.* CARIM-East RR 2013/24, Carim East – Consortium for Applied Research on International Migration. Accessed December 8, 2014. http://www.carim-east.eu/media/CARIM-East-RR-2013-24.pdf.

Katanian, Konstantin. 1998. *Freedom of Movement in the Russian Federation Today: The Propiska and the Constitutional Court.* East European Constitutional Review.

Keck, Margaret E., and Kathryn Sikkink. 1999. "Transnational Advocacy Networks in International and Regional Politics." *International Social Science Journal* 51 (159): 89–101. https://doi.org/10.1111/1468-2451.00179.

Kim, Buyng-Yeon. 2013. "The Unofficial Economy in Russia." In *The Oxford Handbook of the Russian Economy*, ed. Michael Alexeev and Shlomo Weber, 265–85. New York: Oxford University Press. https://doi.org/10.1093/oxfordhb/9780199759927.013.0032.

Kleinman, Mark. 2003. "The Economic Impact of Labour Migration." *Political Quarterly* 74 (s1): 59–74. https://doi.org/10.1111/j.1467-923X.2003.00581.x.

Klimina, Anna. 2014. "Finding a Positive Vision for State Capitalism." *Journal of Economic Issues* 48 (2): 421–30.

Koehler, Kevin. 2008. "Authoritarian Elections in Egypt: Formal Institutions and Informal Mechanisms of Rule." *Democratization* 15 (5): 974–90. https://doi.org/10.1080/13510340802362612.

Kolstø, Pal, and Helge Blakkisrud, eds. 2016. *The New Russian Nationalism.* Edinburgh: Edinburgh University Press. https://doi.org/10.3366/edinburgh/9781474410427.001.0001.

Kononenko, Vadim. 2011. "Conclusions." In *Russia as a Network State: What Works in Russia When State Institutions Do Not?* ed. Vadim Kononenko and Arkady Moshes, 164–71. New York: Palgrave Macmillan. https://doi.org/10.1057/9780230306707_8.

Korobkov, Andrei V. 2008. "Post-Soviet Migration: New Trends in the Twenty-First Century." In *Migration, Homeland, and Belonging in Eurasia*, ed. Cynthia J. Buckley, Blair A. Ruble, and Erin Trouth Hofmann, 69–98. Baltimore: Johns Hopkins University Press.

Korobkov, Andrei V., and Zhanna A. Zaionchkovskaia. 2004. "The Changes in the Migration Patterns in the Post-Soviet States: The First Decade." *Communist and Post-Communist Studies* 37 (4): 481–508. https://doi.org/10.1016/j.postcomstud.2004.09.004.

Kozhevnikova, Galina. 2007. "Iazyk vrazhdy posli Kondopogi [Hate speech after Kondopoga]." In *Iazyk vrazhdy protiv obshchestva* [*Hate speech against society*], ed. Aleksandr Verkhovskii, 10–71. Moscow: Open Society Institute of the Soros Foundation.

Krastev, Ivan, and Stephen Holmes. 2012. "An Autopsy of Managed Democracy." *Journal of Democracy* 23 (3): 33–45. https://doi.org/10.1353/jod.2012.0043.

Kroschenko, Mikhail, and Denis Zibarev. 2009. *Review of Current Approaches in Monitoring and Assessing Labour Shortages in the Russian Federation and Methods/Procedures in Migration Planning*. Moscow: International Labour Organization.

Kryshtanovskaya, Olga, and Stephen White. 2003. "Putin's Militocracy." *Post-Soviet Affairs* 19 (4): 289–306. https://doi.org/10.2747/1060-586X.19.4.289.

Kryshtanovskaya, Ol'ga, and Stephen White. 2005. "Inside the Putin Court: A Research Note." *Europe-Asia Studies* 57 (7): 1065–75. https://doi.org/10.1080/09668130500302830.

Kubal, Agnieszka. 2013. "Conceptualizing Semi-Legality in Migration Research." *Law & Society Review* 47 (3): 555–87. https://doi.org/10.1111/lasr.12031.

Kubal, Agnieszka. 2016a. "Entry Bar as Surreptitious Deportation? Zapret na v'ezd in Russian Immigration Law and Practice: A Comparative Perspective." *Law & Social Inquiry*. https://doi.org/10.1111/lsi.12232.

Kubal, Agnieszka. 2016b. "Spiral Effect of the Law: Migrants' Experiences of the State Law in Russia – a Comparative Perspective." *International Journal of Law in Context* 12 (4): 453–68. https://doi.org/10.1017/S1744552316000215.

Kudelia, Serhiy. 2012. "Society as an Actor in Post-Soviet State-Building." *Demokratizatsiya: The Journal of Post-Soviet Democratization* 20 (2): 149–56.

Kuznetsova, Irina Borisovna, Laisan Muzipovna Mukhariamova, and Guzel' Gakil'evna Vafina. 2013. "Zdorov'e migrantov kak sotsial'naia problema [The health of migrants as a social problem]." *Kazanskii Meditsinskii Zhurnal* [*Kazan Medical Journal*] 94 (3): 367–72.

Lahav, Gallya, and Virginie Guiraudon. 2006. "Actors and Venues in Immigration Control: Closing the Gap between Political Demands and Policy Outcomes." *West European Politics* 29 (2): 201–23. https://doi.org/10.1080/01402380500512551.

Lane, David. 1987. *Soviet Labour and the Ethic of Communism: Full Employment and the Labour Process in the USSR*. Boulder, CO: Westview Press.

Lane, David. 2008. "From Chaotic to State-Led Capitalism." *New Political Economy* 13 (2): 177–84. https://doi.org/10.1080/13563460802018505.

Laruelle, Marlène. 2009. *In the Name of the Nation: Nationalism and Politics in Contemporary Russia*. New York: Palgrave Macmillian. https://doi.org/10.1057/9780230101234.

Laruelle, Marlène. 2010. "The Ideological Shift on the Russian Radical Right: From Demonizing the West to Fear of Migrants." *Problems of Post-Communism* 57 (6): 19–31. https://doi.org/10.2753/PPC1075-8216570602.

Laruelle, Marlène. 2011. "Nationalism and State Control in Russia: A Weakened Social Consensus." *Revista CIDOB d'afers internacionals* 96.

Lazarev, Valery, and Paul R. Gregory. 2002. "The Wheels of a Command Economy: Allocating Soviet Vehicles." *Economic History Review* 55 (2): 324–48. https://doi.org/10.1111/1468-0289.00223.

Ledeneva, Alena. 2006. *How Russia Really Works: The Informal Practices That Shaped Post-Soviet Politics and Business*. Ithaca: Cornell University Press.

Ledeneva, Alena. 2013. *Can Russia Modernize? Sistema, Power Networks and Informal Governance*. New York: Cambridge University Press. https://doi.org/10.1017/CBO9780511978494.

Leighton, Julie. 2013. "The Roizman Phenomenon." Carnegie Moscow Center, September 13, 2013. Accessed July 24, 2017. http://carnegie.ru/commentary/52961.

Lemondzhava, Tatia. 2016. "In Russia, the Doors Are Closing: How — and Why — Russians Are Losing Their Freedom to Travel Abroad." *Foreign Policy*, April 29: online. Accessed February 5, 2017. http://foreignpolicy.com/2016/04/29/in-russia-the-doors-are-closing-tourism-putin-human-rights/.

Levada Center. 2010. "Moskvichi o korrumpirovannosti Yuri Luzhkov [Muscovites on the corruption of Yuri Luzhkov]." *Levada Center.* January 31. Accessed March 15, 2010. http://www.levada.ru/press/2010020103.html.

Levada Center. 2013. "Russian Public Opinion 2012–2013, Yearbook." Accessed January 26, 2015. http://www.levada.ru/books/obshchestvennoe-mnenie-2012-eng.

Levada Center. 2014. "Nationalism, Xenophobia and Migration." August 26. Accessed January 26, 2015. http://www.levada.ru/26-08-2014/natsionalizm-ksenofobiya-i-migratsiya.

Levin, Mark, and Georgy Satarov. 2000. "Corruption and Institutions in Russia." *European Journal of Political Economy* 16 (1): 113–32. https://doi.org/10.1016/S0176-2680(99)00050-6.

Levin, Mark J., and Georgy A. Satarov. 2013. "Russian Corruption." In *The Oxford Handbook of the Russian Economy*, ed. Michael Alexeev and Shlomo Weber, 286–306. New York: Oxford University Press.

Levitsky, Steven, and Lucan Way. 2002. "The Rise of Competitive Authoritarianism." *Journal of Democracy* 13 (2): 51–65. https://doi.org/10.1353/jod.2002.0026.

Lewis, Robert A., and Richard H. Rowland. 1979. *Population Redistribution in the USSR: Impact on Society, 1897–1977*. New York: Praeger.

Light, Matthew A. 2005. "Migration Controls in Russia since 1991: From Centralized Repression to Localized Anarchy." PhD dissertation, Yale University.

Light, Matthew. 2016. *Fragile Migration Rights: Freedom of Movement in Post-Soviet Russia*. London, New York: Routledge.

Lipsky, Michael. 1980. *Street-Level Bureaucracy: Dilemmas of the Individual in Public Services*. New York: Russell Sage Foundation.

Loayza, Norman V., Ana María Oviedo, and Luis Servén. 2005. *The Impact of Regulation on Growth and Informality: Cross-Country Evidence*. Related Publication 05–11, AEI-Brookings Joint Center for Regulatory Studies. https://doi.org/10.1596/1813-9450-3623.

Lukanin, Aleksandr. 2010. "Khoteli kak luchshe [Like the best]." *Migratsiia XXI Vek*, 1: 13.

Machamer, Peter, Lindley Darden, and Carl F. Craver. 2000. "Thinking about Mechanisms." *Philosophy of Science* 67 (1): 1–25. https://doi.org/10.1086/392759.

Mainwaring, Scott, Daniel Brinks, and Aníbal Pérez-Liñán. 2001. "Classifying Political Regimes in Latin America, 1945–1999." *Studies in Comparative International Development* 36 (1): 37–65. https://doi.org/10.1007/BF02687584.

Makarkin, Aleksei, and Peter M. Oppenheimer. 2011. "The Russian Social Contract and Regime Legitimacy." *International Affairs* 87 (6): 1459–74. https://doi.org/10.1111/j.1468-2346.2011.01045.x.

Malashenko, Alexey. 2012. *Illegal Immigration: Can It Be Stopped?* Carnegie Moscow Center. Accessed December 8, 2014. http://carnegie.ru/2012/07/11/illegal-immigration-can-it-be-stopped/dvvu.

Malinkin, Mary Elizabeth. 2013. *A Wary Welcome: Varying Reception of Migrants in Russian Cities*. Washington, DC: Woodrow Wilson International Center for Scholars.

Malle, Silvana. 1987. "Planned and Unplanned Mobility in the Soviet Union under the Threat of Labour Shortage." *Soviet Studies* 39 (3): 357–87. https://doi.org/10.1080/09668138708411700.

Manevich, Efim. 1968. "The Management of Soviet Manpower." *Foreign Affairs* 47 (1): 176–84. https://doi.org/10.2307/20039363.

Mann, Michael. 1997. "Has Globalization Ended the Rise and Rise of the Nation-State?" *Review of International Political Economy* 4 (3): 472–96. https://doi.org/10.1080/096922997347715.

Marat, Erica. 2009. "Migrants' Remittances Fare Better Than Expected in Central Asia." *Central Asia-Caucasus Institute Analyst*. November 11. Accessed March 12, 2010. http://www.cacianalyst.org/?q=node/5215.

Markowitz, Lawrence P., and Vera Peshkova. 2016. "Anti-Immigrant Mobilization in Russia's Regions: Local Movements and Framing Processes." *Post-Soviet Affairs* 32 (3): 272–98.

Marten, Kimberly. 2014. "Crimea: Putin's Olympic Diversion." *Washington Post: The Monkey Cage*. March 26. Accessed August 2, 2017. https://www.washingtonpost.com/news/monkey-cage/wp/2014/03/26/crimea-putins-olympic-diversion/?utm_term=.f0a2ae82ec87.

Martin, Philip L. 2014. "Germany." In *Controlling Immigration: A Global Perspective, Third Edition*, ed. James F. Hollifield, Philip L. Martin, and Pia M. Orrenius, 224–50. Stanford: Stanford University Press.

Massey, Douglas S., Joaquin Arango, Graeme Hugo, Ali Kouaouci, Adela Pellegrino, and J. Edward Taylor. 1993. "Theories of International Migration: A Review and Appraisal." *Population and Development Review* 19 (3): 431–66. https://doi.org/10.2307/2938462.

Massey, Douglas S., Jorge Durand, and Nolan J. Malone. 2002. *Beyond Smoke and Mirrors: Mexican Immigration in an Era of Economic Integration*. New York: Russell Sage Foundation Publications.

Massey, Douglas S., and Karen A. Pren. 2012. "Unintended Consequences of US Immigration Policy: Explaining the Post-1965 Surge from Latin America." *Population and Development Review* 38 (1): 1–29. https://doi.org/10.1111/j.1728-4457.2012.00470.x.

Mayda, Anna Maria. 2010. "International Migration: A Panel Data Analysis of the Determinants of Bilateral Flows." *Journal of Population Economics* 23 (4): 1249–74. https://doi.org/10.1007/s00148-009-0251-x.

McFaul, Michael. 2004. "Democracy Promotion as a World Value." *Washington Quarterly* 28 (1): 147–63. https://doi.org/10.1162/0163660042518189.

McMann, Kelly M. 2014. *Corruption as a Last Resort: Adapting to the Market in Central Asia*. Ithaca: Cornell University Press.

McMann, Kelly M., and Nikolai V. Petrov. 2000. "A Survey of Democracy in Russia's Regions." *Post-Soviet Geography and Economics* 41 (3): 155–82.

Medvedev, Roy. 2004. "The Yuri Luzhkov Phenomenon." *Russian Politics and Law* 42 (5): 50–63.

Memorial. 2002. "Stop Ethnic Cleansing! Statement of the Human Rights Centre MEMORIAL concerning Persecutions of the Meskhetian Turks and Other Ethnic Minorities in the Krasnodar Region of the Russian Federation." April 9. Accessed February 25, 2014. http://www.memo.ru/eng/memhrc/texts/stop.shtml.

Memorial and Grazhdanskoe Sodeistvie. 2014. *Olimpiada v Sochi: liuboi tsenoi* [*Olympics in Sochi: at any cost*]. Sochi and Moscow: Open Society. Accessed

July 17, 2017. https://memohrc.org/monitorings/olimpiada-v-sochi-lyuboy-cenoy.

Merry, Sally Engle. 2016. *The Seductions of Quantification: Measuring Human Rights, Gender Violence, and Sex Trafficking*. Chicago: University of Chicago Press. https://doi.org/10.7208/chicago/9780226261317.001.0001.

Messina, Anthony. 2007. *Logics and Politics of Post-WWII Migration to Western Europe*. New York: Cambridge University Press. https://doi.org/10.1017/CBO9781139167192.

Meyers, Eytan. 2004. *International Immigration Policy: A Theoretical and Comparative Analysis*. New York: Palgrave Macmillan. https://doi.org/10.1057/9781403978370.

Migration Advisory Committee. 2012. "Analysis of the Impacts of Migration." British Home Office. January. Accessed January 28, 2015. https://www.gov.uk/government/uploads/system/uploads/attachment_data/file/257235/analysis-of-the-impacts.pdf.

Mikhailova, Elena, and Elena Tyuryukanova. 2009. "Migranty v roznichnoi torgovle: effekt zapretov [Migrants in retail trade: the effect of bans]." In *Novoe migratsionnoe zakonodatel'stvo Rossiiskoi Federatsii: pravoprimenitel'naia praktika* [*New migration legislation in the Russian Federation: enforcement practices*], ed. Galina Vitkovskaya, Anna Platonova, and Vladimir Schkolnikov, 237–65. Moscow: International Organization for Migration, Federal Migration Service of Russia, Organization for Security and Cooperation in Europe.

Mokhtari, Manouchehr, and Irina Grafova. 2007. "Corruption: Theory and Evidence from the Russian Federation." *Economic Systems* 31 (4): 412–22. https://doi.org/10.1016/j.ecosys.2007.04.003.

Money, Jeannette. 1999. *Fences and Neighbors: The Political Geography of Immigration Control*. Ithaca: Cornell University Press.

Money, Jeannette. 2010. "Comparative Immigration Policy." In *The International Studies Encyclopedia*, ed. Robert Allen Denemark. Chichester, West Sussex: Wiley-Blackwell.

Morawska, Ewa. 2001. "Gappy Immigration Controls, Resourceful Migrants, and Pendel Communities: East-West European Travelers." In *Controlling a New Migration World*, ed. Virginie Guiraudon and Christian Joppke, 173–99. London: Routledge.

Moses, Joel C. 2015. "Putin and Russian Subnational Politics in 2014." *Demokratizatsiya: The Journal of Post-Soviet Democratization* 23 (2): 181–203.

Mudde, Cas. 2004. "The Populist Zeitgeist." *Government and Opposition* 39 (4): 542–63. https://doi.org/10.1111/j.1477-7053.2004.00135.x.

Mudde, Cas. 2007. *Populist Radical Right Parties in Europe*. New York: Cambridge University Press. https://doi.org/10.1017/CBO9780511492037.

Mudde, Cas. 2012. *The Relationship between Immigration and Nativism in Europe and North America*. Washington, DC: Migration Policy Institute.

Mudde, Cas, and Cristobal Rovira Kaltwasser. 2013. "Exclusionary vs. Inclusionary Populism: Comparing Contemporary Europe and Latin America." *Government and Opposition* 48 (2): 147–74. https://doi.org/10.1017/gov.2012.11.

Mukomel, Vladimir. 2005. *Migratsionnaia Politika Rossii* [*Migration policy in Russia*]. Moscow: Institute of Sociology (Russian Academy of Sciences).

Mukomel, Vladimir. 2006. "Immigration and Russian Migration Policy: Debating the Future." *Russian Analytical Digest*, 2–5. Accessed February 12, 2007.

Mukomel, Vladimir. 2009. "Po khodu diskussii [In the course of the debate]." In *Novoe migratsionnoe zakonodatel'stvo Rossiiskoi Federatsii: pravoprimenitel'naia praktika* [*New migration legislation in the Russian Federation: enforcement practices*], ed. Galina Vitkovskaya, Anna Platonova, and Vladimir Shkolnikov, 117–18. Moscow: International Organization for Migration, Federal Migration Service of Russia, Organization for Security and Cooperation in Europe.

Nemtsov, Boris. 2009. *Luzhkov. Itogi.* [*Luzhkov. Results.*]. Accessed July 17, 2017. http://nemtsov.ru/old/indexff2f.html?id=705917.

Nemtsov, Boris, and Leonid Martyniuk. 2013. "Zimniaia olimpiada v subtropikakh [Winter Olympics in the subtropics]." Accessed February 3, 2017. http://www.putin-itogi.ru/zimnyaya-olimpiada-v-subtropikax/.

Neoruss Project. 2014. "Nation-Building and Nationalism in Today's Russia." http://www.hf.uio.no/ilos/english/research/projects/neoruss/.

Nikitin, P. 1969. "The Planned Development of the National Economy under Socialism." In *The Soviet Economy*, ed. Harry G. Shaffer, 364–71. New York: Meredith Corporation.

North, Douglass C. 1990. *Institutions, Institutional Change and Economic Performance*. New York: Cambridge University Press. https://doi.org/10.1017/CBO9780511808678.

OECD. 2013. *OECD Assessment of the Statistical System and Key Statistics of the Russian Federation*. Accessed March 13, 2015. http://www.oecd.org/russia/russia-progress-made-in-improving-the-quality-of-official-statistics-but-challenges-remain.htm.

Office of the Director of National Intelligence. 2017. "Background to 'Assessing Russian Activities and Intentions in Recent US Elections': The Analytic Process and Cyber Incident Attribution." January 6. Accessed

February 19, 2017. https://www.dni.gov/files/documents/ICA_2017_01.pdf.

Opp, Karl-Dieter. 2005. "Explanations by Mechanisms in the Social Sciences. Problems, Advantages and Alternatives." *Mind & Society* 4 (2): 163–78. https://doi.org/10.1007/s11299-005-0013-8.

Orrenius, Pia M. 2001. "Illegal Immigration and Enforcement along the US-Mexico Border: An Overview." *Economic and Financial Review – Federal Reserve Bank of Dallas* 2–11. Accessed December 14, 2016. http://www.dallasfed.org/assets/documents/research/efr/2001/efr0101a.pdf.

Orrenius, Pia M., and Madeline Zavodny. 2012. "Economic Effects of Migration: Receiving States." In *Oxford Handbook of the Politics of International Migration*, ed. Marc R. Rosenblum and Daniel J. Tichenor, 105–31. New York: Oxford University Press.

Ortega, Francesc, and Giovanni Peri. 2013. "The Effect of Income and Immigration Policies on International Migration." *Migration Studies* 1 (1): 47–74. https://doi.org/10.1093/migration/mns004.

Osipov, Alexander. 2002. "New Persecutions against the Meskhetian Turks in Krasnodar Krai." Memorial. Accessed March 6, 2014. http://www.memo.ru/hr/news/turki.htm.

Pachirat, Timothy. 2009. "The Political in Political Ethnography: Dispatches from the Kill Floor." In *Political Ethnography: What Immersion Contributes to the Study of Power*, ed. Edward Schatz, 143–62. Chicago: University of Chicago Press.

Panov, Petr, and Cameron Ross. 2013. "Patterns of Electoral Contestation in Russian Regional Assemblies: Between 'Competitive' and 'Hegemonic' Authoritarianism." *Demokratizatsiya: The Journal of Post-Soviet Democratization* 21 (3): 369–99.

Paspalanova, Mila. 2008. "Undocumented vs. Illegal Migrant: Towards Terminological Coherence." *Migraciones Internacionales* 4 (3): 79–90.

Perlmutter, Ted. 2014. "Italy: Political Parties and Italian Policy, 1990–2009." In *Controlling Immigration: A Global Perspective*, ed. James Hollifield, Philip Martin, and Pia Orrenius, kindle version. Stanford: Stanford University Press.

Perry, Guillermo E., Omar S. Arias, Pablo Fajnzylber, William F. Maloney, Andrew D. Mason, and Jaime Saavedra-Chanduvi. 2007. *Informality: Exit and Exclusion*. Washington, DC: The World Bank. https://doi.org/10.1596/978-0-8213-7092-6.

Petkov, Radoslav K., and Natan M. Shklyar. 1999. "Russian Regions after the Crisis: Coping with Economic Troubles Governors Reap Political Rewards." *Demokratizatsiya: The Journal of Post-Soviet Democratization* 7 (4): 527–43.

Petrov, Nikolay. 2010. "Regional Governors under the Dual Power of Medvedev and Putin." *Journal of Communist Studies and Transition Politics* 26 (2): 276–305. https://doi.org/10.1080/13523271003712633.

Petrov, Nikolay. 2011. "Who Is Running Russia's Regions." In *Russia as a Network State*, ed. Vadim Kononenko and Arkady Moshes, 81–112. New York: Palgrave Macmillan. https://doi.org/10.1057/9780230306707_5.

Petrov, Nikolay, Maria Lipman, and Henry E. Hale. 2014. "Three Dilemmas of Hybrid Regime Governance: Russia from Putin to Putin." *Post-Soviet Affairs* 30 (1): 1–26. https://doi.org/10.1080/1060586X.2013.825140.

Petrov, Nikolai, and Darrell Slider. 2009. "The Regions under Putin and After." In *After Putin's Russia: Past Imperfect, Future Uncertain*, ed. Stephen K. Wegren and Dale R. Herspring, 59–83. Lanham, MD: Rowman and Littlefield.

Pew Research Center. 2014. "A Fragile Rebound for EU Image on Eve of European Parliament Elections. " Accessed January 28, 2014. http://www.pewglobal.org/files/2014/05/2014-05-12_Pew-Global-Attitudes-European-Union.pdf.

Pilkington, Hilary. 1998. *Migration, Displacement, and Identity in Post-Soviet Russia*. New York: Routledge. https://doi.org/10.4324/9780203444436.

Pilkington, Hilary, Elena Omelchenko, and Anton Popov. 2010. "Xenophobic Youth Groups in Krasnodar/Sochi Russia: Cossacks." *Groups and Environments* (2): 117–23.

Piore, Michael J. 1979. *Birds of Passage: Migrant Labour and Industrial Societies*. New York: Cambridge University Press. https://doi.org/10.1017/CBO9780511572210.

Popov, Anton, and Igor Kuznetsov. 2008. "Ethnic Discrimination and the Discourse of 'Indigenization': The Regional Regime, 'Indigenous Majority' and Ethnic Minorities in Krasnodar Krai in Russia." *Nationalities Papers* 36 (2): 223–52. https://doi.org/10.1080/00905990801934322.

Portes, Alejandro, and John Walton. 1981. *Labor, Class, and the International System*. New York: Academic Press.

Porthé, Victoria, Emily Ahonen, M. Luisa Vazquez, Catherine Pope, Andres Alonso Agudelo, Ana M. Garcıa, Marcelo Amable, Fernando G. Benavides, and Joan Benach. 2010. "Extending a Model of Precarious Employment: A Qualitative Study of Immigrant Workers in Spain." *American Journal of Industrial Medicine* 53 (4): 417–24. https://doi.org/10.1002/ajim.20781.

Pryadilnikov, Mikhail Vladimirovich. 2009. "The State and Markets in Russia – Understanding the Development of Bureaucratic Implementation Capacities through the Study of Regulatory Reform, 2001–2008." PhD dissertation, Harvard University.

Putin, Vladimir. 2005. "Vstupitel'noe slovo na zacedanii soveta bezopasnosti po migratsionnoi politike [Opening remarks at the Security Council meeting on migration policy]." March 17. Accessed September 30, 2016. http://kremlin.ru/events/president/transcripts/22861.

Putin, Vladimir. 2006. "Putin na linii [Putin on the line]." *Lenta*. Moscow, October 25. Accessed January 19, 2017. https://lenta.ru/articles/2006/10/25/putin/.

Putin, Vladimir. 2009. "V.V. Putin provel zasedanie Presidiuma Pravitelstva Rossiiskoi Federatsii [Putin held a meeting of the Presidium of the Government of the Russian Federation]." June 1. Accessed March 22, 2010. http://www.government.ru/content/governmentactivity/mainnews/archive/2009/06/01/3056300.htm.

Putin, Vladimir. 2012. "Rossiia: Natsional'nyi Vopros [Russia: the national question]." *Nezavisimaia Gazeta*, January 23. Accessed September 30, 2016. http://www.ng.ru/politics/2012-01-23/1_national.html.

Putin, Vladimir. 2013. "Poslanie Prezidenta Federal'nomu Sobraniiu [President's address to the Federal Assembly]." December 12. Accessed July 16, 2016. http://kremlin.ru/events/president/transcripts/messages/19825.

Quillin, Bryce, Carlo Segni, Sophie Sirtaine, and Ilias Skamnelos. 2007. *Remittances in the CIS Countries: A Study of Selected Corridors*. Chief Economist's Regional Working Paper Series 2/2, World Bank. Accessed December 8, 2014. http://www-wds.worldbank.org/external/default/WDSContentServer/WDSP/IB/2010/02/19/000334955_20100219050652/Rendered/PDF/531060NWP0Remi10Box345597B01PUBLIC1.pdf.

Radnitz, Scott. 2006. "Weighing the Political and Economic Motivations for Migration in Post-Soviet Space: The Case of Uzbekistan." *Europe-Asia Studies* 58 (5): 653–77. https://doi.org/10.1080/09668130600731003.

Ratha, Dilip, Sanket Mohapatra, and Ani Silwal. 2009. "Migration and Remittance Trends 2009: A Better-Than-Expected Outcome So Far, but Significant Risks Ahead." *People Move: A Blog about Migration, Remittances, and Development*. November 3. Accessed March 21, 2010. https://blogs.worldbank.org/peoplemove/migration-and-remittance-trends-2009-a-better-than-expected-outcome-so-far-but-significant-risks.

Reeves, Madeleine. 2013. "Clean Fake: Authenticating Documents and Persons in Migrant Moscow." *American Ethnologist* 40 (3): 508–24. https://doi.org/10.1111/amet.12036.

Reisinger, William M. 2013. "Studying Russia's Regions to Advance Comparative Political Science." In *Russia's Regions and Comparative Subnational Politics*, ed. William M. Reisinger, 1–24. New York: Routledge.

Remington, Thomas F. 2014. *Presidential Decrees in Russia: A Comparative Perspective*. New York: Cambridge University Press. https://doi.org/10.1017/CBO9781139629355.

Renz, Bettina. 2006. "Putin's Militocracy? An Alternative Interpretation of Siloviki in Contemporary Russian Politics." *Europe-Asia Studies* 58 (6): 903–24. https://doi.org/10.1080/09668130600831134.

Reuter, Ora John. 2013. "Regional Patrons and Hegemonic Party Electoral Performance in Russia." *Post-Soviet Affairs* 29 (2): 101–35.

Reuter, Ora John, and Thomas F. Remington. 2009. "Dominant Party Regimes and the Commitment Problem: The Case of United Russia." *Comparative Political Studies* 42 (4): 501–26. https://doi.org/10.1177/0010414008327426.

Reuter, Ora John, and Graeme Robertson. 2012. "Sub-National Appointments in Authoritarian Regimes: Evidence from Russian Gubernatorial Appointments." *Journal of Politics* 74 (4): 1023–37. https://doi.org/10.1017/S0022381612000631.

Richman, Barry M. 1969. "The Planning Process." In *The Soviet Economy*, ed. Harry G. Shaffer, 336–47. New York: Meredith Corporation.

Rivera, Sharon Werning, and David W. Rivera. 2006. "The Russian Elite under Putin: Militocratic or Bourgeois?" *Post-Soviet Affairs* 22 (2): 125–44. https://doi.org/10.2747/1060-586X.22.2.125.

Robinson, Neil. 2013. "The Contexts of Russia's Political Economy." In *The Political Economy of Russia*, ed. Neil Robinson, 15–50. New York: Rowman and Littlefield.

Romodanovsky, Konstantin. 2013. "Migration Strategy of Russia." In *Migration in Russia 2000–2013*, ed. Igor Ivanov, 36–48. Moscow: Russian International Affairs Council.

Ross, C. 2003. "Putin's Federal Reforms and the Consolidation of Federalism in Russia: One Step Forward, Two Steps Back!" *Communist and Post-Communist Studies* 36 (1): 29–47. https://doi.org/10.1016/S0967-067X(02)00057-0.

Ross, Cameron. 2011. "Federalism and Defederalisation in Russia." In *Routledge Handbook of Russian Politics and Society*, ed. Graeme Gill and James Young, 140–52. New York: Routledge.

Ross, Cameron. 2012. *Russian Regional Politics under Putin and Medvedev*. New York: Routledge.

Rowney, Don K., and Eugene Huskey, eds. 2009. *Russian Bureaucracy and the State: Officialdom from Alexander III to Vladimir Putin*. New York: Palgrave Macmillan. https://doi.org/10.1057/9780230244993.

Rubins, Noah. 1998. "The Demise and Resurrection of the Propiska: Freedom of Movement in the Russian Federation." *Harvard International Law Journal* 39 (2): 545–66.

Ruhs, Martin. 2013. *The Price of Rights: Regulating International Labor Migration*. Princeton: Princeton University Press. https://doi.org/10.1515/9781400848607.

Ruhs, Martin, and Bridget Anderson. 2010. "Semi-Compliance and Illegality in Migrant Labour Markets: An Analysis of Migrants, Employers and the State in the UK." *Population Space and Place* 16 (3): 195–211.

Rutland, Peter. 1985. *The Myth of the Plan: Lessons of Soviet Planning Experience*. La Salle, IL: Open Court.

Rutland, Peter. 2008. "Putin's Economic Record: Is the Oil Boom Sustainable?" *Europe-Asia Studies* 60 (6): 1051–72. https://doi.org/10.1080/09668130802180975.

Ryazantsev, Sergey, and Oleg Korneev. 2013. *Russia and Kazakhstan in Eurasian Migration System: Development Trends, Socio-Economic Consequences of Migration and Approaches to Regulation*. CARIM-East Research Report 2013/44, CARIM East: Consortium for Applied Research on International Migration. Accessed June 18, 2014. http://www.carim-east.eu/media/CARIM-East_RR-2013-44.pdf.

Sadiq, Kamal. 2005. "When States Prefer Non-Citizens over Citizens: Conflict over Illegal Immigration into Malaysia." *International Studies Quarterly* 49 (1): 101–22. https://doi.org/10.1111/j.0020-8833.2005.00336.x.

Sakwa, Richard. 2010. *The Crisis of Russian Democracy: The Dual State, Factionalism and the Medvedev Succession*. New York: Cambridge University Press.

Sakwa, Richard. 2014. *Putin Redux: Power and Contradiction in Contemporary Russia*. New York: Routledge.

Samers, Michael. 2004. "An Emerging Geopolitics of 'Illegal' Immigration in the European Union." *European Journal of Migration and Law* 6 (1): 27–45. https://doi.org/10.1163/1571816041518750.

Sandel, Michael. 1984. *Liberalism and Its Critics*. New York: New York University Press.

Sassen, Saskia. 1996. *Losing Control: Sovereignty in an Age of Globalization*. New York: Columbia University Press.

Sassen, Saskia. 1998. "The De Facto Transnationalizing of Immigration Policy." In *Challenge to the Nation-State: Immigration in Western Europe and the United States*, ed. Christian Joppke, 49–85. Oxford: Oxford University Press. https://doi.org/10.1093/0198292295.003.0003.

Savva, Mikhail V., and Valerii A. Tishkov. 2011. "Civil Society Institutions and Peacemaking." *Anthropology & Archeology of Eurasia* 49 (4): 12–39. https://doi.org/10.2753/AAE1061-1959490401.

Schaible, Damian S. 2001. "Life in Russia's 'Closed City': Moscow's Movement Restrictions and the Rule of Law." *New York University Law Review* 76 (344).

Schain, Martin A. 2006. "The Extreme Right and Immigration Policy-Making: Measuring Direct and Indirect Effects." *West European Politics* 29 (2): 270–89. https://doi.org/10.1080/01402380500512619.

Schatz, Edward. 2009. "Introduction. Ethnographic Immersion and the Study of Politics." In *Political Ethnography: What Immersion Contributes to the Study of Power*, ed. Edward Schatz, 1–22. Chicago: University of Chicago Press. https://doi.org/10.7208/chicago/9780226736785.001.0001.

Schenk, Caress. 2010. "Open Borders, Closed Minds. Russia's Changing Migration Policies: Liberalization or Xenophobia." *Demokratizatsiya: The Journal of Post-Soviet Democratization* 18 (2): 101–21. https://doi.org/10.3200/DEMO.18.2.101-121.

Schenk, Caress. 2012. "Nationalism in the Russian Media: Content Analysis of Newspaper Coverage Surrounding Conflict in Stavropol, 24 May–7 June 2007." *Nationalities Papers: The Journal of Nationalism and Ethnicity* 40 (5): 783–805. https://doi.org/10.1080/00905992.2012.705271.

Schenk, Caress. 2013. "Controlling Immigration Manually: Lessons from Moscow (Russia)." *Europe-Asia Studies* 65 (7): 1444–65. https://doi.org/10.1080/09668136.2013.824242.

Schenk, Caress. 2016. "Assessing Foreign Policy Commitment through Migration Policy in Russia." *Demokratizatsiya: The Journal of Post-Soviet Democratization* 24 (4): 475–99.

Schenk, Caress. Forthcoming. "Anti-Migrant, but Not Nationalist: Pursuing Statist Legitimacy through Immigration Discourse and Policy." In *Russia before and after Crimea: Nationalism and Identity, 2010–2017*, ed. Pål Kolstø and Helge Blakkisrud. Edinburgh: Edinburgh University Press.

Schneider, Friedrich. 1997. "The Shadow Economies of Western Europe." *Economic Affairs* 17 (3): 42–8. https://doi.org/10.1111/1468-0270.00041.

Schneider, Friedrich. 2004. *The Size of the Shadow Economies of 145 Countries all over the World: First Results over the Period 1999 to 2003*. IZA Discussion Paper No. 1431, Bonn, Germany: Institute for the Study of Labour (IZA).

Schulze, Günther G., Bambang Suharnoko Sjahrir, and Nikita Zakharov. 2016. "Corruption in Russia." *Journal of Law & Economics* 59 (1): 135–71. https://doi.org/10.1086/684844.

Schuster, Liza. 2011. "Turning Refugees into 'Illegal Migrants': Afghan Asylum Seekers in Europe." *Ethnic and Racial Studies* 34 (8): 1392–1407. https://doi.org/10.1080/01419870.2010.535550.

Semenova, Elena. 2011. "Ministerial and Parliamentary Elites in an Executive-Dominated System: Post-Soviet Russia 1991–2009." *Comparative Sociology* 10 (6): 908–27. https://doi.org/10.1163/156913311X607629.

Sen, Amartya. 1999. "Democracy as a Universal Value." *Journal of Democracy* 10 (3): 3–17.

Shahnazarian, Nona. 2011. "Violence, Politics, and Ethnicity in the 'Russian Riviera.'" PONARS Eurasia Policy Memo No. 191.

Sharafutdinova, Gulnaz. 2010a. *Political Consequences of Crony Capitalism inside Russia*. Notre Dame: Notre Dame University Press.

Sharafutdinova, Gulnaz. 2010b. "Subnational Governance in Russia: How Putin Changed the Contract with His Agents and the Problems It Created for Medvedev." *Publius* 40 (4): 672–96. https://doi.org/10.1093/publius/pjp036.

Sharafutdinova, Gulnaz. 2012. "The Limits of the Matrix: Ideas and Power in Russian Politics of the 2000s." *Problems of Post-Communism* 59 (3): 17–30. https://doi.org/10.2753/PPC1075-8216590302.

Shenfield, Stephen. 2001. *Russian Fascism: Traditions, Tendencies, Movements.* New York: ME Sharpe.

Shevel, Oxana. 2011. "Russian Nation-Building from Yel'tsin to Medvedev: Ethnic, Civic or Purposefully Ambiguous?" *Europe-Asia Studies* 63 (2): 179–202.

Shlapentokh, Vladimir. 2003. "Russia's Acquiescence to Corruption Makes the State Machine Inept." *Communist and Post-Communist Studies* 36 (2): 151–61. https://doi.org/10.1016/S0967-067X(03)00023-0.

Shlapentokh, Vladimir. 2005. "Russia's Demographic Decline and the Public Reaction." *Europe-Asia Studies* 57 (7): 951–68. http://dx.doi.org/10.1080/09668130500301337.

Shleifer, Andrei, and Robert W. Vishny. 1992. "Pervasive Shortages under Socialism." *Rand Journal of Economics* 23 (2): 237–46. https://doi.org/10.2307/2555986.

Slater, Dan, and Lucan Ahmad Way. 2017. "Was the 2016 U.S. Election Democratic? Here Are 7 Serious Shortfalls." *The Washington Post: Monkey Cage*, January 12: online. Accessed January 13, 2017. https://www.washingtonpost.com/news/monkey-cage/wp/2017/01/12/was-the-2016-u-s-election-democratic-we-see-7-serious-shortfalls/?utm_term=.c7a193e1c0c7&wpisrc=nl_cage&wpmm=1.

Slider, Darrell. 2011. "Regional Governance." In *Routledge Handbook of Russian Politics and Society*, ed. James Young and Graeme Gill, 153–63. New York: Routledge.

Slider, Darrell. 2014. "Resistance to Decentralization under Medvedev and Putin." *Region: Regional Studies of Russia, Eastern Europe, and Central Asia* 3 (1): 125–46. https://doi.org/10.1353/reg.2014.0003.

Smyth, Regina, Anna Lowry, and Brandon Wilkening. 2007. "Engineering Victory: Institutional Reform, Informal Institutions, and the Formation of a

Hegemonic Party Regime in the Russian Federation." *Post-Soviet Affairs* 23 (2): 118–37. https://doi.org/10.2747/1060-586X.23.2.118.

Sohoni, Deenesh, and Tracy W.P. Sohoni. 2014. "Perceptions of Immigrant Criminality: Crime and Social Boundaries." *Sociological Quarterly* 55 (1): 49–71. https://doi.org/10.1111/tsq.12039.

Somerville, Will, and Sara Wallace Goodman. 2010. "The Role of Networks in the Development of UK Migration Policy." *Political Studies* 58 (5): 951–70. https://doi.org/10.1111/j.1467-9248.2009.00814.x.

Somerville, Will, and Madeline Sumption. 2009. *Immigration and the Labour Market: Theory, Evidence and Policy.* Migration Policy Institute, Equality and Human Rights Commission.

Soysal, Yasemin. 1994. *Limits of Citizenship: Migrants and Postnational Membership in Europe.* Chicago: University of Chicago Press.

Steel, Daniel. 2004. "Social Mechanisms and Causal Inference." *Philosophy of the Social Sciences* 34 (1): 55–78. https://doi.org/10.1177/0048393103260775.

Stefes, Christoph H. 2007. "Measuring, Conceptualizing, and Fighting Systemic Corruption: Evidence from Post-Soviet Countries." *Perspectives on Global Issues* 2 (1): 1–16.

Steiner, Nils D. 2014. "Comparing Freedom House Democracy Scores to Alternative Indices and Testing for Political Bias: Are US Allies Rated as More Democratic by Freedom House?" *Journal of Comparative Policy Analysis* 18 (4): 1–21.

Stoner-Weiss, Kathryn. 2006. *Resisting the State: Reform and Retrenchment in Post-Soviet Russia.* New York: Cambridge University Press. https://doi.org/10.1017/CBO9780511510403.

Strange, Susan. 1996. *The Retreat of the State: The Diffusion of Power in the World Economy.* New York: Cambridge University Press. https://doi.org/10.1017/CBO9780511559143.

Sundstrom, Lisa McIntosh. 2006. *Funding Civil Society: Foreign Assistance and NGO Development in Russia.* Stanford: Stanford University Press.

Svolik, Milan W. 2012. *The Politics of Authoritarian Rule.* New York: Cambridge University Press.

Swerdlow, Steve. 2006. "Understanding Post-Soviet Ethnic Discrimination and the Effective Use of U.S. Refugee Resettlement: The Case of the Meskhetian Turks of Krasnodar Krai." *California Law Review* 94 (6): 1827–78. https://doi.org/10.2307/20439082.

Taran, Patrick. 2011. "Crisis, Migration and Precarious Work: Impacts and Responses. Focus on European Union Member Countries." ITC-Actrav European Trade Union Conference on Conversion of Precarious Work into Work with Rights. Budapest. Accessed October 12, 2015. http://www.

globalmigrationpolicy.org/articles/decentWork/Crisis,%20Migration,%20 Precarious%20Work-%20impacts%20&%20responses%20focus%20EU,%20 TARAN%202012.pdf.

Tartakovskaya, Irina, and Sarah Ashwin. 2006. "Who Benefits from Network?" In *Adapting to Russia's New Labour Market: Gender and Employment Behaviour*, ed. Sarah Ashwin, 164–92. New York: Routledge. https://doi.org/10.4324/9780203313138_chapter_6.

Taylor, Brian D. 2011. *State Building in Putin's Russia: Policing and Coercion after Communism*. New York: Cambridge University Press. https://doi.org/10.1017/CBO9780511974144.

Tichenor, Daniel J. 2009. *Dividing Lines: The Politics of Immigration Control in America*. Princeton: Princeton University Press.

Tilly, Charles. 2001. "Mechanisms in Political Processes." *American Political Science Review* 4 (1): 21–41. Accessed December 2, 2015. https://doi.org/10.1146/annurev.polisci.4.1.21 http://professor-murmann.info/tilly/2001_Mechs_of_pol_process.pdf.

Tipaldou, Sofia, and Katrin Uba. 2014. "The Russian Radical Right Movement and Immigration Policy: Do They Just Make Noise or Have an Impact as Well?" *Europe-Asia Studies* 66 (7): 1080–1101. https://doi.org/10.1080/09668136.2014.927647.

Tishkov, Valery, Zhanna Zayinchkovskaya, and Galina Vitkovskaya. 2005. *Migration in the Countries of the Former Soviet Union*. A paper prepared for the Policy Analysis and Research Programme of the Global Commission on International Migration, Global Commission on International Migration. Accessed August 6, 2010. http://www.gcim.org/attachements/RS3.pdf.

Toje, Hege. 2006. "Cossack Identity in the New Russia: Kuban Cossack Revival and Local Politics." *Europe-Asia Studies* 58 (7): 1057–77. https://doi.org/10.1080/09668130600926306.

Tolz, Vera. 2001. *Inventing the Nation*. New York: Oxford University Press.

Tolz, Vera, and Sue-Ann Harding. 2015. "From 'Compatriots' to 'Aliens': The Changing Coverage of Migration on Russian Television." *Russian Review* 74 (3): 452–77. https://doi.org/10.1111/russ.12025.

Transparency International Russia. 2002. "Indeks vospriiatiia korruptsii-2002: Rossiia na 71 meste [Corruption Perceptions Index-2002: 71 places in Russia]." Accessed February 3, 2017. http://transparency.org.ru/indeks-vospriiatiia-korruptcii/indeks-vospriiatiia-korruptcii-2002-rossiia-na-71-meste.

Treisman, Daniel. 2010. "Is Russia Cursed by Oil?" *Journal of International Affairs* 63 (2): 85–102.

Triadafilopoulos, Triadafilos. 2011. "Illiberal Means to Liberal Ends? Understanding Recent Immigrant Integration Policies in Europe." *Journal of*

Ethnic and Migration Studies 37 (6): 861–80. https://doi.org/10.1080/1369183X.2011.576189.

Triandafyllidou, Anna. 2003. "Immigration Policy Implementation in Italy: Organisational Culture, Identity Processes and Labour Market Control." *Journal of Ethnic and Migration Studies* 29 (2): 257–97. https://doi.org/10.1080/1369183032000079611.

Triandafyllidou, Anna, and Maurizio Ambrosini. 2011. "Irregular Immigration Control in Italy and Greece: Strong Fencing and Weak Gate-Keeping Serving the Labour Market." *European Journal of Migration and Law* 13 (3): 251–73. https://doi.org/10.1163/157181611X587847.

Troitskii, Konstantin E. 2016. *Administrativnye vydvoreniia iz Rossii: Sudebnoe razbiratel'ctvo ili massovoe izgnanie?* [*Administrative Expulsion from Russia: Court Proceedings or Mass Expulsion?*] Moscow: Komitet Grazhdanskoe Sodeistvie.

Tsuda, Takeyuki. 2003. *Strangers in the Ethnic Homeland: Japanese Brazilian Return Migration in Transnational Perspective*. New York: Columbia University Press. https://doi.org/10.7312/tsud12838.

Turovskii, Rostislav F. 2010. "How Russian Governors Are Appointed: Inertia and Radicalism in Central Policy." *Russian Politics and Law* 48 (1): 58–79. https://doi.org/10.2753/RUP1061-1940480104.

Tyuryukanova, Elena. 2008. "Labour Migration from CIS to Russia: New Challenges and Hard Solutions." *Empires & Nations* (Paris), July 3–5.

Tyuryukanova, Elena. 2009a. "Monitoring Migratsionnoi Politiki: Itogi 2007 i 2008 godov [Monitoring of Migration Policies: Results of 2007 and 2008]." Presentation at Nauchni Sovet FMS [Scientific Council of the FMS], Moscow, April 10, 2009.

Tyuryukanova, Elena. 2009b. *Regularization of Migrant Workers and Discouragement of Employment of Irregular Migrants in the Russian Federation*. Moscow: International Labour Organization.

Uhlin, Anders. 2006. *Post-Soviet Civil Society: Democratization in Russia and the Baltic States*. New York: Routledge.

United Russia. 2009. "Trudoustroistvu migrantov pomogut chastnye agentstvo Zaniatost' [Private employment agencies help migrants find employment]." *Edinaia Rossiia*. May 26. Accessed March 15, 2010. http://www.edinros.ru/text.shtml?8/1415,101820.

Vandyshev, M.N., N.V. Veselkova, L.E. Petrova, and E.V. Priamikova. 2009. "Migranty iz Tadzhikistana v Yekaterinburge. Analiticheskii otchet po rezul'tatam sotsiologicheskogo issledovaniia [Migrants from Tajikistan in Yekaterinburg. Analytical report on the results of sociological research]." In *Obshchestvennyi monitoring i analiz protsessov trudovoi migratsii iz Respubliki*

Tadzhikistan v Sverdlovskuiu oblast' [*Public monitoring and analysis of the process of labour migration from the Republic of Tajikistan to Sverdlovsk oblast*]. A publication of Otdelenie mezhdunarodnoi organizatsii Institut "Otkrytoe Obshchestvo" – Fond sodeistviia v Tadzhikistane i Nekommercheskoe partnerstvo "Mezhnatsional'nyi informatsionnyi tsentr" [Branch office of the International Organization of Open Society Institute – Assistance Foundation in Tajikistan and the non-profit partnership "Interethnic information centre"]. Yekaterinburg.

Veikou, Mariangela, and Anna Triandafyllidou. 2001. "Immigration Policy and Its Implementation in Italy: A Report on the State of the Art." *Mediterranean Migration Observatory*. Accessed January 16, 2010. http://www.mmo.gr/pdf/library/Italy/triandaf.pdf.

Vishnevsky, Anatoly. 2013. "The Impact of Migration on Russia's Demographic Development." In *Migration in Russia 2000–2013*, ed. Igor Ivanov, 194–208. Moscow: Russian International Affairs Council.

Vishnevsky, Anatoly G., and Sergei N. Bobylev. 2009. *Russia Facing Demographic Challenges. National Human Development Report, Russian Federation 2008*. Moscow: United Nations Development Programme.

Vitkovskaya, Galina. 2009. "Novoe migratsionnoe zakonodatel'stvo Rossii: liberalizatsiia v tseliakh legalizatsii [New migration legislation in Russia: liberalization in the aims of legalization." In *Novoe migratsionnoe zakonodatel'stvo Rossiiskoi Federatsii: pravoprimenitel'naia praktika* [*New migration legislation in the Russian Federation: enforcement practices*], ed. Galina Vitkovskaya, Anna Platonova and Vladimir Shkolnikov, 19–36. Moscow: International Organization for Migration, Federal Migration Service of Russia, Organization for Security and Cooperation in Europe.

Vlachoutsicos, Charalambos, and Paul R. Lawrence. 1990. "What We Don't Know about Soviet Management." *Harvard Business Review*. Accessed November 30, 2015. hbr.org/1990/11/what-we-dont-know-about-soviet-management.

Vlasova, N.I., V.V. Kravtsov, I.G. Matveeva, and V.A. Postavnin. 2011. *Vremennaia Trudovaia Migratsiia: Nuzhno Li Sokraniat' Kvoty?* [*Temporary labour migration: do we need to reduce the quota?*] Moscow: Fond: Migration of the 21st Century.

Voronina, Natalia. 2006. "Outlook on Migration Policy Reform in Russia: Contemporary Challenges and Political Paradoxes." In *Migration Perspectives: Eastern Europe and Central Asia*, ed. Roger Rodriguez Rios, 71–90. Vienna: International Organization for Migration.

Walzer, Michael. 1983. *Spheres of Justice: A Defense of Pluralism and Equality*. New York: Basic Books.

Wegren, S.K. 2003. "The Rise, Fall, and Transformation of the Rural Social Contract in Russia." *Communist and Post-Communist Studies* 36:1–27.

Weinthal, Erika, and Pauline Jones Luong. 2006. "Combating the Resource Curse: An Alternative Solution to Managing Mineral Wealth." *Perspectives on Politics* 4 (1): 35–53. https://doi.org/10.1017/S1537592706060051.

Williams, Colin C., John Round, and Peter Rodgers. 2013. *The Role of Informal Economies in the Post-Soviet World: The End of Transition?* New York: Routledge.

Wilson, James Q. 1989. *Bureaucracy: What Government Agencies Do and Why They Do It.* New York: Basic Books.

Wodak, Ruth. 2015. *The Politics of Fear: What Right-Wing Populist Discourses Mean.* Los Angeles: Sage. https://doi.org/10.4135/9781446270073.

World Bank. 2009. "World Bank Lowers Remittances Forecast for 2009 as Financial Crisis Deepens." March 24. Accessed July 18, 2017. http://www.worldbank.org/en/news/feature/2009/03/24/world-bank-lowers-remittances-forecast-for-2009-as-financial-crisis-deepens.

World Bank. 2015. "Personal Remittances, Received (% of GDP)." Accessed March 11, 2016. http://data.worldbank.org/indicator/BX.TRF.PWKR.DT.GD.ZS.

World Bank. 2016. "Migrant Remittance Outflows." Accessed February 8, 2017. https://www.worldbank.org/en/topic/migrationremittancesdiasporaissues/brief/migration-remittances-data.

Yanow, Dvora. 2009. "Dear Author, Dear Reader: The Third Hermeneutic in Writing and Reviewing Ethnography." In *Political Ethnography: What Immersion Contributes to the Study of Power*, ed. Edward Schatz, 275–302. Chicago: University of Chicago Press.

Yudina, Tatiana Nikolaevna. 2005. "Labour Migration into Russia: The Response of State and Society." *Current Sociology* 53 (4): 583–606. https://doi.org/10.1177/0011392105052716.

Zaionchkovskaia, Zhanna. 2009. "Novaia migratsionnaia politika Rossii: pervye itogi [New migration policies in Russia: first results]." In *Novoe Migratsionnoe Zakonodatel'stvo Rossiiskoi Federatsii: Pravoprimenitel'naia Praktika* [*New migration legislation in the Russian Federation: enforcement practices*], ed. Galina Vitkovskaya, Anna Platonova, and Vladimir Shkolnikov, 73–118. Moscow: International Organization for Migration, Federal Migration Service of Russia, Organization for Security and Cooperation in Europe.

Zaionchkovskaia, Zhanna, Nikita Mkrtchyn, and Elena Tyuryukanova. 2009. "Rossiia pered vyzovami immigratsii [Russia facing the challenges of immigration]." In *Postsovetskie transformatsii: otrazhenie v migrantakh* [*Post-Soviet transformations: reflected in migrants*], ed. Zhanna Zaionchkovskaia and Galina Vitkovskaya, 9–62. Moscow: Centre for Migration Research and Institute of Economic Forecasting at the Russian Academy of Sciences.

Zaionchkovskaya, Zhanna. 2013. "Migration in Contemporary Russia." In *Migration in Russia 2000–2013*, ed. Igor Ivanov, 209–31. Moscow: Russian International Affairs Council.

Zayonchkovskaya, Zhanna. 2000. "Recent Migration Trends in the Commonwealth of Independent States." *International Social Science Journal* (UNESCO) 52 (3/165): 343–55.

Laws and Government Documents

Constitutional Court Order (*postanovlenie*) No. 5-P of February 17, 2016. *Po delu o proverke konstitutsionnosti polozhenii puncta 6 stat'i 8 Federal'nogo zakona "O pravovom polozhenii inostrannykh grazhdan v Rossiiskoi Federatsii", chastei 1 i 3 stat'i 18.8 Kodeksa Rossiiskoi Federatsii ob administrativnykh pravonarusheniiakh", i podpunkta 2 chasti pervoi stat'i 27 Federal'nogo zakona "O poriadke vyezda iz Rossiiskoi Federatsii i v"ezda v Rossiiskuiu Federatsiiu" v sviazi s zhaloboi grazhdanina Respubliki Moldova M. Tsurkana* [*In the case of the constitutionality of provisions of paragraph 6 article 8 of the Federal Law "On the Legal Status of Foreign Citizens in the Russian Federation", parts 1 and 3 of article 18.8 of the Code of the Russian Federation on Administrative Offenses", and subpoint 2 part 1 of article 27 of the Federal Law "On the Order of Exit from the Russian Federation and Entry into the Russian Federation", in connection with the complaint of the citizen of the Republic of Moldova M. Tsurkana*].

Federal Law No. 5242-1 of June 25, 1993. *O prave grazhdan Rossiiskoi Federatsii na svobodu peredvizheniia, vybor mesta prebyvaniia i zhitel'stva v predelakh Rossiiskoi Federatsii* [*On the right of citizens of the Russian Federation to freedom of movement, choice of place of stay and residence in the Russian Federation*].

Federal Law No. 196 of December 10, 1995. *O bezopastnosti dorozhnogo dvizheniia* [*On road safety*].

Federal Law No. 63 of June 13, 1996. *Ugolovnyi kodeks Rossiiskoi Federatsii* [*Criminal Code of the Russian Federation*].

Federal Law No. 115 of July 25, 2002. *O pravovom polozhenii inostrannykh grazhdan v Rossiiskoi Federatsii* [*On the legal status of foreign citizens in the Russian Federation*].

Federal Law No. 62 of May 31 2002. *O grazhdanstve Rossiiskoi Federatsii* [*On citizenship in the Russian Federation*].

Federal Law No. 109 of July 18, 2006. *O migratsionnom uchete inonstrannykh grazhdan i lits bez grazhdanstva v Rossiyskoy Federatsii* [*On migration registration for foreign citizens and stateless persons in the Russian Federation*].

Federal Law No. 2487-1 of March 11, 1991. *O chastnoi detektivnoi i okhrannoi deiatel'nosti v Rossiiskoi Federatsii* [*On private detectives and security activities in the Russian Federation*].

Federal Law No. 114 of August 15, 1996. *O poriadke vyezda iz Rossiiskoi Federatsii i v"ezda v Rossiiskuiu Federatsiiu* [*On the order of exit from the Russian Federation and entry into the Russian Federation*].

Federal Law No. 167 of December 15, 2001. *Ob obiazatel'nom pensionnom strakhovanii v Rossiiskoi Federatsii* [*On compulsory pension insurance in the Russian Federation*].

Federal Law No. 197 of December 30, 2001. *Trudovoi kodeks Rossiiskoi Federatsii* [*Labour Code of the Russian Federation*].

Federal Law No. 195 of December 30, 2001. *Kodeks Rossiiskoi Federatsii ob Administrativnykh ravonarusheniiakh* [*Russian Federation Code of Administrative Offenses*, or *Administrative Code*].

Federal Law No. 161 of November 14, 2002. *O gosudarstvennykh i munitsipal'nykh unitarnykh predpriiatiiakh* [*On state and municipal unitary enterprises*].

Federal Law No. 310 of December 1, 2007. *Ob organizatsii i o provedenii XXII Olimpiiskikh zimnikh igr i XI Paralimpiiskikh zimnikh igr 2014 goda. v g. Sochi, razvitii goroda Sochi kak gornoklimaticheskogo kurorta i vnesenii izmenenii v otdel'nye zakonodatel'nye akty Rossiiskoi Federatsii* [*On preparing and conducting the XXII Winter Olympic Games and XI Winter Paralympic Games of 2014 in Sochi, development of the city of Sochi as a mountain resort and amendments to separate legislative acts of the Russian Federation*].

Federal Law No. 210 of July 27, 2010. *Ob organizatsii predostavleniia gosudarstvennykh i munitsipal'nykh uslug* [*On the organizations providing state and municipal services*].

Federal Law No. 108 of June 7, 2013. *O podgotovke i provedenii v Rossiiskoi Federatsii chempionata mira po futbolu FIFA 2018 goda, Kubka konfederatsii FIFA 2017 goda i vnesenii izmenenii v otdel'nye zakonodatel'nye akty Rossiiskoi Federatsii* [*On preparing and conducting in the Russian Federation the FIFA 2018 Football World Championships, the FIFA 2017 Confederation Cup and amendments to separate legislative acts of the Russian Federation*].

FMS Order (*prikaz*) No. 36 of February 26, 2009. *O nekotorykh voprosakh vydachi razreshenii na rabotu inostrannym grazhdanam pribyvshim v Rossiiskuiu Federatsiiu v poriadke, ne trebuiushchem polucheniia visy* [*On a few questions about issuing work permits to visa-free foreign citizens coming to the Russian Federation*].

FMS Order (*prikaz*) No. 147 of June 28, 2010. *O formakh i poriadke uvedomleniia Federal'noi Migratsionnoi Sluzhby ob osushchestvlenii inostrannymi grazhdanami trudovoi deiatel'nosti na territorii Rossiiskoi Federatsi* [*On the forms and order to notify the Federal Migration Service about the labour activities of foreign citizens in the Russian Federation*].

FMS Order (*prikaz*) No. 387 of September 23, 2013. *Ob osobennostiakh oformleniia razreshitel'nykh dokumentov dlia osushchestvleniia inostrannymi grazhdanami i litsami bez grazhdanstva trudovoi deiatel'nosti na territorii munitsipal'nogo obrazovaniia gorod-kurort Sochi v period organizatsii i provedeniia XXII Olimpiiskikh zimnikh igr i XI Paralimpiiskikh zimnikh igr 2014 goda. v g. Sochi* [*On peculiarities of arranging work documents for foreign citizens and stateless persons in the municipality city-resort of Sochi during the period of organizing and conducting the XXII Winter Olympic Games and XI Winter Paralympic Games of 2014 in Sochi*].

FMS. 2016. *Svedeniia po migratsionnoi situatsii v Rossiiskoi Federatsii za 12 mesiatsev 2015 goda* [*Information on the migration situation in the Russian Federation for 12 months of 2015*].

General'naia Prokuratura Rossiiskoi Federatsii. "Portal Pravovoi Statistiki." Accessed October 15, 2015. http://crimestat.ru/.

Gosstandart Order (*postanovlenie*) No. 454-st of November 6, 2001. *O priniatii i vvedenii v deistvie OKVED* [*On the adoption and introduction of OKVED*].

Government Order (*postanovlenie*) No. 574 of September 21, 2005. *O vzaimnykh poezdkakh grazhdan Rossiiskoi Federatsii i grazhdan Respubliki Tadzhikistan* [*On reciprocal trips of citizens of the Russian Federation and citizens of the Republic of Tajikistan*].

Government Order (*postanovlenie*) No. 682 of November 15, 2006. *Ob utverzhdenii na 2007 god kvoty na vydachu razreshenii na rabotu inostrannym grazhdanam, pribyvshim v Rossiiskuiu Federatsiiu v poriadke, ne trebuiushchem polucheniia visy* [*On the approval of 2007 quotas for issuing work permits to visa-free foreign citizens arriving to the Russian Federation*].

Government Order (*postanovlenie*) No. 783 of December 22, 2006. *O poriadke opredeleniia ispolnitel'nymi organami gosudarstvennoi vlasti potrebnosti v privlechenii inostrannykh rabotnikov i formirovaniia kvot na osushchestvlenie inostrannymi grazhdanami trudovoi deiatel'nosti v Rossiiskoi Federatsii* [*On the order of executive bodies of state government for determining the need for foreign workers and establishing quotas*].

Government Order (*postanovlenie*) No. 737 of October 3, 2008. *O vnesenii izmenenii v nekotorye postanovleniia Pravitel'stva Rossiiskoi Federatsii po voprosam opredeleniia potrebnosti v privlechenii instrannykh rabotnikov i utverzhdeniia kvot na osushchestvlenie inostrannymi grazhdanami trudovoi deiatel'nosti v Rossiiskoi Federatsii* [*On amendments to several government orders of the Russian Federation on the question of determining the demand for attracting foreign workers and approval of quotas for the labour activities of foreign citizens in the Russian Federation*].

Government Order (*postanovlenie*) No. 798 of December 23, 2006. *Ob utverzhdenii poriadka podachi uvedomleniia o privlechenii i ispol'zovanii dlia osushchestvleniia trudovoi deiatel'nosti inostrannykh grazhdan, pribyvshikh v Rossiiskuiu Federatsiiu v poriadke, ne trebuiushchem polucheniia visy* [*On the approval of the procedure for submitting notification on the attraction and use for labour purposes of visa-free foreign citizens, arriving to the Russian Federation*].

Government Order (*postanovlenie*) No. 991 of December 29, 2007. *O programme stroitel'stva olimpiiskikh ob"ektov i razvitiia goroda Sochi kak gornoklimaticheskogo kurorta* [*On the program for construction of Olympic objects and development of the city of Sochi as a mountain resort*].

Government Order (*postanovlenie*) No. 183 of March 18, 2008. *Ob utverzhdenii Pravil podachi rabotodatelem ili zakazchikom rabot (uslugi) uvedomleniia o privlechenii i ispol'zovanii dlia osushchestvleniia trudovoi deiatel'nosti inostrannykh grazhdan i (ili) lits bez grazhdanstva, pribyvshikh v Rossiiskuiu Federatsiiu v poriadke, ne trebuiushchem polucheniia visy, i imeiushchikh razreshenie na rabotu* [*On the approval of rules for employers and contractors to submit notice on the attraction and use for labour purposes of foreign citizens and (or) stateless persons, arriving to the Russian Federation without the need for a visa*].

Government Order (*postanovlenie*) No. 758 of October 13, 2008. *Ob uskorennoi i uproshchennoi vydache razreshenii na rabotu insotrannym grazhdanam, zakliuchivshim trudovye ili grazhdansko-pravovye dogovory s avtonomnoi nekommercheskoi organizatsiei "Organizatsionnyi komitet XXII Olimpiiskikh zimnikh igr i XI Paralimpiiskikh zimnikh igr 2014 goda. v g. Sochi" ili Gosudarstvennoi korporatsiei po stroitel'stvu olimpiiskikh ob"ektov i razvitiiu goroda Sochi kak gornoklimaticheskogo kurorta i pribyvshim na territoriiu Rossiiskoi Federatsii v period organizatsii i provedeniia XXII Olimpiiskikh zimnikh igr i XI Paralimpiiskikh zimnikh igr 2014 goda. v g. Sochi* [*On the expedited and simplified issuance of work permits to foreign workers signing labour or service contracts with the autonomous non-profit organization "Organizing committee XXII Winter Olympic Games and XI Winter Paralympic Games of 2014 in Sochi" or the state corporation for construction of Olympic objects and development of the city of Sochi as a mountain resort and staying in the Russian Federation during the period of organizing and conducting the XXII Winter Olympic Games and XI Winter Paralympic Games of 2014 in Sochi*].

Government Order (*rasporiazhenie*) No. 1638-r of November 5, 2009.

Government Order (*postanovlenie*) No. 800 of September 12, 2013. *Ob utverzhdenii Pravil podgotovki predlozhenii po opredeleniiu potrebnosti v prilechenii inostrannykh rabotnikov, utverzhdeniiu kvoty na vydachu inostrannym grazhdanam priglashenii na v"ezd v Rossiiskuiu Federatsiiu v tseliakh osushchestvleniia trudovoi deiatel'nosti, a takzhe kvoty na vydachu inostrannym grazhdanam razreshenie na rabotu* [*On the approval of rules for the preparation of recommendations on the necessity to attract foreign workers, approval of work visa invitation quotas, as well as work permit quotas*].

Government Order (*postanovlenie*) No. 555 of June 17, 2014. *O priznanii utrativshim silu postanovleniia pravitel'stva Rossiiskoi Federatsii ot 21 Sentiabria 2005 g. N 574* [*On taking out of force government order of 21 September N 574*].

Government Order (*postanovlenie*) No. 72 of February 5, 2016. *O vnesenii izmenenii v otdel'nye akty Pravitel'stva Rossiiskoi Federatsii* [*On changes to separate acts of the Government of the Russian Federation*].

International Treaty, February 26, 1999. *Soglashenie mezhdu Respublikoi Belarus', Respublikoi Kazakhstan, Kyrgyzskoi Respublikoi, i Rossiiskoi Federatsiei ob uproshchennom poriadke priobreteniia grazhdanstva* [*Agreement between the Government of the Republic of Belarus, Government of the Republic of Kazakhstan, Government of the Kyrgyz Republic, and Government of the Russian Federation on the simplified procedure for acquiring citizenship*]

International Treaty, November 30, 2000. *Soglashenie mezhdu Pravitel'stvom Respubliki Belarus', Pravitel'stvom Respubliki Kazakhstan, Pravitel'stvom Kirgizskoi Respubliki, Pravitel'stvom Rossiiskoi Federatsii i Pravitel'stvom Tadzhikistana o vzaimnykh bezvizovykh poezdkah grazhdan* [*Agreement between the Government of the Republic of Belarus, Government of the Republic of Kazakhstan, Government of the Kyrgyz Republic, Government of the Russian Federation and Government of Tajikistan on reciprocal visa-free trips for citizens*].

Krasnodar Governor's Order (*postanovlenie*) No. 826 of July 25, 2002. *Ob upravlenii monitoringa migratsionnykh protsessov administratsii Krasnodarskogo Kraia* [*On the managing of monitoring the migration process by the administration of Krasnodar Krai*].

Krasnodar Governor's Order (*postanovlenie*) No. 767 of August 8, 2003. *Ob upolnomochennom ispolnitel'nom organe gosudarstvennoi vlasti Krasnodarskogo kraia po opredeleniiu potrebnosti v prilechenii inostrannykh rabotnikov i podgotovke predlozhenii po ob"emam kvot v Krasnodarskom krae* [*On the authorized executive organs of government power of Krasnodar Krai for defining demand in attracting foreign workers and the preparation of recommendations for the volume of quota in Krasnodar Krai*].

Krasnodar Governor's Order (*postanovlenie*) No. 1094 of November 22, 2005. *O koordinatsii deiatel'nosti organov ispolnitel'noi vlasti Krasnodarskogo kraia po vzaimodeistviiu s territorial'nymi organami federal'nykh organov ispolnitel'noi vlasti v sfere migratsionnykh pravootnoshenii* [*On the coordination of activities of executive power of Krasnodar Krai for cooperation with territorial organs of federal executive bodies in the sphere of migration relations*].

Krasnodar Governor's Order (*postanovlenie*) No. 363 of April 24, 2007. *O kraevoi mezhvedomstvennoi komissii po voprosam privlecheniia i ispol'zovaniia inostrannykh rabotnikov* [*On the krai interdepartmental commission on the question of attracting and using foreign workers*].

Krasnodar Governor's Order (*postanovlenie*) No. 298 of April 22, 2010. *Ob utverzhdenii administrativnogo reglamenta ispolneniia v administratsii Krasnodarskogo kraia gosudarstvennoi funktsii po opredeleniiu potrebnosti v privlechenii inostrannykh rabotnikov i podgotovke predlozhenii' po ob''emam kvot v Krasnodarskom krae* [*On the approval of administrative regulations in the Krasnodar administration for public function for determining the need and attraction of foreign workers and preparation of quota recommendations in Krasnodar krai*].

Krasnodar Law No. 247 of March 13, 2000. *O dopolnitel'nykh merakh sotsial'noi zashchity chlenov kazach'ikh obshchestv Kubanskogo voiskovogo kazach'ego obshchestva, privlekaemykh k neseniiu gosudarstvennoi i inoi sluzhby v Krasnodarskom krae* [*On additional measures of social protection for the members of Cossack societies of the Kuban Cossack army society, involved in public and other service*].

Krasnodar Law No. 460 of April 11, 2002. *O prebyvanii i zhitel'stve na territorii Krasnodarskogo Kraia* [*On stay and residence in Krasnodar Krai*].

Krasnodar Law No. 735 of July 2, 2004. *O Merakh po predotvrashcheniiu nezakonnoi migratsii v Krasnodarskii Krai* [*On measures for the prevention of illegal migration in Krasnodar Krai*].

Krasnodar Legislative Assembly Order (*postanovlenie*) No. 1381-P of March 27, 2002. *O merakh po usileniiu gosudarstvennogo kontrolia za migratsiei i administrativnomu vydvoreniiu lits, nezakonno nakhodiashchikhcia na territorii Krasnodarskogo Kraia* [*On measures to strengthen government control of migration and administrative expulsion of persons illegally located on the territory of Krasnodar Krai*].

Krasnodar Legislative Assembly Order (*postanovlenie*) No. 1532-P of May 29, 2002. *Ob utverzhdenii kraevoi tselevoi programmy "Uchastie kazachestva v okhrane obshchestennogo poriadka i provedenii meropriiatii po presecheniiu nezakonnoi migratsii na territioriiu Krasnodarskogo kraiia"* [*On the approval of the regional program "The participation of Cossacks in maintaining order and carrying out actions for the suppression of illegal migration in Krasnodar Krai"*].

Krasnodar UFMS. 2013. "V vykhodnye na Kubani vyiavleny svyshe 150 Kitaitsev-nelegalov [The weekend in Kuban revealed 150 illegal Chinese]." Press service of the Krasnodar UFMS. July 30. Accessed February 3, 2017. http://www.ufmskrn.ru/site2/news/66245/.

Krasnodar UFMS. 2015. *Itogi sluzhebnoi deiatel'nosti za 9 mesiatsev [Results of service activities for 9 months]* November 16. Accessed March 10, 2016. http://www.23.fms.gov.ru/press/news/item/42924/.

Krasnodar UFMS. 2016. *Doklad "O migratsionnoi situatsii v Krasnodarskom krae i osnovnykh rezul'tatakh deiatel'nosti UFMS Rossii po Krasnodarskomu kraiiu" [Report "On the migration situation in Krasnodar krai and main results of the activities of the UFMS of Russia in Krasnodar krai"]*. Accessed February 17, 2016. http://www.23.fms.gov.ru/document/55785.

Minzdrav Order (*prikaz*) No. 603 of September 17, 2007. *Ob utverzhdenii formy zaiavki rabotodatelei, zakazchikov rabot (uslug), v tom chisle inostrannykh grazhdan, zaregistrirovannykh v kachestve individual'nykh predprinimatelei, o potrebnosti v rabochei sile dlia zameshcheniia vakantnykh i sozdavaemykh rabochikh mest inonstrannymi rabotnikami i poriadka ee zapolneniia [On the approval of application forms for employers, contractors, including foreign citizens registered as individual entrepreneurs, on labour force needs for filling vacant workplaces with foreign workers, and procedures for filling out forms]*.

Minzdrav Order (*prikaz*) No. 604 of September 17, 2007. *Ob utverzhdenii metodiki otsenki effektivnosti ispol'zovania inostrannoi rabochi sily [On approval of the methodology for estimating the effective use of foreign labour]*.

Moscow Mayoral Order (*rasporiazhenie*) No. 243 of May 24, 1994. *O polozhenii o privlechenii i ispol'zovanii v g. Moskve inostrannoi rabochei sily [On the position of inviting and using foreign work force in Moscow]*.

Moscow UFMS. 2016. *O migratsionnoi situatsii v g. Moskve i osnovnykh rezul'tatakh deiatel'nosti UFMS po g. Moskve za 12 mesiatsev 2015 goda [On the migration situation in Moscow and main results of the activities of the Moscow UFMS for 12 months of 2015]*, Moscow.

MVD. 2003–9. *Statistika [Statistics]*. Accessed December 13, 2009. http://www.mvd.ru/stats/.

Presidential Decree (*ukaz*) No. 564 of April 16, 1996. *Ob ekonomicheskikh i inykh l'gotakh, predostavliaemykh kazach'im obshchestvam i ikh chlenam, vziavshim na sebia obiazatel'stva po neseniiu gosudarstvennoi i inoi sluzhby [On economic and other benefits, granted to Cossack groups and their members, committing themselves to public and other services]*.

Presidential Decree (*ukaz*) No. 928 of July 19, 2004. *Voprosy Federal'noi migratsionnoi sluzhby [Questions of the Federal Migration Service]*.

Presidential Decree (*ukaz*) No. 1351 of October 9, 2007. *Kontseptsiia demograficheskoi politiki Rossiiskoi Federatsii na period do 2025 goda [Demographic Policy Concept to 2025]*.

Presidential Decree (*ukaz*) No. 594 of May 7, 2012. *O Prezidentskoi programme povysheniia kvalifikatsii inzhenernykh kadrov na 2012–2014 gody* [*On the presidential program for training engineering personnel for 2012–2014*].

Presidential Decree (*ukaz*) No. 596 of May 7, 2012. *O dolgostrochnoi gosudarstvennoi ekonomicheskoi politike* [*On long-term state economic policy*].

Presidential Decree (*ukaz*) No. 597 of May 7, 2012. *O meropriiatiiakh po realizatsii gosudarstvennoi sotsial'noi politiki* [*On activities for the realization of state social policy*].

Presidential Decree (*ukaz*) No. 598 of May 7, 2012. *O sovershenstvovanii gosudarstvennoi politiki v sfere zdravookhraneniia* [*On improving state healthcare policy*].

Presidential Decree (*ukaz*) No. 599 of May 7, 2012. *O merakh po realizatsii gosudarstvennoi politiki v oblasti obrazovaniia i nauki* [*On measures for the realization of state policy on education and science*].

Presidential Decree (*ukaz*) No. 600 of May 7, 2012. *O merakh po obespecheniiu grazhdan Rossiiskoi Federatsii dostupnym i komfortnym zhil'em i povysheniiu kachestva zhilishchno-kommunal'nykh uslug* [*On measures to ensure citizens of the Russian Federation affordable and comfortable housing and to improve the quality of housing and communal services*].

Presidential Decree (*ukaz*) No. 601 of May 7, 2012. *Ob osnovnykh napravleniiakh sovershenstvovaniia sistemy gosudarstvennogo upravleniia* [*On the main directions for improving public administration*].

Presidential Decree (*ukaz*) No. 602 of May 7, 2012. *Ob obespechenii mezhnatsional'nogo soglasiia* [*On ensuring interethnic harmony*].

Presidential Decree (*ukaz*) No. 603 of May 7, 2012. *O realizatsii planov (programm) stroitel'stva i razvitiia Vooruzhennykh Cil Rossiiskoi Federatsii, drugikh voisk, voinskikh formirovanii i organov i modernizatsii oboronno-promyshlennogo kompleksa* [*On the realization of the plans (programs) for the construction and development of the armed forces of the Russian Federation, other troops, military formations and bodies and modernization of the defense-industrial complex*]

Presidential Decree (*ukaz*) No. 604 of May 7, 2012. *O dal'neishem sovershenstvovanii voennoi sluzhby v Rossiiskoi Federatsii* [*On the further improvements to the armed services in the Russian Federation*].

Presidential Decree (*ukaz*) No. 605 of May 7, 2012. *O merakh po realizatsii vneshnepoliticheskogo kursa Rossiiskoi Federatsii* [*On measures for the realization of foreign policy of the Russian Federation*].

Presidential Decree (*ukaz*) No. 606 of May 7, 2012. *O merakh po realizatsii demograficheskoi politiki Rossiiskoi Federatsii* [*On measures for the realization of demographic policy in the Russian Federation*].

Presidential Decree (*ukaz*) No. 636 of May 21, 2012. *O strukture federal'nykh organov ispolnitel'noi vlasti* [*On the structure of federal organs of executive power*].

Presidential Decree (*ukaz*) of June 13, 2012. *Kontseptsiia gosudarstvennoe migratsionnoi politiki Rossiiskoi Federatsii na period do 2025 goda* [*Concept of State Migration Policy to 2025*].

Presidential Decree (*ukaz*) No. 1304 of September 19, 2012. *Ob ob"iavlenii distsiplinarnogo vzyskaniia Ministru obrazovaniia i nauki Rossiiskoi Federatsii, Ministru regional'nogo razvitiia Rossiiskoi Federatsii Ministru truda i sotsial'noi zashchity Rossiiskoi Federatsii* [*On the declaration of disciplinary sanctions on the minister of education and science of the Russian Federation, the minister of regional development of the Russian Federation, and the minister of labour and social protection of the Russian Federation*].

Presidential Decree (*ukaz*) No. 30 of January 15, 2013. *O nekotorykh voprosakh Ministerstva vnutrennikh del Rossiiskoi Federatsii i Federal'noi migratsionnoi sluzhby* [*On a few questions relating to the Ministry of Internal Affairs and the Federal Migration Service*].

Presidential Decree (*ukaz*) No. 686 of August 19, 2013. *Ob osobennostiakh primeneniia usilennykh mer bezopasnosti v period provedeniia XXII Olimpiiskikh zimnikh igr i XI Paralimpiiskikh zimnikh igr 2014 goda. v g. Sochi* [*On peculiarities of applying enhanced security measures during the XXII Winter Olympic Games and XI Winter Paralympic Games of 2014 in Sochi*].

Presidential Decree (*ukaz*) No. 754 of September 30, 2013. *O sniatii distsiplinarnogo vzyskaniia s Ministra obrazovaniia i nauki Rossiiskoi Federatsii, Ministra truda i sotsial'noi zashchity Rossiiskoi Federatsii* [*On lifting the disciplinary sanctions from the minister of education and science of the Russian Federation, and the minister of labour and social protection of the Russian Federation*].

Rospotrebnadzor Order (*prikaz*) No. 336 of September 14, 2010. *O poriadke podgotovki, predstavleniia i rassmotreniia v sisteme Rospotrebnadzora materialov po priniatiiu resheniia o nezhaletel'nosti prebyvaniia (prozhivaniia) inostrannogo grazhdanina ili litsa bez grazhdanstva v Rossiiskoi Federatsii* [*On the preparation, submission and consideration in the Rospotrebnadzor system of materials for decisions about undesirability of residency of foreigners or persons without citizenship in the Russian Federation*]. Accessed January 23, 2015. http://www.rg.ru/2010/11/03/inostr-dok.html.

Rosstat. 2007a. *Regiony Rossii: Sotsial'no-Ekonomicheskie Pokazateli* [*Regions of Russia: socio-economic indicators*]. Moscow. Federal'naia Sluzhba Gosudarstvennoi Statistiki [Federal State Statistical Service].

Rosstat. 2007b. *Trud i Zaniatost' v Rossii* [*Labour and employment in Russia*]. Moscow. Federal'naia Sluzhba Gosudarstvennoi Statistiki [Federal State Statistical Service].

Rosstat. 2008a. *Regiony Rossii: Sotsial'no-Ekonomicheskie Pokazateli* [*Regions of Russia: Socio-economic indicators*]. Moscow. Federal'naia Sluzhba Gosudarstvennoi Statistiki [Federal State Statistical Service].

Rosstat. 2008b. *Ekonomicheskaia aktivnost' naseleniia Rossii* [*Economic activity of the population of Russia*]. Moscow. Federal'naia Sluzhba Gosudarstvennoi Statistiki [Federal State Statistical Service].

Rosstat. 2009a. *Regiony Rossii: Sotsial'no-Ekonomicheskie Pokazateli* [*Regions of Russia: Socio-economic indicators*]. Moscow. Federal'naia Sluzhba Gosudarstvennoi Statistiki [Federal State Statistical Service].

Rosstat. 2009b. *Trud i Zaniatost' v Rossii* [*Labour and employment in Russia*]. Moscow. Federal'naia Sluzhba Gosudarstvennoi Statistiki [Federal State Statistical Service].

Rosstat. 2010a. *Chislennost' i migratsiia naseleniia Rossiiskoi Federatsii v 2009 godu* [*Number and migration of the population of the Russian Federation in 2009*]. Moscow. Federal'naia Sluzhba Gosudarstvennoi Statistiki [Federal State Statistical Service]."

Rosstat. 2010b. *Ekonomicheskaia aktivnost' naseleniia Rossii* [*Economic activity of the population of Russia*]. Moscow. Federal'naia Sluzhba Gosudarstvennoi Statistiki [Federal State Statistical Service].

Rosstat. 2010c. "Metodologicheskie poiasneniia [Methodological Explanation]." In *Itogi Vcerossiiskoi perepisi naseleniia 2010 goda* [*Results of the 2010 population census*], 493–6. Accessed December 20, 2014. http://www.gks.ru/free_doc/new_site/perepis2010/croc/Documents/vol8/methodology.pdf.

Rosstat. 2010d. *Regiony Rossii: Sotsial'no-Ekonomicheskie Pokazateli* [*Regions of Russia: Socio-economic indicators*]. Moscow. Federal'naia Sluzhba Gosudarstvennoi Statistiki [Federal State Statistical Service].

Rosstat. 2011a. *Regiony Rossii: Sotsial'no-Ekonomicheskie Pokazateli* [*Regions of Russia: Socio-economic indicators*]. Moscow. Federal'naia Sluzhba Gosudarstvennoi Statistiki [Federal State Statistical Service].

Rosstat. 2011b. *Trud i Zaniatost' v Rossii* [*Labour and employment in Russia*]. Moscow. Federal'naia Sluzhba Gosudarstvennoi Statistiki [Federal State Statistical Service].

Rosstat. 2012a. *Chislennost' i migratsiia naseleniia Rossiiskoi Federatsii v 2011 godu* [*Number and migration of the population of the Russian Federation in 2011*]. Moscow. Federal'naia Sluzhba Gosudarstvennoi Statistiki [Federal State Statistical Service]."

Rosstat. 2012b. *Regiony Rossii: Sotsial'no-Ekonomicheskie Pokazateli* [*Regions of Russia: Socio-economic indicators*]. Moscow. Federal'naia Sluzhba Gosudarstvennoi Statistiki [Federal State Statistical Service].

Rosstat. 2012c. *Ekonomicheskaia aktivnost' naseleniia Rossii* [*Economic activity of the population of Russia*]. Moscow. Federal'naia Sluzhba Gosudarstvennoi Statistiki [Federal State Statistical Service].

Rosstat. 2013a. *Sotsial'no-ekonomicheskoe polozhenie federal'nykh okrugov* [*Social-economic situation in the federal districts*]. Moscow. Federal'naia Sluzhba Gosudarstvennoi Statistiki [Federal State Statistical Service].

Rosstat. 2013b. *Trud i Zaniatost' v Rossii* [*Labour and employment in Russia*]. Moscow. Federal'naia Sluzhba Gosudarstvennoi Statistiki [Federal State Statistical Service].

Rosstat. 2014a. *Chislennost' i migratsiia naseleniia Rossiiskoi Federatsii v 2013 godu* [*Number and migration of the population of the Russian Federation in 2013*]. Moscow. Federal'naia Sluzhba Gosudarstvennoi Statistiki [Federal State Statistical Service].

Rosstat. 2014b. *Ekonomicheskaia aktivnost' naseleniia Rossii* [*Economic activity of the population of Russia*]. Moscow. Federal'naia Sluzhba Gosudarstvennoi Statistiki [Federal State Statistical Service].

Rosstat. 2014c. *Regiony Rossii: Sotsial'no-Ekonomicheskie Pokazateli* [*Regions of Russia: Socio-economic indicators*]. Moscow. Federal'naia Sluzhba Gosudarstvennoi Statistiki [Federal State Statistical Service].

Rosstat. 2014d. *Sotsial'no-ekonomicheskoe polozhenie federal'nykh okrugov* [*Social-economic situation in the federal districts*]. Moscow. Federal'naia Sluzhba Gosudarstvennoi Statistiki [Federal State Statistical Service].

Rosstat. 2014e. *Trud i Zaniatost' v Rossii* [*Labour and employment in Russia*]. Moscow. Federal'naia Sluzhba Gosudarstvennoi Statistiki [Federal State Statistical Service].

Rosstat. 2015a. *Chislennost' i migratsiia naseleniia Rossiiskoi Federatsii v 2013 godu* [*Number and migration of the population of the Russian Federation in 2014*]. Moscow. Federal'naia Sluzhba Gosudarstvennoi Statistiki [Federal State Statistical Service].

Rosstat. 2015b. *Regiony Rossii: Sotsial'no-Ekonomicheskie Pokazateli* [*Regions of Russia: Socio-economic indicators*]. Moscow. Federal'naia Sluzhba Gosudarstvennoi Statistiki [Federal State Statistical Service].

Rosstat. 2015c. *Sotsial'no-ekonomicheskoe polozhenie federal'nykh okrugov* [*Social-economic situation in the federal districts*]. Moscow. Federal'naia Sluzhba Gosudarstvennoi Statistiki [Federal State Statistical Service].

Rosstat. 2015d. *Trud i Zaniatost' v Rossii* [*Labour and employment in Russia*]. Moscow. Federal'naia Sluzhba Gosudarstvennoi Statistiki [Federal State Statistical Service].

Rosstat. 2016a. *Chislennost' i migratsiia naseleniia Rossiiskoi Federatsii v 2015 godu* [*Number and migration of the population of the Russian Federation in 2015*].

Moscow. Federal'naia Sluzhba Gosudarstvennoi Statistiki [Federal State Statistical Service].

Rosstat. 2016b. *Regiony Rossii: Sotsial'no-Ekonomicheskie Pokazateli* [*Regions of Russia: Socio-economic indicators*]. Moscow. Federal'naia Sluzhba Gosudarstvennoi Statistiki [Federal State Statistical Service].

Rosstat. 2016c. *Rossiiskii Statisticheskii Ezhegodnik* [*Russian Statistical Yearbook*]. Moscow. Federal'naia Sluzhba Gosudarstvennoi Statistiki [Federal State Statistical Service].

Sverdlovsk Government Order (*postanovlenie*) No. 126 of February 2, 2010. *Ob utverzhdenii Polozheniia o Ministerstve Ekonomiki Sverdlovskoi oblasti* [*On approval of the regulations on the Ministry of Economics of Sverdlovsk Oblast*].

Sverdlovsk Government Order (*postanovlenie*) No. 674 of June 1, 2011. *O Departmente po trudu i zaniatosti naseleniia Sverdlovskoi oblasti* [*On the Department for Labour and Employment of Sverdlovsk Oblast*].

Sverdlovsk Governor's Decree (*ukaz*) No. 402 of May 7, 2007. *Ob upolnomochennom ispolnitel'nom organe gosudarstvennoi vlasti Sverdlovskoi Oblasti po opredeleniiu potrebnosti v privlechenii inostrannykh rabotnikov i podgotovke predlozhenii po ob"emam kvot na osushchestvlenie inostrannymi grazhdanami trudovoi deiatel'nosti v Sverdlovskoi Oblasti* [*On the authorized executive bodies of state power of the Sverdlovsk region for defining the demand for and attraction of foreign workers and preparation of quota for the labour activities of foreign citizens in the Sverdlovsk region*].

Sverdlovsk Governor's Decree (*ukaz*) No. 467 of May 30, 2011. *O pereimenovanii Departamenta Gosudarstvennoi Sluzhby Zaniatosti Naseleniia Sverdlovskoi Oblasti* [*On renaming the Department of State Employment Services of Sverdlovsk Oblast*].

Sverdlovsk Governor's Decree (*ukaz*) No. 285 of April 28, 2012. *O Mezhvedomstvennoi komissii po voprosam privlecheniia i ispol'zovaniia inostranniykh rabotnikov v Sverdlovskoi oblasti* [*On the interdepartmental commission on the question of attracting and using foreign workers in the Sverdlovsk region*].

Sverdlovsk UFMS. 2012. *Obzor Migratsionnoi Situatsii v Sverdlovskoi Oblasti za 2011 god* [*Overview of the migration situation in Sverdlovsk Oblast for 2011*]. Yekaterinburg.

Sverdlovsk UFMS. 2013. *Analiticheskii Obzor, kharakterizuiushchii migratsionnuiu situatsiiu i deiatel'nosti' UFMS Rossii po Sverdlovskoi olbasti po realizatsii gosudarstvennoe migratsionnoi politiki v regione za 2014 god.* [*Analytical overview, characteristics of the migration situation and activities of the Sverdlovsk UFMS towards the realization of state migration policies in the region for 2012*]. Yekaterinburg.

Sverdlovsk UFMS. 2014. *Analiticheskii Obzor, kharakterizuiushchii migratsionnuiu situatsiiu i deiatel'nosti' UFMS Rossii po Sverdlovskoi olbasti po realizatsii gosudarstvennoe migratsionnoi politiki v regione za 2014 god.* [*Analytical overview, characteristics of the migration situation and activities of the Sverdlovsk UFMS towards the realization of state migration policies in the region for 2013*]. Yekaterinburg.

Sverdlovsk UFMS. 2015. *Analiticheskii Obzor, kharakterizuiushchii migratsionnuiu situatsiiu i deiatel'nosti' UFMS Rossii po Sverdlovskoi olbasti po realizatsii gosudarstvennoe migratsionnoi politiki v regione za 2014 god* [*Analytical overview, characteristics of the migration situation and activities of the Sverdlovsk UFMS towards the realization of state migration policies in the region for 2014*]. Yekaterinburg.

Sverdlovsk UFMS. 2016. *O migratsionnoi situatsii v Sverdlovskoi oblatsi, osnovnykh rezul'tatakh deiatel'nosti Upravleniia Federal'noi migratsionnoi sluzhby po Sverdlovskoi oblasti za 2015 god* [*On the migration situation in Sverdlovsk Oblast, results of activities of the Sverdlovsk UFMS for 2015*]. Yekaterinburg.

Index

Page references in **bold** indicate a table or a figure.